Bild und Recht – Studien zur Regulierung des Visuellen

Edited by

Prof. Dr. Thomas Dreier
PD Dr. Dr. Grischka Petri
Prof. Dr. Wolfgang Ullrich
Prof. Dr. Matthias Weller

Volume 11

Thomas Dreier | Tiziana Andina (Eds.)

Digital Ethics

The issue of images

HART

Nomos

The painting – created well before the advent of digital technology and even photography – shows the view from the spot overlooking Lake Cuomo where today the Villa Vigoni is located, and where the Conference, the proceedings of which are contained in this book, took place in autumn 2020.

The Deutsche Nationalbibliothek lists this publication in the Deutsche Nationalbibliografie; detailed bibliographic data are available on the Internet at http://dnb.d-nb.de

ISBN: HB (Nomos) 978-3-8487-8841-5
ePDF (Nomos) 978-3-7489-3401-1

British Library Cataloguing-in-Publication Data
A catalogue record for this book is available from the British Library.

ISBN: HB (Hart) 978-1-5099-6414-7

Library of Congress Cataloging-in-Publication Data
Dreier, Thomas | Andina, Tiziana
Digital Ethics
The issue of images
Thomas Dreier | Tiziana Andina (Eds.)
426 pp.
Includes bibliographic references.

ISBN 978-1-5099-6414-7 (hardcover Hart)

Onlineversion
Nomos eLibrary

1st Edition 2022

Table of Contents

Part 5 Technology, Ethics and Legal Norms

Part 6 Ethics and Fundamental Rights

Part 1
From Drawings to Deep Fakes – Some Introductory Remarks

Chapter 1
Images, Technology, Ethics and Law – An Intricate Relationship

Thomas Dreier/Tiziana Andina

I. Digital Ethics – The Issue of Images: An Introduction

1. Defining the issue

a) What is to be understood by digital image ethics?

As of now, *digital image ethics* may not be a well-established philosophical term or field of systematic research. Hence, before issues related thereto are discussed in the contributions to this book, some clarification of what is meant by digital image ethics is required. While, roughly speaking, *digital ethics* comprises the totality of ethical issues and rules regarding actions of digitisation, the use of objects and services, and communication in a digital format, *image ethics*, on the other hand, comprises the totality of ethical issues and rules regarding the production, dissemination and ultimately, consumption of visual images.[1] In view of these brief and admittedly, summary descriptions, it can be said that *digital image ethics* is both a part of digital ethics and likewise a part of image ethics, thus marking the intersection between these larger areas of applied ethics.

In view of the increasing penetration of society by digital and networking technologies, *digital ethics* is confronted with a continuously increasing number of issues. At present, in line with current development of technology, most books on digital ethics focus on different aspects of digital and networking technology, as well as on particular uses of different digital technologies. These include digital media ethics, computer or information ethics via the ethics of memory to the ethics of artificial intelligence appli-

---

1 Interestingly, the Stanford Encyclopedia of Philosophy lists neither "digital ethics", nor "image ethics". Rather, "digital" is only mentioned in connection with the philosophy of digital art, and "image" only in connection with mental imagery (https://plato.stanford.edu/contents.html). – However, for a summary of image ethics ("Bildethik") in Germany see, e.g., Tappe (2016).

cations (AI) and, last but not least, the ethics of digital sex and of cyber warfare.

The array of issues addressed by *image ethics* is similarly wide. This is particularly true if, regarding images, one considers as images, besides depictions of real or imagined objects and non-figurative representations, still (drawings, photographs, computer generated and hybrid forms of images) and/or moving images, language metaphors and, ultimately, perhaps even mental images of human role model appearances. Ethical issues range from which images can be taken to under what circumstances and by whom images may be taken. They also concern the ways images are or should be used, including the legitimacy of image alteration and manipulation. Aditionally, there are ethical questions as to who shall or shall not look at certain images. So far, image ethics literature has identified areas as diverse as privacy vis-à-vis curiosity and spectacle, surveillance, images of the pain of others,[2] copying and copyright-relevant acts, manipulation of images, the credibility of photojournalism, advertising and projected images of certain groups of persons and of the body, pornography, computer games, to name just the most prominent ones. In many, if not all areas, the prevailing issue is one of control over images, of external view and of self-representation both in individual cases and in society.[3]

At the intersection of both digital ethics and image ethics, *digital image ethics* on the one hand focuses from the vast area covered by digital ethics only on ethical issues raised relating to digital *visual* material. On the other hand, within the area of image ethics, it only deals with *digital* visual material. Consequently, issues which deal with digital issues in general, such as, e.g., the protection of personal data are not addressed by digital image ethics. Further, issues which exclusively concern images in general or actions which only concern analogue images are also not addressed. Of course, the separation of the issues is not as clearcut as it may seem at a first glance, since many digital image ethics issues are of a general nature

---

2 Sontag (2003); Fishman (2003).

3 See the attempts by both billionaires Bill Gates (with Corbis since 1989) and Mark Getty (with Getty Images since 1995) who had taken over many of the existing picture agencies, thus assembling a huge repertoire of visual images in order to serve a world-wide market; for the subsequent history – Corbis was sold, in 2006, to a Chinese Company, with Corbis retaining the right to license material from the image database outside of China. Getty Images, after it had changed ownership several times, was bought back by the Getty family. See Frater (2016); https://en.wikipedia.org/wiki/Branded_Entertainment_Network, and https://en.wikipedia.org/wiki/Getty_Images.

and hence important for visual and non-visual objects (such as, e.g., the issue of automated decision-making and the regulation of algorithms) as well as for digital and non-digital ethics (such as, e.g., the issue of image manipulation) alike.

b) Changes brought about by digital and networking technologies

Before some issues central to digital image ethics are discussed in this book, the impact of digitisation and digital communication technologies shall briefly be recalled.

Common metaphors such as the one of "flood of images" may, of course, be explained as merely defensive reflexes caused by fear due to the increased number of pictures made following the democratization of digital cameras which today are to be found in every smartphone. More precisely, networking technology and, most notably, the development of exchange platforms has led to a revolution in terms of who can distribute images and how images are distributed. This development has increased both the number of persons whose actions are subject to moral judgement and the number of ways that images can be used. In addition, automated search, identification and, to an increasing extent, even recognition of the semantic content of images makes it possible to automatically block access to or even delete unwanted images. Moreover, all of this is now possible without any direct human judgement but merely on the basis of predefined criteria or – even more detached from a direct human decision – on the bases of criteria search engines have "learned" through deep-learning techniques. The impact of digital and networking technologies is thus not only of a quantitative, but likewise of a qualitative nature, which completely transforms existing ethical issues and adds new issues unexamined by image ethics in times of analogue images.

Similarly, despite its use in "television", the notion of "vision" was traditionally limited to on-sight vision of the material carrier of the images (the paper, but also the TV-screen). It was also complemented and enlarged by "supervision" which permits the observer to observe actions from a distance (the police station, the satellite control center etc.). The ethical issues raised in this respect may not be totally new. Indeed, Foucault's "Surveiller et punir – Naissance de la prison" was published already in 1975, well before the advent of mass digitization, and the description of Jeremy Bentham's "Panopticum" even dates to the late 18th century. But the digital development of tele-surveillance of everybody at any time has taken on another quality and with it raised a substantial number of additional ethical issues.

In economic terms, the most significant effects of digital and networking technologies are evidenced in the possibility to copy and transmit images at marginal cost without loss of quality in almost no time. At the same time, regarding the value chain, a marked shift of revenues generated due to image consumption is clear from those who produce and sell the images (professional and non-professional photographers, picture agencies, media enterprises) to the online content-sharing platform providers (YouTube, Instagram etc.). In ontological terms, what was once one individual analogue image, i.e., one object, has dissolved in its digitized form into a great number of discrete pixels which can be recombined in any possible new way. Even though digital photography still works with classical lenses, photo theorists generally diagnosed an end to photography,[4] emphasising the special, non-indexical properties of digital photography and of computer-generated images over the indexical properties that analogue and digital photography still have in common. But even if the indexical link between what is depicted and what can be seen in a given picture, is undeniably weakened, it is not lost in all instances. Therefore, digital image ethics does not completely replace the ethics of analogue images. Rather, they complement and, in some instances, modify, the moral rules formulated regarding the production, communication and use of analogue images.

2. *Issues of digital image ethics*

As artefacts, "images do not in themselves make any assertions about the world, do not make any demands and do not make any judgements".[5] Rather, these actions are performed by the persons who produce, make use of or look at images. Since ethics only deals with actions, not with objects, it is these actions which must be judged according to their moral standards. In other words, when colloquially speaking of images that are dangerous for certain people, what we are really saying from an ethical perspective is that the act of showing images to people who should not see them is unethical due to the negative impact looking at them might cause to the individual or society at large.

4 For references see, e.g., Dreier (2019) 31 et seq.

5 See only Tappe (2016).

Digital image ethics is thus concerned with the ethical judgement of the actions of humans when it comes to acts of making, distributing and viewing certain images. If one of these acts is performed automatically, it is then the decision to use the automatic device and to opt for its particular design that should be scrutinised. However, additionally it should be noted this action-centerd perspective of ethics is not shared by all disciplines. Thus, although an image has neither intentionality, will nor character, some authors in art history have recently attributed some form of "agency" to images. According to these authors who thus ultimately ascribe some form of "personhood" to images, in the communication between the person who makes or uses an image and the viewer, it is not primarily the latter who plays the active part in the construction of an image's meaning, nor do images merely stare back at the gaze of their viewers.[6] Rather, it is emphasised that it's the images that look at their potential onlookers, provoking them to look back.[7]

However, such a focus on "acting" images does not exclude the necessity to evaluate the morality of the reasons to make and use images, nor the purposes of looking at an image. Hence, as an applied ethics, the focus of digital image ethics is, to a large extent, on the level of practice. However, as will be shown, ethical issues also exist regarding the semantical level of digital images.

a) *Practical level*

Generally, practical ethical issues concern all acts performed on all stages, from the production of images to their use and consumption. Considering the great number of persons which are involved today in the communication of images, acts undertaken not only by image producers but also by gatekeepers, agencies, editorial offices and, last but not least, by image-sharing platforms come into focus. After all, an image is not just taken and presented. Rather, every single step from the selection of the motif to the selection of a photograph and its cropping represents a decision, the exercise of which can be judged according to moral criteria. This concerns both the content of an image and the question of its potential falsification, misrepresentation or misinterpretation of its message by any of the stakeholders mentioned. Even the camera is not simply a neutral

6 Elkins (1996).
7 Mitchell (2005); Bredekamp (2018).

recording device, but, in many cases, changes the scene depicted which, in the absence of the camera, would often have been different.

The kind of questions that arise on a practical level shall only be briefly outlined here, by way of example, in relation to image manipulation and the use of filters. As it has often been stated, digital photography means the end of the indexicality of the photographic image. In other words, the trace between the object depicted and its representation is interrupted due to the discrete character of the digital form of the representation.[8] This interruption creates room for subsequent image manipulation which is by far larger than in the case of analogue photography. Additionally, there is room for images that look like depictions of an object that never actually existed. The main problem with ethically judging acts of manipulating images is that it requires finding a discrepancy between what is considered as "true" or "authentic" and what is considered an ethically unacceptable alteration. In addition, it must be noted that over time and in different cultures, the expectations placed on the truth and authenticity of images vary quite substantially. What exactly is considered "authentic" under certain circumstances in a specific cultural environment seems to be less an objectively verifiable fact but rather the result of certain ascribed properties. Moreover, even before the advent of digital imaging technology, the expectation of image "authenticity" was exaggerated. Lenses have always preferred a certain vision over another and the chosen chemical configuration of color film was responsible for the hue of the resulting images.[9] Contrary to what one might think, these differences were not a direct and uncontrolled result of chemo-technical differences of the respective film material. Rather, even in those earlier days these differences were a matter of conscious design decisions that reacted to assumed different color preferences in the U.S., in Europe and in Japan.

Already before the making of individual images, camera manufacturers configured camera software so that, even in low light, one can take images one could not take with an analogue camera. However, this would generally not be regarded as producing an in-authentic photograph. But what about other image modifications caused by the camera's internal settings? If, e.g., it is most likely legitimate for private users to exercise their personal freedom and manipulate images in any way, why should

8 See, e.g., Mitchell (1992). – Of course, not only digital images, but all technically produced images brought about a radical change to images that were manually created; see Flusser (1983) 13 et seq.; Belting (2011) 27–28.

9 E.g., colour slide films manufactured by Kodak had a tendency to red cast, whereas Agfa films had a rather green and Fuji films a more bluish cast.

the hardware's configuration which enables users to do so be regarded as unethical? Does that allow for the installation of pre-defined so-called filters, the use of which enables the camera-user to embellish the picture taken? Is it objectionable if in-built software for selfies automatically makes us appear younger or our skin fairer, because the software programmer or its producer considers that wrinkles and a darker skin are undesirable? Ethically, are there absolute or at least relative limits to what should be considered a permitted embellishment, and what should not be permitted as an unacceptable distortion? Most likely, the decisive criterion will be whether the user is informed and if they have a choice to apply the specific filter.

As a matter of fact, Google has recently addressed this issue when it announced, in October 2020, its guidelines for face retouching filters. Previously, they were applied on Google Android devices by default, but following the announcement their default status should be off, so users can decide whether he or she wants to use them. Google reasoned that "when you're not aware that a camera or photo app has applied a filter, the photos can negatively impact mental wellbeing. These default filters can quietly set a beauty standard that some people compare themselves against. ... We've steered away from references to 'beauty', by using iconography and language that is value-neutral, so you can decide what retouching means to you." In other words, "if face retouching filters are on, this should be clearly indicated in the product experience. And when it's off, it should stay off".[10] Indeed, if more than 70 percent of photos taken on an Android device are made using the front-facing camera, i.e., which are selfies, this policy change constitutes a major shift towards transparency and ultimately leads to greater self-determination for users. A similar issue is raised regarding digital images generated by artificial intelligence (AI) which may convey bias of gender or race, particularly if the training uses biased data.

b) Semantical level

Contrary to ethical issues at the practical level, ethical issues at the semantical level may, at first, be somewhat surprising. After all, as already stated, ethics concern actions and not objects. However, when judging acts of making, using and consuming images, the respective actions cannot be

10 Modi (2020).

judged from the perspective of their ethical value without considering their semantic meaning. On the one hand, it is true that unlike language, images generally may not need translation. On the other hand, like language, images are open to interpretation. According to a proverb often quoted, a picture is worth a thousand words. But what exactly does an image communicate? Does it say anything at all, or does it mainly transport and evoke emotions? Any interpretation of an image will encounter the problem that the semantic meaning of images is vague and ambivalent. This is even more true when moving between different cultural contexts. Interpreting and understanding an image's semantic content, on the one hand, highly depend on the cultural conventions shared by those who use images and those who view at them. On the other hand, it depends on each individual viewer's personal experience as well as his or her individual visual memory. Just as a verbal statement's ethical quality cannot be ascertained by simply analysing the speech itself but requires one to consider the statement's subject, speaker and circumstances, the ethical analysis of actions relating to images must also consider the images' semantic meaning.

3. *Method and aim of the book*

Whereas it is well possible to circumscribe the core of *digital image ethics*, it's exact boundaries and content still must be more precisely defined.[11] Although this book's contributions shall provide some groundwork to formulate a digital image ethics, they cannot chart the totality of issues that may arise. Additionally, this book may even less provide answers to all the ethical issues one might naturally consider as belonging to digital image ethics. Rather, quite like this brief introduction, the contributions of this book only highlight certain isolated aspects of a digital image ethics.

The Villa Vigoni conference organisers and editors of this book share the conviction that meaningful discussion of digital image ethics cannot be conducted from a philosophical perspective alone. Rather, since a whole series of the questions that require answering have already been regulated by law, it seems sensible to include the legal perspective as well.[12]

11 For an overview of the current state of research relating to digital image ethics as a partial applied ethics, see Schmücker (2022) in this volume.

12 Note that due to the limited territorial scope of national legislation, any discussion of existing legal rules can only, on an exemplary basis, refer to a particular national legal order. Given the origin of the conference participants, reference is

Hence, the conference participants and the book's contributors were not exclusively philosophers, but, in equal numbers, lawyers.[13]

a) Questions to be asked

The leading question could be formulated as follows: If pictures play an important role in contemporary social communication, how should the actions relating thereto be judged from an ethical perspective? And, from the legal perspective, how should existing legal norms be ethically assessed? Additionally, it is important to note that digital technology defines what users can do with images, thus enabling and structuring, but simultaneously limiting the individual user's scope for action. The technical configuration of the internet, the architecture of platforms, the design of filtering technologies and technical access controls exemplify this important issue. Hence, the design and use of such technical devices as well as the relevant existing regulation must be ethically scrutinised. In view of the importance of such technical devices and their freedom enabling and limiting configuration, the focus of this book is on digital image ethics' structural issues. This contrasts to special uses of digital images which are usually at the core of image ethics (which images may be shown in the media, the extent to which alterations are permissible, whether the depicted person's personality rights are infringed, which images should be accessible to children and minors, etc.). This focus does not exclude, however, a small number of contributions dealing with the ontological structure of virtual images or the significance of digital images for the freedom to consume images and society's collective memory.

b) Consequential ethics

Clearly, when searching for moral solutions to these questions, a consequentialist ethics seems to dominate the discourse. According to this approach, actions appear ethically acceptable/unacceptable in terms of their

---

mostly made to German, Italian and EU law, with a possible sideways glance at US law.

13 The conference brought together expert scholars and interested doctoral and post-doctoral students from a variety of disciplines, namely from philosophy, law, legal theory, information technology, sociology and image sciences.

consequences, i.e., of the effects they may cause. If even today possible negative consequences are imputed to images, this conforms to the Platonic tradition to mistrust images. According to Plato, after the abstract idea and its representation in the physical world, images of the latter constitute only a third level truth which by pretending to be more than they are, lie. According to this view, not only do pictures lie, but because they lie, they are regarded as potentially dangerous. In view of this fundamental distrust of images, the question to ask is whether a rule with negative effects can be replaced by a rule that would have less serious negative consequences.

A consequential ethics asks questions such as who may be harmed by an action concerning the making, use and consumption of images, and whether the specific type of image impacts the harm? Who should be entitled to protection (e.g., the person depicted, the potential onlooker)? Should some persons such as children, victims of accidents, terrorist attacks and warfare, or ethnic minority groups receive more protection than others? How should one respond to images' intended or unintended effects on the formation of the human image, the image and construction of the body and, generally, those effects which discriminate "the other" through visual stereotyping or denigration? Examining these questions, in Western cultures initially,[14] the construction of the image of women mainly in advertising was dominant. Later, the image of other minorities became prevalent and for some time now, post-colonial cultural studies examine the stereotypes of non-colonial populations in Western visual communication,[15] at times reversing the perspective by writing "photography's other histories" from a non-Western point of view.[16]

When answering ethical questions from a consequential view, one likewise must ask what could justify an otherwise unacceptable making or showing of images. If photographing warfare victims always seems problematic, can it be justified by the fact that without such documentation, human suffering would remain unnoticed, outside the place and time it was afflicted? To name just one example: It is now a commonly shared belief that Nick Út's famous photograph of the naked girl after the US napalm attack on a village in Vietnam played a crucial role in changing the attitude of the US population towards the Vietnam War. Moreover, without the publication of the photograph, the girl (Phan Thị Kim Phúc)

14 It should be noted, however, in Germany the debate about personality rights to one's own image dates back to a photograph illegally taken in 1898 of Germany's ex-chancellor Bismarck on his deathbed; see Koetzle (2002).

15 E.g., see only Herdin/Faust/Chen (2020); Cohen (2003).

16 Pinney/Peterson (2003).

would probably not have been transferred to a special clinic and would not have survived. In turn, does the commercial motive for taking such photographs alter the ethical judgement of the taking? Will the ethical judgement be different if the photograph is reproduced even half a century later? When it is filtered out for nudity on a Social Media platform? What about the use of such images of victims in art?[17]

Concerning all these questions, the debate is still ongoing. In both traditional forums and social media diverging claims are made and attacked, especially when it comes to the disputes fought out under fighting terms such as "political correctness", "culture cancelling" and "identity politics". The sometimes fiercely led debates revolve precisely around the fundamental questions of who may communicate and share – via text or images – what, to whom, about whom, in what manner and when. However, these questions are not the subject of the contributions to this book.

4. *Law and ethics*

Finally, another issue which is underlying most of the contributions to this book, but which is not addressed as such, shall briefly be touched upon here. It is the question of the relationship between ethical and legal rules. It is certainly possible to answer all digital image ethics questions from a purely philosophical perspective without considering existing and corresponding legal norms. However, to do so would seem a little odd. Admittedly, there may be issues that will always be outside of legal regulation as well as others which so far have not been addressed by legal regulation. However, to the extent that legal rules have already been formulated, the formulation of ethical rules would not have to start from scratch. Rather, these existing legal regulations could serve as a starting point for a discussion on what ethical rules should look like if they are not regarded as formulations of ethical rules altogether. Examples are the already mentioned right to one's own image, copyright as well as the protection against the circumvention of digital technical protection measures, to name just a few of the areas that will be dealt with in more depth in this book.[18]

17 For a more recent example, see Brinkmann (2020) 94 et seq.

18 Other major examples not discussed in this book are the legal ban found in many jurisdictions of making, distributing and even possessing images of child pornography; age restrictions or warning and labelling duties for showing certain images to specific groups of onlookers such as children and teenagers, as well as,

The existence of legal rules for images raises the question of the relationship between them and the corresponding ethical rules. On the one hand, one could argue that provided the legal norms were adopted by a democratically legitimized lawmaker, they reflect societal consensus on how these issues should be regulated. On the other hand, the majority may not share a view in line with ethical principles. Moreover, the legislative process might be flawed and thus not reflect the majority's moral conviction, but rather only the interests of a powerful and influential individual group or group of individuals. That is why it is indicated to also analyse actions which do not morally conflict with legal rules. For example, one may ask whether it is ethically permissible to publish an unfavourable picture of a person, even if it does not violate the law. But not only legal norms – be they imposed by authoritarian governments or adopted by democratic procedures – may conflict with sound ethical rules. Rather, the same can be said of court decisions. Since judges are bound by the legal norms adopted by the lawmaker, even if judges are impartial, any ethical flaw of a legal norm continues in court decisions.

However, at least in countries where the Constitutional Court has the legal power to declare legal norms adopted by Parliament null and void if they violate fundamental human rights, things appear different. Here the legality of the scrutinised legal norm is not ascertained because of the mere act of adoption in Parliament. Rather, the standard of measurement against which legal norms must be measured, are the human rights as enshrined in the Constitution. In such cases it appears at least plausible to assume that the Constitutional Court has already considered all the ethical aspects when interpreting individual fundamental rights and weighing them against each other. But even if carefully argued Constitutional Courts' decisions take due account of all ethical issues, one should emphasize that they hardly ever hold that only one legal norm is correct from a constitutional perspective. This is somewhat surprising to the philosopher who is used to assuming that any given ethical issue has only one single definitive answer. But from a constitutional perspective, the reason that more than one specifically worded legal rule can meet the constitutional threshold test is that some scope for political decision making must be left, by the judiciary, to both the legislative and the executive. In other words, since fundamental rights generally allow for more than one political decision, more than one legal rule implementing a specific political

---

last but not least, the obligation to affix certain images showing health hazards of smoking when selling packages of cigarettes.

decision satisfies the balance of fundamental rights. On another occasion, it was suggested by one of the book's editors to accept, quite like in constitutional law, a margin of appreciation also when it comes to defining ethical rules.[19] In other words, it could no longer be concluded that a legal norm which does not correspond with the preferred ethical rule is by definition unethical. Rather, any legal norm that remains within the constitutional margin of appreciation would have to be considered equally ethically justified. This assumption of a margin of appreciation should not be confused with ethical relativism.[20] Other than ethical relativism which allows for only one answer from each individual perspective, the model of a margin of appreciation suggested here would allow for several possible answers from one and the same perspective.

II. The Contributions of This Book

The book's contributions are the result of a three-day symposium at Villa Vigoni near Lake Como in Menaggio, held from 28 September to 1 October 2020 between two waves of the Corona pandemic. The conference was organized by the editors and sponsored by the German Research Foundation. This context explains the painting reproduced on the book's cover which was painted in 1939/1949 by American painter Sophia Amelia Peabody well before the advent of digital technology and even photography, but from the spot overlooking Lake Como where the Villa Vigoni stands today.

1. Transalpine considerations

Due to the format of conferences and symposia organized at Villa Vigoni, which serves as a German-Italian Center for the European Dialogue, about half of the participants of the conference and contributors to this book were from Italy, and the other half from Germany. The focus on the Italian-German cultural exchange is also the reason why the first of the contributions by *Werner Gephart* concentrates on the role of images from drawings to online communication in the transalpine context. Taking the

---

19 See Dreier (2018) 54.

20 For ethical relativism recognizing and taking stock of cross-country cultural differences, see, e.g., Ess (2009) 183 et seq.

Malcesine episode of Goethe's "Italian Journey"[21] as the starting point, Gephart adopts a sociological lens and proposes that the text can be viewed "as a reconstruction of a sociological space of observation and experience". From there on, Gephart examines "whether Goethe also used this objective space of experience 'sociologically', i.e., to what extent did [Goethe] not only discover himself, but also 'society' in Italy". This contribution analyses the extent to which the image of the "foreign" is indissolubly connected to the image of the "self", be it the personal self or the self of the traveller's own culture and society he lives in. Simultaneously, Gephart highlights how carefully and intentionally Goethe used both his drawings and his writings to initiate and undertake a highly complex transalpine transcultural communication. Images and their production, it becomes clear, are by no means static ontological objects, nor are they to be regarded as anthropological constants. Rather, as forms of communication in society, Gephart concludes, they "are placed in the realm of the normative and surrounded by commandments and prohibitions. They also exude their own deontic power, which we find difficult to grasp theoretically."

2. *The parts of this book*

Despite its limited focus on images as experienced by the famous traveller in the late 18th century, this initial contribution opens the view to the ethical questions raised by today's production and communication of digital images. These are developed by the subsequent contributions and can be divided into five parts.

To begin with, Part 2 on the *ethical foundations* starts with an overview of existing research in the field of visual digital ethics and an attempt to describe what an applied digital image ethics might have to say. This includes, on an exemplary basis, the formulation of three ethical rules. A second contribution of this part sketches out the relationship between form and norm in images.

Following, Part 3 centers on an array of ethical issues relating to *images in art and society*. It begins with the suggestion that to ensure that our societies are fair, rather than focussing on the issue of privacy we should focus on the benefits derived from a better understanding of the functioning of digital technology and the surplus value it creates via the web. Also, a helpful starting point could be a better understanding and ontological analysis

21 von Goethe (1816/1817).

of both the identification and the properties of immersive artistic forms. Additionally, one could focus on the shift in the understanding of images as objects to an understanding of images as a means of communication. On an exemplary basis, this is further highlighted by a discussion of the issues raised by referencing cultures. This part closes with two contributions discussing ethical issues regarding the importance of safeguarding digital images for the future, one focussing on the orientation of future generations, and one more specifically on issues surrounding the restoration of conceptual audiovisual material.

Part 4 examines the *effects of digital technology on the individual image*, which tends to dissolve into an array of isolated pixels. This begins with a more theoretical elaboration of the semiotics of the visual fake, followed by a more practical look at digital collaging and image manipulation. The next contributions focus on the existing legal regulation which already transmits certain ethically motivated choices, and hence could serve as a blueprint for the formulation of corresponding ethical rules. First, a description of the different legal regimes protecting the multiple layers of information in a digital image is made. Second, an explanation is given of the difficulties faced by legal regulation when regulated objects can be looked at as either one image or an array of personal data. Finally, the issue of human authorship is discussed when objects are made using artificial intelligence.

Subsequently, the contributions of Part 5 reflect some of the *effects of digital technology on both ethical and legal norms*. This begins with a thorough examination of the moral issues and constraints concerning cloud-based image storage, a chapter which raises more – highly relevant – questions than it is yet able to answer but clarifies to what extent these answers are influenced by the configuration of the storage devices. Particularly access controls, the following contribution argues, have the effect of replacing what users are legally allowed to do with what they can do, thus making the effect of both legal and ethical norms obsolete. The following contribution in this chapter draws the readers' attention to the fact that all norms – and, in particular, algorithmic decisions – which hold that certain images should be inaccessible involve some sort of censorship in a broad sense and hence must be based on ethical, political, and economic rationales. The last contribution in this part discusses the issue of the image of algorithms and provides an overview of the possibilities to regulate algorithms to ensure that they perform the decision making as envisaged.

Finally, the contributions of Part 6 attempt to shed some light, on an exemplary basis, on the intricate relationship between *ethical rules and fundamental rights*. One of these examples retraces the ethical considerations and arguments in decisions from both the German and Italian Constitutional Courts relating to the scope of the right to one's own image vis-à-vis the freedom of the press. From a similar perspective, the other contribution examines how the freedom of the art is currently being delimited from the proprietary interest protected by copyright in conflicts involving works of appropriation art.

3. *The contributions in detail*

a) *The ethical framework*

Following Part 1, in Part 2 of the book *Reinold Schmücker* begins with a differentiated overview of what the term "digital ethics" means or should mean from different perspectives and in view of different cognitive interests. Being critical of mere "guidebook" literature masquerading as ethics, Schmücker outlines the different approaches so far taken in ethical research. After providing an admittedly subjective snapshot of the current state of the multitude of positions and arguments on very different individual aspects of digital ethics, Schmücker discusses the difficulty of formulating normative foundations for what in his opinion could be an applied digital ethics. Also, he considers the functions a digital applied ethics could have and how it might differ from our everyday moral judging. In doing so, Schmücker draws a parallel between formulating an applied ethics and the application of legal rules. This complements the brief analysis of the substantive relationship between legal and moral rules found in the book's introduction by focussing on the procedural similarities of legal and ethical rules. Finally, Schmücker focuses on an "image ethics" that sees itself as part of digital ethics and considers the differences between analogue and digital images to be only of a gradual nature and hence doubts the need for a special digital image ethics. Rather, Schmücker argues, it is the social practices regarding digital images which raise normative questions that digital image ethics should aim to answer. The mid-level ethical principles Schmücker proposes – the "Principle of Unconditionally Permissible Use of All Vocabulary of a Visual Language", the "Principle of the Legitimacy of Taking Photographs in Museums" to allow for documenting one's own life, and the "Principle of Prohibiting Deception by Manipulated Photographs" – regarding digital images could all be applied to analogue images as well. However, Schmücker concludes that in the analogue age, there was simply no need for those principles specifically tied to the characteristics of digital images.

Following Schmücker's contribution, *Enrico Terrone* proposes an hylomorphic account of pictures. Assuming hylomorphism is the view according to which objects are constituted by both their form and their matter, Terrone argues that the matter of a picture is a colored surface while its form is a norm that prescribes how to use that surface, that is, what one should see in that surface. Moreover, the hylomorphic account of pictures can be deployed to evidence both the analogies and the differences between depiction and language.

b) Images, art and society

The first contribution in Part 3 on various issues of the production, dissemination and use of images in art and society by *Maurizio Ferraris* starts from the observation of the current societal crisis and particularly how our work life and our private life has changed due to digital technology and the web ("smartworking"). Ferraris contends that this is an ongoing and accelerating trend which can be observed over the past few years. This trend is said to make us consider our own features and appreciate the opportunities the Web gives us, without, however, being fully aware of the information asymmetries between the mobilisers and the mobilised, which Ferraris analyses in great detail. He then proposes that we should reduce the importance of privacy to better understand the potential of benefits gained from a true and transparent understanding of the Web, of big data, and its uses. This could lead us to dealing with what Ferraris calls "documedia capital", the surplus value of which will help us to make our societies fairer, provided it is properly distributed. However, there are, of course, two main objections made against this approach, which Ferraris attempts to debunk.

The contribution of *Davide Dal Sasso* offers an account of the origins and features of "immersive artistic forms" by proposing a list of identifying criteria. The first part of this contribution is dedicated to the topic of technology and focuses on the relationship between art, knowledge and operational practices. The second part addresses some issues in the metaphysics of art, the relationship between form and structure. Likewise, it presents possible criteria for identifying "immersive artistic forms". It is suggested that rather than classifying a kind of art, the term can reference the outcomes achieved through different artistic practices that favour users' immersion in works of art. Based on these identification criteria, immersive artistic forms are thus works of art structured in different ways and which may offer immersive experiences in virtual reality as well as in the real world.

Wolfgang Ullrich subsequently discusses the consequences of a new image culture that has emerged in recent years because of digitization and can be described as a shift from works to lively means of communication. For the first time in their history, images are no longer static entities, but can be reproduced, sent, and above all, changed as often and quickly as desired. Following language, one could thus say that there are no longer only written, i.e., fixed, but also oral forms of pictoriality. Until now, such forms existed mainly to the extent that facial expressions and gestures have a pictorial-variable character. Correspondingly, many forms of digital images also have primarily communicative functions. Only rarely, are they still associated, Ullrich argues, with the idea of an (art) work.

Stating that today, not only do images gain their prominence through mass reproduction on social media, but that referencing images has become a general means of communication, *Eva-Maria Bauer* concludes that existing copyright law does not adequately reflect the importance of references such as Memes or GiFs. Contrary to the U.S., where most – and certainly non-commercial – referencing uses of images in social media are covered by the so-called "fair use"-exception, under European copyright law there is no corresponding exception to the exclusive rights of the original creators of images. Even the exception for pastiches, recently adopted in Germany based on EU legislation dating from 2001, will – notwithstanding the fact that the official memorandum, accompanying the draft bill explicitly considers memes as a case of pastiche – not solve the problem. This is because such a broad understanding of pastiche was likely not intended at a time when communication with images via social networks was simply beginning. In Bauer's view, the societal importance of referencing cultures justifies eliminating the discrepancy between a rigid legal assessment of appropriation on the one hand, and referencing techniques and the changed communication behaviour in social media on the other hand. Without the creation of a legal exemption for communicative appropriations, Bauer argues, the legitimacy crisis of copyright law will intensify, for if copyright law no longer reflects social reality, it will no longer be supported by social consensus.

The remaining two contributions focus on aspects of preservation of digital art works and their importance for future generations. To begin with, *Tiziana Andina* focuses on the aspect of transgenerationality of digital images, outlining a new ethic regarding the role of digital images to orient the future. In view of the need of Western democracies to direct the future, Andina proposes that tools must be strengthened to orient the future towards a direction of development, greater equity and sustainability. To this end, Andina examines the technological possibilities offered by digital images and demonstrates how they can easily become tools of memory as well as vehicles of detailed information to help us to understand the human at a level of detail never reached before. This informational capital could become the empirical basis for backcasting experiments that could later be used to model future societies.

In the second of the two contributions on aspects of preservation of digital art works and their importance for future generations, *Cosetta Saba* examines the impact of preserving analogue audiovisual material in a digital format. Building upon a distinction from the French philosopher, anthropologist and sociologist Bruno Latour, between iconoclasm (which aims at the destruction of a work of art) and iconoclash (which designates the forces behind different modes of representation), Saba demonstrates to what extent iconoclash is inherent in both the activities of preservation and digital restoration of analogue moving images. Indeed, the apparent indistinction between destructive and constructive actions aimed at the cultural transmission of analogue images reveals a principle of assimilation underlying the current "software culture". What we are faced with is a "selective-elective" process, i.e., selection by similarity and election to oneself – a "making similar to oneself" – that removes the aesthetic and historical difference of analogue moving images regarding their context of production and reception. The practice that qualifies the digitisation process for preservation purposes thus activates issues that have less in common with the variation of the aesthetic and historical properties of analogue motion pictures, than with their "erasure".

c) *Binary encoding and artificial intelligence: The dissolution of the visual object*

In a way, the contributions of the following Part 4 revisit the iconoclash theme regarding the representation of the human face. What is gauged is the difference between the real face and a deep fake which is no longer indexically linked to and does not represent a particular individual's face, but which, through algorithmic machine learning references a great number of faces. In this respect, *Massimo Leone* proposes a semioethics of visual fakes and argues that the ethics of images differs from that of words because images have an intrinsic motivation that words lack. There is of course something conventional in images, as there might be motivation in words, yet the materiality of visual signs anchors them to reality and perception in a different, more cogent way. That is why, in Leone's opinion, images do not lie as words do. Even when they are farfetched, they transmit an idea of real possibility that words can hardly evoke. There are two different ideological stances regarding the relation between images and the reality they manifest. Humanities, including semiotics, tend to emphasize the weight of the cultural context; increasing evidence, however, shows that images evoke certain responses because they match the innate neurophysiology of cognition. Humans are biologically inclined to react to images, and representations trigger different perceptions depending on their technology, which accumulatively evolves throughout human history. Semiotics is therefore called to debunk the realistic propaganda of new devices for representation and display, emphasizing their conventionality, but also considering how new advances in the production of simulacra tend to introduce emerging phenomena between images and the human perception. The visual fake of today is indeed somewhat more powerful than those of past epochs because it is constructed through machines whose outcome can be debunked only by other machines. Furthermore, the evolution of digital cultures now blurs fictional and non-fictional genres. The visual fake starts to circulate like a virus, multiplying the occasions for ambiguous suspensions of disbelief. Instead, Leone argues, a new ecology of the fictional that can foster a reasonable semioethics of the visual fake is needed.

On a slightly more concrete and practical level, *Olivia Hägle* then retraces how the basic principle of digital information processing, binary encoding, yields a variety of new possibilities for the manipulation of visual objects. By breaking down images to their components and recomposing these parts with parts of other images, existing visual objects can be manipulated and entirely new objects can be created. Recent technical advances in artificial intelligence enable such image manipulations to be created almost autonomously and already achieve deceptively realistic results. This so-called deep fake technology offers numerous potential applications. It could revolutionise the film industry and it provides countless opportunities for art, satire and economy. But in the wrong hands, like any technology, it has a potential for misuse. All too often, deep fake technology is used to defame people, for example by inserting them into pornographic material. And due to their simplicity and persuasiveness, deep fakes are powerful weapons for targeted disinformation campaigns. Given the technology's inherent threats, according to Hägle, there is a strong need for regulation. Therefore, not only should legal and technical measures be considered, but also ethical considerations.

Shifting the focus to existing legal regulation, *Benjamin Raue's* contribution provides an overview of the multi-layered – structural, syntactical, semantical – information in a (digital) image, and describes the legal regulations attached to each of these layers. In his view, the information layer model is a tool to structure and analyse the varying interests that exist within a digital image. While the model does not provide definitive answers, it does allow the identification of the appropriate layer of information for mediating the different interests. Accordingly, the regulation can be limited to specific aspects of information and, consequently, restrict the conflicting interests as little as possible.

Another legal aspect of the dissolution of images into discrete digital pixels is discussed by *Lorenz Müller-Tamm* in his contribution on the legal protection of images through personality rights (right to one's own image) versus data protection legislation. For a long time, there had been broad agreement that pictures depicting people are subject to image protection law. However, the introduction of data protection laws, especially the European General Data Protection Regulation (GDPR) in 2016, which also encompasses the processing of image data, questioned the relationship between the two regulatory regimes. After giving an overview of the image protection law in Germany and the data protection law in the EU, the contribution investigates the question whether the GDPR opening clauses still allow for the applicability of the German image protection law despite the general precedence of EU law. The account of this vital legal debate then leads to the follow-up question of whether the – national or European – legislator should intervene and what could be considered an ethically appropriate solution.

Apart from rasing many additional questions, the advent of artificial intelligence used when making artefacts urges the law to reconsider the traditional concepts of authorship, originality, and creativity both in- and outside of copyright. As *Gianmaria Ajani* shows, current copyright laws only offer the public domain or outdated regulatory mechanisms as solutions. The inertia of the law, he argues, is rooted in the romantic idea of a solitary individual as the master of creativeness. While this idea still inspires theoretical elaborations and normative choices, the art world is discovering the perspective of an art made without the intervention of human authors. Facing these technological advancements, in Ajani's view, policy makers should reconsider the role of artificial intelligence in copyright law and be inspired by innovative theories in robot law where new frames for a legal personhood of artificial agents are being proposed.

d) Technology, ethics and legal norms

Opening Part 5 which focuses on the relationship between and mutual dependency of, technology, ethical and legal norms, *Wybo Houkes*' contribution emphasizes that, increasingly, businesses turn to subscription-based, service-oriented models for digital products instead of traditional models which transfer ownership of a product. One instance of this "servitization" trend is cloud storage of personal images, such as family photos. Here, justifiable business interests must be weighed against basic consumer (or end-user) rights. Woukes explores ways to examine and assess this complicated balance from a moral perspective. According to him, the first option is to focus on seeking continuity with non-digitized practice. Consumer acceptance of digitized products crucially depends on how they are used to view such products. Existing consumers' perceptions create reasonable expectations regarding consumer rights, but also difficulties to identify how best digitized products should be viewed. After proposing that the perception of digitized objects be examined in relation to high-level activities, Woukes specifies moral constraints for the basic activities of accumulating, accessing, curating, and deleting personal images in cloud-based storage. These constraints result from personal image collections acting as "technologies of memory" that support formation of and reflection on individual and collective identity.

Next *Thomas Dreier*, in his contribution draws the readers' attention to the phenomenon that whereas the law tells us what we may do, technology defines what we can do. While technology enables users to act in a new way, it does not enable users to act in any way they want. Whereas this is the case with any technology, it presents a problem if technology prevents its users from performing acts which they are legally allowed to perform. In such cases, Dreier argues, law and even ethical norms lose their regulatory function when technology takes the lead. This is a phenomenon described by Lawrence Lessig in the famous expression "code as law" and one which Dreier names the deontic power of technology. Copyright limitations are prime examples as they grant users certain communicative freedoms which, due to copy control mechanisms and automatic filtering systems applied by platform operators, can no longer fully be exercised digitally. Similarly, so-called end-user license agreements implemented as digital contracts reduce the users' freedom of response to the "love it or leave it" approach. After retracing the legal reactions of the legislature, the courts and legal literature, Dreier outlines the key elements for developing both ethical and legal rules to counterbalance the factual force of technology. As long as competition is not unduly restricted and since technical protection measures allow useful product diversification, an appropriate solution, Dreier argues, cannot be found in an ex ante ban nor in a mere ex post control of technology. Rather, it is proposed that the aim should be greater transparency and more detailed information of users about the existence and properties of technology applied to digital content, including images.

Reminding the reader that any regulation which allows the circulation and accessibility of images constitutes a form of censorship in the wider sense, *Eberhard Ortland* first explains that censorship is neither good nor bad, as it can be used for both bad (suppressing certain opinions) and good (protecting children from images detrimental to the child's personal development) purposes. However, in all instances the central question is who should decide according to which criteria under which circumstances which images may and which may not be shown? In view of both the increasing number of circulated images due to the increase of cameras, digital communication technologies generally, and conflicts regarding circulation and accessibility of certain images, this task is increasingly assigned to more or less automatic censorship algorithms. Concerning the moderation of visual contents, algorithms, Ortland argues, need supervision by accountable human moderators so long as they cannot cope with the pragmatics of "pictorial speech acts", among other challenges.

Finally, *Lisa Käde* takes a closer look at algorithms and discusses how they could be regulated in a way that automatic decision-making could be left to them. In other words, what has to be done to guarantee that AI algorithms are in line with regulation? The most important issue to consider in this respect, Käde argues, is to ascertain the exact societal impact of algorithms, and why and in which cases algorithms must be regulated. How can images, Käde asks, be useful for the regulation of algorithms? How should algorithms dealing with images be regulated? And how does the negative image of algorithms influence their regulation? The author discusses the ethical issues and legal context as well as their mutual influences. Answers to these questions are provided by means of practical examples. Finally, Käde reviews existing legislative approaches, guidelines and regulations, both in Germany and the EU as well as practical tools to foster algorithm transparency.

e) Ethics and fundamental rights

In Part 6, the two final contributions of the book focus on how ethical issues regarding images are treated by constitutional law.

In the first of these contributions, *Johannes Eichenhofer* highlights various issues related to the constitutional protection of images. The starting point is the proposal for a terminological and phenomenological distinction between "inner" and "outer" images on the one hand, and "self" and "external" images on the other hand. In the following, Eichenhofer aims to show how these different conceptions of "images" are treated under both German and Italian constitutional law. The focus of his analysis is on a German-Italian case study on the legality of the dissemination of images of prominent persons, namely Princess Soraya of Persia and Princess Caroline of Hanover (formerly Monaco). He then uses this case study to propose some constitutional standards for the use of images and discusses the extent to which digitization justifies modifying these standards. The contribution concludes with some remarks on the handling of digital images.

In the final contribution, *Christophe Geiger* reviews a set of recent court decisions convicting famous contemporary artists for copyright infringement in cases of appropriation art. It is argued that these decisions not only totally disregard the artistic context in which these takings from previous works occur, but also wrongly assess the legitimacy of these artistic expressions regarding fundamental rights protection in our democratic society. Denying art the possibility to construct a discourse about a previous copyright protected work, the act of copying itself, or even the copyright system and its conception of ownership, amounts to a misuse of copyright for the purpose of censorship. This is, Geiger argues, because it is the essence of art to be able to express ideas without seeking for permission by the state or by private entities. Moreover, in Geiger's opinion, these decisions endanger the worldwide exhibition of contemporary art as often museums or art galleries have been jointly convicted with the appropriation artists. Consequently, there is a serious risk that cultural institutions in the future will be overcautious when choosing to expose certain artists to avoid repeated and costly copyright claims. To address these shortcomings of the copyright system, Geiger proposes to rethink the boundaries of copyright law and to introduce into the European legal framework a flexibility clause based on criteria developed by the freedom of expression-case law of European courts.

References

Belting, Hans (2011): *An Anthropology of Images – Picture, Medium, Body* (Princeton/Oxford: Princeton University Press 2011)

Bredekamp, Horst (2018): *Image Acts – A Systematic Approach to Visual Agency* (Berlin: De Gruyter 2018)

Brinkmann, Franziska (2020): 'Formen der Kopie von der Fälschung bis zur Hommage', in: Dreier, Thomas/Jehle, Oliver: *Original – Kopie – Fälschung* (Baden-Baden: Nomos 2020) 57–104

Cohen, Hart (2003): 'Moral copyright – Indigenous People and Contemporary Film', in: Gross, Larry/Katz, John Stuart/Ruby, Jay: *Image Ethics in the Digital Age* (Minneapolis/London: University of Minnesota Press 2003) 313–325

Dreier, Thomas (2018): 'The Ethics of Citations and Partial Copying', 26 Annual Review of Law and Ethics (2018) 39–55

Dreier, Thomas (2019): *Law and Images*, Brill Paper Art and Law 3.1 (Leiden/Boston: Brill 2019)

Elkins, James (1996): *The Object Stares Back – On the Nature of Seeing* (San Diego/New York/London: Harcourt 1996)

Ess, Charles (2009): *Digital Media Ethics* (Cambridge: Polity Press 2009)

Fishman, Jessica M. (2003): 'News Norms and Emotions' – Pictures of Pain and Metaphors of Distress', in: Gross, Larry/Katz, John Stuart/Ruby, Jay (2003): *Image Ethics in the Digital Age* (Minneapolis/London: University of Minnesota Press 2003) 53–69

Flusser, Vilém (1983): *Towards A Philosophy of Photography* (Göttingen: European Photography 1983)

Frater, Patrick (2016): 'Bill Gates' Corbis Images Sold to Visual China Group', Variety, Jan 25, 2016, https://variety.com/2016/digital/asia/bill-gates-corbis-images-sold-to-visual-china-1201687743

Gross, Larry/Katz, John Stuart/Ruby, Jay (2003): *Image Ethics in the Digital Age* (Minneapolis/London: University of Minnesota Press 2003)

Herdin, Thomas/Faust, Maria/Chen, Guo-Ming (2020): *De-Westernizing Visual Communication and Cultures – Perspectives from the Global South* (Baden-Baden: Nomos 2020)

Koetzle, Hans-Michael (2002): *Photo Icons – Die Geschichte hinter den Bildern* (Köln et al: Taschen 2002) 108–115

Mitchell, William John Thomas (1992): *The Reconfigured Eye – Visual Truth in the Post-photographic Era* (Cambridge/Mass.: MIT Press 1992)

Mitchell, William John Thomas Mitchell (2005): *What do pictures want? The Lives and Loves of Images* (Chicago: University of Chicago Press 2005)

Modi, Vinit (2020): 'More controls and transparency for your selfies – Control and transparency for selfie filters', Google Blog Outreach Activities Digital-Wellbeing, 1 October 2020, https://blog.google/outreach-initiatives/digital-wellbeing/more-controls-selfie-filters

Pinney, Christopher/Peterson, Nicolas (2003): *Photography's Other Histories* (Durham/London: Duke University Press 2003)

Schmücker, Reinold (2022): 'Digital Image Ethics – How it Could be Pursued and What It Might Have to Say', in: Dreier, Thomas/Andina, Tiziana: *Digital Ethics – The Issue of Images* (Baden-Baden: Nomos 2022) 49–73

Sontag, Susan (2003): *Regarding the Pain of Others* (New York: Farrar, Straus and Giroux 2003)

Tappe, Inga (2016): 'Bildethik', in: Heesen, Jessica, *Handbuch Medien- und Informationsethik* (Stuttgart: J.B. Metzler 2016)

von Goethe, Johann Wolfgang (1816/1817): *Italienische Reise (Italian Journey)*, in: *Werke*, Vol. XI (Hamburg: Christian Wegner Verlag 1950; first published 1816–1817 as "Zweite Abteilung" of his autobiography *Aus meinem Leben*, Tübingen: Cotta'sche Verlagsbuchhandlung 1816–1817)

Chapter 2
From Goethe's *Italian Journey* to Transalpine Online Navigation – Narrative Changes and Transnational Stereotypes

Werner Gephart

I. Preface

Among Goethe scholars, there is consensus that the poet's journey to Italy marks a turning point for his self-discovery, the development of his studies of nature, and the unfolding of his poetic work. It seems to me, however, that less attention is given to this journey also yielding a "social researcher" – someone who has yet to be discovered and explored.[1] Goethe's statements are unambiguous, as we shall see. Besides "nature" and "poetry", there is the analysis of the "customs of peoples". The trip to Italy presented an opportunity for an elementary sociological experience. This is true for any kind of travel, but did Goethe also ponder this? Why do the more or less professed "Goetheans" among the founders of sociology refrain from referencing this literary burden of sociology in Germany?

No poet of German classicism has left such deep traces in classic sociological work as Goethe. Georg Simmel[2] wrote a book about Goethe that barely gained attention in Goethe research circles[3] which he dedicated to Marianne Weber, the sociologist's wife. In one of his most presuppositional pictures, he draws upon *Die Wahlverwandtschaften* (*Elective Affinities*)[4] specifically when dealing with the interactions of ideas and interests. This leaves us to wonder whether these references are based on subcutaneous bourgeois recollections, as is largely the case in German intellectual history concerning Olympians,[5] or whether their reasoning differs: the secret con-

1 Ideas on this can, of course, be found in Werner (1988).

2 Simmel (1913).

3 Mandelkov (1997) expressedly points out the need to catch up; insights on the link between Goethe's image and Simmel's sketch of modernity can be found in Gephart (1998) 25 et seq.

4 Cf. for example Weber (1920) 82.

5 On Goethe's reception in Germany cf. Mandelkow (1980 and 1989).

tent of sociological, intuitive thought, which hides societal analysis behind the literary form of the *Italian Journey* (*Italienische Reise*)[6] and has a similar meaning for the shape of sociology in Germany – just like the French novel undoubtedly did for the emergence of sociology in France.

I would like to proceed in two steps: First, I will sociologically examine the *Italian Journey* as a reconstruction of a sociological space of observation and experience. In a second step, I will examine whether Goethe also used this objective space of experience "sociologically", i.e., to what extent did he not only discover himself but also "society" in Italy.

II. "Travelling" as a Medium of Communication and Discovery

> "The pleasure of a journey is, if you want it pure, an abstract pleasure [...]"[7]

... Goethe writes in his diary intended for Charlotte von Stein, which, in the literary version, is free from Protestant dross, and contains only rudiments of a travel ethic, labelling travelling primarily as *work*. The diary's original text reads: "Jeder denckt doch eigentlich für sein Geld auf der Reise zu *genießen*. Er erwartet alle die Gegenstände von denen er so viel hat reden hören, nicht zu finden, wie der Himmel und die Umstände wollen, sondern so rein wie sie in seiner Imagination stehen und fast nichts findet er so, fast nichts kann er so genießen."[8] Achieving this pure "experience" of the idea of the journey requires work – hard and relentless "travel work"[9] – from which Goethe can only free himself from when he goes beyond the Brenner Pass, leaving Lake Garda and Rome behind as he continues on to Sicily and Naples to experience an emerging and uninhibited "travel happiness".

A sociological analysis, which can only be hinted at here, clarifies how a formal analysis of the constitution of the travelling "me" is applied at the intersection of social circles – meaning between the *society of origin*,

6 Von Goethe (1816/1817).

7 Von Goethe (1786/1991) 75 ("Der Genuß einer Reise ist wenn man ihn rein haben will, ein abstrackter Genuß [...]"; English translation by the author).

8 Ibid.

9 How close Goethe's connection to the Puritan work ethic is, becomes visible not least in Weber, who emphasizes the mutual condition of 'deed' and 'renunciation' as an insight of the late Goethe especially in his study on Protestantism; Weber (1920) 203; the passage referring to Goethe is missing in the first version of 1904/1905.

the travelling society, and the "*travelled society*". In this model – which is a given for travel research conducted from a cultural studies perspective – attention is not initially cast on the *foreign*, but rather on the *self* of the abandoned society, which the traveller is bound to via a network of relationships of ongoing entanglements. And even before any actual contact with the "foreign", there are the ephemeral *casual socializations*[10] of travel, as well as the more or less perennial local social formations which the traveller, as a stranger for his own part, partially grows into. Goethe's journey can now be applied to "social circles" where the social rebirth of the travelling "me" first occurs. But how does the traveller remain connected to those whom he left? How do we communicate with each other when the lockdown robs us of the sociality of physical co-presence?

III. Letters, Circulars, and Broadcast Chains

As regards the official Weimar – whose benevolence Goethe must continue to strive for – the numerous and painstakingly consistent monthly letters to Duke Karl August quantitatively stand out. In contrast, the letter to the Duchess, which was not reflected upon at all in the *Italian Journey*, provides a refreshing irony which even caricatures the Arcadian motto of the *Italian Journey*: "The traveller can seldom go out of himself, what he has to report of fates is of little importance and mostly he writes with

10 Theoretically illuminating is the sketch by Luhmann (1972). – In Simmel's work, the importance of non-institutionalized social connections is particularly clearly emphasized. Thus it says in his "Exkurs über das Problem: wie ist Gesellschaft möglich" ("*Excursus on the problem: How is society possible?*"): "Es bestehen außer jenen weithin sichtbaren, ihren Umfang und ihre äußere Wichtigkeit allenthalben aufdrängenden Erscheinungen eine unermeßliche Zahl von kleineren, in den einzelnen Fällen geringfügig erscheinenden Beziehungsformen und Wechselwirkungsarten zwischen den Menschen, die aber von diesen Fällen in gar nicht abzuschätzender Masse dargeboten werden, und, indem sie sich zwischen die umfassenden, sozusagen offiziellen sozialen Formungen schieben, doch erst die Gesellschaft, wie wir sie kennen, zustandebringen", Simmel (1908/1968a) 14 et seq. ("Apart from those widely visible phenomena which impose their extent and external importance everywhere, there exist an immeasurable number of smaller forms of relationships and modes of interaction between people, which in the individual cases appear to be insignificant, but which are presented by these cases in an incalculable mass and, by interposing themselves between the comprehensive, so to speak official social forms, only bring about society as we know it"; translation by the author).

smug delight: that he now also enters those long-desired regions, sees those hearty regions with his eyes and enjoys them after his own kind."[11]

Let us consider the confidants and friends of the Weimar Circle – a Weimar which had just 6,000 citizens and was to become the center of world literature. It's not just Charlotte von Stein who stands out in this circle, but also – and with a completely different significance – the servant and confidant, assistant and administrator Seidel, as well as Gottfried Herder, for whom the Göschen edition is being compiled. In addition to Knebel, Voigt, and Kayser, letters addressed to the anonymous *Weimar Circle of Friends* also deserve special sociological attention – circulars, circulars ad *incertam personam*, insofar as the circle of friends is not yet defined, or at least determinable. It is Goethe's *communicative genius* that provides for an unbelievable multiplication of fruitful bonds which eventually leads to the fact that the circle of friends seems to determine the progress of the journey seemingly consensually. Indeed, Goethe even asks Charlotte to excuse him from the places he does not write![12]

The letter is thus a medium in which both the distance intended – not least by the traveller – and the communicative proximity can be modulated.

To me, correspondence[13] appears thus not only particularly appealing to literary scholars. Rather, it can also be interpreted as an indicator of the journey's communicative *socio-gram*. Travelling thereby places extraordinarily complex communicative demands which go in two directions: both in relation to one's own world, which is left behind, and to the new, "foreign" world. Perhaps we're only "touched"[14] by "foreign objects and people" – as Goethe authoritatively postulates for his son – if the traveller meets both requirements: as a traveller, one becomes a mediator between worlds and cultures to the extent that one remains connected to the abandoned world and allows oneself to be touched by the new, as another world.

Does this also apply to travelling on the internet? With communication streams that go back and forth via Gmail, WhatsApp, I-Chat, and in fo-

---

11 Von Goethe (1786/1890) 96 ("Der Reisende kann selten aus sich selbst herausgehen, was er von Schicksalen zu melden hat ist wenig bedeutend und meistens schreibt er mit selbstgefälligem Entzüken: daß er nun auch jene langgewünschten Gegenden betrete, jene herzlichen Gegenden mit Augen sehe und nach seiner Art davon und dabey genieße"; English translation by the author).

12 Ibid.

13 Cf. Simmel (1908/1968b) 287 et seq.

14 Von Goethe (1830/1999) 235.

rums between Germany and Italy? And what kind of digital ethics prevails here, or is it unethical?

IV. How We Participate in Foreign Life

Here, the Malcesine scene, as noted by Goethe in his daily report from September 14, has an exemplary significance.[15] The basic experience of sociological travel, of entering an ambiguous observer's situation, not only comprises irony and subcutaneous allusions, but is a key communicative experience.

The "incognito traveller" settles in an old castle and begins to sketch the tower (Fig. 1), and a crowd forms. But then: someone pushes their way to the traveller, asking what he was doing. Goethe confesses to having sketched it "in order to preserve a memory of Malcesine". This is followed by the imperative comment that this is not permitted and that he should refrain from doing so. When Goethe doesn't seem to understand what is said in Venetian dialect, the following happens: "At this, with typical Italian nonchalance he tore the page up though he left it on the pad"[16] (which is how we still have it today). The rest of the story deserves to be analyzed sentence by sentence.

Fig. 1: Johann Wolfgang von Goethe, Castello Scaligero, Malcesine (torn), 14.9.1786

15 Von Goethe (1817/1950).

16 "Er ergriff darauf mit wahrer italienischer Gelassenheit mein Blatt, zerriß es, ließ es aber auf der Pappe liegen" (English translation by the author).

Goethe's memories of the Italian community influenced his search for communicative "agreement" with the man who had taken offence. Following, Goethe asks why the ruins, functionless buildings of a decaying fortress, are not worthy of being painted by a "spy", but by a traveller who – as Goethe writes in this very passage – "anything strange is not strange at all".[17] But one must first of all assume the role of the foreigner, i.e., that peculiar position that denotes both an inside and an outside of society. Not every outsider is a "stranger" as Georg Simmel explained in his famous digression: "Strangeness is [...] a very positive relationship, a special form of interaction [...]. The stranger is an element of the group itself [...]."[18] But the stranger is quite distanced from the group; "he occasionally comes into contact with each individual element but is not organically bound to any one of them by kinship, local, professional fixities".[19] Thus, the mixture of closeness and distance requires the "stranger" to "immerse" him or herself into the life-world of the "other" to grant him or her, through necessary distance, a special opportunity for objectivity: "Because he is not fixed from the root for the singular constituents or the unilateral tendencies of the group, he faces all these with the special attitude of the 'objective', which does not mean a mere distance and a lack of involvement, but is a special construction of distance and proximity, indifference and commitment."[20]

Analyzing the Malcesine scene, we could go even further and read into an externally induced experimental situation – a field experiment, so to say – which we know, of course, Goethe later decorated in a colorful fashion.[21] Especially if we accept Goethe's interpretation of the scientific

17 "etwas Fremdes nicht fremd ist" (English translation by the author).

18 Simmel (1908/1968a) 510 ("das Fremdsein ist [...] eine ganz positive Beziehung, eine besondere Wechselwirkungsform [...]. Der Fremde ist ein Element der Gruppe selbst [...]"; Englisch translation by the author).

19 Ibid. ("er kommt gelegentlich mit jedem einzelnen Elemente in Berührung, ist aber mit keinem einzelnen durch die verwandtschaftlichen, lokalen, beruflichen Fixiertheiten organisch verbunden"; English translation by the author).

20 Ibid. ("Weil er nicht von der Wurzel her für die singulären Bestandteile oder die einseitigen Tendenzen der Gruppe festgelegt ist, steht er allen diesen mit der besonderen Attitüde des 'Objektiven' gegenüber, die nicht etwa einen bloßen Abstand und Unbeteiligtheit bedeutet, sondern ein besonderes Gebilde aus Ferne und Nähe, Gleichgültigkeit und Engagiertheit ist"; English translation by the author).

21 The original entry is much more brittle: "Die Lust dir das Schloß zu zeichnen, das ein ächtes Pendant zu dem böhmischen ist, hätte es mir übel bekommen können. Die Einwohner fanden es verdächtig, weil hier die Gränze ist und sich alles vorm Kayser fürchtet. Sie thaten einen Anfall auf mich, ich habe aber den Treufreund

experiment as a *mediator between object and subject*, and apply it to the analysis of "society", the potential richness of the Malcesine experiment, even in poetic imagination, becomes immediately obvious.

The scene also plays, in two ways, with the notion of a hidden identity. It is only the incognito traveller who exposes himself to the danger of being mistaken for a spy, a suspicion whose refutation is both cumbersome and pleasurable for the knowledgeable reader – after all, the identity of the accused, as author of *Werther*, is known to him.

V. The Power of the "Image"

The Malcesine scene is also of paradigmatic value because the "suspicion" was linked to the activity of drawing, a medium in which the view of art, nature, and society unfolds. The appropriation of the "foreign", and of the yet so "familiar", occurs in a medium that simultaneously creates a visual communicative link to the abandoned society: drawing. Thus, Goethe writes the following in a letter on February 17, 1787, which, by the way, did not find its way into the literary text: "A packet of drawings or rather scribblings after nature, to give you at least a view of the country in general." He continues: "request Mrs. v. Stein that she distribute the pictures when you arrive, and that Prince August and Franckenberg also see them. Finally, however, they are to be returned to her [...]".[22]

This function of drawing for Goethe's perception and visual communication should be considered when the lines facilitate any idea of sensual things, because, and I quote: "The more closely and precisely one observes particulars, the sooner one arrives at a perception of the whole".[23]

I would like to conclude the "Malcesine experience" with Goethe's prophetic statement that this report could one day be of touristic value. Just listen to his words in the *Italian Journey*: "The keeper of the inn where

---

köstlich gespielt, sie haranguirt und sie bezaubert. Das Detail davon mündlich." Von Goethe (1786/1991) 37.

22 Von Goethe (1890) 187 ("Ein Päckchen Zeichnungen oder vielmehr Krabeleyen nach der Natur, um Euch wenigstens einen Blick des Landes im allgemeinen zu geben. [...] ersucht Fr. v. Stein, daß sie die Bildchen wenn Sie kommen circulieren laße, auch Prinz August und Franckenberg sie sehen. Zuletzt aber sollen sie wieder bey ihr zurück kommen [...]"; English translation by the author).

23 Von Goethe (1817/1950) 137 ("man erhebt sich ja eher zum Allgemeinen, wenn man die Gegenstände genauer und schärfer beobachtet"; English translation by the author).

I had engaged a room – after the misunderstanding had dissolved into nothingness – now joined us and was delighted at the prospect of foreigners flocking to his inn, once the attractions of Malcesine were properly known."[24]

VI. Conclusion

During these times, pandemic borders must be overcome to relive the Malcesine scene on site. But I hope it has become clear how images and their production can acquire situational power. They are placed in the realm of the normative and surrounded by commandments and prohibitions. They also exude their own deontic power which we find difficult to grasp theoretically. What we can expect from the distance experienced by those at home was very precisely reflected between the lines in Goethe as a communicative epistolary ethic. And we also know that one may even offend the sensitive minds by de-individualizing group messages, only using them for certain content, circulars, and broadcasts.

The uncanny realm of the normative also extends to the most subtle forms of communication: the love letter, including the love email, and the prohibition of breaking up over text, even though in some legal cultures, one can now divorce by email.

I am firmly convinced that we can still learn from the highest levels of the epistolary arts, including for their application to questions of a digital ethic.

References

Gephart, Werner (1998): *Bilder der Moderne – Studien zu einer Soziologie der Kunst- und Kulturinhalte* (Opladen: Leske and Budrich Verlag 1998)

Luhmann, Niklas (1972): 'Einfache Sozialsysteme', Zeitschrift für Soziologie (1972) 51–65

Mandelkow, Karl Robert (1980 and 1989): *Goethe in Deutschland – Rezeptionsgeschichte eines Klassikers* (2 Vol. München: C.H. Beck Verlag 1980 and 1989)

24 Ibid. 35 ("Der Wirt, bei ich eingekehrt war – nachdem sich das Missverständnis in Wohlgefallen aufgelöst hatte – gesellte sich nun zu uns und freute sich schon auf die Fremden, welche auch ihm zuströmen würden, wenn die Vorzüge Malcesines erst recht ans Licht kämen"; English translation by the author).

Mandelkow, Karl Robert (1997): 'Das Goethebild Georg Simmels', in: Baßler, Moritz/Brecht, Christoph/Niefanger, Dirk (eds): *Von der Natur zur Kunst zurück – Neue Beiträge zur Goethe-Forschung* (Tübingen: Max Niemeyer Verlag 1997) 219–233

Simmel, Georg (1913): *Goethe* (Leipzig: Klinkhardt & Biermann Verlag 1913)

Simmel, Georg (1908/1968a): *Soziologie – Untersuchungen über die Formen der Vergesellschaftung* (Berlin: Duncker und Humblot, 5th ed. 1968; first ed. 1908)

Simmel, Georg (1908/1968b): 'Exkurs über den schriftlichen Verkehr', in: Simmel, Georg: *Soziologie – Untersuchungen über die Formen der Vergesellschaftung* (Berlin: Duncker und Humblot, 5th ed. 1968b; first ed. 1908) 287–288

von Goethe, Johann Wolfgang (1890): 'Letter of (12–) 23 December 1786', in: *Goethes Briefe*, Vol. 8 der IV. Abt. of his Works, edited by order of the Grand Duchess Sophie of Saxony (Weimar: Böhlau 1890)

von Goethe, Johann Wolfgang (1816/1817): *Italienische Reise* (*Italian Journey*), in: *Werke*, Vol. XI (Hamburg: Christian Wegner Verlag 1950; first published 1816–1817 as "Zweite Abteilung" of his autobiography *Aus meinem Leben*; Tübingen: Cotta'sche Verlagsbuchhandlung 1816–1817)

von Goethe, Johann Wolfgang (1830/1999): 'Letter of 29 June 1830', reprinted in: von Goethe, August: *Auf einer Reise nach Süden – Tagebuch 1830*, First printing after the manuscripts, ed. by Beyer, Andreas/Radecke, Gabriele (München/Wien: Hanser 1999)

von Goethe, Johann Wolfgang (1786/1991): 'Reisetagebuch für Frau von Stein – First piece', in: Eibl, Karl: *Sämtliche Werke,* II. Abteilung, Vol. 3 (Frankfurt a.M.: Deutscher Klassiker Verlag 1991; dedicated 1786)

Weber, Max (1920): *Die protestantische Ethik und der 'Geist' des Kapitalismus – Gesammelte Aufsätze zur Religionssoziologie I* (Tübingen: Mohr 1920)

Werner, Hans Georg (1988): 'Goethes Reise durch Italien als soziale Erkundung', 105 Goethe-Jahrbuch (1988) 27–41

Photo credits

Fig. 1: https://de.m.wikipedia.org/wiki/Datei:Goethe_Malcesine.jpg

Part 2
Ethical Foundations

Chapter 3
Digital Image Ethics – How it Could be Pursued and What It Might Have to Say

Reinold Schmücker

I. Introduction

Digital ethics is a broad field. It encompasses a wide range of even more specialised ethical disciplines: Information ethics, data ethics, ethics of Big Data, ethics of algorithms, digital media ethics, ethics of digital journalism, ethics of geo-blocking and, last but not least, an ethics of copying which also deals with digital reproductions.[1] Given this breadth, it is not surprising that there is no consensus on what exactly digital ethics is and how it should proceed, nor is its claim to validity clear.

I will therefore start with a snapshot that sheds light on the current state of digital ethics and highlights some of the difficulties that digital ethics currently faces (II.). My overview will be rather subjective and – since the multitude of positions and arguments on very different individual aspects of digital ethics cannot be reproduced in detail – necessarily superficial. It will become obvious, however, that the status and function of digital-ethical conclusions are not yet clear. To remedy this, I will defend the possibility and explain the task of digital image ethics. First, I elaborate on how normative ethics is challenged by both a problem of justification and a problem of application (III.). I then outline the possibility and specific function of an applied ethics (IV.), before defining the task of digital image ethics in more detail (V.) and giving three examples to illustrate what a digital image ethics might have to say (VI.).

Before beginning, however, I would like to make two comments about the terminology used in this chapter. In the law of English-speaking countries, the term "moral rights" has a different, more specific meaning than, for example, the German term "moralische Rechte". In the context of

1 See, e.g., Hick/Schmücker (2016); Joerden/Schmücker/Ortland (2018); Dreier (2019). – For the ethics of copying see the 2015–2016 Research Group at the Bielefeld Center for Interdisciplinary Research (ZiF), https://www.uni-bielefeld.de/(en)/ZiF/FG/2015Copying/.

copyright, moral rights (in German: "Urheberpersönlichkeitsrechte") are understood to be the inalienable rights of the creators of original works which are generally recognised in civil law and differ from the economic rights associated with copyright. Therefore, even if an artist has assigned use rights or, if permitted by national legislation, the copyright in a work to a third party, he or she retains the moral rights in the work. In contrast, in ethics the term "moral rights" today refers to those subjective rights of individuals and groups of individuals that give rise to a moral claim against third parties. In this chapter, I will use the term "moral rights" in the latter sense. I will also use the term "ethics" to refer to normative theories of what is morally right and not in a descriptive or sociological sense such as the epitome of norms established in a particular social group or as a term for theories of the good life.

II. Digital Ethics Today: A Snapshot

Digital ethics is a multifaceted field. On the World Wide Web as well as in the relevant literature, one can find definitions that mean very different things. On quite a number of websites you can find – without a reference – the following definition, which apparently enjoys some popularity: "Digital Ethics is the study of how to manage oneself ethically, professionally and in a clinically sound manner via online and digital media".[2] This definition was obviously inspired by the idea that ethics is the theory of the good life. Other definitions consider digital ethics to be more of a domain ethics. It can then be understood as a branch of ethics that concerns "moral standards for digitalization and Big Data". Such an understanding has become increasingly accepted over the last ten years. The book *Digital Media Ethics* (1st ed. 2009) by Charles Ess pioneered this approach because the author broadened digital ethics beyond the area of information and computing ethics and focused on ethical problems that arise in the everyday use of digital media and digital devices.[3] Since then, like Ess' book, many books on digital ethics – at least as far as they come

2 See, e.g.: https://www.assemblymade.com/2021/12/why-do-we-need-ethics-as-an-it/; https://brainly.ph/question/9879339; https://www.endnowfoundation.org/all-about-the-new-digital-ethics-code-php/; https://www.zurinstitute.com/clinical-updates/digital-ethics-101/; http://www.losfelizledger.com/cosfyo/importance-of-digital-media-ethics; https://www.coursehero.com/file/24313350/Project-3-Ethical-Dilemmasdocx/.

3 Ess (2009/2020).

from philosophy, theology or media studies – are not aimed exclusively at a specialist audience, but at a broader readership, consisting in particular of end users of digital media and devices. This also applies to the most recent German-language studies that seek to depict the subject area of digital ethics in its full scope, for example the small compendium *Digitale Ethik. Leben in vernetzten Welten (Digital Ethics. Living in Networked Worlds)* edited by Grimm, Keber and Zöllner and published in 2019 by Philipp Reclam jun. or the study *Digitale Ethik. Ein Wertesystem für das 21. Jahrhundert (A Value System for the 21st Century)* by Sarah Spiekermann.[4]

This focus on a broader readership has at least two consequences:

On the one hand, it leads to a focus on ethical questions that arise for individual actors or that affect the lifestyle and well-being of individuals. It is symptomatic of this tendency that an early book on ethical problems of informatics was entitled *Gewissensbisse (Pangs of Conscience)*.[5] In contrast, questions that arise, for example, from an ethical perspective relating to the normative "Richtigkeit" ("rightness"; Jürgen Habermas[6]) of positive-legal norms, are rarely considered.

On the other hand, this is all the more true since the focus on a broader readership also has the consequence that digital ethics is often conducted at a very high operating altitude. Indeed, instead of developing convincing solutions to difficult concrete questions and conflicts of interest, digital ethics often limits itself to ascribing to well-known ethical theories the competence to provide us with appropriate solutions, which they would first have to prove in concrete cases.

Thus, digital ethics often boils down to commonplace wisdom and platitudes, which are presented with a raised index finger, without it always being entirely clear what the ethical authority being claimed is based on. A good example of this are the *10 Gebote der Digitalen Ethik* (*10 Commandments of Digital Ethics*), which were developed in the interest of protecting minors at the Institute for Digital Ethics at Stuttgart Media University (Fig. 1)[7]:

4 Grimm/Keber/Zöllner (2019/2020); Spiekermann (2019/2021).
5 Weber-Wulff/Class/Coy/Kurz/Zellhöfer (2009).
6 Habermas (1973) 220 et passim.
7 https://www.hdm-stuttgart.de/digitale-ethik/lehre/10_gebote.

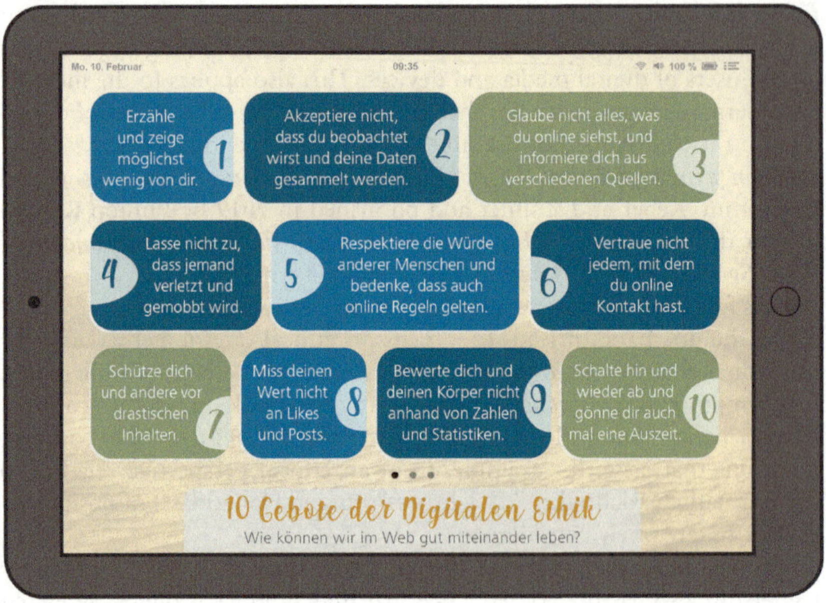

Fig. 1: Institute For Digital Ethics, Stuttgart Media University Stuttgart – 10 Gebote der Digitalen Ethik

1. Tell and show as little of yourself as possible.
2. Do not accept being watched and your data being collected.
3. Do not believe everything you see online and get information from a variety of sources.
4. Do not allow anyone to be hurt or bullied.
5. Respect the dignity of others and remember that rules apply online as well.
6. Do not trust everyone you have contact with online.
7. Protect yourself and others from drastic content.
8. Do not measure your worth by likes and posts.
9. Do not assess yourself and your body based on numbers and statistics.
10. Switch off now and then and allow yourself some time out.

Of course, these are tips that may well be useful for young people. Except for rules no. 4 and 5, however, they are rules that serve a specific purpose: the protection of young people. Kant famously called such rules "hypothetical imperatives".[8] Such rules are often very useful – but they are not moral rules in the sense in which we usually speak of moral rules. So, what is being sold here as "digital ethics" is not ethics at all. Evidently, rule no. 3 suggests that the authors themselves may have been aware of this.

But even in recent studies and study materials, digital ethics is often pursued on the level of guidebook literature. In the previously mentioned German books from 2019, for example, there are chapters with headings such as "Tugendhafte Manager für tugendhafte Kunden", "Werte in der Technik sind das neue ‚Bio' im Internet", "Wertträger sind Firmen mit Herz" ("Virtuous managers for virtuous customers", "Values in technology are the new 'organic' on the Internet", "Value carriers are companies with a heart").[9] A good example of this kind of digital ethics in English is the book *Media Ethics and Global Justice* by Clifford G. Christians, also published in 2019 by Cambridge University Press. Here, everything from Aristotle to Heidegger's *Dasein* and the Tao is brought into play to develop, as the author claims, "an international, cross-cultural, gender inclusive and ethnically diverse media ethics of justice".[10]

Digital ethics that is pursued like this is limited to advising individual actors, most of whom are end users of digital media and technologies and wish for a good, successful or happy life. Consequently, in the Reclam volume mentioned above, an entire chapter is devoted to the topic of "happiness". In this way, however, digital ethics capitulates to ethics' genuine task of finding solutions to conflicts of interest that take into account the widely recognised moral rights of individuals and groups and seem fair from an impartial point of view. It also capitulates to the complexity of its subject matter, which is characterised by the manifold effects of different factors. The interplay of these factors is not easy to grasp, and their consequences and side effects, especially for third parties and society, are not easy to assess.

Digital ethics can shirk the difficult task of developing principles and ideas for regulating the conflicts of interest caused by digitisation. The legal system, in contrast, cannot avoid the regulation of these conflicts and therefore has a far greater awareness of complexity, from which digital ethics should learn. Under pressure from economically powerful actors, however, the legal system does not always succeed in finding morally defensible solutions. It could therefore benefit from a discussion with a

8 Kant (1788/2015) A 37; AA, vol. V, p. 20 (p. 18 of the English translation).
9 Spiekermann (2019/2021) Ch. 2.1, Subheadings.
10 Christians (2019) 329.

digital ethics that is able to argue at eye-level. Thus, though digital ethics is still in its infancy, in order to outgrow it, it could (and should) learn – as explained below – from similar applied ethics such as medical ethics and other domain-specific ethics.

This diagnosis is, of course, somewhat too one-sided: there are several studies, especially from recent years, that address concrete normative questions raised by digitisation. Significantly, however, as bibliometric research has discovered,[11] most of them are not the work of philosophical, so to speak full-time ethicists, but rather of computer scientists and lawyers. The *Research Handbook on Human Rights and Intellectual Property*, edited by Christophe Geiger, is one of the most important of these contributions.[12]

Regarding this branch of digital ethics from the outset, questions about the scope of morally required data protection and the preservation of the privacy of users of digital media are on the agenda. An example is the volume *Towards a Digital Ethics* by the European Data Protection Supervisor (EDPS) Ethics Advisory Group (2018).[13] In order to indicate the broad spectrum of topics that digital ethics deals with today, I would like to also mention some more recent instructive works: Luciano Floridi (*The Ethics of Information*, 2013) as well as Jonathan Beever, Rudy McDaniel and Nancy Stanlick (*Understanding Digital Ethics. Cases and Contexts*, 2020) are working on the foundation of a digital ethics.[14] Data ethics, as formed by Floridi and Mariarosaria Taddeo, analyses the moral issues that arise regarding the acts of generating, collecting and processing of data, access to them, their use and algorithmic evaluation.[15] The ethics of Big Data[16] and the ethics of algorithms[17] can be assigned to them. The area of data ethics also includes studies on the moral responsibility of online service providers[18] or the ethics of the design of interfaces and online platforms.[19] The Ethics of Information Warfare is the focus of several recent studies.[20] Ess' book on *Digital Media Ethics* has already been mentioned; the volume

11 Mahieu/van Eck/van Putten/van den Hoven (2018).

12 Geiger (2015).

13 European Data Protection Supervisor (EDPS) Ethics Advisory Group (2018).

14 Floridi (2013); Beever/McDaniel/Stanlick (2020). See also Luciano/Taddeo (2018 et seq.); Otto/Gräf (2018).

15 Floridi/Taddeo (2016).

16 Mittelstadt/Floridi (2016a) and (2016b).

17 Mittelstadt/Allo/Taddeo/Wachter/Floridi (2016).

18 Taddeo/Floridi (2016).

19 See, e. g., Reyman/Sparby (2020).

20 See, e. g., Floridi/Taddeo (2014); Taddeo (2016); Lukas (2017); Christen/Gordijn/Loi (2020).

Ethics for a Digital Era, edited by Deni Elliott and Edward Spence (2018) is devoted to basic problems of digital journalism ethics.[21] The anthology *Digital Ethics. Research and Practice*, edited by Don Heider and Adrienne Massanari in 2012, discusses among other issues ethical problems of computer gaming such as the moral status of grieving, but also permissible piracy.[22] Last but not least I should mention two volumes on image ethics: *Image Ethics. The Moral Rights of Subjects in Photographs, Film, and Television*, and *Image Ethics in the Digital Age*, both edited by Larry Gross, John Stuart Katz and Jay Ruby.[23]

It is worth noting that the above-mentioned studies (and many other studies on digital ethics which cannot be mentioned here) do either not address the underlying reasons supporting the validity of their normative statements or determine them in very different ways. Therefore, the status and function of digital-ethical conclusions remain unclear and it is this ambiguity that leads me to the core of my contribution to the present book.

III. Ethics: Challenged by Both a Problem of Justification and a Problem of Application

How can digital ethics be pursued in such a way that its statements can claim normative rightness? Such claims are fundamental to any ethics. For anyone who cannot claim normative rightness for his statements is not practising ethics. At best, as a moral sociologist, one could put the term "ethics" in quotation marks and speak of an "ethics" that someone holds. But even that is difficult if the conviction of its normative rightness cannot be attributed to the person or group who holds it.

1. The problem of justification

Because ethics is about normative rightness in practical questions, it is challenged by both a problem of justification and a problem of application. Ethics faces a problem of justification because it does not only exist

21 Elliott/Spence (2018).

22 Heider/Massanari (2012).

23 Gross/Katz/Ruby (1988) and (2003). To my knowledge, the most recent book on image ethics is Schicha (2021).

in the singular. In modern, ideologically pluralistic societies, there are a multitude of partially incompatible systems of moral belief. Perhaps such an ethical plurality existed, albeit under a non-individualistic sign, even before the modern age. However, there is a lack of a generally accepted procedure that would allow the correct moral view to be filtered out from the multitude of empirically available moral views. It therefore appears difficult to justify the normative rightness or – as it is often said in German literature – the validity of ethical statements in such a way that they appear to be normatively right not only to those who share certain fundamental values.

However, if it is assumed to be a conceptual truth that ethical statements should not only be valid for like-minded people, this problem of justification seems to generally endanger the possibility of ethics. Is there a way to justify it at all? The most promising way seems to be to refer to those moral beliefs which are shared, if not by all, at least by the great majority. Such beliefs, however, can only be identified either in very general moral norms or with regard to very specific situations. For example, it is plausible to assume that at least most of the ten moral rules stated by Bernard Gert – such as "Do not kill" or "Do not cause pain" – are accepted to be moral rules by the vast majority of people. However, this is true only if they are restricted by a proviso: "except when a fully informed, impartial rational person can publicly allow violating it [this rule]".[24] Likewise, it can be assumed that hardly any person who is familiar with the meaning of the term "moral" would contradict the following judgement: It is morally forbidden to use force to prevent a person risking his or her own life when saving a two-month-old child from drowning in deep water from coming ashore with the child and thereby causing the person to drown along with the child.

Apparently, there are some very general moral norms that are very widely accepted, and some actions that are very widely considered morally required or forbidden. This indicates that there is a universal, linguistically and culturally invariant core of the meaning of "morality". This finding is also indicated by the fact that there are areas of overlap between all ethics, despite their partial divergence, which allow them to arrive at some unanimous judgements from partially different premises.

---

24 Gert (1998) 216 (italics removed).

2. *The problem of application*

However, ethics seeking an answer to the problem of justification is also confronted with a fundamental problem of application. For the universal, culturally and linguistically invariant core of meaning of the term "morality" (if it exists) is very abstract; indeed, so abstract that it often seems almost impossible to derive practical orientation from moral norms whose universal recognition can plausibly be assumed. At the same time, it is rarely possible to relate an action to this core of meaning in such a way that an unambiguous judgement can be made about its morality that is shared by almost all speakers who are language competent.

A particularly promising candidate for such a norm, belonging to the universal core meaning of the term "morality", is undoubtedly the norm: "Do not kill an innocent person!" Another candidate would be the rule: "Save the innocent in distress whenever possible!" But even these two seemingly simple norms raise considerable problems of definition: Does the concept of killing include letting others die? Under what conditions is someone guilty by omission? Does the talk of innocent or innocently refer only to human beings? When is it possible for someone to rescue someone else and when is it not? Would a rescue action still be moral if it were, at the same time, harming innocent third parties?

Without answers to such questions, even such norms, which we are inclined to assume being part of the universal core of the concept of morality, cannot be applied to concrete actions. But even the widely accepted norm "Do not kill an innocent person" shows how difficult their practical application can be. The interpretation of terms that play a central role in such norms is already controversial. Obviously, a decision cannot always be made between conflicting views based on generally understandable reasons. This is all the more true when members of different cultures or citizens of different states disagree on the interpretation of normatively relevant terms. For example, without a specific concept of attribution – which some neurobiologists in our culture would probably already refuse to agree to today – it would not even be possible to decide who is innocent or guilty.

But that is not all. Even if it were possible to unambiguously and indisputably define the terms essential to abstract principles of universal morality, it would not be possible to pass a judgement on the morality of a concrete action whose claim to universal validity can only be disputed with obviously unfounded objections. The reason is that most given situations of action can be viewed from different angles and therefore described very differently. Thus, it will often remain contentious which of several possible norms is to be applied with priority. Even if it is possible to reduce such divergences by establishing moral principles of medium range – as I will describe in more detail below – there will still be dissent about the completeness, adequacy or normative rightness of descriptions of concrete situations of action. This is so, because every description of a concrete situation of action always incorporates the perceptual perspective of the person making that description, and every such description is hence shaped by that person's experiences, interests and desires. Several people therefore often disagree on how to describe a situation of action correctly.

IV. The Possibility of Applied Ethics

1. The need for applied ethics

However, technological progress, and today digitisation in particular, raise normative questions for which two things can be said: firstly, these questions have not yet become the subject of legal regulation at the time they arise, nor is it immediately clear what such legal regulation should look like. Secondly, they cannot be answered convincingly by potential actors simply asking their conscience. This is either because the situation in which we are supposed to act is so complex that we cannot easily relate it to our moral beliefs and intuitions, or because it mobilises different moral beliefs or intuitions that suggest different and incompatible actions.

"Applied ethics" attempts to provide answers to normative questions of this kind. The term is often used to describe domain-specific ethics that claims to specify moral norms tailored to a particular sphere of action. However, the term "applied ethics" is not a mere misnomer only if it denotes an attempt to understand moral judgements as the application of principles or norms, i.e. by analogy with the application of law. This chapter argues that applied ethics is in many ways characterised by projecting processes characteristic of the legal system onto moral judgement.

Such an understanding of moral judgement analogous to the application of law has several implications. In particular, it presupposes that it is possible to determine a set of norms applicable in situations in which moral judgement is required. This assumption is not trivial. For such norms can neither be obtained through meta-ethical reflection, nor does it seem possible to simply deduce them from any of the normative-ethical theories established in philosophical discussion. Certainly, if the question arises in a concrete situation whether one should overtake a vehicle in a blind curve, one can be guided by the moral norm that it is immoral to unnecessarily endanger other road users. And this norm, which refers to a particular domain of everyday human activity, can also be traced back to the more fundamental moral principle: "Do not endanger a third party unless you have a justifying reason for doing so!" This principle can then be understood as one that can be justified by an ethical theory – for example, by the Kantian ethics of the categorical imperative or a variant of utilitarianism.

However, this principle cannot be derived from one of the relevant ethical theories without reference to an object of moral reflection. For as a conclusion it only arises when a certain description of action – which in turn is abstracted from a concrete situation in a suitable manner and usually to a very high degree – is added as a minor premise. In our example case, such an abstract description of action could read: "endangering a third party without sufficient reason". However, this description cannot be deduced from an ethical theory, but only by an abstraction – possibly in stages – of concrete circumstances of an actual or possible action. Such an abstraction, in turn, always includes normative judgements about which aspects of a concrete situation of action should be abstracted from a moral standpoint, and it is conceivable that such judgements are in turn influenced by ethical theories on which the person making the judgement is guided. However, this does not mean that our everyday moral judging could be characterised as the application of an ethical theory.

This finding is confirmed when we consider where and how the law is applied. Legal norms are applied on the one hand in jurisprudence, and on the other hand in the administrative actions of the state and its subsidiary institutions. In both contexts there is an institution judging given actions or situations in a normative sense, and doing so on the basis of a description, or more precisely: of either a single description or a plurality of descriptions of one and the same action or situation, which can diverge and, under certain circumstances, also contradict each other. The institution itself is not usually affected by the consequences of its decisions. Further, it can base its decisions on a more or less clearly defined canon of norms whose validity is secured by institutionalised procedures.

The procedures that guarantee the validity of the norms to be applied by legal practitioners in court or in public administration are, moreover, of such a nature that they guarantee a certain minimum degree of social acceptance of the norms in question. In democratic societies, the validity of positive law is thus a manifestation of a normative consensus of a society, which, although not absolute, is broad enough to guarantee a degree of acceptance that makes it rational for potential actors to assume the validity of the norm in question when planning their actions.

Moreover, the application of law is usually done from the point of view of an impartial third party whose decisions relate to acts or situations that have been carried out by or that affect others. Furthermore, the impartial third party is usually not affected by the consequences of his or her decisions. If this expression also includes the perspective of decision-makers in public administration institutions, the relevant perspective can be characterised as the point of view of a judge. From such a judge's point of view in the broad sense, a more or less clearly identifiable canon of norms is applied, the validity of which is at least indirectly supported by a social consensus. We can therefore characterise the application of law as (1) an evaluation of (2) actions or facts given by descriptions, and which (3) is carried out from a judge's point of view in the light of a more or less clearly identifiable canon of norms, the validity of which is at least indirectly supported by a social consensus.

With regard to the consideration of processes of moral judgement, it is natural to speak of the standpoint of a moral judge. This term also expresses that it is a point of view that implies a very high degree of impartiality of the judging person as well as unaffectedness from the consequences of an action to be judged, which differs from the point of view of a potential actor considering an action. Since applied ethics can only be understood as the application of moral norms, we can now add a fourth condition. Thus, in ethics, we would be dealing with an application if the following four conditions were fulfilled: (1) an action or fact is assessed (2) on the basis of descriptions (3) from the standpoint of a moral judge and (4) in the light of a more or less clearly identifiable canon of moral norms whose validity is supported by a sufficiently large social consensus.

Note that the condition formulated here as the fourth necessary condition of an application of ethics does not contain any statement about the reason for the validity of a moral norm. It merely expresses that one can meaningfully speak of application in ethics only in relation to those moral norms whose validity is supported by a sufficiently large social consensus. Indeed, if the foundations of morality are controversial, then applied ethics can only refer to those moral norms about whose validity there is a consensus, regardless of how controversial the reason for them is. This fact allows us to assume their validity as a factual given and it is a central prerequisite for the possibility of applied ethics. For it would not seem reasonable to speak of an application of norms whose validity cannot plausibly be assumed.

In my opinion, this understanding of applied ethics has two consequences. First, it allows us to distinguish applied ethics from the kind of reference to moral norms and ethical theories that is characteristic of moral reflections of potential actors in everyday life. Second, it allows us to identify contexts within which applied ethics can have a specific function.

2. *Applied ethics is different from everyday moral judging*

Obviously, our everyday referencing to moral norms is not limited to applied ethics in this sense. For in the moral evaluation of actions and facts, we do not have to orientate ourselves to a canon of moral norms whose validity is supported by a sufficiently large social consensus. Rather, we usually orientate ourselves to norms that we consider to be valid moral norms, regardless of whether our belief in them is shared by many or only a few others. This applies in particular to the assessment of one's own actual and potential actions. Because what counts in front of our conscience is our own moral beliefs – regardless of whether they are supported by a broad social consensus or not. Insofar, applied ethics is a normative practice that differs significantly from our everyday moral judging. As a solution to the problem of the application of normative ethics, it is only suitable for non-ordinary, especially scientific and law-political contexts of moral judgement.[25]

3. *The "seat in life" of applied ethics*

If the everyday forms of moral reflection and moral thinking are clearly different from applied ethics, the question naturally arises as to the "seat in life" (as the theologians call it) of applied ethics. Where, if not in everyday life, does this form of moral judgement have its place? And what is its function? In my view, there are indeed (non-ordinary) contexts of a certain type in which moral judgements can and should take the form of applied ethics. Contexts of this type are characterised by the following features: (1) The objects of moral judgement are matters that could in principle also be normatively regulated by positive law, but for the judgement of which positive law cannot be resorted to, either because no corresponding legal norms exist or because the corresponding positive law is not or no longer regarded as normatively right by a sufficiently large part of the respective

25 Carissa Véliz (2019) has therefore already expressed the view that digital ethics can and should learn from medical ethics; in doing so, however, she only has in focus the forms in which a domain ethics can and should institutionalise itself.

society. Moral evaluation takes place (2) on the basis of descriptions (3) from the impartial standpoint of a moral judge and (4) in the light of moral norms whose validity is supported by a sufficiently large social consensus.

V. *The Task of Digital Image Ethics*

Applied ethics, in the sense explained here, has a specific function: it provides practical orientation in non-ordinary, particularly scientific and legal-political contexts in which the four conditions mentioned above are met. It also serves as an argumentative test of the normative rightness of legal norms that relate to specific domains. In my view, both are the two central tasks of *digital ethics* in general and *digital image ethics* in particular. They deal with domains for which it can be assumed that either sufficiently specific legal norms do not yet exist or that the relevant positive law is not completely regarded as normatively right by a sufficiently large proportion of people who, for example, frequently use digital reproductions of copyrighted images without asking the rights holders for permission.

However, digital image ethics cannot be performed by simply applying generally accepted moral rules belonging to a specific domain. For there are no such moral rules that are widely accepted and considered uncontroversial. The moral rules we have are so abstract that it is *not* possible to simply *derive* from them judgements regarding conflicts about digital images.

How can digital image ethics deal with this result? In medical ethics, e.g., one considers concrete problems of a certain domain in the light of general moral norms and, conversely, concretises general moral norms with regard to concrete problems of the certain domain. In this way, ethical principles of a certain kind can be developed. These principles are often called mid-level principles because they do not claim general validity but validity for typical cases of the respective domain and cannot be easily transferred to another domain. Such principles are of course themselves open to change. This already follows from their relation to the specifics of their domain, which, on the one hand, can change, e.g., through technological developments, and whose moral evaluation by a sufficiently large number of people, on the other hand, can also change in the course of time, due to changes of the context, which suggest the consideration of new points of view.

In the last part of the chapter, as examples, I now present three such mid-level principles of a digital image ethics.

VI. What Digital Image Ethics Might Have to Say: Three Examples

How are digital images different from analogue images? For our present purpose, it is sufficient that we consider three obvious differences. Firstly: digital images can usually be produced, passed on to third parties and made public with much less effort than analogue images. All that is needed is a simple smartphone (or similar electronic device) which is now commonly available all over the world. Secondly: digital images, as Thomas Dreier has succinctly stated, "unlike content in analogue form, can be reproduced without loss of quality and at marginal cost – that is, at the pure cost of copying"[26]. To copy them, all that is needed is a storage facility and a very simple mini-computer, as is now integrated in smartphones and other electronic devices. And thirdly: digital images can be changed much more easily than analogue images, in such a way that the change can only be detected as such with considerable technical effort – if at all. They are therefore much easier and more effective to forge.[27]

No defining characteristic for digital images can be derived from any of the three differences. This is because all three differences are only of a gradual nature. They refer to characteristics that analogue images also possess. Analogue images are also produced, passed on to third parties, published, copied and forged. However, doing so with regard to analogue images involves greater effort, and the result is usually less "perfect" in the sense of the intended purpose – be it the possibility of easy distribution, the largest possible audience to be reached by publishing the images, the aimed-for accuracy of a copy, or the intended deceptive effect of a forgery.

Does the merely gradual difference that separates digital from analogue images in these three respects really call for a digital image ethics? One might doubt it. For the ethical principles I am about to propose could all be applied to analogue images as well. In the analogue age, however, there was no need for such principles. For they all refer to social practices that as such either only emerged in the digital age because they were only made possible by the difference in degree between digital and analogue images, or it is only in the digital age that they have become so widespread raising normative problems which did not play an important role before.

26 Dreier (2019) 62; translation by the author.

27 Without doubt, the development of Non Fungible Tokens (NFTs) results from the desire to counter this unprecedented ease and effectiveness of forging digital artefacts.

1. *The Principle of Unconditionally Permissible Use of all Vocabulary of a Visual Language*

Brought about by the digital transformation of sharing and reproducing, these social practices raise normative questions that digital image ethics should aim to answer. Think about pictures, especially extraordinarily successful ones, which we know from postcards or because they have been copied millions of times and distributed widely if not globally on the Internet – haven't they taken on the status of vocabulary of a visual language? Can it be right that such images, if copyrighted, cannot simply be used without permission by anyone in any situation as media of visual communication? Shouldn't such images be in the public domain even if their creators have been dead for less than 70 years? It seems to me that digital image ethics must answer this question in the affirmative and thus critically question the copyright laws of most countries. Those who think this is an absurd assumption should ask themselves how they would answer the same question if it referred not to the vocabulary of a visual language but to the vocabulary of a written language. Would it be morally acceptable to legally require people to pay compensation or even seek permission for the use of words from their mother tongue or a foreign language that they use to express something? And if you think that we are comparing apples and oranges here and that the comparison is limp, just realise that in the digital age we are dealing in both cases with information that can be copied: with data.

Image ethics, which, as outlined above, starts with normative intuitions of which most people are highly confident, and examines new cases in particular to what extent they resemble cases for which we have clear moral intuitions, will therefore hardly be able to come to a different conclusion here. This conclusion is also supported by the fact that – without any awareness of wrongdoing – we freely use even words that are registered as trademarks and legally protected in everyday language contexts, i.e., we talk about having put on Nivea cream and needing a Kleenex tissue to clean the lenses of our glasses. Moreover, it does not violate any fundamental ethical requirement of fairness. For a picture can only be granted the status of a visual vocabulary if it has achieved an extraordinarily high popularity. It must therefore already have been used quite unusually often. An image to which this applies will, however, as a rule have already earned its creator such high usage fees that he can be expected to forego this income in the future, if he has not generally waived the collection of royalties already in advance.

Provided what has been said is convincing, a mid-level principle of a (digital) image ethics can be formulated: It is morally permissible to make free use of all vocabulary of a visual language for (digital) visual communication without obtaining permission and without paying a fee. We can call this the *Principle of Unconditionally Permissible Use of all Vocabulary of a Visual Language*. Following from this principle copyright must be limited to ensure that digital images that have become vocabularies of a visual language in which people communicate in the digital age through the transmission of images can be used (i.e., copied, sent, posted, varied, etc.) by anyone without permission, without cost, and without threat of sanction.

2. *The Principle of the Legitimacy of Taking Photographs in Museums*

The social practices that have established themselves in the course of the digital transformation also include the photographic documentation of one's own life. Because digital photographic images are much easier to produce than analogue images, and almost easier to produce than a written note or short text, the smartphone has become the new note-taking pen. Many people use their smartphone camera to record a variety of perceptions they make and thus document a multitude of events that happen to them. Today, it is no longer necessary to record what you find noteworthy and memorable about your life and your experiences in (hand)written form in a diary because you can keep a visual diary that manifests itself in a plethora of image files. If we consider this not only legitimate but a contemporary form of a principally desirable way of forming a stable self-identity by remembering and reflecting on one's own biography, one will have to acknowledge a fundamental moral right to record one's own perceptions photographically. However, such a moral right can only be a *prima facie* right; it has its limits where the photographic documentation of one's own perception threatens to violate genuine moral rights of third parties. This will have to be assumed not only in many cases where third parties have unintentionally and through no fault of their own ended up in a situation in which they would never present themselves willingly to someone observing them. Photographing an accident victim is therefore probably not legitimised in most cases by the moral right to record one's own perceptions photographically.

In other cases, on the other hand, one will be able to assume that the photographic documentation of one's own perception would not infringe any genuine rights of third parties. A particularly clear example of such a case seems to be the photographic documentation of those impressions that the visitor of a publicly accessible museum gains of the exhibits on display while walking through the exhibition rooms. In this case, the moral right to record one's own perceptions photographically is particularly important because the perceptions made there form an essential part of the life of the visitor who visits the museum for the sake of gaining these impressions. Above all, however, the enabling of such perceptions is a vital part of the purpose of every museum open to the public. We can therefore state as a further mid-level principle of (digital) image ethics that it is morally permissible for anyone to take photographs of cultural objects on display in publicly accessible museums, if this does not damage them. I call this the *Principle of the Legitimacy of Taking Photographs in Museums*.

One might consider this principle to be too far-reaching a principle of permission that does not sufficiently consider the interests of the creators and owners of museum objects. But this is not the case. For as long as the photographed object is not damaged, the creators and owners of museum objects do not suffer any damage when museum visitors photograph them.[28] At most, they could suffer damage from the exploitation of photographs that visitors have taken of museum objects. However,

---

28 The photographing itself would only be morally problematic if it created a substitute for the photographed item. This can be derived from the ethical *Principle of Permissible Non-substitutional Copying*. According to this principle, acts of copying are morally permissible if they do not result in an entity that could substitute the template to at least one of its principal purposes. I first proposed this principle in 2016 (Schmücker [2016] 367 et seq.), and I justified and defended it in detail elsewhere (Schmücker [2018]). I will therefore assume here that it is a well-founded principle of copying ethics. As such, it is relevant for digital image ethics as well because photographing artefacts can be seen as a form of copying or reproducing: every camera can be used to produce a photocopy. At the same time, however, the principle also shows why the possibility of substitutional copying cannot call into question the Principle of the Legitimacy of Taking Photographs in Museums. Photographing does not, as a rule, produce new instances of an artefact, but only images. Photographing is therefore, apart from very special cases, not a form of generating an entity that could substitute the template to at least one of its principal purposes. It is worth noting that the Principle of Permissible Non-substitutional Copying does not imply that there are no further moral restrictions for copying. It only permits the production of copies that cannot substitute the template to one of its principal purposes. This does not mean that the production of copies that could substitute the copied object is always morally forbidden. There might be reasons for allowing the production of copies that could be used instead of the template. The principle also does not allow for any production of copies that cannot substitute the template. The principle rather includes two important restrictions: it does not permit acts of non-substitutional copying that

the Principle of the Legitimacy of Taking Photographs in Museums only morally permits the taking of photographs of museum objects, not the exploitation of the photographs.[29]

This conclusion could be countered by arguing that mere permission to photograph harms museums (or the creators or owners) because museum visitors who want to be reminded by photographs of the perceptions they made during their visit to the museum might take such photographs themselves, in other words, because they are no longer forced to purchase the photographs sold by the museum (or the creator or owner of a museum object). I consider this to be an implausible view. If one were to regard the non-establishment of a prohibition norm that would create an economic monopoly as harming those who therefore cannot profit from a monopoly position, every non-granting of privileges and economic advantages by the legislator would have to be understood as resulting in economic harm and hence as an injury.

However, the counterargument is not a suitable objection to the Principle of the Legitimacy of Taking Photographs in Museums, even if one does not agree with this assessment. Morally, even if the non-establishment of a monopoly were an injury, it would have to be weighed against the injury suffered by a visitor who, in the case of a ban on photography, cannot document his or her own perception of the museum items for his or her own visual diary, but can only be reminded of a place he or she visited for the sake of his or her own perception of certain objects by images of these objects that show them from a perspective chosen by someone else. It is obvious that this weighing will not be in favour of those who would profit from a monopoly position. For we would consider it morally reprehensible if the making of notes and sketches were forbidden in a museum in order to promote the dissemination of those descriptions or interpretations of the exhibited objects which the museum director (or whoever) considers to be the only correct ones and therefore wishes to enforce.

---

would damage the template – and it does not allow acts that would entail a serious violation of generally accepted moral rules.

29 The Principle of the Legitimacy of Taking Photographs in Museums is therefore not sufficient for the ethical assessment of most of the conflicts over the use of photographs of museum objects that have become the subject of legal proceedings in recent years. For a profound analysis and assessment of the most prominent recent litigations that has ensued, see Petri (2014) and (2018). See also the ruling of the German Federal Court of Justice (BGH), 20 December 2018 – I ZR 104/17.

Moreover, by imposing photography bans, often within the framework of house rules, many museums have tried to promote the sale of images offered in the museum shop, to create a monopoly for in-house photographers or even to make the publication of images of works in the public domain de facto dependent on the permission of the exhibiting museum. However, such a practice cannot be justified on the grounds that the revenue it generates is necessary to cover the costs of the museums concerned. For it is possible for museums – both public and private – to charge an entrance fee to cover costs; and it is fairer to (partially) cover the costs of a museum in this way than with the help of a photography ban because then all the museum's visitors contribute to the revenues created, rather than only those who want to remember certain exhibits with the help of photographs. This practice cannot therefore be proven to be morally justified with this argument either. Hence, there do not seem to be any valid reasons to argue against the Principle of the Legitimacy of Taking Photographs in Museums. Indeed, the "Kulturgesetzbuch Nordrhein-Westfalen" (Cultural Code of North Rhine-Westphalia, KulturGB NW), which was unanimously passed by the North Rhine-Westphalian state parliament on 25 November 2021 and came into force on 1 January 2022, takes this finding of the ethical analysis into legal account in an exemplary manner by stipulating in § 40 para. 2: "The taking of photographs of items of museum collections which are permanently on display is to be permitted for private purposes".[30]

3. *The Principle of Prohibiting Deception by Manipulated Photographs*

My last example of a mid-level principle of a digital image ethics ties in with the third gradual difference between digital and analogue images. Photographs are highly valued as evidence in everyday contexts, but also in relation to fines and court proceedings.[31] However, digital photographs can be altered much more easily than analogue photos, and in many cases,

30 Official Journal (Gesetz- und Verordnungsblatt) of Northrhine-Westphalia 2021 No. 84 of 14 December 2021, 1345 (online at https://recht.nrw.de/lmi/owa/br_vbl_detail_text?anw_nr=6&vd_id=19996&ver=8&val=19996&sg=0&menu=0&vd_back=N); translation by the author.

31 The legal weight of pictorial evidence has been documented in a remarkable exhibition "La preuve par l'image. Archives de la justice et de la police" at the Musée gruérien in Bulle (Fribourg, Switzerland) from 30 October 2021 to 22 February 2022; cf. https://musee-gruerien.ch/events/la-preuve-par-limage.

it is much more difficult (sometimes even impossible) to clearly determine whether a digital photograph has been altered. This provides new possibilities for the artistic use of photographs and even enables new forms of artistic expression and artistic criticism, such as photographic caricature. However, it also facilitates deception about facts through manipulated photos, whose supposed evidential value often makes people believe that what can be seen in a photograph did indeed happen although it did not happen (or did not happen the way a manipulated photo seems to prove). With the help of face swapping techniques, it is even possible to provide supposed picture evidence that a person has committed an act that he or she in fact has not committed. To produce so-called deepfakes, artificial neural networks can be used, which automatically generate such fakes.[32]

Of course, by giving rise to new forms of artistic articulation, the potentiation of the manipulability of photographic images promotes ongoing cultural development. Combined with the "uncomplicated possibilities of sharing 'digital images' with third parties"[33] (and indeed with a numerically barely limited multitude of third parties), it also enables the rapid and mass dissemination of visual political critique, especially via social media. By using manipulated digital photos, this critique can now be articulated through visual irony or through forms of visual mockery that were not possible before. This greatly increases the punch of such criticism, as was demonstrated in the Arab Spring and in other political contexts since. In this respect, the increase in the manipulability of photographic images that comes with the digital transformation contributes to the preservation and probably even the increase of artistic freedom and freedom of expression.

However, photographs are still commonly considered as evidence: Notwithstanding the fact that by virtue of the choice of cropping, perspective, lighting conditions, focal length, etc., every photograph represents a certain *perspective* on reality, photographs are still the most influential means of evidence in everyday life. The possibility of a hitherto unknown easy, fast and mass distribution of manipulated images, which make many people believe something that never happened, therefore enables a much more effective establishment of fake facts than was previously possible – namely a much faster simultaneous deception of a much larger number of people. It is obvious that this greatly increases the possibilities of "effective" exposure and defamation of third parties. But, also for processes of democratic decision-making, the possibility of the rapid simultaneous

32 See Pawelec/Bieß (2021); Hägle (2022); Leone (2022).

33 Dreier (2019) 243; translation by the author.

deception of many people about facts bears the danger that decisions will be made which those who make them would not have made in the same way if they had not started from fake facts suggested to them by supposed photographs of evidence.[34]

Taking this ambivalent ethical finding into account, one cannot assume that even the *production* of manipulated photographs, which under certain circumstances can make fake facts appear to be facts, is illegitimate. For we do not in principle consider the production of artefacts that can be used both for morally blameless purposes and for morally reprehensible acts to be illegitimate.[35] From a moral point of view, however, it must seem reprehensible and therefore forbidden to use manipulated photographs in such a way that they make people believe events that did not happen or make them believe that someone performed or omitted an action that they did not perform or omit. My third example of a mid-level principle of digital image ethics can therefore be reduced to a brief formula: It is morally forbidden to deceive third parties about facts by publishing, reproducing or distributing manipulated photographs that are neither marked as such nor recognisable as such in the context of their use. Unlike the first two principles I have presented, this *Principle of Prohibiting Deception by Manipulated Photographs* does not require most national legislatures to do much rework. For criminal law, by sanctioning defamation, fraud and falsification of data relevant to evidence (cf. the German Criminal Code §§ 187, 263, 269), already largely takes into account the moral reprehensibility of deception about facts by means of manipulated photographs. Indeed, at most, it remains to be discussed whether the morally reprehensible deception about facts that influences a person's decisions about their own way of life or their vote should also be sanctioned under criminal law (I am sceptical about this.) For the rest, moral judges – and, in relation to legal consequences, courts – will have to decide in each individual case whether manipulated photos are labelled as such or are recognisable as such in the

34 This is probably even more true for all forms of direct democracy that dispense with representation and instead rely on voting "by mouse click or wipe" than for parliamentary democracies. For the vision of such a democracy "by mouse click or wipe" see Sommer (2022), quoted from the blurb of the book to be published on 11 April 2022.

35 As John Stuart Mill already stated in the 5th chapter of *On Liberty*, see Mill (1859/1991) 106: "If poisons were never bought or used for any purpose except the commission of murder, it would be right to prohibit their manufacture and sale. They may, however, be wanted not only for innocent but for useful purposes, and restrictions cannot be imposed in the one case without operating in the other". I owe this reference to Lukas Daum.

context of their use and whether they are actually misleading about facts or not. Digital image ethics cannot relieve them of the responsibility for assessing the concrete individual case in this regard.[36]

References

Beever, Jonathan/McDaniel, Rudy/Stanlick, Nancy (2020): *Understanding Digital Ethics – Cases and Contexts* (Abingdon/New York: Routledge 2020)

Christen, Markus/Gordijn, Bert/Loi, Michele (eds) (2020): *The Ethics of Cybersecurity* (Cham: Springer 2020)

Christians, Clifford G. (2019): *Media Ethics and Global Justice in the Digital Age – A New Theory of Communication* (Cambridge: Cambridge University Press 2019)

Dreier, Thomas (2019): *Bild und Recht – Versuch einer programmatischen Grundlegung* (Baden-Baden: Nomos 2019)

Elliott, Deni/Spence, Edward H. (eds) (2018): *Ethics for a Digital Era* (Hoboken, N. J./Chichester: Wiley Blackwell 2018)

Ess, Charles (2009/2020): *Digital Media Ethics* (Cambridge/Malden, Mass.: Polity Press 2009, 3rd ed. 2020)

European Data Protection Supervisor (EDPS) Ethics Advisory Group (2018): *Towards a Digital Ethics* (2018, https://edps.europa.eu/sites/default/files/publication/18-01-25_eag_report_en.pdf)

Floridi, Luciano (2013): *The Ethics of Information* (Oxford/New York: Oxford University Press 2013)

Floridi, Luciano/Taddeo, Mariarosaria (2014): *The Ethics of Information Warfare* (Cham: Springer 2014)

Floridi, Luciano/Taddeo, Mariarosaria (2016): 'What is data ethics?', Philosophical Transactions R. Soc., Series A 374: 20160360 (28 December 2016, https://royalsocietypublishing.org/doi/pdf/10.1098/rsta.2016.0360)

Floridi, Luciano/Taddeo, Mariarosaria (eds) (2018 et seq.): *The Yearbook of the Digital Ethics Lab* (Cham: Springer 2018 et seq.)

Geiger, Christophe (ed) (2015): *Research Handbook on Human Rights and Intellectual Property* (Cheltenham/Northampton, Mass.: Edward Elgar 2015)

Gert, Bernard (1998): *Morality – Its Nature and Justification* (Oxford/New York: Oxford University Press 1998)

Grimm, Petra/Keber, Tobias A./Zöllner, Oliver (eds) (2019/2020): *Digitale Ethik – Leben in vernetzten Welten* (Ditzingen: Reclam 2019, 2nd ed. 2020)

---

36 I would like to thank Lukas Daum, Thomas Dreier, Herta Gehr and Georgia Jenkins for their critical comments on earlier versions of this chapter and their many suggestions for improvement.

Gross, Larry/Katz, John Stuart/Ruby, Jay (eds) (1988): *Image Ethics – The Moral Rights of Subjects in Photographs, Film, and Television* (New York: Oxford University Press 1988)

Gross, Larry/Katz, John Stuart/Ruby, Jay (eds) (2003): *Image Ethics in the Digital Age* (Minneapolis, Minn./London: The University of Minnesota Press 2003)

Habermas, Jürgen (1973): 'Wahrheitstheorien', in: Fahrenbach, Helmut (ed): *Wirklichkeit und Reflexion – Festschrift für Walter Schulz* (Pfullingen: Neske 1973) 211–265

Hägle, Olivia (2022): 'From Copy & Paste to Deep Fakes – Digital Collaging and Image Manipulation', in: Dreier, Thomas/Andina, Tiziana (eds): *Digital Ethics – The Issue of Images* (Baden-Baden: Nomos 2022) 207–227

Heider, Don/Massanari, Adrienne (eds) (2012): *Digital Ethics – Research and Practice* (New York: Peter Lang 2012)

Hick, Darren H./Schmücker, Reinold (eds) (2016): *The Aesthetics and Ethics of Copying* (New York/London: Bloomsbury 2016)

Joerden, Jan C./Schmücker, Reinold/Ortland, Eberhard (eds) (2018): 'Recht und Ethik des Kopierens – Law and Ethics of Copying', 26 Annual Review of Law and Ethics (2018) 1–264

Kant, Immanuel (1788/2015): *Critique of Practical Reason* (Cambridge: Cambridge University Press 2nd ed. 2015)

Leone, Massimo (2022): 'Semioethics of the Visual Fake', in: Dreier, Thomas/Andina, Tiziana (eds): *Digital Ethics – The Issue of Images* (Baden-Baden: Nomos 2022) 187–205

Lukas, George R. (2017): *Ethics and Cyber Warfare – The Quest for Responsible Security in the Age of Digital Warfare* (New York/Oxford: Oxford University Press 2017)

Mahieu, René/van Eck, Nees Jan/van Putten, David/van den Hoven, Jeroen (2018): 'From Dignity to Security Protocols – A Scientometric Analysis of Digital Ethics', 20 Ethics and Information Technology (2018) 175–187

Mill, John Stuart (1859/1991): 'On Liberty', in: Mill, John Stuart: *On Liberty and Other Essays*, ed. with an Introduction and Notes by John Gray (New York/Oxford: Oxford University Press) 1–128

Mittelstadt, Brent Daniel/Allo, Patrick/Taddeo, Mariarosaria/Wachter, Sandra/Floridi, Luciano (2016): 'The Ethics of Algorithms – Mapping the Debate', Big Data & Society (July–December 2016, https://journals.sagepub.com/doi/pdf/10.1177/2053951716679679) 1–21

Mittelstadt, Brent Daniel/Floridi, Luciano (eds) (2016a): *The Ethics of Biomedical Big Data* (Cham: Springer 2016)

Mittelstadt, Brent Daniel/Floridi, Luciano (2016b): 'The Ethics of Big Data – Current and Foreseeable Issues in Biomedical Contexts', 22 Science and Engineering Ethics (2016) 303–341

Otto, Philipp/Gräf, Eike (eds) (2018): *3TH1CS – Die Ethik der digitalen Zeit* (Berlin: iRights media 2nd ed. 2018)

Pawelec, Maria/Bieß, Cora (2021): *Deepfakes – Technikfolgen und Regulierungsfragen aus ethischer und sozialwissenschaftlicher Perspektive* (Baden-Baden: Nomos 2021)

Petri, Grischka (2014): 'The Public Domain vs. the Museum – The Limits of Copyright and Reproductions of Two-dimensional Works of Art', 12 Journal of Conservation and Museum Studies No. 1 (2014, http://dx.doi.org/10.5334/jcms.1021217)

Petri, Grischka (2018): 'La propriété, c'est le vol? – Reproducing Art at the Museum', 26 Annual Review of Law and Ethics (2018) 99–123

Reyman, Jessica/Sparby, Erika M. (eds) (2020): *Digital Ethics – Rhetoric and Responsibility in Online Aggression* (New York/London: Routledge 2020)

Schicha, Christian (2021): *Bildethik* (München: UVK 2021)

Schmücker, Reinold (2016): 'Normative Resources and Domain-Specific Principles – Heading for an Ethics of Copying', in: Hick, Darren H./Schmücker, Reinold (eds) (2016): *The Aesthetics and Ethics of Copying* (New York/London: Bloomsbury 2016) 359–377

Schmücker, Reinold (2018): 'What is Wrong with Non-substitutional Copying?', 26 Annual Review of Law and Ethics (2018) 57–66

Sommer, Andreas Urs (2022): *Eine Demokratie für das 21. Jahrhundert – Warum die Volksvertretung überholt ist und die Zukunft der direkten Demokratie gehört* (Freiburg: Herder 2022)

Spiekermann, Sarah (2019/2021): *Digitale Ethik – Ein Wertesystem für das 21. Jahrhundert* (München: Droemer 2019, 2nd ed. 2021)

Taddeo, Mariarosaria (2016): 'Just Information Warfare', 35 Topoi (2016) 213–224

Taddeo, Mariarosaria/Floridi, Luciano (2016): 'The Debate on the Moral Responsibilities of Online Service Providers', 22 Science and Engineering Ethics (2016) 1575–1603

Véliz, Carissa (2019): 'Three Things Digital Ethics Can Learn from Medical Ethics', 2 Nature Electronics (2019) 316–318

Weber-Wulff, Deborah/Class, Christina/Coy, Wolfgang/Kurz, Constanze/Zellhöfer, David (2009): *Gewissensbisse. Ethische Probleme der Informatik. Biometrie – Datenschutz – geistiges Eigentum* (Bielefeld: transcript 2009)

Photo credits

Fig. 1: https://www.hdm-stuttgart.de/digitale-ethik/lehre/10_gebote

Chapter 4
Form and Norm in Pictures

Enrico Terrone

Hylomorphism is a metaphysical view, traced back to Aristotle, that holds that things are constituted by both their form and their matter. For example, a statue may have clay as its matter and the shape of the subject portrayed as its form. In a recent book,[1] Simon Evnine revisited Aristotle's metaphysics, arguing that the notion of form is unified with those of origin and function, while the notion of matter subsumes not only stuff such as clay or marble, but also more complex components which comprise the form. For example, the matter of a bicycle might consist of wheels, frame, tires etc. while its form is how those components are arranged by a certain process of making, namely the origin, for a certain purpose, namely the function.[2] Artifacts, from this perspective, are "the impress of mind on matter".[3] In this paper I will argue that pictures also can be analysed from a hylomorphic perspective along these lines. Specifically, I will argue that the matter of a picture is a colored surface while its form is a norm which prescribe a certain use of that surface.

The claim that the matter of a picture is a colored surface paves the way for a unitary account that concern both concrete pictures such as paintings and more abstract pictures such as the digital images. What matters is the distribution of colors on a surface, regardless of whether this distribution is recorded by means of paint on a canvas or by means of an array of digits. Note that black-and-white pictures are also included in as black, white, and grey also are considered as colors in this analysis.

From a hylomorphic perspective, having a colored surface as the matter is necessary for something to be a picture, but not sufficient. A further component is required, namely the form. There are many colored surfaces which are not pictures because they lack the pictorial form. I propose to cast the latter as a norm that prescribes one to enjoy a peculiar visual experience of things that are not in one's immediate surroundings.

---

1 Evenine (2016).
2 See Evnine (2016) 9.
3 Ibid. 100.

One sees a colored surface as an object which has its place here and now, but when one uses that colored surface as a picture, thereby abiding by its norm, one also sees other things that have not their place here and now. It is worth characterizing the experience of the things depicted as a visual experience since things appear as organized in space just as they do in an ordinary visual experience. Yet, the pictorial experience differs from ordinary vision since things do not appear as organized in a space which surrounds and encompasses ourselves.

Thus, pictures are artifacts whose function consists in triggering visual experiences of things that are not in front of the viewer. While the matter of a picture is the colored surface that can trigger such an experience, the picture's form is the norm that prescribes the use of that surface which is to enjoy that experience.

Each picture may supplement the general norm that prescribes to see something in the colored surface with a specific norm that specifies what to see. Richard Wollheim calls the latter norm "the standard of correctness" of a picture, arguing that it depends on the history of making of the picture.[4] For example, the standard of correctness may specify the kind of things that a picture portray, or the place and time of the scene portrayed.[5] On the one hand, the standard of correctness is constrained by the picture's matter: the standard cannot force one to have visual experiences which could not be elicited by the colored surface. On the other hand, the standard can enrich the visual experience elicited by the colored surface, enabling one to properly understand what one sees. That is what Wollheim calls the "appropriate experience" of a picture.[6]

By means of its standard of correctness, a picture can play a communicative role. The viewer does not only enjoy the visual experience that the picture elicits, but also recognizes that this experience was elicited by a maker for a communicative purpose in a certain context. What is seen in the pictures is thus supplemented by what is communicated by it. The distinction between what is seen in and what is communicated by a picture matches the distinction between what is said and what is communicated linguistically, namely, the distinction between semantics and pragmatics. What is said only depends on the syntactic and semantic rules of a certain language, while what is communicated also depends on the

---

4 Wollheim (1980).

5 See Terrone (2021).

6 Wollheim (1980).

mental attitudes deployed in a certain context.[7] Yet, a difference remains between depiction and language due to the difference between the matter of pictures and that of linguistic utterances. The matter of an utterance is a sequence of words, while the matter of a picture is a colored surface. Consequently, the form of an utterance prescribes one to understand the meaning of the sequence of words which is the utterance's matter, while the form of a picture prescribes one to enjoy the visual experience elicited by the colored surface which is the picture's matter. However, both the meaning of an utterance and the visual experience elicited by a picture can be exploited for further communicative purposes.

As explained by John Austin, utterances can make different kinds of speech act, for example, assertions, directives, interrogatives.[8] In principle, the same holds true for pictures. One can use a picture to make assertions about how certain things look or about the occurring of a certain event, but one can also use a picture to give directives for assembling a piece of furniture,[9] or to invite imaginings by means of a speech act of "fiction-making".[10] However, pictures are less flexible than language since they lack connectives such as "or", "if", "because", or indicators such as question marks. Still, this is just a difference in degree which should not obscure the fact that both pictures and language can be used to make speech acts.

The place of pictures is somewhere in between language and perception. On the one hand, pictures resemble perception since their matter is a colored surface that can elicit a visual experience. On the other hand, pictures resemble language as for their form, which is a norm that enables communication by coordinating the intentions of pictures' makers with the cognitive responses of the viewers.

Ordinary perceptual experience involves content which is open-ended, requiring us to adopt our own perspective. However, when we look at a picture, our vision is constrained by the intentions of the picture's maker. We see things from a given perspective which is not up to us but rather is the same for all the picture's viewers. Moreover, in a pictorial experience we can see the same scene from the same perspective how many times we want, while in ordinary perception every moment is unique. Pictorial experience is closed and repeatable while ordinary perception is rather unrepeatable and open-ended.

7 Recanati (2004).
8 Austin (1962).
9 See Frixione/Lombardi (2015).
10 See García-Carpintero (2013).

Pictures turn perception into a form of communication which resembles linguistic communication. Yet, the perceptual root of pictures differentiates them from language. While linguistic sentences are sequences of words which match the conceptual structure of high-level cognition, pictures are colored surfaces which match the spatial structure of the visual field. Consequently, there are no dictionaries and grammatical rules for pictures. While the speaker of a language combines words from the dictionary by means of the rule of the grammar to enable the listener to grasp the intended meaning, the maker of a picture only organizes colors on a surface to elicit the proper visual experience from the viewer.

Although only the sequences of words that abide by the dictionary and grammar count as utterances of a certain language, any distribution of colors on a surface may count, in principle, as an image. That is why there can be abstract images and not abstract utterances. An abstract image is a colored surface which does not enable us to see things in it, as pictures usually do, and yet has a form which is a norm that prescribes us to enjoy a visual experience of that surface. In this sense, abstract images are borderline cases since they have the matter of paradigm pictures, namely a colored surface, but also a peculiar form which prescribes us to visually scrutinize that very surface as an object in our space rather than to see in it other things arranged in a different space.

References

Austin, John L. (1962): *How to Do Things with Words* (Cambridge, MA: Harvard University Press 1962)

Evnine, Simon (2016): *Making Objects and Events – A Hylomorphic Theory of Artifacts, Actions, and Organisms* (Oxford: Oxford University Press 2016)

Frixione, Marcello/Lombardi, Antonio (2015): 'Street Signs and Ikea Instruction Sheets – Pragmatics and Pictorial Communication', 6 Review of Philosophy and Psychology (2015) 133–149

García-Carpintero, Manuel (2013): 'Norms of Fiction-Making', 53 British Journal of Aesthetics (2013) 339–357

Recanati, François (2004): *Literal Meaning* (Cambridge: Cambridge University Press 2004)

Terrone, Enrico (2021): 'The Standard of Correctness and the Ontology of Depiction', 58 The American Philosophical Quarterly No. 4 (2021) 409–422

Wollheim, Richard (1980): *Art and its Objects – An Introduction to Aesthetics* (Cambridge: Cambridge University Press 2nd revised ed. 1980)

Part 3
Images, Art and Society

Chapter 5
Who Cares About Privacy? – The Documedia Surplus Value

Maurizio Ferraris

I. Prologue: The Virus and the Web

These Covid-19 crisis times are also times of 'smart working', and the question arises as to what is 'smart' about it. Let's start from an unquestionable point. As always, the current crisis is an ongoing and accelerating trend. For example, the transition from labour to mobilisation, occurring for at least twenty years, has blurred the distinction between working time and living time. Initially this meant the working as if you were on vacation, but of course it now signifies that you *also* work on vacation. There are two ways to view this phenomenon, and they are not mutually exclusive. However, the first is confined to the past, while the second looks towards the future.

Firstly, capital is expanding its dominion by no longer overseeing the means and places of production, a trend decisively driven by the virus outbreak's security requirements. There is some truth in this view, as one can easily understand. The problem, though, is that it involves a scheming and plotting supernatural entity, i.e., capital, or a modern Satan (wasn't it Marx who insisted on the Faustian character of capital?). But the collapse of stock markets, the unpreparedness of governments, and the current general turmoil should at least raise the legitimate suspicion that Satan was not quite in command of things and failed to promptly warn his followers so that they could take full advantage of the outbreak.

The second perspective, which is perhaps more complicated, does not involve Satan, but the human being. This view can give us not only hope, but actual solutions for the future – a future that will obviously look very little like the past, since the current crisis is of an epochal character, bringing together the two great components of the world, souls and mechanisms, life and technology.

Let's start from a simple observation: if computers could only be used in the office, at certain times and places, would we actually 'live' at home, leaving computers behind? Of course not. At work, at home, and when commuting between home and work, we always look at our mobile phones, both for work and for other reasons. This is because mobilisation is not a command that comes from outside, but the fundamental characteristic of every soul. In fact, every soul is driven by vital urges, be they the remote consciousness of death or the very pressing need to have lunch.

We humans are particularly maladapted organisms because we grow slowly and are poorly endowed by nature. However, we also have mechanisms to enhance our scarce resources. To put it succinctly, we are organisms related to a series of automata which are indispensable to us. This is why even when we could be inert *à la* Oblomov[1] we tinker with our mobile phones instead.

The difference between organisms and automata is very simple. An organism has only two positions, on or off, dead or alive. An automaton, on the other hand, works serially: on/off, on/off, and so on, until the bulb burns out or the battery deteriorates. An organism has an internal purpose, its end is its end, so to speak, and in between there is life. An automaton has an external purpose: knives are made to cut, books to be read, fines to be paid.

This mass of external purposes enriches the life of the soul, giving it a little more meaning. Indeed, this is why pensioners often get depressed: depression is but the revelation of bare life, of the organism without automata. This is also why the human organism desperately requires automata, from clubs to fire to society to culture. But – and this is the main point – if we remove the organism, the soul, then the automata make no sense. Imagine the British Library or Times Square in a world without a soul (something that we can imagine quite easily today).

However, let's get back to Earth. Remote working is still the offshoot of a vanishing old world, a world where souls produce by using automata. But in the meantime, for about ten years now, automata have become capable of recording the souls' smallest gestures, recording them and replicating them. This is what artificial intelligence is. Instead of focusing on automata usurping control and stealing our jobs, let us view the matter more carefully, though not smartly as this term always involves a catch. Firstly, we should note that automata have no reason to usurp control as despite their name, they require souls to function. Secondly, if we lived in a fully automated world, the Covid-19 crisis would have been less serious.

Big Internet platforms are huge automata that record the souls' smallest gestures in an exchange that seems fair (I give you free information, and you give me free information). Yet, this quid pro quo is not fair as automa-

---

1 Goncharov (1859/2005).

ta can capitalise the information and translate it into automation and distribution, as well as profit, whereas souls cannot. However, automata cannot live and produce wealth without souls. They have certainly never produced as much wealth as this very moment when all souls are on the Internet. Automata need souls just as souls need food. And if souls die, automata are finished. Therefore, the survival of souls is indispensable on the end of all things, the end of time – total apocalypse. Of course, this only applies to the association of souls and automata – the rest of the world will get along great without us, but we won't be there.

Let me explain what the only kind of 'smart working' entails: doing nothing, 'far niente', that is, living, cultivating one's hobbies and interests, studying, writing, exercising and eating. Each of our acts, today, is recorded and produces value, precisely because it instructs the automata that live by imitating souls. This value must be redistributed, but first it must be acknowledged. Think of the groups that are the most exposed today, namely all those who are employed and poorly paid. What can be done for them? Those who fought against automation, in their case, may have done so for the noblest of reasons, but ultimately caused their own misfortune.

And what will support the souls once they have been replaced by automata? Digital welfare: the taxation of the enormous surplus value that souls, by the mere fact of living, generate in their interaction with automata. I repeat, the great Internet platforms have never earned as much as they do today, and if we think about it, the answer to the questions 'who will pay Corona bonds?' and 'what is the EU doing?' is very simple. Platforms will pay Corona bonds and the EU will collect the taxation and redistribute it in terms of welfare. Welfare means freedom from material needs, but also from ignorance and prejudice – therefore, it also means culture, i.e., a resource that seems particularly valuable in these weeks of quarantine.

If the virus, as is to be expected, accelerates these ongoing processes, then the immense amount of blood shed will not have been for nothing. But for this to happen we need to think of the future not as the projection of the past (that's what 'smart working' amounts to) but as a radically new era that is coming forward unceremoniously and will really change the world for the better.

II. Privacy, Post-Truth, and Documedia Surplus Value

92 per cent of young people do not read privacy terms and conditions but maintain that doing so is important. I do not know how many old

people like me do *not* read the terms and conditions nor believe it to be important, but I wouldn't be surprised if the percentage was even higher. Not only because many people are willing to give up their privacy to share their thoughts, words and works for free on social networks, but because, and above all, the centrality of privacy is a thing of the past. It belongs to the world of bourgeois freedoms and civil rights.

We have excellent reasons to regret the intrinsic values of that world, the values of Weber and Mann, but that world is no longer ours, and it hasn't been ours for a long time. Totalitarianisms, world wars and especially the mass media have generated a different world, one where the relationship between people and their public image, as well as the concept of 'privacy', has completely changed. Privacy is obviously the least of problems for those (over half of the world) who post content on social networks, and those (almost all the world) who consent to the use of cookies, eager to get on with it and access the given service. It is not a question of bourgeois confidentiality, of decorum, of minding one's own business with due discretion: it is a question of labour.

Similarly, the relationship with the truth has also changed. The fact that one is willing to accept the existence of 'alternative facts' is the result of multiple circumstances: ideological ones, like the postmodern critique of objectivity; sociological ones, like the formation of the 'society of the spectacle'; and above all technological ones, which have determined what I call 'documedia revolution'. The latter is the boom of recording that has determined an unprecedented multiplication of documents – the so-called 'big data' – and a horizontalization of the media through social networks. Now, instead of focusing on the phenomenon itself, I think it is important to look at its context and at what has made it possible.

The real problem, in the perspective I propose, is neither privacy nor truth, but the disproportion between the data available to the general users (the 'mobilised') and the companies that manage the web platforms (the 'mobilisers') which I define 'documedia surplus value'. As we carelessly give up our privacy and navigate in the waters of post-truth, we produce wealth. This, in my opinion, is the essential core and the preliminary condition to focus on, to gain a correct understanding of epiphenomena such as the transformations of privacy and post-truth. How much does an unemployed person care about their privacy? Consider the smartphone-owning beggars we see today: would they be happier if their privacy were protected, or if their mobilisation were recognised as work, and paid, recognising the documedia surplus value? Or think of those who view the web as a space to vent their dissatisfactions, most often motivated, but blamed on often imaginary causes: what do they care about post-truth?

Now, privacy is priceless, even in the sense that it does not necessarily matter to many, and it is not clear how it can be protected. The same applies to truth which is certainly a great good, but only for the few (usually scientists) who care about it, while for most of humanity post-truth (the current version of myth) works just fine. But the value produced by our mobilisation on the web which involves the renunciation of privacy as well as production and distribution of post-truth, has a price. It can be quantified and paid by platforms without impacting national budgets. This would decrease social discontent, and perhaps make politics more palatable, making it more honourable, feasible, and rewarding to serve less scared and angry people.

III. From the Superstructure to the Structure

With a move that Marx would have defined typical of bourgeois economics, the ongoing revolution debate concentrates on its superstructures, not its actual structure. In Europe, the United States and progressively around the world, daily acts that until a very recent past would have disappeared into thin air today are recorded and therefore capitalised upon. Note that China has a huge competitive advantage, its one billion and three hundred and seventy million inhabitants with one billion mobile phones. Social objects, those that would not exist without society such as money, titles, and status, require recording. That is, they follow the Object = Recorded Act rule. A social object is the result of a social act which involves at least two people, or a person and a delegated machine, or two delegated machines that can be recorded. The recording boom involves a proportional growth in social objects, thus generating the most ubiquitous and informed capital in history. Every byte, for those few with the means to interpret it (i.e., web platform managers and web analysts) is a bearer of knowledge and generates value.

Even assigning a very low value, for example a thousandth of a euro to every byte generated daily, the total value would be € 4 billion per day. Because of this enormous data production, our world is not liquid and elusive, as postmodernists claimed. It is perhaps the most financially stable world that history has ever known since everything is recorded, everything is considered, and everyone can be held accountable. Ultimately, everything is transferred to the Documedia Capital account, the heir of financial capital and industrial capital which replaced goods and finance with an abundant and more manageable asset-documents.

Documedia Capital does not provide the means of production, but the means of interpretation. It correlates and confers meaning from the data which it owns to resell or reuse. Today's workers are not subjected to monotonous or tiring tasks, unlike the industrial age, but they must pay for the means of production, i.e., the web terminals. Production is at the bottom, knowledge at the top, although obviously the mobilised can access knowledge (for example, books or encyclopaedias), except by doing so they produce further and much more precious knowledge about themselves that they cannot access. This unprecedented and largely unforeseen way of producing wealth through documents needs to be recognised and understood. This is necessary to establish a new social contract. In particular, in Europe and the United States where the advancement of populism triggered by a formal unemployment is as extensive as real mobilisation is capillary.

This gap in accessing data is key to understanding the present. In theory, the relationship between the mobiliser and the mobilised is fair: the first offers services, the second pays with information. However, it differs in practice. There is a crucial asymmetry between what the mobiliser gives and the actions of the mobilised which can also be represented in terms of truth and post-truth. While the mobilised have considerable post-truth, the mobiliser has substantial. 'Hyper-truth' refers to the quality of the knowledge that the mobiliser acquires about the mobilised. From this point of view, the difference between the data available to the mobiliser (who owns the platforms) and the mobilised (who simply have access to it) could not be more astounding.

From the point of view of the mobilised, documedia surplus value produces a monadisation of knowledge. Each of us is a monad in the sense that we see the world, the World Wide Web, from our own very personal perspective, determined by the coordinates that the web algorithms have attached to us. So, that World Wide Web becomes the description of our home, and universal communication becomes the interlocution with the unhappy few with whom we share prejudices and preferences. We all live in different worlds – as sleepwalkers, it would seem, if we follow Heraclitus, since 'The awake share a common world, but the asleep turn aside into private worlds'.[2]

The image of the world available to the mobilisers, the managers of the platforms, is completely different. If we follow the Kantian categorisation, in terms of quantity, the platform's data is enormous, while the mobilised

2 Diels/Kranz (1951) 12B89.

are comparatively poor. This is despite our impression of being inundated with information. In terms of quality, the platform's data is rich. This is because they are individual and entail very detailed profiling, while the data available to the mobilised is general-generic and refers not to individuals, but general notions. In terms of transparency, the mobilisers' data is secret, while the mobilised's data is blatant and in the public domain. Finally, in terms of modality, the mobilisers' data is real as it records actual behaviours on the net, while the data accessible to the mobilised is a combination of real information and fake news (Table 1).

	Mobilisers	Mobilised
Quantity	*Big data*	*Small data*
Quality	*Rich data*	*Poor data*
Relation	*Secret data*	*Public data*
Modality	*Real data*	*Virtual data*

Table 1: Quantity, Quality, Relation and Modality of Data for Mobilisers and Mobilised

So, let's proceed to an analysis of this disproportion to highlight the documedia surplus-value.

1. *Quantity: big data*

Let's start with quantity. For every bite of information on the mobilised there are several recordings on the part of the mobiliser. Google Translate has capitalised on all the existing texts on the web, and Tesla cars improve their software by collecting data through Autopilot, Tesla's semi-automatic driving system. While providing a service, you acquire information that is not found in the simple passive documentation of commodities. For example, a wine's label informs only us, while an online purchase informs us, and additionally others about us. The power of Google or Amazon lies in an innovative scheme based on the development of old things (the register, in the case of Google; the postal market, in the case of Amazon). However, in a new context this scheme has exponentially increased through the possibility of recording, and subsequently, so has capitalisation. It may not be immediately clear to what extent the accumulation of data, regardless of the knowledge it provides,[3] constitutes capitalisation per se, but this will be perfectly evident if we consider that money itself is data.

If money is a commodity like any other, as economists remind us about, it is primarily because it is a document like any other such as a passport which also has complicated doodles and characteristic colours. With a passport, a state authorises a citizen to leave the country (as it was originally) and with a banknote it authorises him to buy things. Since there are many more citizens willing to buy than those wishing to leave, banknotes are more numerous than passports. Also, since money changes hands, banknotes are not nominal, and – since the exchanges are done quickly and may involve illiterate agents – to prevent misunderstandings about their value, in most States (albeit with the significant exception of the United States) banknotes have different sizes and colours. This allows money to be used as documents by illiterate persons. Moreover, regarding both passports and banknotes, the state did not invent anything new. It simply allowed paper to set services and quantify value, a practice that originates from our past and coincides with the evolution of human cultures.

Many economists have noted that money is a recordal system, although they often speak of 'information',[4] namely a low-cost means to keep track of previous resource allocations.[5] Further, that money is superfluous when agents have access to all their previous mutual interactions[6] because ultimately money is nothing but memory. This thesis has been developed in particular by American economist Narayana Kocherlakota.[7] The memory is an agent's knowledge of the acts of all the agents that he has had direct or indirect contact with previously. Money is an object that, unlike commodities, you cannot manufacture yourself and is available in fixed quantities. And yet, these amounts of money somehow form the limits of human memory and represent an artificial informational deposit which ultimately results in a form of primitive memory. Instead of noting a given or rendered service, a universally accepted document is created that sums up the annotation in an anonymous form which is particularly interesting for the 'narcos' and the mafia.

In an environment where memory replaces money, every social actor has an imaginary account. When an actor gives assets to another actor, his

3 This issue I will discuss in relation to quality (III.2).
4 Ostroy (1973).
5 Lucas (1980).
6 Aiyagari/Wallace (1991).
7 Kocherlakota (1996).

account increases, along with his future ability to receive assets. When an actor receives assets from another actor, her account decreases, and this decreases her ability to receive assets in the future. In an environment endowed with memory, an agent's account does not only depend on her transfers. If Tom gives something to Dick, and Dick's account is empty, Tom's account does not increase. So, Tom's account is not only based on his actions, but also on those of the actors he is in contact with and their contacts. This environment is the web. The environment in which money is replaced by memory also has the advantage of being able to account for finer transactions: favours, reputation, physical pleasures (intellectual assets, on the other hand, are an exception to this exchange system, in agreement with Franklyn's principle that sharing an idea does not mean losing it). At this point, big data is the absolute memory and the absolute currency, and the exchanges that take place on the web are exchanges in the strictest sense of the term. That is, they produce value by being recorded in the great worldwide calculation of give and take.

In fact, between traditional currency and documedia money – 'documoney' if you will – there is no match. The credit guarantee and the exchange can be implemented in a much more effective way through the collection of data. This informs the state of the market (not only economic, but political, demographic, etc.) incomparably better than currency can. In fact, the latter only provides economic information through a rough summary of the price of products. As for the value reserve, it is still left to currency, for now, though in the context of a growing marginalisation of banks, which are increasingly becoming value deposits and must renounce their consulting functions. The progress of cryptocurrencies suggests, however, that soon even the credit guarantee will cease to be a privilege of the banks and even, in the last instance, sovereign states. But here we are already moving from the realm of quantity to that of quality.

2. *Quality: rich data*

So, let's come to quality. Currency is a datum. But, more importantly, data is qualitatively much richer than money. Or, more accurately, the mobiliser's data is rich since it holds information regarding the individual's details. Conversely, the data available to the mobilised comprises general information, the kind available on the web, products labels, and price tags. The rise of data as knowledge of the individual is an event that has far greater social and political repercussions than those related to the mere protection of privacy. Though formally, our privacy is preserved by big data collecting and collating everything about us, except our name. However, true transformations do not occur on the basis of privacy, but regarding industry and capital.

Under the profile of industry, rich data entails a decisive transformation.[8] A world that for centuries had believed that the individual was unknowable could only be captured via types, classes and species has now discovered that the individual is not ineffable and that the production of the individual is not unfeasible. On the one hand, we now know individuals including their heartbeats and musical preferences. Indeed, perhaps the only thing that remains unknown is their name: but what does it matter at this point? On the other hand, the production of individualised commodities is economically sustainable again as it was in pre-industrial times. This is true both in traditional industries and for digital artisans (makers) that produce items with 3D printers using individualised parameters. This relationship between production and knowledge of the individual, once again, makes documents much more powerful than money.

But above all, rich data entails a radical transformation of the economy. Traditionally, documents had commemorative value: they oversaw an agreement, maintained a social object in existence. But in the case of big data, the point of interest shifts from the past to the future. The value of documents is now predictive which can multiply as now machine learning methods not only use data to predict data, but to verify previous predictions, precisely by learning autonomously. The data that documents contain can provide general information on large sections of society and on the market, such as big data or specific information on individual consumer behaviour (who, it has to be noted, is also a producer), and this is the case with rich data.

In short, documents as commodities allow for unprecedented individual profiles, knowledge, and production – just think of the homepage of large online sites that cater to the consumer by providing individualised suggestions, decreeing the end of the standardised market. The phenomenon appears to be the opposite of the shadow economy. The shadow economy is a commodity production that secures a hidden profit to the producer and is not quantified in the nation's gross domestic product. Here, instead, we have a production of commodities that are even more profitable than money itself, that is – as we have seen when talking about big data – highly informative and individualised documents generated through mobilising web users. Though, this mobilisation does

8 Carpo (2017).

not bring economic benefits to the producer, whose activity is not even conceptualised as labour.

This process has a definite impact on the whole market. The classic industry has a pyramidal structure, and this makes it unsuitable to compete with the new internet giants. While these companies only have very few employees (since we are the ones who do the work), they are better positioned, when companies lose favour on the market, to wide-spread intermediation by the web. Traditional, but forward-looking industries such as Daimler in Germany, have realized this reality and integrate the hierarchical management pyramid with interdisciplinary and cross-functional groups. That is, transversal groups endowed with humanistic skills, will gradually form the new core of the company.[9] On the production side, which is more closely related to the passage from commodities to documents, a transition from company to market has occurred. The latter, in fact, constantly increases its self-awareness (whereas before it was short of information compared to companies), and therefore becomes increasingly efficient while companies must run after it.

3. *Relation: secret data*

Once again, the privacy violation appears as a secondary problem compared to a more general framework, which relates to the production of value rather than the protection of secrecy. This appears particularly evident precisely when one examines the category of the relation which more directly relates to privacy. From this perspective, the mobiliser has secret or at least exclusive data in the sense that only he has them, while the mobilised accesses data in the public domain, which from a strategic perspective is infinitely less relevant. Indeed, one can distinguish two levels of recording that account for the asymmetry of web exchanges in terms of secrecy.[10] On the one hand, the infrastructure recording is accessible to a hacker or to the police but also to the companies that manage web platforms. On the other hand, conversational recording is explicit and accessible to the mobilised.

The latter is therefore the only recording with respect to which the mobilised are aware of dealing with privacy issues, as it is the extension of classical communication contexts. But already at this level the mobilisers tend

9 Mayer-Schönberger/Ramge (2018).
10 Domenicucci (2018).

to underestimate the advantages that come from owning a continuous, centralised and always active archive. To make an example, an Austrian law student, resorting to a European law, has asked Facebook for all the material collected on him and received a CD with 1200 PDF pages, including the comments he had deleted. And even in the case of IM services[11] where the message disappears once read by the recipient, the content remains accessible to the company that manages the platform, clearly another obvious case of asymmetry between mobilisers and mobilised. Even in the competition between companies, digital technologies create a huge cognitive asymmetry that allows capital to first destroy existing forms of business and then manage entire sectors of the economy in a monopolistic way.

But it is infrastructural recording that provides the mobilisers with the greatest benefits. They accumulate data about the mobilised of which the latter are not even aware. This includes the brightness of the place they happen to be, not to mention all the bodily data that are recorded by devices like the Apple Watch which, again, is bought by the mobilised and has the obvious effect of giving a huge amount of free data to the mobilisers. Whether we are awake or asleep, the gigantic archive that we familiarly call the web is always growing and producing. If we assume that 90 per cent of all data currently stored in the world has been generated only in the last two years, it is already clear that the digital transformation's impact will soon be equivalent, if not superior, to the industrial revolution. In that case, the driving force was given by steam and mechanical devices. Here the revolution makes no noise: it leaves *traces* and creates *documents*.

These documents are secret in many ways, but in a different form from those involved in conversational recording. The latter, so to speak, were 'plain' secrets, expressed in natural language, whereas here we are dealing with secrets that are often unrecognisable and require tools to interpret them. Once again, this reality constitutes more than a privacy violation. Indeed, can privacy really be unknown to those directly involved? Of course, this does not correspond to the traditional concept of privacy, and most likely to no general concept of privacy at all. Rather than a violation of the private sphere, therefore, we are dealing with a new form of capitalisation (and labour) whose dimensions have not yet been defined.

11 'IM' refers to instant messaging.

4. Modality: real data

So, let's come to the last category, that of modality, which is the category most directly concerned with post-truth. From the perspective of modality, the mobiliser has real data because they reflect the actual behaviours of the mobilised. Obviously, you could create algorithms to confuse the results, and maybe you do, but quantitatively speaking most of the documents would remain truthful. On the other hand, the mobilised navigate in a sea of true, false or purely verisimilar information. This is the world of post-truth.

This suggests once again that the web is a document rather than an information context:[12] a docusphere rather than an infosphere. According to the theoreticians of the infosphere,[13] information is essentially made up of well-formed, true and meaningful data, so that false information is not really information. However, on the web there is also post-truth which is anything but true. Recording can explain it as it is a written act, although it refers to things that are not true,[14] and information cannot. So, even in this case we are dealing with a phenomenon that finds its condition of possibility in the unprecedented formation of Documedia Capital, and we must bear this in mind to understand the profound nature of post-truth.

Post-truth, in other words, is explained by the documedia revolution and is one of the side effects of the formation of Documedia Capital, just like the mobilisation on the web. As for the way it works, I propose to outline it once again using the Kantian categories, but this time – this being a communicative sphere – I will use them in the version offered by the four 'conversational maxims' enunciated forty years ago by English philosopher Paul Grice.[15]

The principle of quality says: be genuine and provide truthful information to the best of your knowledge. Trump says that Obama spied on him, but it is not true. A simpleton would say that Trump is a liar; a man of the world would say that what Trump expresses is an alternative truth. The term 'alternative truth' is the tribute that vice pays to virtue, but it is also a formally radical chic construct which raises the suspicion that the truth is fascist and dogmatic and claims to emancipate while deceiving. The man of the world might have learnt this trick in a good university

12 Ferraris (2013).
13 Floridi (2014).
14 Ferraris (2017).
15 Grice (1975).

where liberal and naive professors preach that truth should be farewelled in the name of justice like the professor of *The Blue Angel*. They impart that solidarity is more important than objectivity, and democracy, more important than truth. There are at least two weaknesses to this idealistic defence of democracy, or, if you will, two precious lessons that can be drawn from post-truth. The first is that the audience addressed by the philosophers is already trained to worship the truth but must be sensitised to respecting solidarity and otherness. The second is that, after having offered an involuntary ideological assist to populists and having deprived the intellectuals of their only weapon (the pride, if not the courage, of the truth), postmodernists did not consider that a democracy without truth is not a democracy, and likewise if solidarity prevails over objectivity. This produces an uncontrollable drift (after all, the mafia or amoral familism are notable examples of the prevalence of solidarity over objectivity).

Grice's maxim of quantity recites: Do not be reticent or redundant. Aware of the fact that the best reticence is redundancy, post-truth engages in the industrial production of nonsense. In terms of quantity, post-truth is favoured by technology. There is a ceaseless production of documents on the web and each receiver can become a transmitter and even, a re-transmitter (the nonsense reaches its critical mass thanks to the re-tweet, the forwarding that inaugurates virality). Is this production systematic and intentional as claimed by the Marxist doctrine of ideology, according to which those who control the means of production control the ideas? The answer is no: behind such nonsense there is no great puppeteer, no intelligent and strategic capital. What we inadequately call 'capital' is precisely a documedia system, that is, I repeat, the union between the constitutive power of documents ('documentality') and the mobilising power of the media, generating behaviours that are difficult to explain with age-old categories belonging to a different world. Hence, a second teaching of post-truth is the following: let's try to explain what happens with different criteria, in particular by seeing the convergence (very accidental and not very intelligent) between a technological organisation and a natural human weakness. We might understand something more about the world we live in.

The maxim of relation is: Be pertinent. But pertinence is a rare, burdensome and obnoxious quality, whereas the hoax is mediagenic and viral. It is gossip, heir of the fairy-tale, the fantastic, and the futurist words in freedom. But once again, postmodernism contributed too, by claiming that the world depends on our language and our conceptual schemes. Which, if said in a seminar, can make you smile or think (do dinosaurs really depend on the word 'dinosaur'?), but which outside of the classroom can justify the idea that things are the docile subordinates of words. If you say that there are weapons of mass destruction in Iraq, then there are weapons of mass destruction in Iraq, and if you say, on 1 May 2003, that the war in Iraq is over, then it's over. These hoaxes are much more demanding than the claim that a restaurant in Padua serves human flesh, but at the same time they manifest the human lordship over language that philosophers and non-philosophers were so passionate about in the twentieth century. Of course, now during the third teaching of post-truth, we recognise the vanity.

Finally, the maxim of modality is: 'Avoid ambiguity' and *fashionable nonsense*. However, people like nonsense – this is an unquestionable truth. It is neither true nor post-true that humans naturally seek knowledge, as Aristotle claimed. Rather they hate the potential consequences of their lack of knowledge which is a very different thing. Although the truth sooner or later comes out, the search for truth can hardly be carried out with bare hands and no cultural training. Augustine says so in his Confessions: I want to *do* the truth, not only in my heart, but also in writing and in front of many witnesses.[16] What does he mean? Can you do the truth like you do a sport? Again, the answer is no. I would propose we interpret this sentence as follows: truth is not granted and requires technical training as well as a good dose of goodwill and sometimes even personal courage. While post-truth can be constructed by means of nonsense and illogicality, the truth asks for more but also has much more to offer. If we really cannot give up post-truth and, for example, are too attached to the concept of 'bad hombre', it is better to acquiesce than perform minimal fact checking. As the challenging test proposed by William James states, "True ideas are those that we can assimilate, validate, corroborate, and verify. False ideas are those that we cannot".[17]

5. The unfair exchange

Let's return to our general goal, to understand the determination of the documedia surplus value. As pre-Marxian economists discounted that workers were only paid for part of their work, today we tend to overlook that the mobilisation is paid only in part by the free services offered on the web. Here it is difficult not to grasp the asymmetry between give and take. The documents that the archives provide to the mobilised are general

---

16 Augustine, *Confessions*, X 1.1.

17 James (1907).

and accessible to everyone, by definition. Therefore, they do not offer competitive advantages. The information that the mobilised offer to the archives is individual and accessible only to the archives. Therefore, they offer enormous competitive advantages. Of this advantage I only receive the negative part, the one that pushes me to spend due to the probabilistic prediction of my habits. Additionally, as I recalled above, the mobilised also pay for the means of production, i.e., devices and internet provider subscriptions (not unlike what happens for the house in Airbnb or the car in Uber). Trying to draw a general law from the various categorisations proposed so far, I have obtained a law on the formation of documedia surplus value that can be formulated as follows:

Let's call the documedia value v, the amount of generic data received from the mobilised Q and the amount of specific data provided by the mobilised X.

(1) The way things appear to the mobilised: receiving a free amount of Q seems to coincide with the documedia value

$v^* = Q$

(2) What actually happens: the mobilised receives Q in exchange for X (whether they know it or not), therefore the true documedia profit is:

$v = Q - X$

(3) We can quantify X as quantitatively and qualitatively superior to Q, therefore expressed by the formula

$X = (1 + k)Q \quad \text{(with } k>0)$

Therefore the true documedia profit is

$v = Q - X = Q - (1 + k)Q = -kQ$

And consequently the surplus value obtained by the system (social network or else):

$p = X - Q = -v = kQ$

In particular, if we say that the mobilised receives 50 from the platform in generic data and gives 100, this is equivalent to saying $k = 1$, which means that $X = 2Q$

Therefore, the documedia profit is

$v = -Q$

And consequently the surplus value is

$p = -v = Q$

In short, we have $v = -Q = -v^*$, i.e., the mobilised person believes they have a documedia profit v^*, instead they face a documedia loss of the same value. On the contrary, the surplus value of the system is equal to the data that it has apparently given to the mobilised user.

As long as this law is not clear, I fear that we will continue to operate with inadequate categories and to nurture social hatred – which is the most serious problem of an age that, in many ways, is the richest and most evolved in human history.

IV. Epilogue: Objections and Answers

I will conclude by replying to two objections made respectively by a reviewer and by an article that appeared in *Wired*.

The reviewer, whom I thank, writes the following:

> "I would question certain assertions, such as that of consumers not benefitting from web services that exploit big data. For example, increased competition can drive down prices and increase consumer surplus: this leaves customers with more money in their pocket to spend elsewhere (and not just on more 'stuff', i.e., they could save for a child's education, for example). As such, there are a few assumptions I challenge. Further, I question whether large tech companies employ only a few people. Amazon, FB and Google all employ tens of thousands of employees each. It's perhaps then a question of whether the revenues per company employee are unusually large (?), e.g., FB's revenue per employee per year is circa $1.6m (Global turnover is circa $70bn, 45k employees).[18] Are retail banks today any different? They have large revenues, but increasingly few employees (as operations shift online and are automated). Are tech companies very different?".

My answer is that consumers obviously benefit from these services, otherwise they would not use them. And it is also true that the big Internet platforms hire tens of thousands of employees, though mainly in the United States (which is why they are reluctant to tax the web, unlike in Europe). However, these companies' profit margins compared to the number of their employees is unusually high, and this should make us think. The crux of the matter is that what these platforms do is profit from something that would otherwise go to waste, thus minimising the weight of human input and maximising their profit.

18 Van Romburg (2019).

Let me explain what I mean with an example given by a colleague, the philosopher Fausto Corbini:

> "I get my hair cut by a gentleman who (excuse the example) collects the hair he cuts and sells it to a company that makes insulating material out of it (or something like that, I don't really remember). Hair, like data, is a resource out of which I would not know how to get a penny, unlike the resources that are the object of classical capitalist accumulation. And that makes it pretty complicated to argue that my barber gets added value from my hair. In fact, he doesn't ask customers if they want to take their hair home, he just sells it. A similar argument could perhaps apply to data. As soon as I click 'accept' I'm deprived of something that has no economic value to me".

I object. There is no value if the barber didn't collect them and sell them. Since it's valuable to him, it's valuable to you too. Visit a different barber or ask for a discount, I'd say.

Now to *Wired*'s objection, which is not addressed to me, but to the idea that platforms should be taxed as data is the new oil.[19] I reply that it is a mistake to view data as the new oil. This, in turn, makes it very easy to challenge and state that there is no reason to demand payments of any kind from the tech companies since data are not easily monetised, and it is not clear how redistribution would occur. Though, what we are dealing with here is both a conceptual and political error.

The conceptual error consists in equating data with assets (in this case, resulting from the decomposition of organisms that died millions of years ago) rather than as the result of the mobilisation of living human organisms, without which the tech companies would collapse. There is therefore an excellent reason for Internet platforms to ensure the survival of users because without them, they would halt and lose any reason to exist.

Secondly, coming to the political error, data cannot be monetised by users. Though users are very much monetised by tech companies which form the sector that has earned the most for some years now. It makes no sense to imagine a system of modest wages for our mobilisation on the web, but it is sensible to imagine taxing the documedia surplus-value to favour a digital welfare system managed by governments, or even better, supranational entities like the EU.

In conclusion, I reiterate my thesis. At first glance the exchange between users and Internet platforms (including not only social networks which

---

19 García Martinez (2019).

are a marginal problem because no one forcibly uses them, but also small businesses, restaurants and artisans that without use would suffer a serious competitive disadvantage) is a fair exchange: the platform offers free information to users, and users provide free information to platforms.

However, I would also like to emphasize that such reasoning could also apply to the feudal mode of production, as the feudal lord grants a free field to the serf so long as the serf works in the lord's field for free. It also applies to the industrial mode of production where the capitalist offers free means of production and livelihood to workers who work for free, the salary corresponding to the capitalist's need to ensure the reproduction of the labour force. If we find this description of the feudal and the industrial modes of production grotesque and caricatured, then we must recognise that there is a documedia surplus value that is generated in the relationship between users and tech companies. I will only indicate the most obvious reasons for this.

Firstly, the data that users receive is in the public domain, while those that the platforms receive become (*de facto* or *de jure*, little changes) property of the platform. So, we are dealing with a primary accumulation of the capitalist type. That this accumulation is made possible by the platforms themselves (no one could have capitalised on, say, the number of steps we take every day prior to the introduction of pedometers) does not take away the fact that the primary accumulation takes place, and is profitable.

Secondly, the data that tech companies receive from a user can be compared by them to millions of other users' data which the single user cannot do. Data can be recorded and calculated with algorithms and computers that users do not have. And so, data can give rise to behavioural profiling which generates savings for users but much larger gains for tech companies. Data can give rise to the automation of production processes with the progressive reduction of the need for manpower (which is actually happening). It can be sold like any other asset, to other platforms, agencies, or to individuals who aspire to become the President of the United States or of Luxembourg (I think there is a price difference involved here).

Thirdly, in an entirely data-based economy – such as the one that will no doubt soon be implemented, because it guarantees enormous economic advantages and the reduction of human input in production and distribution – data will perform all the functions traditionally performed by money: value reserve, accounting unit, means of exchange. But, it should be noted, this is only true for tech companies, not for users, who do not have the advantages set out in the two previous points.

References

Augustine (1960): *Confessions* (New York: Image Books 1960)

Aiyagari, S. Rao/Wallace, Neil (1991): 'Existence of Steady-States with Positive Consumption in the Kiyotaki-Wright Model', 58 The Review of Economic Studies (1991) 901–916

Carpo, Mario (2017): *The Second Digital Turn – Design Beyond Intelligence* (Cambrige MA: MIT Press 2017)

Diels, Hermann Alexander/Kranz, Walther (1951): *Die Fragmente der Vorsokratiker*, Vol. 1 (Berlin: Weidmann 6th edition 1951)

Domenicucci, Jacopo (2018): 'Trust, Extended Memories and Social Media', in: Romele, Alberto/Terrone, Enrico (eds), *Towards a Philosophy of Digital Media* (Basingstoke: Palgrave Macmillan 2018) 119- 142

Ferraris, Maurizio (2013): *Documentality – Why It Is Necessary to Leave Traces* (New York: Fordham University Press 2013)

Ferraris, Maurizio (2017): *Postverità e altri enigmi* (Bologna: il Mulino 2017)

Floridi, Luciano (2014): *The Fourth Revolution – How the Infosphere Is Reshaping Human Reality* (Oxford: Oxford University Press 2014)

García Martinez, Antonia (2019): 'No, Data Is Not the New Oil', Wired, 26 February 2019 (available at www.wired.com/story/no-data-is-not-the-new-oil)

Grice, H.P. (1975): 'Logic and Conversation', in: Cole, Petre/Morgan, Jerry L.: (eds), *Syntax and Semantics, Vol. 3 – Speech Acts* (New York: Academic Press 1975) 41–48 (reprint available at https://www.ucl.ac.uk/ls/studypacks/Grice-Logic.pdf)

Goncharov, Ivan (1859/2005): *Oblomov* (Petersburg 1859, cited after the edition London: Penguin 2005)

James, William (1907): *Pragmatism* (London/New York: Longmans, Green & Co. 1907; cited after the edition Mineola: Dover 1995)

Kocherlakota, Narayana R. (1996): *Money is Memory* (Minneapolis: Federal Reserve Bank of Minneapolis, Research Department Staff Report 218, October 1996)

Lucas, Robert. E. Jr. (1980): 'Equilibrium in a Pure Currency Economy', in: Kareken, John H./Wallace, Neil (eds): *Models of Monetary Economies* (Minneapolis: Federal Reserve Bank of Minneapolis, 1980) 131–145

Mayer-Schönberger, Viktor/Ramge, Thomas (2018): *Reinventing Capitalism in the Age of Big Data* (New York: Basic Books 2018)

Ostroy, Joseph M. (1973): 'The Informational Efficiency of Monetary Exchange', 63 American Economic Review (1973) 597–610

van Romburg, Marlize (2019): 'Facebook Makes More Profit Per Employee Than Other Fortune 500 Tech Companies', The Business Journals, 8 July 2019 (available at https://www.bizjournals.com/bizwomen/news/latest-news/2019/07/facebook-makes-more-profit-per-employee-than-other.html?page=all; see also https://csimarket.com/stocks/FB-Revenue-per-Employee.html)

Chapter 6
Immersive Artistic Forms – What They Are and How to Identify Them

Davide Dal Sasso

I. Introduction

This text presents an account of what we might call 'immersive artistic forms' by proposing a list of criteria to identify them. The first part is dedicated to the topic of technology and consists of two sections focused on the relationship between art, knowledge and operational practices. The second part, also divided into two sections, addresses some issues in the metaphysics of art, the relationship between form and structure, and presents the identification criteria to use the term 'immersive artistic forms'.

II. Technology

1. Knowledge

Numerous aspects concerning the nature of the arts, their current condition and the experiences they can offer are linked to the use of the latest-generation technologies as well as to resources offered by research in the computer and electronic fields and to those made available by the Internet and its tools. Many of the achievements in contemporary arts – for example, in New Media Art, in the fields of video art and Net Art, in certain works of theatre, dance and in some types of installations and performances – are due to the recognition of the role of technology in the framework of the possibilities of artistic production.[1] Far from being a

1 For more on the relationship between art, science and technologies, and the fruitful possibilities it yields in different artistic fields, see Wilson (2003); on the relationship between technology and medium, with particular attention to the issue of time in the field of video art, see Rush (2005) and (2007); about the implementation of technological resources and their achievements in areas such as theatre,

recent question, the question of technology is an ancient one that refers to an assumption at the base of all artistic practices: human activity.

Two factors characterize human activity: decisions and industriousness. Both refer to the relationship between knowledge and practice that also guides artistic production, and both are pivotal for the relationship between technology and human activity. Therefore, these elements are important to investigate in order to clarify the meaning of 'immersive artistic forms', a term referring to the outcomes of those practices that foster viewers' immersion in works of art. As these are not a definite kind of art but rather the *outcomes* that can be achieved through different artistic practices, instead of using the general term 'art forms' I propose the more specific 'artistic forms'.

a) Planning

For studies on the nature of the arts, the subject of technology is one of the most important to examine, as it allows new means of expression through research in the computer and electronic fields. Today, works that allow us to have immersive experiences – namely 'to enter' scenarios that, although essentially visual, offer various degrees of practicability, exploration, and interaction through the aid of VR helmets and other devices – are based on the implementation of several technological resources. On closer inspection, however, long before reaching its virtual version, it was precisely in reality that important results were achieved in several artistic fields, both on the technological front and on that of 'immersivity'. The latter term mainly refers to the possibility of entering a work of art, of being able to experience it differently than usual. This was based on an important change, the reduced distance between work and viewer. Indeed, instead of observing the artwork from the outside, one can discover it, so to speak, from the inside.[2] However, 'entering a work of art' can mean very different things. Although today this possibility is primarily encouraged by

dance, installations and performance art, see Dixon (2007); for an overview of the relationship between art and technology useful for clarifying the developments of artistic practices based on the changes that occurred in the twentieth century, see Popper (2009); for an overview of the most recent directions in new media art and digital art, see Paul (2016).

2 To learn more about immersive images and the new experiences of practicability and habitability that they can offer, see Pinotti (2017) for the essential elements concerning their nature of 'an-icons', and Pinotti (2020), to go in deep about the

new technological devices, it has already been offered in more traditional works. Following important changes occurring in the twentieth century, immersive experiences were brought back to the fore. Above all, this was due to research by numerous artists in the 1960s and 1970s, well before the worldwide spread of the web and the latest immersive technologies.

The first example of immersive experiences in artworks of the past is described by the art historian Oliver Grau in his important study dedicated to virtual art.[3] Grau emphasizes how immersive experiences were first made possible by achievements that occurred primarily in the field of painting. More precisely, this occurred by painting the walls of certain rooms of physically accessible prestigious buildings. Two instances made by Grau are particularly emblematic: the *Camera degli Sposi* (1465–1474) created by Andrea Mantegna in a room in the tower of the Castello di San Giorgio in Mantova, and the panorama of *The Battle of Sedan* (1883) created by Anton von Werner depicting a scene from the 1870 Battle of Sedan.

In both cases, the link between technology and immersion stands out. In other words: if the work is considered immersive, it is because it was created by the artist to also offer other experiences than those provided by the mere visual observation of the work. However, and this is one of the most important aspects highlighted by Grau, the potential of immersion – namely the access to the work – requires us to consider the increase in the virtual dimension of art. This increase was the result of images research. Through a considerable implementation of technological resources, it now possible to further emphasize their virtual character. This is crucial for works of art to offer illusions, namely visual experiences through the configuration of a two-dimensional surface while not being limited to it. These possibilities are also decisive for the relationship between vision and imagination.[4]

This connection – evidently of technological nature – between image, the virtual dimension of the artwork, and illusion[5] had already been brought into focus in the mid-twentieth century by the philosopher Su-

---

boundaries of icons, the 'environmentalization' of images and its impact on their experiences.

3 Grau (2003).

4 As the philosopher Richard Wollheim observed while investigating what he called 'seeing in' and the nature of representations in relation to the imagination. See Wollheim (1998).

5 To learn more about this connection and many other issues related to the nature of images, see in particular Grau/Veigl (2011).

sanne K. Langer, who focused on the idea that works are *symbols* that convey ideas of feeling.[6] In her successive studies on the theme of creation in the arts, Langer wonders what it is that an artist creates. Considering the role of the image – in particular, the kind resulting from pictorial production – she describes it in ontological terms as "an apparition", "a vision". Indeed, she writes that "[t]he whole picture is a piece of purely visual space".[7] Shortly after, Langer specifies that it "is an apparition of virtual objects (whether they be 'things' in the ordinary sense or just coloured volumes), in a virtual space".[8] Developing her explanation, she compares a mirror image and a painting. Unlike the former, the latter offers a different appearance: "[t]he space beyond the mirror is really an indirect appearance of actual space. But the virtual space of a painting is *created*".[9]

The first aspect to consider for our reflection on the relationship between technology and art, and in particular on the role of the image in the context of the immersive possibilities offered by the arts, precisely concerns this inclination of artists to arrange everything so that the work can succeed. Art is primarily an organizational activity. Artists identify the conditions of possibility to create their work and try to implement them. They do several things for this purpose. Indeed, as Langer writes, "[t]he illusion of space is created".[10]

b) Processing

Why should the organization of the artwork interest us? Mainly because it allows us to recognize that what the artists do are essential for their work to be in one way or another. Of course, their initial decisions may be very different from what the final outcome. However, the production and form of the latter are certainly influenced by the former. Thus, this means that we should not only consider the final appearance of the work, but also the assumptions that guided its creation.[11] Should the artist choose to work on image processing – as Langer finely observes – these assumptions would also include the premise of creating illusions, of offering virtual objects in

---

6 See Langer (1953).
7 Langer (1957) 28.
8 Ibid. 29.
9 Ibid.
10 Ibid.
11 I will return to this in the second part of this text, in the section dedicated to the relationship between form and structure.

a virtual space. This is in line with Grau's reflection on the achievement of illusion in relation to what he calls "aesthetic distance", i.e., how close the experience allows users to be to the work.

Indeed, this distance (or proximity) is determined by the creation process, the illusion it offers and the degree of immersion possible. Of course, these results ultimately concern the type of work that the artist carries out on the medium. As Grau proposes, this allows artists to move from offering illusions to creating experiences based on immersion in their works through the implementation of different technological resources. As the history of the arts shows, the artist can carry out this activity by emphasizing the role of the image, as Grau also points out. "At best, the medium of virtual reality can be objectified through knowledge and critique of the image production methods and an understanding of their technical, physiological, and psychological mechanisms, for *everything* is an image".[12] For everything to be an image and an immersive experience, including illusions and virtual spaces, it is essential that the artist's practice proceeds according to resources that are cognitive and operational.

The second aspect that is important to consider is to shed light on the relationship between art and technology concerns these resources which are crucial for the *processing* that makes artistic production possible. The implementation of technological resources is performed based on knowledge. This includes not only the knowledge that, allows an artist to create works that involve virtual reality experiences through helmets and other devices but also *operational knowledge*. This is the basis of many human activities and in particular of what we call 'artistic practices'. Such knowledge can be applied differently in each area and does not necessarily require a hierarchy between the cognitive and executive levels. 'Operational knowledge' means both the set of theoretical and cognitive references that an artist uses to create works and those applied directly by experimenting, doing, and working even without any knowledge guiding the practice. There are in fact numerous cases in which artists start from the practical level and make discoveries on the theoretical one, or the other way around. Among other human activities, artistic processing can be easily characterized by either procedural direction.

A crucial theme one needs to address to recognize and further clarify some aspects of artistic activity is that of organization, which was highlighted by the philosopher Alva Noë. Underlying the arts, Noë writes, there are human activities which he considers essentially as organized ac-

12 Grau (2003) 202.

tivities. They can be conducted individually or socially, on a large or small scale, and are related to our organic nature in what can be considered a fruitful relationship between the human being and the environment. In particular, organized activities indicate our biological condition characterized by its own structure.[13]

According to Noë, artistic practices could be considered as reorganizational practices. More precisely, they allow us to highlight the very fact that we are organized in a certain way – as he points out by taking dance as an example. As human beings, we organize our activities in a certain way and are organized by them. When we make art, we can reorganize them and make manifest the organizational character that distinguishes us. The link with technology is determined by what Noë calls "evolving patterns of organization"[14] that we can implement based on the technological tools we can use. Indeed, as he remarks, taking up an already established idea, "technologies are natural for us. People use tools naturally, in something like the way bees build hives and birds make nests. We are designers by nature".[15]

In the arts, especially through the research and practices conducted during the 1960s and 1970s, the natural technological attitude that characterizes us is highlighted. But – it is important to reiterate it again – this happened long before virtual reality devices or the tools made available by the Internet and the web. The latter are certainly important. However, they were obtained in parallel and in some cases even *after* some of those obtained in the arts – as shown by the immersive possibilities examined so far.

2. *Practices*

Art practices are based on human practices. While this may seem elementary, in the light of the evolutions of the arts, our attention to what is 'artistic' is primarily directed to the visible results of human practices,

---

13 Precisely as Noë writes: "We are organized. We get organized. We are organisms! Our lives are structured by organized activities, in the large, in the small. Our lives are one big complex nesting of organized activities at different levels and scales. Talking, walking, eating, perceiving, driving. We are always captured by structures of organization. This is natural, indeed our biological, condition. It is the basic fact about us."; Noë (2015) 10.

14 Ibid. 18.

15 Ibid. 20.

rather than to the practices themselves. One of the most important teachings offered by numerous artists who have contributed to transforming the arts in depth, especially since the second half of the twentieth century, was precisely this: besides the visual outcome, it is even more important to consider *how* this outcome was obtained.

To explain the relationship between human and artistic practices, Noë considers technology and the possibility that through artistic practices, human beings reorganize themselves because they are absorbed by them. Indeed, he also considers artistic practice as a way to examine our *absorption* in it.[16] This indication is valuable because it allows us to recognize that artistic practices can also reveal the very relationship between technology and human activity. Usually, especially in traditional artistic practices, this link is crucial in functional terms but not in terms of content. That is to say, the technology is functional for the purpose of a certain result that can be obtained through a certain human activity. The link between technology and human activity is therefore crucial for the purposes that artists aim to achieve, being a decisive element for the *means* they can use. These changes made possible by the research conducted by numerous artists in the second half of the twentieth century offer a different perspective: artistic practices can manifest the link between technology and human activity. Showing it means making it an *end* and not just a means for artistic practice. The latter, in fact, can consist of different activities shown for what they are, phases of a human activity carried out at different times.

a) Dispositions

Practices can be arranged in different ways. The artistic practices that manifest human activity are those carried out between the 1960s and 1970s, which developed new and alternative methods to traditional art making. These practices can be called 'conceptualist'. Their specificity lies in the artists' choice to emphasize the processes rather than the form and the production methods rather than the results. Art is conceptual since

16 Noë explains this possibility considering, for instance, dance and the role of choreography as follows. "Choreography is concerned with the ways we are organized by dancing. Crucially, dancing is natural for us. It is our nature to be absorbed into organized activities, and dancing is an organized activity; it is one of the activities that absorb us. Choreography is a practice for investigating our absorption."; Noë (2015) 14.

it expresses the role of processes through forms which are reduced to a minimum.

Let us consider some artworks. *The Shortest Day at My House in Amsterdam* is a work made by Jan Dibbets in 1970. It consists of a series of photographs taken by Dibbets from dusk to dawn from a room in his house. After installing the camera in front of a window, the artist took numerous photographs over a period of twenty-four hours. The photographs show the darkness and the first light at dawn, the increase in brightness during the morning hours and its progressive decrease in the afternoon and evening, eventually going back to darkness. Dibbets's work manifests indeed the different phases of a human activity – taking a photograph – carried out at different times. What matters is not the form but the process that makes it possible. Through it, Dibbets records the change of time and, at the same time, the light variations during his "shortest day".

One can understand what it means to emphasize the process or a method of artistic production rather than the result by considering a second example. The importance of human activity is crucial in *Hand Catching Lead*, a work made by Richard Serra in 1968. The video details a hand opening and closing in the foreground as it attempts to grab some pieces of falling lead. This gesture is repeated for the entire duration of the short video (about three minutes).

The mentioned works share the same trait: the artistic practice is not simply a production activity, namely a medium, but an 'end'. What matters in these works is what the artist means and does, the concept and the action. The result is that the form, viewed as an external aspect of the work, is of secondary importance.

This difference between practice as a medium and practice as an end is further clarified by distinguishing between artistic practices. 'Traditional artistic practices' are those conducted by humans in the arts that have spread throughout history and are recognized thanks to the modern classification proposed by the philosopher Charles Batteux[17]: painting, sculpture, dance, poetry, and music. Next to these there are also architecture, literature, cinema, and photography. Broadening Batteux's interpretation, we can recognize that these kinds of art are characterized by three traits: imitative, expressive, and representational. Each trait may be more significant in certain art than others. For example, the imitative and representational traits are less incisive in music and architecture, in which the expressive

17 For further details on the modern classification of arts, its features and main theses presented in it, see Batteux ([1746] 2015).

trait is much more important. The latter is fundamental for conceptualist practices where processes, creation methods and human activity are brought to the fore. Indeed, in traditional arts, absorption – determined by the degree of reorganization, according to Noë[18] – is usually decisive for the link between technology and human activity to be functional. Conversely, in conceptual arts absorption is crucial because the link itself becomes the content of the work. The purpose of conceptual artworks is to emphasize the technological resources, the possibilities of human activity, and the ingenuity that guides the countless new art making methods proposed since the second half of the twentieth century.

b) *Reality*

The aspects addressed so far allow us to recognize that, in the arts, practices can be arranged in different ways, considering them as medium or also as ends. Thanks to technological resources, the possibilities for making art has changed. These resources can be regarded in two ways: (i) as means additional to human activities and which, as Noë[19] proposes, allow for an increase in absorption, making their reorganization possible; and (ii) as elementary devices that naturally belong to the human being. In the second case, they are linked to operational knowledge, to the range of creative possibilities that allow artists to make art according to their work programs. In this way, the reorganization would occur based on means already available to the human being: making art then becomes a way to make this condition visible, to show making as making.

This latter artistic attitude naturally belongs to alternative or – as happens in many cases, radically new – practices compared to traditional ones. These practices are precisely those of a conceptualist orientation. They allow the artist to manifest the idea they wish to express or represent and, depending on the case, also the activity they must perform to create their work. I will return to conceptualist practices in the next sections, addressing some themes in the metaphysics of art. Now, I wish to conclude the reflection on technology by highlighting the following issues.

An artist can use traditional technology such as painting to make an immersive work because, as Grau[20] shows, they can work on the surfaces

---

18 Noë (2015).
19 Ibid.
20 Grau (2003).

of a room and on the image dimensions to achieve immersion. An artist can also choose alternative tools. Instead of processing images, they can resort to what already exists in the world, working on a space that exists in reality. Using traditional artistic practices, an artist can both add tools and use those that they naturally have as a human being: poetry, dance and theatre are excellent demonstrations of this second possibility. Conceptual arts such as performance, relational and participatory practices, certain ways of making installations and certain uses of video art as video documentation, show equally well what results can be achieved based on the technological resources implemented. Using the human body in its entirety, making gestures, saying something out loud, performing an action in a certain (natural or artificial) environment, involving other human beings in shareable activities, etc.: these are all implementable technological resources in artistic practices. This is because, as the philosopher Maurizio Ferraris writes, technology is characterized by two aspects in particular: (*a*) its median position between what there is (ontology) and what we can know about what there is (epistemology); and (*b*) its iterative trait: the basis of the production and reproducibility of works of art is the possibility of repeating the practices, of implementing and re-implementing technologies.[21] As Ferraris remarks, technology can be decisive because "it ensures the transition from ontology to epistemology".[22] Indeed, in his view, 'technology' is the name of multiple operations that enable the relationship between what there is and what we can say about the things of the world which, before being true or false, are present or absent.[23]

III. Metaphysics

1. Structures

Along with many others, the things we call 'works of art' decorate our world. They are characterized by their aesthetic properties (which make them the objects of our appreciation, and thanks to which they arouse pleasure, interest and emotions), representationality (the artworks stand

---

21 To learn more on this, see Ferraris (2019) 5–12, and, in particular, ibid., § 1.2.3, 11–12.

22 Ferraris (2017) 119.

23 For further details see ibid. 123–128 (English translation of the quoted text by the author).

for the contents and subjects they represent), expressiveness (they convey content, emotions and information), and the relational property of aboutness (works of art have a meaning and are about something that the artist intentionally chooses to express or represent through them).[24] These are just a few criteria that identify works of art. In fact, in addition to these we could add another one: their formal essence. Numerous scholars, critics, artists, and philosophers share the idea that artworks are essentially forms, namely conclusive manifestations of activities that are carried out by artists, who work precisely to develop new forms.[25] On closer inspection, however, this reading does not work as well as it seems.

a) Forms

Aristotle's metaphysics theory has long informed the discussion regarding form. By examining the relationship between form and matter, Aristotle confirms the indissoluble link (the *synolon*) between the organization of things and the appearance they have in accordance with their form. However, numerous questions arise from this link about the very nature of form which, as he writes, comes before matter, configures it, and is more than it.[26] Matter is organized in a certain way, in accordance with its form. However, the latter is not only transposed into the external appearance of matter, precisely because form is also its organizing principle. Drawing from the Aristotelian teaching, form is considered in both ways, as the organization and as the external aspect of things. However, there are also other aspects. As an organization, form determines the appearance of a certain entity. This determination, being a resolution, therefore also implies the essence of the latter: the form of x determines what x will look like. This also means that through its form, x will have a certain appearance to the extent that it materially translates a certain organization project.

24 The best-known philosophical research dedicated to the semantic nature of works of art, which defended the thesis that aboutness is one of the necessary conditions to define what art is, was developed by the philosopher Arthur C. Danto. To learn more on this, see Danto (1981).

25 Form has often been the subject of reflection also in the writings of numerous artists: in Kandinsky (1911) form is a constant reference; form is also present in the reflections on the nature of theater, in the writings collected in Kantor (1977). In the history of art, important accounts on this topic have been presented. Two examples are Focillon (1934) and the reflection on the history of art as the history of things developed by Kubler (1962).

26 Cf. Aristotle, Metaphysics, Z, VII, 1029a, I-5.

Furthermore, this organization *defines* the entity that is formed in a certain way: a thing (*x*) is in a certain way because it is formed in that way; it is so because its form establishes it. In fact, the form allows one to answer the question 'what is the substance' of a certain entity because the latter is as it is by virtue of the form it has.[27]

As a principle, the form entails the 'planning and articulation' of things and ultimately, their resolution. This condition characterizes form, in its autonomy, both in natural processes and in those that feed the activities of human beings – including artistic ones. The idea that artworks are also forms emphasizes that they are the results of processes, outcomes of activities that lead to the development of a certain configuration. This conception is fairly shared by commentators, although it is crucial to agree on the meaning of the concept of 'form'. The philosopher Władysław Tatarkiewicz identified at least five meanings of 'form',[28] showing an oscillation between what we can consider as two 'dimensions' that naturally belong to it, one internal and one external. The first, the internal dimension is that of form as organization. The second is that of form as the external aspect of things.

These two dimensions are very important. Indeed, when we consider the arts, the internal dimension of form – the organization of the work – anticipates and orientates the artistic practice. Conversely, the external dimension characterizes the outcome that can be obtained through the latter. Now, in art as in many other human activities, not only is it possible that what one envisages may lead to unexpected results – therefore that there is no coincidence between the two dimensions – but that a form is also an expression of the dynamism that animates the work, or even be open rather than closed.

Langer was inclined to consider form in the first way, attributing two additional characteristics to it. Firstly, that it is an "organic unity"[29] that can be perceived and manifests the vital dynamism that makes it possible. Since it is perceptible, the work as a form is a semblance: it is a set of aspects that can be seen in different ways. Furthermore, to manifest the vital dynamism that animates it, a work of art expresses ideas of feeling or the subjective condition of those who made it: "a work of art presents

27 To learn more on this, see also Berti (2013).

28 Among others, Tatarkiewicz mentions the following meanings of form: composition or relationship between the parts; concrete definition of an object; its outline; the essence of a substance; the contribution of the intellect. For further information see Tatarkiewicz ([1975] 1980), in particular chap. 7, 220–243.

29 Langer (1966) 7.

something like a direct vision of vitality, emotion, subjective reality".[30] But that the work of art is considered a form, or rather an organic unity, also means that it is thought as a closed result, namely as the determination of a certain setting – also in accordance with the presupposition of entelechy made by Aristotle, according to whom it is possible that entities have their own end in themselves. Therefore, their forms determine their essence. However, Langer also considered another aspect of the form that allows for further considerations: its abstract dimension, which shows the connection with structure.[31]

In his first studies dedicated to various themes concerning arts, the theory of communication and the assumptions for his researches in semiotics,[32] Umberto Eco examined the connection between form and structure, highlighting important findings. His proposal was to consider the work of art not as a form but as a system of relations between several elements, i.e., precisely as a structure. In this way, it would be possible to recognize numerous aspects of it, linked both to its organic planning and to the vital dynamism that makes it possible. This is because the structure would be the main reference also to evaluate the relationships between the different formal dimensions of the work: between its organization and the appearance it has; between what the artist does by creating it and what the user can add to it with their experience.

The structure includes several elements, among which form as organization and as semblance.

From a metaphysical point of view, considering works as structures is very advantageous. In particular, for one reason: as structures, they can be investigated in relation to the variability that can characterize them. Structure is a crucial reference because it reveals that things are transformable and that the sense of being is not unique but multiple.[33] Being a system of relations, structure collects this mutability and the form, as an external semblance, can offer traces of it. Eco considered this aspect in relation

---

30 Ibid. 9. For more detail see ibid., in particular 7–9.

31 Exactly as Langer writes: "[…] 'form' in its most abstract sense means structure, articulation, a whole resulting from the relation of mutually dependent factors, or more precisely, the way that the whole is put together. The abstract sense, which is sometimes called 'logical form' is involved in the notion of expression, at least the kind of expression that characterizes art. That is why artists, when they speak of achieving 'form', use the word with something of an abstract connotation"; Langer (1957) 16.

32 See, in particular, Eco (1962), (1964) and (1968).

33 In this regard, see also Berti (2001).

to the opening of the work. Extending his proposal,[34] defining works of art essentially as structures allows us to shed light on numerous aspects concerning the relationships between their organization, the appearance they have and their profound link with human nature.

b) Hybridizations

That human nature – or rather, as Noë proposes,[35] our biological condition – is structured in a certain way, also means that it can be considered in terms of a system of relationships between several elements which has also been observed in other studies.[36] This system is characterized by its continuous transformability and sensitivity with respect to our position in the world, our experiences, the possibilities of interaction that it offers us, and the relationships we can have with it. This dense network of relationships is naturally influenced by the flow of events and by the variability that characterizes the complex and vast set of processes that determine reality. Symmetrically, even works of art – being structures – can express or represent these and many other aspects. Here, again, there is good reason to evaluate the median position that characterizes technology – in agreement with Ferraris[37] – and that allows works of art to be different based on the decisions and activities carried out by the artists.

---

34 I worked on this possibility in Dal Sasso (2021a), in which I presented the main characteristics of Eco's position and showed some first directions for setting up a positive philosophy of the arts based on the conception of the work of art as a structure; I further developed the hypothesis in Dal Sasso (2021b), formulating an ontology of works of art conceived essentially as structures developed on the basis of different rules for artistic creation.

35 Noë (2015).

36 In this regard, two essential references are Alfred North Whitehead's philosophy of the organism and the systemic conception developed by the biologist Ludwig von Bertalanffy, with the identification of fruitful applications in various theoretical and cultural fields. The main reference for Whitehead's philosophy is Whithead (1929); the reference study for understanding von Bertalanffy's position is von Bertalanffy (1968). The two references are precious because they show the growing interest of the philosophical and scientific fields in a structural conception of reality and biological human nature. Such conception is based on the recognition of the considerable role played by the processes, the relationships between numerous elements that characterize them, and the variability that naturally influences them.

37 Ferraris (2017).

Making art is a matter of rules. Much more than we tend to believe, what artists do is based on rules. These rules have a pragmatic value and guide artistic work, making it possible to begin and complete it. One might object that if there is one area among human activities where there is no place for rules, that is precisely what we call 'art'. Note that this remark presupposes that we intend art only in the (restricted) sense derived from the modern concept that we still share today. This is, in fact, the concept of 'fine arts' that Batteux presented in his treatise, stating that what unites the practices we call 'artistic' would be the principle of imitation since they all aim to create similarities. According to Batteux, artists do not invent anything. Rather, they follow the patterns offered by nature and instead of the true, their goal is the probable. Perhaps we could say that in this limited sphere of activity, the role of rules does not immediately become apparent. On closer inspection, however, this is not the case. Each artistic field is based on its own rules – which also allow artists to learn their craft, in line with traditional academic teaching. Furthermore, if we consider especially conceptualist practices, we can recognize that it is precisely the rules that come to the fore in them.

To get a better idea of this aspect, it is important to start by clearing the field. Rather than being philosophical, dematerialized or based on sophisticated analyses focused above all on language and thought, 'conceptual' is a kind of art that can be specified in different ways precisely because it is based on operational rules that differ from traditional ones. What we can call 'conceptualism' is precisely an operational code, a set of rules that allow artists to create works based on the use of ordinary objects, industrial materials, or performances through their own bodies or those of others.[38]

The implementation of technology can include both repetition (of practices, resources, operational choices, etc.) – in agreement with Ferraris[39] – and the introduction of variants. In both cases the metaphysical definition of works as structures is pivotal to proceed with the investigations. Creativity in particular, brings variability to artistic practices. In general, creativity also entails the human capacity to make an idea possible. Above all, it allows us to propose something new[40] by introducing

---

38 The first study on this conception of conceptual art is the basis of Dal Sasso (2020); further developments are offered in Dal Sasso (2021b).

39 Ferraris (2019).

40 These aspects of creativity have been examined in various studies: for a general philosophical overview on the matter see Tatarkiewicz ([1975] 1980), in particular, chap. 8, 244–265; on the possibility of introducing innovation and in particular on the relationship between art and creativity, see Boden (2012); on the

variations. Whenever an artist introduces new rules, they can make works differently than usual. In fact, the variants are linked to the rules that the artist accepts, rejects, or combines to make their work. In this sense, creativity is the principle of variability that allows the identification of new resources. Thus, it favours the introduction of variants in the structures created by artists. Some structures resemble each other – for example those of the works of traditional arts – despite presenting variations. For instance, the works of Pablo Picasso, Tiziano Vecellio and Jackson Pollock are all paintings; each, however, has different variations (the decomposition of the subjects, scenic lyricism, the sole presence of the colour dripped on the canvas). We can say the same for the products of cinema, theatre, sculpture, etc. Other structures, however, are *essentially different*: these are the outcomes of conceptualist practices. Rather than a result of activities aimed to achieve a high degree of complexity (what we can call 'maximalism'), conceptual works are based on the opposite possibility: to achieve a lot by working with the essential (what we can call 'reductionism').[41]

Herbert E. Cory wrote that art could be a continuation of nature because it shows some aspects of it. He therefore considered it as "a fulfilment of some of nature's groping tendencies".[42] For this reason, he emphasized *the relativity of form* from its energy and matter in nature, to its organization and activities that make artistic production possible, among others. The meaning of 'artistic form' therefore lies in a relationship, which is that between what we call 'art' and human nature. Works of art are structures precisely because they are systems that gather multiple relationships. The term 'artistic form' is useful to point out this trait: it highlights this system of relations that metaphysically characterizes the work of art.

The works made through traditional practices are maximalist structures, whereas the products of conceptualist practices are reductionist structures. However, artists may very well make different choices as well. In fact, there are also works that are the result of combinations of several practices: hybrid structures. These can result from the combination of different kinds of art (between theatre and dance, video and installations, sculpture and video, etc.). The outcomes are therefore partly traditional and partly conceptual works. The combination occurs at different levels. The basic hypo-

conception of creativity as a search for originality and innovative enterprise see Wilson (2017).

41 For further clarification of the concepts of 'maximalism' and 'reductionism' see Dal Sasso (2021b).

42 Cory (1926) 324–25.

thesis is that each work, being a structure, can be composed of different modules. Hybridization is therefore based on the possible combination of different modules.

Hybrid structures have one specific characteristic: they cannot be classified in any kind of art. For example, consider *Ello* (2003), a work by Tony Oursler composed of a video projection on a fiberglass tridimensional prop: it is neither only video nor only sculpture. It is even less clear whether it is possible to include John Bock's *1 = 2 + Kleinod* (1999) as a kind of sculpture. The work consists of different objects: a table with fabrics, other models above and below it, but also pots, bottles, vases and more. It is no coincidence that terms such as 'installation' or 'mixed media' are used for these works: both indicate that they are hybrid structures. In many cases, it was precisely the practices of hybridization that made the production of immersive works possible (even the *Camera degli Sposi* and the *Sedan panorama* could be called *ante litteram* installations). This happens because, as Stephen Wilson writes, the research conducted by artists "might simultaneously use systematic investigative processes to develop new technological possibilities or discover new knowledge or perspectives".[43]

What we can call 'immersive artistic forms' arise from the artists' choices, from their researches and ways to implement technologies in creating their works, thus offering new possibilities of experience. Immersive artistic forms can result from hybridizations for two reasons. Firstly, since they are actually composed of several modules, and secondly, as they develop the illusory and virtual potentials of a module through the processing of its structure which is based on technological implementation. In this second case, the image processing performed to make two-dimensional environments explorable, favouring immersion in simulated three-dimensional environments, is a change that occurs on a structural level. Thus, concretely, there may be a helmet and another device that ensure user access in a scenario that is based on a highly complex modular structure, precisely because it is a hybridization.

43 Wilson (2003) 49.

2. *Immersivity*

The two traits of technology highlighted by Ferraris[44] are significant because they clarify some aspects concerning artistic practices and the immersive possibilities they offer. The median position of technology, between reality and knowledge, makes it decisive for artistic practices for their development, continuous evolutions and the experiences they offer. Note that the very passage from reality to its virtual version is explainable precisely in these terms. The intervention of technology – namely of resources made available based on research conducted in the fields of computer science, electronics and contemporary sciences – has enabled various degrees of immersion where users can enter works of art in a different way from what happens in actual reality.

a) Interaction

In particular, there are two aspects that are important to consider to further clarify the nature of immersive possibilities: *scale* and *accessibility*.

Scale is the system of relationships established by the artist based on the technology they implement to create their work. This system therefore determines the size of the artworks and the experiences it offers. Images painted on walls are the result of the technologies of the past, whereas those made available for today's immersions are the result of more recent technological tools. The difference between them ultimately lies in their scale. The former are based on an *environmental scale*, determined by relationships of magnitude established by the real relationship with the environment (for example the walls on which a painting is made). The latter are based on a *visual scale*, namely on relationships determined by results established parameters about the possibilities of visual perception (as happens when helmets and visors are worn to interact with virtual scenarios).

Based on its scale, and therefore on the technologies used by the artist to make it, a work can be more or less immersive, namely it can favour a greater or lesser integration of the user in it. And this depends on its degree of accessibility. Access to a work can vary: paintings on a wall are not accessible, while the room in which they are located is; the scenario of experience is accessible to the viewer, but what can be seen cannot al-

44 Ferraris (2017).

ways be fully accessed. This second accessibility (the one that characterizes virtual reality) has two characteristics: the exploration and accessibility of the work which vary depending on the production method of the work. The success of an immersive work – in the second sense, namely works that based on the implementation of the latest generation technological resources – is ultimately due to the degree of simulation. Indeed, a virtual reality experience allows different degrees of exploration and practicability which are however subject to the settings and the technological organization of the work.

Another important aspect is related to the differing degrees of accessibility offered. *Unpredictability* is the trait that distinguishes our experiences in reality. In virtual reality it is linked to the elaboration of scenarios and, above all, to the potential of simulation. We can grasp this difference by considering an example based on the experience of reality. For his solo exhibition held in 1971 at the Tate Gallery in London, Robert Morris chose to present some interactive works. His goal was to engage visitors by allowing them to use the materials on display, to step onto the platforms and touch the ropes, surfaces and other available elements. The interactive nature of the works, however, encouraged incorrect behaviour on behalf of the visitors. This caused the temporary closure of the exhibition which was rearranged and opened at a later time. Together with fostering new ways of interaction, precisely because people were able to immerse themselves in the works, Morris' choice also encouraged other ways of experiencing and relating to works of art.

In relation to reality, it is possible to recognize that immersive works allow different experiences. Interaction, i.e., the possibility of encountering something by acting and triggering a reaction, can therefore be differentiated as follows. We have what we might call 'mediated interaction' when there is a device that makes it possible: in the past it was images, today it is helmets and other tools. Mediated interaction is based on the possibility of relating with environments and elements present in them. This interaction can be described in terms of simulated viability of scenarios based on sampling of two-dimensional visual fragments. Otherwise, it would be termed 'immediate interaction' which occurs when one actually enters a space and experiences it. Immediate interaction is based on the possibility to relate to the work, and potentially change, environments and elements that are really present – which may not always be available for modifications or alterations – in spaces that are actually practicable through the use of our body. This occurs when we enter a work of art and the experience it offers.

b) Identification Criteria

As anticipated in the previous sections, the immersive possibilities of art have already been explored by artists with works based on the intervention in reality. *HON – en katedral* is a work by Niki de Saint Phalle and Jean Tinguely in collaboration with Per Olof Ultvedt and Pontus Hultén, the director at that time of the Moderna Museet in Stockholm, the site of its exhibition in 1966. *Hon* was an installation based on a large sculpture of a reclining woman that one could physically walk inside where there were several explorable environments, including a bar, and many objects like some works of visual art. *Hon* is a great example of a hybrid structure that offers an immersive artistic form based on interactions in a real space. A different case, since it is a reductionist structure, which is however just as valuable for our investigation, is that of the excellent environmental work of art the *Grande Cretto* made by Alberto Burri between 1984 and 1989 and completed in 2015 on the ruins of Gibellina. The work was born from a tragic event, the terrible earthquake that destroyed the old city of Gibellina in 1968, and that claimed numerous victims. The rubble was compacted and submerged by a large pour of concrete with which Burri created several geometric modules that occupy an area of about 80,000 square meters. Between the modules there are numerous slits about two to three meters wide that one can walk into. Visitors can thus enter those spaces and move within what are ideal lines of a three-dimensional map but, above all, cracks in the earth.

The use of the term 'immersive artistic forms' today seems to be especially profitable to clarify the specificities of the intense experiences offered, for example, by a work such as *Carne y Arena*, a virtual reality installation created by the film director Alejandro González Iñárritu in 2017. This is a simulation lasting little more than six minutes in which the user, by wearing a helmet, finds themselves among a group of immigrants on the Mexican border with the United States. The illusory and immersive potential of the work is given by several elements that characterize its structure: the images of the film, the bodily experience of the installation in which you can really walk on the sand while wearing a helmet with visor, the ambient sounds.

The mentioned works are based on at least two main assumptions. First, to point out the possibilities offered by interaction and the exploration of the environments – possibilities that are naturally given by actual experiences in real environments. Second, to underline the relationship with the continuous mutation of forms: events happen in the ordinary flow of the unpredictable processes of reality, that make them possible and transform them. Both assumptions have been decisive in the arts as well as in other areas since, in different ways, they make it possible to work on immersive possibilities and on the link between reality and appearance.[45]

The key word needed to grasp the nature of virtual reality and recognize the potential of immersion is 'simulation'. But how can we orient ourselves with respect to different immersive works? And how can we recognize the links – assuming there are any – between, say, *Hon*, the *Grande Cretto*, and *Carne y Arena*?

A good way to address these questions is, first and foremost, to recognize what such works have in common. To do this, I propose a list of criteria[46] which, in my view, allow us to use the term 'immersive artistic forms' and to identify many of their characteristics, despite their different structures. There are seven criteria: (*i*) immersive accessibility, (*ii*) subjective engagement, (*iii*) structural exploration, (*iv*) interactivity, (*v*) extensional offer, (*vi*) formal mutability, and (*vii*) immersive unpredictability. I introduce each with a short description in what follows.

i. *Immersive accessibility*: the user enters the work and experiences it from the inside. Users form part of the work because it offers an access mode that can be differentiated based on its structure. Depending on the work done by the artist on the structure, it can offer different degrees of immersive accessibility.
ii. *Subjective engagement*: instead of being an observer, the user becomes an active participant; entering the work users can be part of it and involved in different ways, depending on the decisions made by the artist and the structure of the work, sometimes also entering a relationship with the components of the latter.
iii. *Structural exploration*: from inside the work, the user explores and investigates its spaces by walking through them according to the possibilities granted by the artist who created the structure. This explorato-

45 In fields such as universities and museums, these conditions are important for the significant results that can also be achieved on an educational and didactic level. To learn more, see, for example, Garoian (2018) and Roldan/Lara Osuna/Gonzalez-Torre (2019).

46 My choice to proceed with the formulation of a list of criteria is based on a significant lesson drawn from Stanley Cavell's philosophy, according to which the investigation of a concept requires to proceed with the identification of criteria for its use. Identifying the latter is therefore crucial to better clarify the use and meaning of the concept to be examined. For further details about his analysis see Cavell (1979).

ry possibility derives from the artist's choice to offer different degrees of immersion determined by the role of reality or its virtual version.

iv. *Interactivity*: by entering the work, the user interacts with the environment, its parts and the different elements that may be available; based on the work's structure, different degrees of interaction are offered: moving some of its components, using them, triggering cause-effect relationships, etc.

v. *Extensional offer*: the work is composed of one or more modules. In the latter case, the modules are combined in different ways, partly material and partly immaterial, two-dimensional, and three-dimensional. The aim is to increase the perceptive experience of the user to involve them on a cognitive level and allow them to enjoy the work in terms of extensional possibilities – from their body to the experienced environment.

vi. *Formal mutability*: unlike static two-dimensional images, numerous aspects and compositional elements of immersive works are subject to continuous modification. In real environments, these are actual changes determined by the flow of processes that make the plot of events possible. In virtual environments, they result from mutations of shapes obtained above all on a visual level. In both cases, the formal changes belong to the structure of the work and do not necessarily contribute to altering its integrity. It depends on the artist's choices, and also on what happens.

vii. *Immersive unpredictability*: the experiences offered by immersive works are based on different possibilities of access and immersion and characterized by different degrees of unpredictability. In virtual reality, the latter is the result of an organization already contained in the structure of the work: something occurs in an unpredictable way, despite being foreseen among the events offered by the work. In immersive works elaborated in reality, be they reductionist or hybrid, the degrees of experiential unpredictability are higher: something happens without the possibility of control, precisely because reality is experienced.

The seven criteria identified make it possible to use the term 'immersive artistic forms' to reference works where the aspects mentioned are recognizable. They aim to show two aspects in particular: (a) the connection between immersive works based on analogue technologies in real environments and immersive works based on digital technologies that offer virtual environments; (b) an increase in the possibilities of accessibility compared to other types of works. The guiding principle for drawing up the list was the difference between experiences in reality and experiences in fictional contexts, based on the potential of the human faculty of imagination. The key assumption of this list is effective presence, which is real in immersive works based on real environments and simulated in immersive works based on virtual environments.

IV. Conclusion

The present study offers an account about the origins and features of immersive artistic forms. To formulate it, I addressed the relationship between technology and art by highlighting the link between art, knowledge and operational practices. Through reflection on some issues on the metaphysics of art, I evaluated the connection between form and structure and presented a list of identification criteria to use the term 'immersive artistic forms'. The term can be used referring to the outcomes achieved through different artistic practices that foster users' immersion in works of art, rather than to classify a kind of art. Immersive artistic forms are works of art structured in different ways that can offer immersive experiences not only in virtual reality but also in the real world.

References

Aristotle (2002): *Metaphysics* (translated by Joe Sachs; Santa Fe, N.M.: Green Lion Press 2002)

Batteux, Charles (2015): *Les Beaux Arts réduits à un même principe* (Paris: Durand 1746; translated with an Introduction and Notes by Young, James O.: *The Fine Arts Reduced to a Single Principle*, Oxford: Oxford University Press 2015)

Berti, Enrico (2001): 'Multiplicity and Unity of Being in Aristotle', 101 *Proceedings of the Aristotelian Society* (2001) 185–207 (online available at https://www.jstor.org/stable/4545345)

Berti, Enrico (2013): *Aristotele* (Milano: Editrice La Scuola 2013)

Boden, Margaret A. (2012): *Creativity and Art: Three Roads to Surprise* (Oxford: Oxford University Press 2012)

Cavell, Stanley (1979): *The Claim of Reason: Wittgenstein, Skepticism, Morality and Tragedy* (New York: Oxford University Press, 1979)

Cory, Herbert E. (1926): 'The Significance of Artistic Form', 23 The Journal of Philosophy, No. 12 (1926) 324–328 (online available at https://doi.org/10.2307/2014113)

Dal Sasso, Davide (2020): *Nel segno dell'essenziale – L'arte dopo il concettualismo* (Torino: Rosenberg & Sellier 2020)

Dal Sasso, Davide (2021a): 'On Form and Structure: Umberto Eco and the Basis for a Positive Philosophy of the Arts', 76 Rivista di Estetica, LXI (2021) 180–203

Dal Sasso, Davide (2021b): *The Ground Zero of the Arts: Rules, Processes, Forms* (Boston/Leiden: Brill 2021)

Danto, Arthur C. (1981): *The Transfiguration of the Commonplace: A Philosophy of Art* (Cambridge/Mass.: Harvard University Press 1981)

Dixon, Steve (2007): *Digital Performance: A History of New Media in Theater, Dance, Performance Art, and Installation* (Cambridge MA: MIT Press 2007)

Eco, Umberto (1962): *Opera aperta: Forma e indeterminazione nelle poetiche contemporanee* (Milano: Bompiani 1962, 7th ed. 2006)

Eco, Umberto (1964): *Apocalittici e integrati* (Milano: Bompiani 1964, 13th ed. 2017)

Eco, Umberto (1968): *La struttura assente: La ricerca semiotica e il metodo strutturale* (Milano: Bompiani 1968, 5th ed. 2002)

Ferraris, Maurizio (2017): *Postverità e altri enigmi* (Bologna: il Mulino 2017)

Ferraris, Maurizio (2019): *From Fountain to Moleskine: The Work of Art in the Age of Its Technological Producibility* (Boston/Leiden: Brill 2019)

Focillon, Henri (1934): *Vie des formes* (Paris: Librairie Ernest Leroux 1934)

Garoian, Charles R. (2018): 'The Performative Virtuality of Art and Its Education', in Hickman, Richard/Baldacchino, John/Freedman, Kerry/Hall, Emese; Meager, Nigel (eds), *The International Encyclopedia of Art and Design Education*, Vol. 1 (Hoboken: Wiley-Blackwell 2018) 1–12

Grau, Oliver (2003): *Virtual Art – From Illusion to Immersion* (Cambridge MA: The MIT Press 2003)

Grau, Oliver/Veigl, Thomas (eds) (2011): *Imagery in the 21st Century* (Cambridge MA: The MIT Press 2011)

Kandinsky, Wassily (2011): *Über das Geistige in der Kunst, Insbesondere in der Malerei* (München: Piper 1911)

Kantor, Tadeusz (1977): *Le theatre de la mort* (Lausanne: Editions L'Age d'Homme 1977)

Kubler, George (1962): *The Shape of Time* (New Haven/CT: Yale University Press 1962)

Langer, Susanne K. (1953): *Feeling and Form: A Theory of Art Developed from Philosophy in a New Key* (London: Routledge & Kegan Paul Limited 1953)

Langer, Susanne K. (1957): *Problems of Art – Ten Philosophical Lectures* (London: Routledge and Kegan Paul 1957)

Langer, Susanne K. (1966): 'The Cultural Importance of the Arts', 1 The Journal of Aesthetic Education, No. 1 (1966) 5–12 (available at https://www.jstor.org/stable/3331349)

Noë, Alva (2015): *Strange Tools – Art and Human Nature* (New York: Hill and Wang 2015)

Paul, Christiane (ed) (2016): *A Companion to Digital Art* (Hoboken: Wiley-Blackwell 2016)

Pinotti, Andrea (2017): 'Self-Negating Images: Towards An-Iconology', 1 Proceedings, No. 9: 856 (2017) 1–9 (online available at https://doi.org/10.3390/proceedings1090856)

Pinotti, Andrea (2020): 'Towards an-iconology – the image as environment', 61 Screen, No. 4 (Winter 2020) 594–603

Popper, Frank (2009): *From Technological to Virtual Art* (Cambridge MA: MIT Press 2009)

Roldan, Joaquin/Lara Osuna, Rocio/Gonzalez-Torre, Antonio (2019): 'The Project "Art for Learning Art" in Contemporary Art Museums', 38 International Journal of Art & Design Education, No. 3 (2019) 572–582 (online available at https://doi.org/10.1111/jade.12245)

Rush, Michael (2005): *New Media in Art* (London: Thames & Hudson 2nd edition 2005)

Rush, Michael (2007): *Video Art* (London: Thames & Hudson 2007)

Tatarkiewicz, Władysław (1980): *Dzieje sześciu pojęć*, Warszawa: Wydawnictwo Naukowe (published 1975; English translation by Christopher Kasparek, *A History of Six Idea: An Essay in Aesthetics*, Warszawa: PWN-Polish Scientific Publishers 1980)

von Bertalanffy, Ludwig (1968): *General System Theory: Foundations, Development, Applications* (New York: George Brazillier 1968)

Whitehead, Alfred North (1929): *Process and Reality: An Essay in Cosmology* (New York: Macmillan Publishing 1929)

Wilson, Edward O. (2017): *The Origins of Creativity* (New York: W.W. Norton & Company 2017)

Wilson, Stephen (2003): *Information Arts – Intersections of Art, Science, and Technology* (Cambridge MA: MIT Press 2003)

Wollheim, Richard (1998): 'On Pictorial Representation', 56 The Journal of Aesthetics and Art Criticism, No. 3 (1998) 217–226 (online available at https://doi.org/10.2307/432361)

Chapter 7
From Works to Living Means of Communication – The Digital Image and the 'Iconic Turn'

Wolfgang Ullrich

I. The Democratization of the Image Tools

In the long history of images, a new epoch is just beginning. Although printmaking techniques, photography, film and television have already significantly changed in recent centuries, digitization and the Internet, smartphones and social media have led, within two decades, to upheavals on a scale that far eclipses anything we have seen before.

The most striking innovation is that technologies used to produce and distribute images are no longer exclusive, instead, today many people have access to them. Although smartphones and computers, Internet access and image editing programs are costly and require a developed infrastructure, i.e., although they are not freely available to everyone, it makes a qualitative difference whether – as in previous cultural history – only a small minority of people take pictures and an even smaller minority can publish these pictures, or whether everyone who does not completely refuse digital and telecommunications technology is able to both produce and publish pictures.

Even those who had the technical means to produce pictures, such as pens, paints and paper, quickly reached the limits of their abilities and were unable to realize their ideas. Without clear talent, many people also lost the desire to try further as image producers. In addition, there were always only a few places where pictures could be shown to a larger audience. Even professional and highly talented image makers often had little opportunity to make their works publicly visible.

With photography and more developed reproduction methods, the situation improved and led to the production of postcards and especially, illustrated books. Increasingly, more people could take respectable pictures. Hence, photo albums, which until the early 20th century contained almost only pictures taken by professional photo studios, gradually included more and more photos taken by amateurs. Professional image makers also reached a much wider audience as they could no longer circulate just one original, but equally countless reproductions thereof. Nevertheless, image-making remained defined by experiences of scarcity and, as a result, exclusivity. Still, every exposed negative, every photographic print, every print costs money.

Those days are over. Whether you take a few or many pictures, it does not matter financially. Moreover, today many people take countless pictures as image editing programs and applications almost exclude the possibility of creating bad pictures. Rather, as image quality is at least partially decoupled from the talent of those producing the images, the difference between professionals and amateurs is becoming blurred. In addition, the time required to produce an image has been minimized. The software allows images to be made ready for publication in a matter of seconds and to be changed just as quickly, almost at will. Social media has also created an infrastructure that allows the distribution of a vast number of images, communicating and marketing them from a harmless 'like' among friends to a viral hit throughout the entire social network.

For the first time in cultural history, a generation is growing up where the exchange of images is just as unhindered and just as natural as the exchange of words. It is therefore justified to diagnose the 'Iconic Turn' and claim that knowledge and world views are now increasingly generated, grasped and communicated via images.[1] At least, the logocentrism that has long prevailed undergoes relativization.

This is all the more true because images become more versatile, i.e., they are less defined by a binding form. If, due to the use of various filters and programs, one can articulate oneself with images as quickly, variously and smoothly as with language, then there is no reason not to assign them many functions that could previously only be performed with spoken or written words.

The fact that once an image was made, it could at most be painted over, retouched, or censored in the pre-digital era may have given it the merit of permanence and thus the status of a work, admired at best. However, this situation was too inflexible for changing communication methods and expressive ambitions. Moreover, the material basis of traditional images – be it wood, paper, or celluloid – was too cumbersome to organize their exchange across larger spaces quickly and easily. In contrast, in digitized form, images have now become nimble in every respect. They can be varied, reformulated, recombined, and used situationally, as well as simultaneously at any place in the world.

---

1 For detail, see Maar/Burda (2005).

II. From Analogue Images to Forms of Orality

While images were previously as stable and fixed as language in the form of writing, they are now increasingly analogous to forms of orality. Digital images can be as spontaneous and fleeting as spoken words. However, they do not represent the first appearance of oral imagery. Rather, we can already see natural oral imagery in every facial expression and gesture.[2] To converse with someone is never just to talk, but also to see the facial expressions the other person shows and the gestures which accompany said the words. It means expressing oneself not only with words, but through continuous changes in facial features as well as posture. Even if this dimension of articulation is usually called body language, it actually consists of images, or at least of forms of expression that are accessible to the eye and can be visualized.

The extent to which facial expressions and gestures are understood as natural oral images is also shown by the fact that cultural practices aimed at concealing faces can be interpreted as a form of image prohibition. Interpreted in this way, people affected by such a practice are then perceived as having their expressive possibilities curtailed. A part of their orality is erased.

Though there are always efforts to suppress people in their free articulation, conversely, writing and fixed images may have had their origin precisely in the desire to somehow capture what a particularly valued person says and expresses. The liveliness, which would otherwise be completely absorbed in the respective moment, was to be preserved, perhaps even condensed in the fixation. However, this only succeeded at the price of not being able to react to changing circumstances with what had once been recorded. The texts and images could still be interpreted, the captured moment could be recapitulated again and again, but all hermeneutics ultimately served to console was oneself over the absence of any dialogue.

III. Aby Warburg's "Pathosformeln"

It was Aby Warburg's great theme to reconstruct how facial expressions and gestures were visualized in antiquity and individual facial expressions and postures, by visualization. Above all, he demonstrated that while facial expressions and postures are by no means completely immobilized by their

2 For detail, see Belting (2013).

fixation, they can be effective. Warburg researched how a strong gesture in a picture can also trigger strong affects and reactions in recipients, but above all, how other image producers can be influenced by the gesture. By image producers focusing on one visualized body expression and creating variations, they simultaneously contribute to the image becoming a fixed pictorial pattern. Warburg called such patterns – ultimately, i.e., fixed gestures and facial expressions – "pathos formulas" (*Pathosformeln*).

He formulated this concept in contrast to the long-prevailing understanding in antiquity, at least since Winckelmann, that the Greeks had embodied above all 'noble simplicity' and 'quiet grandeur' (*edle Einfalt* and *stille Größe*) in their pictorial works. Warburg, on the other hand, points to the "pathetically heightened facial expressions" (*pathetisch gesteigerte Mimik*) of many depictions, by which the artists of the Renaissance were influenced.[3] Using the motif "Death of Orpheus" as an example, he shows how a pathos formula originating from antiquity became effective anew in Mantegna, Dürer and others in ever more variations and how it was transferred to other subjects, thus confirming itself as such in the first place.

If pathos formulas were originally based on oral images, but then fixed, the new digital techniques allow them to be brought to life again. To the extent that it becomes possible to adapt any image instantaneously to a situation, a purpose, an expressive interest, and to use it purely as a medium of communication, an existing formula is filled with new life. After about two and a half millennia, there is finally a clear answer to Plato's criticism, which is another impressive sign of the epochal change that is currently taking place. At the same time, Warburg's theory deserves new and additional attention, because thanks to digitalization it has become much easier than ever before to express the affectation caused by an image again in the form of images. Thus, pathos formulas also find all the greater resonance. They can become even more striking formulas as much as they can be adapted and used even more variably.

If people exchange themselves with ever new variants of the images that have become available, thus reacting to images with other images, their use does not create any new works, i.e., nothing that has the claim to be completed and removed from time. As often as the fixation of facial expressions and gestures towards pathos formulas might have already related to an idea of artwork, the images that result from the vivification of pathos formulas are limited to communicative functions. They have as little the

---

3 Warburg (1906) 55.

character of works of art as when someone contorts his mouth or makes a defensive gesture with his hands. For the most part, they also come from people who have no concept of a work of art at all. For this reason, images produced and shared in social media should not be measured by the complexity of works of art, but by their communicative function. Perhaps this communicative turn must first be learned, since – contrary to language, where it is self-evident that most of what people say every day in their conversations is not suitable for literary prizes – for the longest time there were no oral traditions with images. In other words, we'll have to adopt the habit of no longer regarding the many users of visual material in social media as bad or half-artists, but to accept that they deal with images with varying degrees of differentiation, but increasingly in a way similar to the use of a native language.

IV. Selfies and Emojis

It is certainly no coincidence that the first image forms to emerge in social media, which have become as widespread as they are prominent, are still based directly on human facial expressions and gestures. These images are selfies and emojis.[4] In both cases, the aim is to express an emotional state as quickly and succinctly as possible. With a selfie, you show whether you are momentarily happy, proud or lonely. You can also report where you are, who you are with, what you are doing. An emoji is like a codified selfie reduced to the expression of feelings and in turn signals the current state of mind. By combining several emojis, a more differentiated mood picture can be drawn. In addition to the emojis, which in turn characterize the "pathetically heightened facial expressions" (*pathetisch gesteigerte Mimik*) Warburg was interested in, and which can thus also be described as particularly formulaic pathos formulas, there are other emojis that reproduce certain hand gestures or consist of objects from everyday life, making it possible to depict standard situations with them.

Moreover, on the one hand, there are apps that allow their user to convert selfies into emojis. In this conversion process as well, one might recognize a consolidation of pathos formulas. On the other hand, other apps are used to change one's facial expression. Thus, if the mood or the occasion and type of communication has changed, one does not even need to take a new selfie. Rather, it may suffice to just manipulate an

4 For detail, see Ullrich (2019); Rebane (2021).

already existing selfie as desired. Above all, it is possible to heighten an emotion inherent in a facial expression and to intensify it in a signal-like, striking manner, not least with the aim of also triggering strong feelings and corresponding reactions in the addressees. The same happens through other effects that have gained considerable importance in recent years. For example, numerous apps offer filters that can be used to change the character of images, add certain elements, or alienate them. It is popular, for example, to mix photographic and graphic image parts with each other. The resulting cartoonish overdrawing not only makes it easier to communicate in a witty and fun way, but is also suitable as the theme of the conversation itself.

V. *The Vivification of the Images: Memes*

However, many more types of images than just selfies are caught up in the maelstrom of vivification. In recent years, the term "meme" has become established for all types of motifs that circulate quickly and generate numerous variants, i.e., which are a living expression of emotions.[5] The term was taken from Richard Dawkins, who coined it in 1976 as an evolutionary biologist. Unlike a gene, a meme is not biologically inherited information, but is grasped and passed on via cultural artifacts. Memes are contents of consciousness, such as ideas or image patterns that bear an imprint on many people at the same time or one after the other. Thanks to the etymology, "meme" (from Latin *memoria*, Greek *mneme*) also recalls Aby Warburg, or more precisely, his *Mnemosyne Atlas*, which is dedicated to several of the pathos formulas he identified, and which contains diverse variants of their visualization, variants that usually originate from different centuries and genres.

As much as memes are thus pathos formulas of digital image culture, they also encompass images from the pre-digital era and not least works from art history. In this way, these images and works of art in turn experience a vivification. This vivification, however, means much more than just an acceleration of the speed at which new variants, translations, and parodies of models occur. Whereas traditionally images were themselves mostly created with a claim to create a work, within the logic of social media, it is much more a matter of quick-wittedness and repartee. Recognition is gained by those who create and circulate a witty, cheeky, absurd

5 For detail, see Von Gehlen (2020).

or provocative image as quickly as possible. From the perspective of a representative of classical high culture, who prefers to interpret complex works by great artists rather than analyse everyday dialogues by average people, most of these pointed meme variants seem ludicrous or obscene, and more so when they are based on works from the canon of art.

VI. The Application of Social Media Tools to Classical Artworks

But even apps that primarily serve to transform facial expressions from selfies in a codified way are now being applied to figures from the art history canon, who appear thus suddenly as laughing or being in a bad mood. They are given donkey ears or wear glasses, surrounded by wreaths of flowers or pop-cultural accessories. Often this is no more than a gag, and it is mainly a matter of using the new possibilities of image processing arbitrarily, be it out of curiosity or of boredom. However, these transformations of existing image material are just as much an expression of the need to set something in motion that was previously immovably fixed. Still and thus lifeless images are being transformed into something that is moving and alive.

This happens all the more when works from art history are digitally animated, i.e., when figures suddenly turn their heads or change their facial expressions, which is now also possible without too much effort. One is led to believe that one can see the events before or after the moment captured by the artist. Some people get their hopes up that in the future it will not only be possible to see one or two seconds, but that significantly longer sequences will be brought to life.

As it is likely to become, in the near future, even easier and thus even more common to modify and animate images, it will also become even easier to use them to convey moods or messages. Those who already use a variation of Munch's "The Scream" to communicate a political or private event and express their own emotions will soon have further opportunities to express themselves orally in the form of images. The technical oral images complement and enhance the natural oral images, so that, in the future, facial expressions and gestures will be externalized as a matter of course. Instead of just looking serious or signalling contempt with a gesture, every movement will be recorded by a camera at the same time and linked at will with predefined image patterns which are no longer limited to just emojis. In this way, every gesture can be transmitted to any place in the world in a matter of seconds, both individually and depending on the addressee. Every gesture can be picked up, amplified and exaggerated in an image. New techniques of expression are to be expected, resulting in a culture in which, now more than ever before in history, the expression of effects and attitudes is becoming an important and differentiated cultural technique.

VII. ...and The Future? – Consequences for Authorship and Copyright

People who are gifted at presenting themselves pictorially and who were previously unaware of their talent will suddenly become prominent, while other talents – such as verbal articulation skills – will lose relative importance. Overall, however, the fact that a great many people will articulate themselves in various digitizable formats – not only by way of images, but also by way of, e.g., sounds – is a dramatic expansion of expressive possibilities. This development leads to a democratization of attention opportunities, but at the same time to a profanation of traditional forms of expression and design.

However, insofar as oral images are no longer works, no copyrights apply – or should apply[6] – to them. As original and witty as an oral image may be, it will not be considered a work and will not be linked to a particular author. Just like a new idiom, a neologism, or even a joke immediately detaches itself from its author, animated images become common property when they are well received. They can no more be patented or placed under copyright protection than a certain facial expression.

Of course, there will be many cases of doubt. Artists, in particular, who do not close their minds to the digital possibilities and who create new images or image variants, may on the one hand still want to see themselves in the tradition of creators of works who are appreciated, protected and honoured as authors. However, on the other hand they will know that their impact and success will be measured by how often their postings are re-blogged, reposted, re-commented and varied. The artist and theorist Brad Troemel not only posits the equation that the more famous an art image becomes, the less its author will be attributed to it, but also makes it clear that in times of social media, art is perceived "not as a commodity so much as a recyclable material". In this way, however, art also "is rein-

6 However, for the current debate on copyright issues with regard to user-generated content, see Dreier (2019).

troduced into everyday life", thus having a completely different and even more important role than before.[7]

It is foreseeable that some artists will become absorbed in developing ever new image variants, while at the same time producing saleable post-Internet art with works materialized from them. Their primary measure of success, however, will be less the amount of money they make from these sellable artworks than the number of viral hits, i.e., the number of postings that become common property. Other artists, however, may still aim to create images that resist usability and vivification, i.e., that do not break away from their creator. In all cases, however, the fact that a rich oral pictorial culture exists for the first time will have a repercussion on art. Just as literature has always grown, not least out of everyday language, which is conversely refined and expanded by it, so visual art will in the future also feed on an oral culture. As much as it has so far been primarily related to its own tradition, and for that reason alone has tended toward forms of exclusivity, it will now benefit from the fact that images are used millions and billions of times every day during live digital communication.

References

Belting, Hans (2013): *Faces – Eine Geschichte des Gesichts* (München: C.H. Beck 2013)

Dreier, Thomas (2019): 'Bilder im Zeitalter ihrer digitalen Kommunizierbarkeit', in: Dreier, Thomas, *Bild und Recht – Versuch einer programmatischen Grundlegung* (Baden-Baden: Nomos 2019) 188–199

Maar, Christa/ Burda, Hubert (2005): *Iconic Turn. Die neue Macht der Bilder* (Köln: Dumont 2005)

Rebane, Gala (2021): *Emojis* (Berlin: Wagenbach 2021)

Troemel, Brad (2013): 'Art after Social Media', Art Papers (Juli/August 2013) 10–15

Ullrich, Wolfgang (2019): *Selfies* (Berlin: Wagenbach 2019)

Von Gehlen, Dirk (2020): *Meme* (Berlin: Wagenbach 2020)

Warburg, Aby (1906): 'Dürer und die italienische Antike', in: *Verhandlungen der 48. Versammlung deutscher Philologen und Schulmänner in Hamburg vom 3. bis 6. Oktober 1905* (Leipzig 1906) 55–60 (online available at http://archiv.ub.uni-heidelberg.de/artdok/volltexte/2011/1630)

7 Troemel (2013) 13.

Chapter 8
Fairness Aspects of Techniques of Referencing Cultures

Eva-Maria Bauer[1]

I. Referencing as a Cultural Phenomenon

Today, images gain their power and prominence through mass reproduction on social networks. The emergence of new digital technologies and apps means that our social relationship to images and originality is changing.[2] There are unprecedented opportunities to copy an original with minimal effort without losing quality. But it is only with the circulation of these images on social networks and their accompanying storage in cultural memory that images gained significance. With digitalization, not only the possibility of appropriation und referencing has changed, but also the general attitude towards it: The new media promote the "flow of images, ideas, and narratives across multiple media channels and demand more active modes of spectatorship".[3] The culture of participation on the Internet has led to appropriation and referencing becoming an everyday phenomenon.[4]

Despite this widespread culture of referencing, there is still a legal risk for those using other people's images. For example, the photographer of the well-known meme "Socially Awkward Penguin" has forbidden the use of the penguin's image.[5] Memes are image-text combinations shared on the Internet where the image often represents extraneous material.[6] The

1 This contribution draws from and is building upon previous work by the author on the same subject, see Bauer (2020).

2 As was already the case, for example, with the discovery of photography.

3 Jenkins (2006) 138.

4 For more detailed information on digital image culture, see Bauer (2020) 104 et seq.

5 Dobusch (2015).

6 Maier (2016) 397. Cultural studies scholar Shifman has defined digital memes as "(a) a group of digital entities that share common characteristics in content, form, and/or attitude, (b) created in conscious engagement with other memes, and (c) disseminated, imitated, and/or transformed by many users on the Internet", Shifman (2014) 44. See also von Gehlen (2020).

term meme originates from Richard Dawkins who defined it as a cultural counterpart to evolution, thus understanding memes as cultural entities that are like genes to genetics.[7] The "Socially Awkward Penguin" was used in different variations for three years by the tech blog GetDigital and in April 2015, they received a 785.40 Euro cease-and-desist warning from Getty Images, the photo agency that holds the rights to the image.[8] Originally, George F. Mobley was commissioned by National Geographic to photograph the Adélie penguin. The "Socially Awkward Penguin" meme uses this photo and positions it against a different background. Memes generally work by using a pre-existing image supplemented with their own text. The texts of the meme are modified again and again, so that the meme always produces new contexts and new meanings. While the text changes, the image or graphic remain the same. Thus, the concept of the meme becomes entrenched and takes on a life of its own and as a metatext. The metatext is the abstract properties of its content and form, how to add a meme correctly in a conversation and how to expand its meaning.[9] This metatext belongs to a meme type.[10] Meme types can be perpetuated by tokens that are generated repeatedly. The image is thus used to generate a new meme – and this meme is in turn to be used communicatively within Internet culture and social networks.[11]

Appropriation and referencing are explicitly seen as a feature of memes.[12] Yet copyright law has prevented this referencing culture regarding the use of the socially awkward penguin.[13] Copyright law assigns the rights to use an image to an individual who can control with its copyright whether and how such an image may be used. But if the image is now necessary for communication, why should the creator of the image still be allowed to control its use? If the creator uploads an image online, should it not be expected that other people will use it?

---

7 "Examples of memes are tunes, ideas, catch-phrases, clothes fashions, ways of making pots or of building arches. Just as genes propagate themselves in the gene pool by leaping from body to body via sperms or eggs, so memes propagate themselves in the meme pool by leaping from brain to brain via a process which, in the broad sense, can be called imitation", Dawkins (1976/2006) 192.

8 See Kühl (2015).

9 Grünewald-Schukalla/Fischer (2018) 7.

10 See also Herwig (2018) 4.

11 Cf. in more detail on digital network culture Bauer (2020) 75 et seq.

12 See Grünewald-Schukalla/Fischer (2018) 7.

13 Meanwhile, a new public domain version of the "Socially Awkward Penguin" is also available (https:// www.getdigital.de/blog/getty-images-wants-license-fees-for-the-awkward-penguin-meme/).

Prior to the introduction of Art. 17 of the DSM-Directive 2019/790[14], these questions led to major debate and protest regarding user rights and the obligation to use upload filters. Opponents of this reform feared the end of the free Internet[15] and made their discontent known through petitions[16] and in Europe-wide demonstrations, using the hashtag #savethememe.[17] The demonstrators advocated an open referencing culture on the Internet to allow the use of other people's works through memes, GIFs, User Generated Content etc. The importance of referencing and appropriating should also play a role in copyright assessment – the rights to use an image should be distributed more fairly.[18] If copyright law does not take into account the conditions and norms of communication,[19] thus not considering the legal reality of users, the legitimacy crisis of copyright law will be exacerbated.[20] Copyright law can only effectively regulate interpersonal relationships if it is also accepted and followed.[21] Thus, if copyright law no longer reflects social reality and is therefore no longer supported by social consensus, the effectiveness of copyright law is also at risk.[22]

---

14 Directive (EU) 2019/790 of the European Parliament and of the Council of 17 April 2019 on copyright and related rights in the Digital Single Market and amending Directives 96/9/EC and 2001/29/EC.

15 See Kaesling (2019) 587.

16 In particular by the SavetheInternet campaign, https://savetheinternet.info.

17 See Mewes (2019). – In Munich alone, about 40,000 demonstrated at the action alliance #saveyourinternet, cf. '40 000 protestieren in München gegen EU-Urheberrechtsreform', SZ vom 23.03.2019, https://www.sueddeutsche.de/muenchen/demo-muenchen-urheberrecht-1.4380419.

18 For the differences in self-perception of the opposing digital cultures (community of internet users on the one hand, and copyright holders on the other hand), the mutual ignorance and the resulting misunderstandings on both sides, see Dreier (2022b).

19 Peukert (2014) 82.

20 Cf. on the crisis of legitimacy in relation to appropriations Bauer (2020) 222 et seq. Regarding the notion of legitimacy crisis in copyright law, cf. Marl (2017) 1; Hansen (2009) 40 et seq.; Stallberg (2006) 25 et seq.; Raue (2013) 280; Leistner/Hansen (2008) 479; Geiger (2008) 468.

21 There have always been legal regulations that have not been followed, but are nevertheless necessary, such as in fare dodging or tax evasion. Non-compliance with the law does not automatically lead to the loss of the justification of the legal regulation. However, one cannot keep law away from the social reality and assume that legal reality does not remain without repercussions on the legitimacy of a norm, cf. Hansen (2009) 74 et seq.

22 Hansen (2009) 75.

II. The Importance of Referencing Cultures

1. Historical use of referencing and appropriation

Appropriation and referencing have always been artistic devices. Originally, they served to achieve closeness to an artistic model by consciously adopting similarities or by learning artistic techniques through copying. Various artistic techniques were used to try to get as close to the original as possible. The Romans, for example, emulated the Greek ideal and created their marble statues after Greek bronze casts.[23] The concept of *aemulatio* is particularly interesting, meaning the emulation after a model – and through this emulation enabling the surpassing of the model.[24] Here, too, appropriation conveys closeness to the original. Importantly, referentiality also allowed artists to learn through copying the workshop master or later at art academies. Within the workshop it was important for artists to paint in the style of the master to ensure uniform standards of quality and by appropriating the master's, the co-workers and apprentices could show how close their skills were to their workshop masters'. Art academy students copied to learn from the original and thus be able to paint as similarly as possible the artist of the original work.[25] One's own art could also be enhanced by associating it through appropriation to other artists who were already significant. In this context, appropriation was also an expression of admiration as well as a teaching tool: by appropriating the picture, the necessary artistic skills could be acquired.

2. Appropriation art[26]

In modern times, art evolved towards non-objectivity and self-reflection on the nature of art. Appropriating and referencing were used to express one's own reflections on the original. Finally, Appropriation Art, in which someone else's complete work was appropriated, can be seen as the culmination of this development. This art movement elevated the adoption of other creators' images to an artistic concept.[27]

---

23 Stähli (2008) 15.

24 Blunck (2011) 19.

25 Rebbelmund (1999) 47.

26 For a more detailed analysis of Appropriation Art and Copyright, see Geiger (2022).

27 Rebbelmund (1999) 13.

The term Appropriation Art was first used to describe a group of artists around Sherrie Levine, Mike Bidlo and others in New York in the 1980s[28]. It is also fundamentally used for artists that appropriate other images. It works with all means that can be used for appropriation, such as the copy, imitation, collage and others. Appropriation comes from the Latin *appropriare*, which means "to make one's own". Appropriation thus describes the process of adopting existing artworks or their parts into one's own artwork. It can either be directly physically integrated or indirectly reproduced through one's own production. In the latter case, the foreign imagery can be appropriated in such a way that the format, technique, motif and style are repeated as exactly as possible[29] not to plagiarize, however, but to create independent works of art. "The copy is the original", proclaimed the appropriationist Elaine Sturtevant.[30] Thus, Appropriation is an artistic concept: it's programmatically directed towards the most exact possible repetition of a work.[31]

3. *Referencing as a medium of communication*

With digitization, appropriation evolved from an isolated artistic strategy with a theoretical foundation to a means of communication. Communication through appropriation now represents everyday user behaviour in the digital world. Images are used as raw material in digital culture: they are constantly changed, combined and placed in new contexts. In times of mass communication, people increasingly communicate with images instead of text. Photos are constantly being snapped and shared with

---

28 Crimp (1977). The group originated with the exhibition "Pictures" at the New York Artists Space in 1977, in which the works of Sherrie Levine, Robert Longo, Jack Goldstein, Troy Brauntuch and Philip Smith were shown. In the meantime, the term Appropriation Art is no longer used only for the original exhibition group of 1977, but also comprehensively for postmodern art that deals with copying and quotation in art (cf. Rebbelmund (1999) 11), so that other artists can also be understood as Appropriationists. The terms "pictures generation", "pictures generation of appopriation" or "iterativism" have also been used for them, but ultimately the term Appropriation Art has prevailed. "The Art of Appropriation" was the title of an exhibition at the Alternative Museum, New York, year 1985.

29 Zuschlag (2012) 127.

30 Sturtevant (1999) 155.

31 Zuschlag (2012) 127.

smartphones. Instead of a detailed description, emojis[32] or memes are sent that summarize in a reduced way what one wants to express. The image speaks for itself. For this, images are constantly being produced and transformed. The iconic turn[33] has led to a new significance of imagery in communication – the "hegemony of images"[34] means that the predominant role of spoken and written language in our culture is being replaced by the image.

The productive and flexible use of images makes them particularly suitable as a means of communication on the Internet. Communication is therefore not only shifting to the digital sphere, but how people communicate is also changing. Both exploitation techniques and interactive procedures greatly simplify the transformation and combination of works[35] and make appropriation an everyday phenomenon. Appropriating and referencing are now undertaken for the purposes of communication and have become a communicative medium. With digital media, every user now produces and alters images for the purpose of communication – and thanks to digital communication possibilities, these images are now continuously available everywhere. Appropriating and referencing are detached from the context of art and used functionally as a medium of communication.

---

32 An emoji is a pictogram similar to an emoticon that refers to emotional states, objects, animals, places, etc., see Dudenredaktion (ed), Emoji, in: Duden. Deutsches Universalwörterbuch, 2015. On the use of emojis in digital image culture, see Rebane (2021) and Ullrich (2019) 39.

33 "Iconic turn" is a term by Gottfried Boehm, which he introduced in 1994, and which denotes a turn towards image science and the examination of how images influence people in their perception of the world and their behaviour, cf. Boehm (1994) 11. In 1992, W.J.T. Mitchell proclaimed the "pictorial turn", which has similar cultural changes in mind, but is more iconological (following Erwin Panofsky) than the "iconic turn", which seeks to establish a hermeneutics of the image, cf. Mitchell (1992). Cf. in detail also the correspondence between Boehm and Mitchell (2014) and fundamentally Maar/Burda (2004); Mitchell (1994); Burda (2010); Belting (2011); Sachs-Hombach (2013) and the website www.iconicturn.de of the Hubert-Burda-Stiftung.

34 Bredekamp (1997) 230.

35 Klass (2015) 298.

III. Under German Copyright Law

Under German copyright law, the lawful use of memes is still unclear. German copyright law considers communication in social networks such as Facebook groups or Instagram as public communication, even if it is often perceived as private.[36] Therefore, the use of a meme usually constitutes an interference with the copyright owner's right to make the work publicly available pursuant to § 19a German Copyright Law (UrhG).

This use arguably requires consent pursuant to § 23 (1) sentence 1 UrhG, as it is not a free use pursuant to § 23 (1) sentence 2 UrhG (see following 1.). It is also not justified by the exception of citation pursuant to § 51 UrhG (see following 2.). A justification via the newly introduced exception for caricature, parody or parody pursuant to § 51a UrhG also seems questionable (see following 3. and 4.).

1. Consent pursuant to § 23 (1) sentence 2 UrhG

The use of works without permission, now regulated in § 23 (1) sentence 2 UrhG, makes it possible to use a work without the permission of the copyright owner, provided that a sufficient distance ("Abstand") to the work used is maintained. Conversely, if this distance is not maintained, this constitutes an adaptation which requires the consent of the copyright owner for publication.

This distance is established, on the one hand, by the external "fading" of the work used, i.e. when, in view of the idiosyncrasy of the new work, the borrowed idiosyncratic features of the protected older work fade away ("verblassen").[37] Memes as a picture-text combination do indeed add a new, additional or even contradictory level of meaning to the adopted picture by adding a text. However, this is not evident in the outward fading of the image's features – even with the addition of a text, the image remains in its entirety with all its individual features. On the other hand, however, a distance can also be achieved with so-called inner distance ("innerer

36 Marl (2020) 150 et seq.

37 German Federal Court of Justice (BGH), case I ZR 42/05 of 20 December 2000, para. 29, Gewerblicher Rechtsschutz und Urheberrecht (GRUR) (2008) 693 – TV Total; BGH case I ZR 264/91 of 11 March 1993, Gewerblicher Rechtsschutz und Urheberrecht (GRUR) (1994) 191, at 193 – Asterix-Persiflagen; Bullinger (2019) para. 10; Schulze (2018) para. 8; Loewenheim (2022) para. 11. This so-called "fading formula" ("Verblassens-Formel") goes back to Ulmer (1980) 275.

Abstand") from the work used. This criterion of inner distance, "fading in the broader sense", was developed by the Federal Court of Justice of Germany (Bundesgerichtshof, BGH) for parody cases.[38] It is applicable if the distance is achieved in a way other than outward fading and if the new work is regarded as independent in its essence.[39]

Such an inner distance can be achieved through an art-specific interpretation ("kunstspezifische Auslegung") if an independent work of art is created by adopting the idiosyncratic features of the older work.[40] The freedom of art pursuant to Art. 5 (3) of the German Constitution (Grundgesetz, GG) creates a legal free space for art which must necessarily be considered within the framework of copyright law. This free space can also be considered as inner distance. For this to be the case, however, techniques of online referencing cultures such as memes or GIFs must be art within the meaning of Art. 5 (3) GG. This cannot be assumed because according to the material concept of art[41], art is the result of free creative design and

38 BGH, case I ZR 264/91 of 11 March 1993, Gewerblicher Rechtsschutz und Urheberrecht (GRUR) (1994) 191, at 193 – Asterix-Persiflagen. However, the inner distance is not only applied in cases of parody but is also considered a criterion for other art forms in which a third party's work is dealt with in an independent form, cf. Schulze (2018) para. 16; Bullinger (2019) para. 14.

39 BGH, case I ZR 264/91 of 11 March 1993, Gewerblicher Rechtsschutz und Urheberrecht (GRUR) (1994) 191, at 193 – Asterix-Persiflagen.

40 See on an art-specific interpretation of § 24 UrhG old version, on which § 23 (1) sentence 2 UrhG is based, German Constitutional Court (BverfG), case 1 BvR 1585/13 of 31 May 2016, para. 86, Gewerblicher Rechtsschutz und Urheberrecht (GRUR) (2016), 690 – Metall auf Metall; BVerfG, case 1 BvR 825/98 of 29 June 2000, Gewerblicher Rechtsschutz und Urheberrecht (GRUR) (2001) 149, at 151 – Germania 3. The decision Metall auf Metall, however, refers to the adoption of the smallest parts (scraps of sound) as an infringement of the rights of the producer of the sound recording and thus precisely not to an infringement of copyright. However, the principles of the judgment on the art-specific interpretation of § 24 (1) UrhG old version apply not only to neighbouring rights but also to copyright. Although the Germania 3 decision refers to the freedom of citation pursuant to § 51 UrhG, the principles established can be transferred, cf. Schulze (2018) para. 25; Summerer (2015) 94; Wegmann (2013) 195; Huttenlauch (2010) 153/154; for a different opinion see Ohly (2017) 967, who rejects a balancing between protection of the copyright owner and artistic freedom beyond the recognised case group of inner distance.

41 The material concept of art recognises as "the essence of artistic activity the free creative design in which impressions, experiences and experiences of the artist are brought to immediate perception through the medium of a specific formal language"; see BVerfG, case 1 BvR 435/68 of 24 February 1971, Neue Juristische Wochenschrift (NJW) (1971) 1645 – Mephisto, and case 1 BvR 765/66 of 7 July 1971, Neue Juristische Wochenschrift (NJW) (1971) 2163 – Schulbuchprivileg.

the expression of one's own personality.[42] However, communicative appropriations are not intended precisely to express the personality itself but to communicate effectively. From the very beginning, the production of these pictorial phenomena is geared towards sharing in communication structures: It is thus not about the representation of the appropriator's personality. Therefore, an art-specific interpretation is not applicable for communicative appropriations such as memes, GIFs and image montages.[43] Since memes thus do not maintain the necessary distance within the meaning of § 23 (1) sentence 2 UrhG, they constitute an adaptation within the meaning of § 23 (1) sentence 1 UrhG, so that consent to publication would be necessary.

2. *Citation according to § 51 UrhG*

A citation pursuant to § 51 UrhG requires, in addition to other requirements, the existence of a citation purpose ("Zitatzweck"). This means that there is an "inner connection" between the quoted and the quoting work.[44] The cited work must be used to explain the content of the citing work, not the cited work.[45] The citation must not have the aim of sparing the author's own explanations[46] or serve solely as an illustration.[47]

An art-specific interpretation, also made within the framework of § 51 UrhG, recognises the citation as an aesthetic medium on the basis of the right to the freedom of art pursuant to Art. 5 (3) GG and eases the requirements of "inner connection" for works of art.[48] For this, however, the

---

In this context, artistic creation is understood as an expression of the artist's individual personality and less as a communicative act of communication.

42 See also Wandtke (2019) 143.

43 See as to the same conclusion Maier (2016) 379.

44 BGH, case I ZR 83/66 of 3 April 1968, Gewerblicher Rechtsschutz und Urheberrecht (GRUR) (1968) 607, at 609 – Kandinsky I.

45 Court of Appeals (Oberlandesgericht, OLG) Munich, case 29 U 1204/2 of 14 June 2012, Archiv für Presserecht (AfP) (2012) 395 – Mein Kampf; Dreier (2022a) para. 3; Spindler (2020) para. 30.

46 Court of Appeals (Kammergericht, KG) Berlin, case 5 U 1457/69 of 13 January 1970, Gewerblicher Rechtsschutz und Urheberrecht (GRUR) (1970) 616, at 618 – Eintänzer.

47 BGH, case I ZR 69/14 of 17 December 2015, para. 25, Gewerblicher Rechtsschutz und Urheberrecht (GRUR) (2016) 368 – Exklusivinterview.

48 BVerfG, case 1 BvR 825/98 of 29 June 2000, Gewerblicher Rechtsschutz und Urheberrecht (GRUR) (2001) 149, at 151 – Germania 3; BGH, case I ZR 42/05

citation must be used as a means of artistic expression and artistic design to make its own artistic statement. In the case of memes, this requirement is not fulfilled, as mentioned before.[49] The inner connection to the cited image will usually not suffice. In memes the image has no supporting function[50] since it does not serve to cite one's own remarks but is the main component of the meme.

3. *Caricature or parody according to § 51a UrhG*

The exception provision of § 51a UrhG was introduced as a consequence of the CJEU ruling in the case *Pelham/Hütter* by the Act on the Adaptation of Copyright Law to the Requirements of the Digital Single Market (Gesetz zur Anpassung des Urheberrechts an die Erfordernisse des digitalen Binnenmarktes[51]). Here, the CJEU held that a Member State may not provide in its national law for an exception or limitation – such as the provision of § 24 (1) UrhG old version – with regard to the right of the phonogram producer which is not provided for in Art. 5 Information Society (InfoSoc) Directive 2001/29/EC.[52] The exception of § 51a UrhG corresponds to Art. 5 (3) lit. (k) of the InfoSoc-Directive.

At first glance, § 51a UrhG appears to be applicable to justify the use of third-party copyright works by means of an exception provision. This is because the exception allows for the use of pre-existing copyrighted works.[53] There is, however, a fly in the ointment at a closer examination.

According to recent CJEU case law, it is not necessary that a new personal intellectual creation within the meaning of § 2 (2) UrhG is created by the use of the third party's work when invoking the § 51a UrhG exception in contrast to the older version pursuant to § 24 UrhG.[54] Therefore, the re-

---

of 20 December 2008, para. 44, Gewerblicher Rechtsschutz und Urheberrecht (GRUR) (2008) 693 – TV Total; OLG Brandenburg, case 6 U 14/10 of 9 November 2010, Gewerblicher Rechtsschutz und Urheberrecht (GRUR) (2011) 141, at 142 – Literarische Collage.

49 BVerfG, case 1 BvR 825/98 of 29 June 2000, Gewerblicher Rechtsschutz und Urheberrecht (GRUR) (2001) 149, at 151 – Germania 3.

50 Cf. also Maier (2016) 397.

51 German Official Journal (Bundesgesetzblatt, BGBl) Part I of 4 June 2021, 1204.

52 CJEU case C-476/17 of 29 July 2019, para. 65, ECLI:EU:C:2019:624 – Pelham/Hütter.

53 Cf. German Government (2021) 89.

54 Ibid.; see also CJEU case C-201/13 of 3 September 2014, para. 21, ECLI:EU:C:2014:2132 – Deckmyn und Vrijheidsfonds; BGH case I ZR 9/15 of

sult of the permitted use does not need to reach the level of creation of a copyright work. The legally permitted derivative uses under § 51a UrhG are all reminiscent of one or more pre-existing works. In order to distinguish them from plagiarism (which is inadmissible under copyright law), they must at the same time show perceptible differences from the original work.[55] However, a "fading" of the original work is not required, in contrast to § 23 (1) sentence 2 UrhG for uses which do not require consent. Finally, the use of the pre-existing work must serve a substantive or artistic engagement of the user with the work or another object of reference.[56] This is generally the case with memes, as they express the freedom of expression and communication pursuant to Art. 11 (1) of the Charter of Fundamental Rights of the European Union (CFR).

However, memes are neither parodies nor caricatures. Parody is an autonomous term of EU law and is therefore to be interpreted uniformly.[57] The characteristics of a parody are that it is reminiscent of an existing work, while simultaneously displaying perceptible differences from it. Additionally, it must be an expression of humour or mockery.[58] Thus, it is no longer necessary that the parody relates to the original work itself or indicates this work[59], as was previously required by the Federal Court of Justice of Germany (BGH).[60] It is true that memes can be regarded as Internet jokes which use the foreign material in a surprising and humorous way.[61] However, their main function is to communicate, not to be a humorous work.[62] Only in a few individual cases, then, will a meme satisfy the requirements of parody.

Yet the essential characteristics of a caricature have not yet been clarified at the level of EU law. A caricature usually involves a drawing or other pictorial representation which, by satirically highlighting or exaggerating

---

28 July 2016, para. 28, Gewerblicher Rechtsschutz und Urheberrecht (GRUR) (2016) 1157 – auf fett getrimmt.

55 German Government (2021) 89.

56 Concerning parody see CJEU case C-201/13 of 3 September 2014, ECLI:EU:C:2014:2132 – Deckmyn und Vrijheidsfonds.

57 CJEU case C-201/13 of 3 September 2014, para. 17, ECLI:EU:C:2014:2132 – Deckmyn und Vrijheidsfonds.

58 Ibid. para. 33.

59 Ibid.

60 The so-called anti-thematic treatment as a prerequisite of parody is thus no longer necessary.

61 Maier (2016) 398.

62 See Ullrich (2016).

certain characteristic traits, exposes a person, thing or event to ridicule.[63] In the case of memes, this – if at all existent – is not the main focus of using the pre-existing image.

4. Pastiche according to § 51a UrhG

The pastiche exception provision has so far received little attention in German legal literature.[64] It was modelled on Art. 5 (3) lit. (k) of the InfoSoc-Directive, which originates from French copyright law (Art. L 122–5 Code de la propriété intellectuelle). The French copyright law assigns the three terms to three categories of work: caricature concerning pictorial art, parody concerning music, and pastiche concerning literature.[65] For one thing, this distinction is not very useful, since European and also German copyright law do not differentiate between the genres of art, music and literature, but all fall under the same concept of a copyright work. In addition, parody is already not understood in a genre-specific manner according to previous CJEU case law: in the *Deckmyn* judgment, a drawing, i.e., a pictorial work of art, was classified as a parody.[66] The pastiche is thus not limited to a specific genre of referential work.[67]

If the terms caricature, parody and pastiche are therefore not assigned to different genres, the question arises as to how they can otherwise be distinguished from one another and what they have in common. In common usage, the term pastiche is not very widespread in the German language, unlike in French or English.[68] In the English language, pastiche is used as a generic term for a wide variety of forms of adoption and similarity.[69] In music theory, the term pastiche is more common and refers to a work that

63 German Government (2021) 91.

64 See Ohly (2017) 969; Stieper (2015) 304, who argued for a usability of the pastiche exception even before the CJEU decision in C-476/17 of 29 July 2019, para. 65, ECLI:EU:C:2019:624 – Pelham/Hütter.

65 See Vlah (2015) 43. Similarly, Hess (1993) 95, who also distinguishes between the three terms according to the genres of the originals understanding caricature as the imitation of persons, parody as the imitation of genres/styles or works of art history, and satire as using situations and customs.

66 CJEU case C-201/13 of 3 September 2014, para. 18 et seq., 29, ECLI:EU:C:2014:2132 – Deckmyn und Vrijheidsfonds.

67 Pötzlberger (2018a) 680.

68 On this subject, see Stieper (2015) 304.

69 Brinkmann (2021) 68/69 with further references.

is mainly or entirely composed of existing music.[70] Pastiche is also used in legal literature to refer to new musical forms such as remix or sampling.[71] The literary pastiche term refers to a process of stylistic imitation of an author or group of texts by different authors, e.g. of a particular period or genre.[72] The pastiche reveals its intertextual structure.[73] Such a notion of pastiche cannot be used when interpreting Art. 5 (3) lit. (k) InfoSoc-Directive. This is because the style of a work is not protected by copyright law[74], consequently there is no need for a legal exception for stylistic imitations.[75]

It remains open which interpretation of pastiche underlies the new § 51a UrhG. Since it is an autonomous term of EU law, the CJEU must ultimately decide this. Therefore, possible interpretations of the term pastiche are now examined.

a) A broad understanding of pastiche in the Explanatory Memorandum to the German Act implementing the DSM-Directive

The Memorandum of the German draft bill ("Gesetzesentwurf") on the Adaptation of Copyright Law to the Requirements of the Digital Single Market (Gesetz zur Anpassung des Urheberrechts an die Erfordernisse des digitalen Binnenmarktes) of 9 February 2021 is based on such a broad understanding of the term pastiche that it is being transformed into an open-ended general clause. Accordingly, pastiche – just like parody or caricature – deals with a pre-existing work. Unlike parody and caricature, which require a humorous or mocking component, a pastiche may also contain an expression of appreciation or reverence for the original, for example as a homage.[76] In particular, pastiche permits, pursuant to § 5 (1) no. 2 of the new "Law on the Copyright Responsibility of Service Providers for Shar-

70 Stieper (2015) 304.

71 Pötzlberger (2018a), 680/681; Ohly (2017) 968.

72 See Stieper, Fan Fiction als moderne Form der Pastiche, AfP 2015, pp. 301, 304 with reference to Antonsen in Müller (Hrsg.) Reallexikon der deutschen Literaturwissenschaft Bd. III, 2003, p. 34.

73 Stieper (2015) 305.

74 BGH, case I ZR 135/87 of 8 June 1989, Neue Juristische Wochenschrift (NJW) (1990) 1986, at 1987/8 – Emil Nolde; Schack (2017) para. 235.

75 See also Stieper (2015) 305; Pötzlberger (2018a) 676; of a different opinion Walter (2010) who argues that pastiche in the sense of Art. 5 (3) InfoSoc-Directive only means imitations of style.

76 German Government (2021) 91.

ing Online Content" (Gesetz über die urheberrechtliche Verantwortlichkeit von Diensteanbietern für das Teilen von Online-Inhalten, Urheberrechts-Diensteanbieter-Gesetz, UrhDaG), use without the rightholder's consent of certain user-generated content which cannot be classified as parody or caricature. Such use also maintains an appropriate balance when assessing copyright interests, namely owners and users.[77]

The draft bill memorandum even assumes that memes constitute a pastiche and thus, are covered by the exception: "Quoting, imitating and borrowing cultural techniques are a defining element of intertextuality and contemporary cultural creation and communication on the 'social web'. In particular, practices such as remix, meme, GIF, mashup, fan art, fan fiction or sampling come to mind."[78] This is the case, as EU law expressly justifies in § 17 (7) subpara. 2 DSM-Directive and recital 70 DSM-Directive the obligation to introduce the exceptions which protect freedom of expression and artistic freedom, now enshrined in § 51a UrhG. This broad understanding of pastiche can be justified by the fact that the new § 51a UrhG is meant to replace old § 24 (1) UrhG (old version), which was repealed due to its unlawfulness under EU law.[79] However, § 51a UrhG does not even require latter works to keep an appropriate (inner or outward) distance from the copyrighted work used, thus stipulating fewer requirements than the old version.

b) A narrow understanding of pastiche

However, there are many arguments against this broad interpretation. Most importantly, there are major doubts as to whether it is consistent with the meaning of the pastiche exception at the European level.[80] The pastiche exception was only implemented in a few member states, and if at all implemented it is not understood to have such a fundamental, almost general clause-like meaning. As seen above, the introduction of the pastiche exception in Art. 5 (3) lit. (k) of the InfoSoc-Directive originates from French law which does not view it as a general clause for referencing. Even when it was introduced into EU law, pastiche was not intended to be an exception for creative uses – rather, the pastiche exception did not play any

77 Ibid.
78 Ibid.
79 Döhl (2020) 380.
80 Ibid. 413.

role in in the legislative documents on the InfoSoc-Directive[81] or in the numerous decisions of the courts in the cases concerning the litigation under the names of *Metall auf Metall* and *Pelham/Hütter*.[82] The sampling at issue in these judgements would probably now be a prime example of what the draft bill memorandum intended pastiche to mean.[83] If it were so obvious that referencing and creative appropriation were to be included under the pastiche term, this would have been discussed in this year-long dispute about the meaning of sampling.

Even when § 5 (3) lit. (k) of the InfoSoc-Directive was introduced, the aim was not to introduce a general clause for creative referencing for the simple reason that social media, user-generated content and referencing culture on the Internet were not an issue in 2001. Rather, the main objective of the InfoSoc-Directive was to prevent digital piracy and file sharing.[84] Thus, there is no unintentional regulatory gap within the term pastiche, which cannot now be converted into a general clause exception. In the draft bill memorandum however, pastiche becomes a synonym for recombining existing material of any kind and quality, regardless of the scope, purpose or commercial nature of the reference. All of this suggests that the concept of pastiche is not suited to claim such a broad, overarching, and fundamental exception as the draft bill memorandum determines.

Döhl derives from the use of the term of pastiche in art science and musicology that in § 51a UrhG it probably means "a kind of disclosed forgery, writing in a foreign aesthetic language, which admittedly does not want to be fraud, but thus serves an interacting artistic purpose".[85] An understanding of pastiche as an artistic transformation that serves the exercise of the

81 Ibid. 414.

82 BGH, case I ZR 115/16 of 30 April 2020, Gewerblicher Rechtsschutz und Urheberrecht (GRUR) (2020) 843 – Metall auf Metall IV; CJEU, case C-476/17 of 29 July 2019, para. 65, ECLI:EU:C:2019:624 – Pelham/Hütter; BVerfG, case 1 BvR 1585/13 of 31 May 2016, Gewerblicher Rechtsschutz und Urheberrecht (GRUR) (2016), 690 – Metall auf Metall; BGH, case I ZR 112/06 of 20 November 2008, Gewerblicher Rechtsschutz und Urheberrecht (GRUR) (2008) 403 – Metall auf Metall I; BGH, case I ZR 182/11 of 13 December 2012, Gewerblicher Rechtsschutz und Urheberrecht (GRUR) (2013) 614 – Metall auf Metall II; BGH, case I ZR 115/16 of 1 June 2017, Gewerblicher Rechtsschutz und Urheberrecht (GRUR) (2017) 895 – Metall auf Metall III.

83 Sampling is explicitly mentioned, see German Government (2021) 91; Döhl (2020) 389.

84 Döhl (2020) 416.

85 Ibid. 439.

fundamentally protected artistic freedom in Art. 13 CFR[86] seems to be the interpretation preferred by legal history and the will of the EU legislator. Since the CJEU in *Pelham/Hütter* provided a much narrower requirement for sampling by requiring perceptible differences to a work, this artistic understanding of pastiche can already be understood as broad.

c) *Pastiche does not achieve a systemic change*

The pastiche exception in § 51a UrhG does not bring about the systemic change in copyright law that the German legislator envisaged according to the draft bill memorandum. Since § 51a UrhG is based on Art. 5 (3) lit. (k) of the InfoSoc-Directive, the term must be interpreted as an autonomous term of EU law. It can be assumed that the CJEU and probably also the German courts will adopt a narrow interpretation of the term. This is because the pastiche exception was not intended to create a general clause for referencing techniques.

Even if an exception for referencing techniques is desirable,[87] it is not yet achieved by the pastiche exception in § 51a UrhG. This is because the introduction of the pastiche term would otherwise protect techniques which, according to unanimous legal literature and case law, were not previously permitted by way of free use pursuant to the older version of § 24 UrhG. It is not acceptable that the implementation of a hitherto vague and unclear exception from the InfoSoc-Directive should lead to a systemic change in copyright law, which has often been called for, but which has not been legally anchored in any way. In particular, it is not possible to impose an exception for creative usages on other EU member states through the back door by way of norm interpretation on which no political consensus has yet been reached.[88]

---

86 See also Bauer (2020) 288.

87 As already called for in numerous cases by Bauer, Die Aneignung von Bildern, 2020, p. 293 ff.; Bauer (2011) 392 et seq. (exception provision for user-generated content); Ziegler (2016) 253 (exception for social sharing); Pötzlberger (2018b) 298 et seq. (exception for creative remixing); the initiative "Recht auf Remix", https://rechtaufremix.org, (exception for remixes); Kreutzer (2011) 73; (exception for transformative uses of works); Geiger (2008) 463/464 and 467 (exception for creative uses); Vlah (2015) 194 et seq. (exception for parodies); Döhl (2016) 314 et seq. (exception for creative usages).

88 See also Döhl (2020) 440.

For memes, this means that they are not justified as pastiche pursuant to § 51a UrhG. For even if one adopts an artistic conceptual understanding of pastiche, memes are not to be classified as artistic, as already mentioned above, and are also not protected by artistic freedom pursuant to Art. 5 (3) GG or Art. 13 CFR.

V. Concluding Remarks

Summing up, the assessment of memes under German copyright law remains a highly relevant problem even after the introduction of § 51a UrhG. There are no exceptions applicable, so they will continue to constitute copyright infringements. The pastiche exception in § 51a UrhG will not be able to solve this problem even though the draft bill memorandum explicitly mentions memes as a case of pastiche. However, this broad understanding would represent a change in the copyright law system which was not intended when implementing Art. 5 (3) lit. (k) InfoSoc-Directive into the German Act and equally, was not possible. Since pastiche is an autonomous term of EU law, only the CJEU can ultimately clarify how the exception provision should be interpreted. However, there are no indications that the introduction of an exception for creative repurposing and referencing was intended.

Thus, there continues to be a discrepancy between the rigid legal assessment of appropriation and referencing techniques on the one hand, and the changed communication behaviour in social media on the other. Without a legal exemption for communicative appropriations, the legitimacy crisis of copyright law intensifies. For if copyright law no longer reflects social reality, it will no longer be supported by social consensus. Thus, the assignment to introduce an exception provision for non-commercial appropriations remains with the EU legislator.[89]

References

Bauer, Christian Alexander: *User-generated Content – Urheberrechtliche Zulässigkeit nutzergenerierter Medieninhalte* (Berlin/Heidelberg: Springer 2011)

89 Cf. in detail Bauer (2020) 288 et seq.

Bauer, Eva-Maria (2020): *Die Aneignung von Bildern – Eine urheberrechtliche Betrachtung von der Appropriation Art bis hin zu Memes* (The Appropriation of Images – A Copyright View from Appropriation Art to Memes (Baden-Baden: Nomos 2020)

Belting, Hans (2011): *An Anthropology of Images* (Princeton: Princeton University Press 2011); German Original Bild-Anthropologie (München: Fink Verlag 2001)

Blunck, Lars (2011): 'Wann ist ein Original?', in: Nida-Rümelin, Julian/Steinbrenner, Jakob: *Kunst und Philosophie – Original und Fälschung* (Ostfildern: Hatje Cantz 2011) 9–29

Boehm, Gottfried: 'Die Wiederkehr der Bilder', in: Boehm, Gottfried: *Was ist ein Bild?* (München: Fink 1994) 11–38

Boehm, Gottfried/Mitchell, W.J.T. (2014): 'Ein Briefwechsel', in: Rimmele, Marius/Sachs-Hombach, Klaus/Stiegler, Bernd: *Bildwissenschaft und Visual Culture* (Bielefeld: transcript 2014) 19–40

Bredekamp, Horst (1997): 'Das Bild als Leitbild – Gedanken zur Überwindung des Anikonismus', in: Hoffmann, Ute/Joerges, Bernward/Severin, Ingrid: *LogIcons – Bilder zwischen Theorie und Anschauung* (Berlin: Ed. Sigma 1997) 225–245

Brinkmann, Franziska (2020): 'Formen der Kopie von der Fälschung bis zur Hommage – Eine Begriffsbestimmung und ihre Grenzen', in: Dreier, Thomas/Jehle, Oliver: *Original – Kopie – Fälschung* (Baden-Baden: Nomos 2020) 57–104

Bullinger, Winfried (2019): 'Commentary on § 24 UrhG', in: Wandtke, Artur-Axel/Bullinger, Winfried: *Urheberrecht* (München: C.H. Beck 5th edition 2019)

Burda, Hubert (2010): *In medias res* (Paderborn: Wilhelm Fink Verlag 2010)

Crimp, Douglas (1977): *Pictures – an exhibition of the work of Troy Brauntuch, Jack Goldstein, Sherrie Levine, Robert Longo, Philip Smith* (New York: Committee for the visual Arts 1977) (online available at https://monoskop.org/images/1/10/Pictures_1977_catalogue.pdf)

Dawkins, Richard (1976/2006): *The Selfish Gene* (Oxford: Oxford University Press 1976; cited after the 30th Anniversary edition 2006)

Digital Single Market Directive (2019): 'Directive (EU) 2019/790 of the European Parliament and of the Council of 17 April 2019 on copyright and related rights in the Digital Single Market and amending Directives 96/9/EC and 2001/29/EC', OJ EU L 130 of 17 May 2019, 92–125

Dobusch, Leonhard (2015): 'Urheberrecht auf Memes? – Getty Images, der "Socially Awkward Penguin" und eine Lösung aus dem Markenrecht', Netzpolitik.org of 04 September 2015 (online available at https://netzpolitik.org/2015/urheberrecht-auf-memes-getty-images-der-socially-awkward-penguin-und-eine-loesung-aus-dem-markenrecht)

Döhl, Frédéric (2016): *Mashups in der Musik* (Bielefeld: transcript 2016)

Döhl, Frédéric (2020): 'Pastiche zwischen Generalklausel und Auffangtatbestand', Zeitschrift für geistiges Eigentum (2020) 380–442

Dreier, Thomas (2022): 'Commentary on § 51 UrhG', in: Dreier, Thomas/Schulze, Gernot: *Urheberrechtsgesetz* (München: C.H. Beck 7th edition 2022)

Dreier, Thomas (2022): *Copyright – Streit zweier Bildkulturen* (Berlin: Wagenbach 2022)

Geiger, Christophe (2008): 'Die Schranken des Urheberrechts als Instrumente der Innovationsförderung', Gewerblicher Rechtsschutz und Urheberrecht – Internationaler Teil (2008) 459–468

Geiger, Christophe (2022): 'Contemporary Art on Trial – The Fundamental Right to Free Artistic Expression and the Regulation of the Use of Images by Copyright Law', in: Dreier, Thomas/Andina, Tiziana: *Digital Ethics – The Issue of Images* (Baden-Baden: Nomos 2022) 387–415

German Government (2021): 'Explanatory Memorandum to the Gesetz zur Anpassung des Urheberrechts an die Erfordernisse des digitalen Binnenmarktes' (Berlin: Bundestags-Drucksache 19/27426 of 9 March 2021)

Grünewald-Schukalla, Lorenz/Fischer, Georg (2018): 'Überlegungen zu einer textuellen Definition von Internet-Memes', 19 kommunikation@gesellschaft, No. 2 (2018) (online available at https://journals.sub.uni-hamburg.de/hup2/kommges/article/view/602/236)

Hansen, Gerd (2009): *Warum Urheberrecht?* (Baden-Baden: Nomos 2009)

Herwig, Jana (2018), 'Viralität als Sonderfall – über Selfies, Serialität und die Wahrscheinlichkeit der Kommunikation im Social Web', 19 komunikation@gesellschaft, No. 2 (2018) (online available at https://journals.sub.uni-hamburg.de/hup2/kommges/article/view/600/230)

Hess, Gangolf (1993): *Urheberrechtsprobleme der Parodie* (Baden-Baden: Nomos 1993)

Huttenlauch, Anna Blume (2010): *Appropriation Art – Kunst an den Grenzen des Urheberrechts* (Baden-Baden: Nomos 2010)

Jenkins, Henry (2006): *Fans, Bloggers, and Gamers – Exploring Participatory Culture* (New York: NYU Press 2006)

Kaesling, Katharina (2019): 'Die EU-Urheberrechtnovelle – Der Untergang des Internets?', Juristen Zeitung (2019) 586–591

Klass, Nadine (2015): 'Werkgenuss und Werknutzung in der digitalen Welt – Bedarf es einer Harmonisierung des Urheberpersönlichkeitsrechts?', Zeitschrift für Urheber- und Medienrecht (2015) 290–308

Kreutzer, Till (2011): 'Verbraucherschutz im Urheberrecht' (iRights 2011, available online at https://irights.info/wp-content/uploads/userfiles/2011-05-03_Verbraucherschutz_im_Urheberrecht.pdf)

Kühl, Eike (2015): 'Socially Awkward Copyright', Die Zeit, 04 September 2015 (online available at https://www.zeit.de/digital/internet/2015-09/getty-images-urheberrecht-meme-socially-awkward-penguin/komplettansicht)

Leistner, Matthias/Hansen, Gerd (2008): 'Die Begründung des Urheberrechts im digitalen Zeitalter. Versuch einer Zusammenführung von individualistischen und utilitaristischen Rechtfertigungsbemühungen', Gewerblicher Rechtsschutz und Urheberrecht (2008) 479–490

Loewenheim, Ulrich (2020): 'Commentary on § 24 UrhG', in: Schricker, Gerhard/Loewenheim, Ulrich: *Urheberrecht* (München: C.H. Beck 6th edition 2020)

Maar, Christa/Burda, Hubert (2004): *Iconic Turn – Die neue Macht der Bilder* (Cologne: DuMont 2004)

Maier, Henrike (2016): 'Meme und Urheberrecht', Gewerblicher Rechtsschutz und Urheberrecht – Praxis im Urheber- und Immaterialgüterrecht (2016) 397–398

Marl, Johannes (2017): *Der Begriff der Öffentlichkeit im Urheberrecht* (Tübingen: Mohr Siebeck 2017)

Mewes, Bernd (2019): 'Save the Internet – Europaweite Demos gegen neues Urheberrecht und Artikel 13', Heise online of 23 March 2019 (online available at https://www.heise.de/newsticker/meldung/Save-the-Internet-Europaweite-Demos-gegen-neues-Urheberrecht-und-Artikel-13-4347138.html)

Mitchell, W.J.T. (1992): 'The Pictorial Turn', Art Forum No. 30 (1992) 89–95

Mitchell, W.J.T. (1994): *Picture Theory – Essays on Verbal and Visual Representation* (Chicago: University of Chicago Press 1994)

Ohly, Ansgar (2017): 'Hip Hop und die Zukunft der "freien Benutzung" im EU-Urheberrecht', Gewerblicher Rechtsschutz und Urheberrecht (2017) 964–969

Peukert, Alexander (2014): 'Das Urheberrecht und die zwei Kulturen der Online-Kommunikation', Gewerblicher Rechtsschutz und Urheberrecht, Beilage (2014) 77–93 (english: 'Copyright and the Two Cultures of Online Communication', in: Torremans, Paul L.C.: *Intellectual Property Law and Human Rights* (Cheltenham: Edward Elgar 3rd ed. 2015) 367–395

Pötzlberger, Florian (2018a): 'Pastiche 2.0 – Remixing im Lichte des Unionsrechts', Gewerblicher Rechtsschutz und Urheberrecht (2018) 675–681

Pötzlberger, Florian (2018b): *Kreatives Remixing – Musik im Spannungsfeld von Urheberrecht und Kunstfreiheit* (Baden-Baden: Nomos 2018)

Raue, Benjamin (2013): 'Informationsfreiheit und Urheberrecht', Juristen Zeitung (2013) 280–288

Rebane, Gala (2021): *Emojis* (Berlin: Wagenbach 2021)

Rebbelmund, Romana (1999): *Appropriation Art – Die Kopie als Kunstform im 20. Jahrhundert* (Frankfurt/M.: Peter Lang 1999)

Sachs-Hombach, Klaus (2013): *Das Bild als kommunikatives Medium – Elemente einer allgemeinen Bildwissenschaft* (Cologne: Herbert von Halem 3rd edition 2013)

Schack, Haimo (2017): *Kunst und Recht* (Tübingen: Mohr Siebeck 3rd edition 2017)

Schulze, Gernot (2018): 'Commentary on § 24 UrhG' in: Dreier, Thomas/Schulze, Gernot: *Urheberrechtsgesetz* (München: C.H. Beck 6th edition 2018)

Shifman, Limor (2013): *Memes in Digital Culture* (Cambridge/MA.: MIT Press 2013)

Spindler, Gerald (2010): 'Commentary on § 51 UrhG', in: Schricker, Gerhard/Loewenheim, Ulrich: *Urheberrecht* (München: C.H. Beck 6th edition 2020)

Stähli, Adrian (2008): 'Die Kopie – Überlegungen zu einem methodischen Leitkonzept der Plastikforschung', in: Junker, Klaus/Stähli, Adrian/Kunze, Christian: *Original und Kopie – Formen und Konzepte der Nachahmung in der antiken Kunst* (Wiesbaden: Reichert 2008) 15–34

Stallberg, Christian (2006): *Urheberrecht und moralische Rechtfertigung* (Berlin: Duncker & Humboldt 2006)

Stieper, Malte (2015): 'Fan Fiction als moderne Form der Pastiche', Archiv für Presserecht (2015) 301–305

Sturtevant, Elaine (1999): 'Fälschung/Original', in: Deecke, Thomas: *Originale echt/ falsch – Nachahmung, Kopie, Zitat, Aneignung, Fälschung in der Gegenwartskunst*, Ausstellungskatalog, Neues Museum Weserburg (Bremen: Neues Museum Weserburg 1999) 149–155

Summerer, Claudia (2015): *Illegale Fans – Die urheberrechtliche Zulässigkeit von Fan Art* (Berlin/Boston: de Gruyte, 2015)

Ullrich, Wolfgang (2016): 'Das Wetteifern der Bilder – Eine Archäologie der Mem-Kultur', irights info of 26 April 2016, https://irights.info/artikel/das-wetteifern-der-bilder-eine-archaeologie-der-mem-kultur/27306

Ullrich, Wolfgang (2019): *Selfies – Die Rückkehr des öffentlichen Lebens* (Berlin: Wagenbach 2019)

Ulmer, Eugen (1980): *Urheber- und Urhebervertragsrecht* (Berlin/Heidelberg/New York: Springer 3rd edition 1980)

Vlah, Tudor (2015): *Parodie, Pastiche und Karikatur – Urheberrechte und ihre Grenzen* (Frankfurt/M.: Peter Lang 2015)

von Gehlen, Dirk (2020): *Meme* (Berlin: Wagenbach 2020)

Walter, Michel/von Lewinski, Silke (2010): 'Comment on Article 5 (3) (k) InfoSoc-Directive', in: Walter, Michel/von Lewinski, Silke: *European Copyright Law – A Commentary* (Oxford: Oxford University Press 2010) Information Society Directive 2001/29/EC, para. 11.5.67

Wandtke, Artur-Axel (2019): 'Persönlichkeitsschutz versus Internet – Politiker und Prominente im Fadenkreuz der Persönlichkeitsrechte', Multimedia und Recht (2019) 142–147

Wegmann, Katrin (2013): *Der Rechtsgedanke der freien Benutzung des § 24 UrhG und die verwandten Schutzrechte* (Baden-Baden: Nomos 2013)

Ziegler, Katharina (2016): *Urheberrechtsverletzungen durch Social Sharing* (Tübingen: Mohr Siebeck 2016)

Zuschlag, Christoph (2012): 'Die Kopie ist das Original – über Appropriation Art', in: Mensger, Ariane: *Déjà-vu? – Die Kunst der Wiederholung von Dürer bis Youtube*, Exhibition Catalogue, Staatliche Kunsthalle Karlsruhe (Bielefeld: Kerber 2012) 126–135

Chapter 9
Towards a New Ethic: Building Transgenerationality – Digital Images to Orient the Future

Tiziana Andina

Can digital images help build a stronger transgenerational bond? One of the most interesting features of human sociality is the disposition to transgenerationality. Transgenerationality is the willingness to organise aspects of social reality by devising mechanisms for the passage of material and immaterial goods from one generation to another. This disposition evidently constitutes one of the foundations that have contributed to the development of our species.

Images, especially digital ones, have two particularly interesting features: they can be reproduced quickly and easily, and they can also be easily archived and preserved. This means that they are a very effective tool for conveying information and memory. This is confirmed by the increasingly pervasive spread of social media (e.g., Instagram) that use images as their essential communicative vectors.

The present article consists of four parts. In the first part, I will briefly examine the ontology of digital images. In the second and third parts, I will analyse the notion of transgenerationality to highlight the main characteristics of the transgenerational bond and transgenerational actions. In the fourth and last part, I will discuss the photos of sculptures found at the Memorial Hall of the Victims in the Nanjing Massacre, developing some reflections on the transgenerational scope of this kind of images. But let us start by clarifying what we mean when we talk about digital images.

I. Digital Images

Images represent a particularly interesting object from an ontological point of view. The ancients were already fascinated by them. The myth of Narcissus, in addition to its many symbolic implications, captures the enigmatic nature of the image.[1] As is well known, Narcissus saw his image for the first time on a reflective surface, discovered his own face and tried to capture this irresistible figure. Psychoanalysis has built a fundamental part of its narrative on the interpretation of this myth. Narcissus is someone unknown to himself, so he does not recognise himself when he sees his reflection in the water. He is also constantly engaged in exploring his own self, while being doomed to never find it. As we know, this fate awaits all who are affected by pathological narcissism, where narcissism is a dominant trait, so that the fixity of the image becomes a bubble from which the subject generally cannot get out.

The image reveals two important characteristics. It is fixed, but at the same time it is elusive. It is fixed – and in fact, Narcissus remains stuck in contemplation of it – because it gives an account of the fixity of the personality that is incorporated in it. The element of elusiveness, on the other hand, is the deepest truth of the myth. The image, in fact, resembles the thing, but is not the thing. More generally, we can identify at least two types of images. Images of things like chimeras and images of material objects that exist in space and time. In other words, images of things that do not exist in reality (chimeras), and images of things that do exist. The latter are characterised by specific properties and suitable for the purpose of imitation.

That the image is not the same as the thing is therefore somehow evident. This is similar to the fact that although there is a link between a thing and its image, there is always a gap between them, just as between Narcissus and his reflected image. This gap is interesting because it bears all the meanings that are conveyed by the image, while not necessarily belonging to the thing. All this is to say that the image of a thing is never a re-proposition of the simple thing but is rather "about" the thing that is represented in the image, because it ultimately constitutes a sort of gaze on the thing. Even in the most faithful of representations, the image – whether pictorial or photographic – is always an added meaning to the thing.[2] For example, it is the thing seen through the particular instrument that allows for its representation.

Now, the question is roughly the following: can we argue that the digital image differs from traditional images, i.e., those reflected in mirrors,

1 Cf. e.g. Filippi (2020).

2 The works of Eduard Stieglitz are significant in this regard. He often points out that photography is both a tool aimed at the mere reproduction of reality, and (most of all) a tool for the artistic representation of the thing, i.e., in Stieglitz's words, a tool that allows one to display the essence of the thing photographed.

painted by painters, or captured by photographs? The medium, i.e., digital technology, certainly does make a significant difference. A photographic image created using digital technology has many uses. It can be archived, classified, duplicated, and diffused in incomparably more effective ways than in the pre-digital era. Photographs taken with a Polaroid required a rather laborious and time-consuming process to make copies of the original. Today, instead, every photo we take with our phone can be reproduced a virtually infinite number of times and can be disseminated in extremely powerful ways via social platforms that, unsurprisingly, specialise primarily in distributing images.

On the other hand, we also know that images created using digital tools and technologies not only convey meanings in the same way as Polaroid photos or paintings, but also carry *information*. This information is made available in the form of metadata which, in turn, are related in part to the contents of the image, in part to the image itself (when, where and who took the photo, the tool that determined the photographic rendering, etc.). In short, digital images bear all the information that belongs to the photographic object, the author and the relationship between the object, the author, and the global environment.

Therefore, images represent an extremely powerful communication tool. They can be duplicated endlessly, they are more direct and quicker than words, and they are distributed through powerful tools such as social platforms that produce serial images. This type of seriality enables a communication that, though generally unsophisticated, is fast and effective. By displaying his *Brillo Box* in a series, Andy Warhol highlighted the serial production mode typical of modern industry. However, the seriality Warhol refers to was very little compared to the ability to produce, reproduce, catalogue and archive images made possible by digital technologies today.

So, let us try to summarise: we said that the characteristic of most images is that they refer to the thing they represent, while having different properties with respect to the thing. The image maintains this characteristic independently of the medium used to create it. The medium, however, has a significant impact on two aspects: on the one hand, the possibility of duplicating and circulating the image; on the other, the wealth of metadata that the image conveys. This depends both on the tool used, and that this tool is generally connected to a network that makes it possible to identify and trace the author of the image, the image itself, and its web of relationships by the tools of digital communication.

Which means that this type of image not only says something about the thing that it captures, but also provides a range of potentially interesting information about the author of the image, their location, habits, tastes, the world related to the image and so on. In other words, any digital image is an object that says something about its object and, at the same time, provides a lot of information about the context it belongs to, the uses made of the image, and the world in which it exists. When Narcissus contemplated his own image reflected in the mirror made of water, filled with love and admiration, he is unable to recognise himself. Clearly, the traces of what he has been do not take the shape of his reflected image.

Therefore, I would like to suggest the following idea: digital images can strengthen the transgenerational bond in effective ways by virtue of two fundamental characteristics. First, they convey content about what is being reproduced, always referring to something else. Second, they also carry much information about the world to which the image belongs. Digital images are therefore, at the same time, bearers of meaning and information, which are both fundamental aspects for the construction of the transgenerational bond.

II. The Transgenerational Bond

By "transgenerationality"[3] I mean the bond that unites different generations. This bond takes two forms. Firstly, the biological bond relates parents to their children and is characterised by a peculiar psychological structure in the relationship between mother and child. Secondly, the bond that unites different generations in the course of history. This bond characterises some social actions that we shall define as "transgenerational actions". The basic idea is that transgenerational actions have a peculiar structure that must be understood and described to adequately portray social reality.

When we reflect on the transgenerational bond, we focus on the diachronic structure of social reality, i.e., the conditions that allow societies to last over time. As has been widely noted by philosophers,[4] this means that the question of the passing of generations is a matter of primary importance for at least two reasons. The first is that it is a necessary transition, to which there is no alternative except atom-like societies, which would not last long enough to develop complex social actions. Secondly, because this model involves a presumed but not required consensus on a given

3 More detailed considerations can be found in Andina (2016).

4 Cf., e.g., Kant (2011), 250; Hume (1994).

course of action. Now, current generations generally consider it obvious that those who will follow, i.e., the generations that will be called to continue what they have started, will agree to do so. This model's background has delicate questions on transgenerational justice,[5] related to the structure and dynamics of transgenerational relations and actions. Let us therefore briefly consider what I mean by transgenerational actions.

III. Transgenerational Actions

By transgenerational actions I mean a particular class of social actions that have the characteristic of lasting considerably over time. The existence of these actions has important implications. The first concerns a fact of reality: the decision makers of these actions set in motion long-term processes that require the collaboration of social actors different from those who have undertaken these processes. Now, let us suppose that a certain action (which we will call "a") is initiated by a certain generation. Presume that "a" implies the massive exploitation of fossil fuels to electrify a country with a low development rate. This action requires a rather long process to be fully realised. So, the political decision makers who authorise the series of actions that are "part of a" nourish the belief that future generations will continue "a", Further, that the actions required are linked to "a" through a spirit and intentions similar to their own, i.e., sharing their underlying values and strategies. Therefore, current generations implicitly assume that future ones will give their consent to "a" and to the actions required for the realization of "a".

In this regard, it is useful to observe two things. The first observation is that future generations are a fictional subject. This is because when they are imagined by present generations they obviously do not yet exist, so they cannot express their consent. Therefore, to simply suppose that they will consent to "a" is a stretch in every respect. However, this stretch comes with a degree of practical utility because, ultimately, it allows decision makers to implement "a" with the belief that it will be completed by future generations. It is worth noting that the fictional subject "future generations" plays a decisive role. The subjects who decide to do "a" not only need future generations (and in fact bet on their future existence), but

5 For a first approach to the issue of transgenerational justice see Tremmel (2009); Gosseries/Meyer (2009); Tremmel (2006); Westra (2006); Dobson (1999).

also need the fictional subject, when it becomes real, to behave in the way they have predicted.

The second point is that future generations are a fictional subject to which we have attributed peculiar characteristics. Their ontological status involves the passage from potentiality to actuality (sooner or later, in fact, they will exist). Moreover, they are necessary for the completion of transgenerational actions. Therefore, let us suppose that a certain future generation commits itself to complete "a" or to take on the consequences of "a", without – I repeat – ever having decided to initiate "a" or anything necessary for the realization of "a". This point obviously has important consequences on both a practical and ethical level.

It is easy to see that there are several areas in which actions with a transgenerational structure emerge with particular clarity. We can think of climate change, or of those decisions, which take the form of actions, which lead to more public debt – depending on how they are implemented, these actions can be either positive or negative, i.e., they can or cannot protect the transgenerational bond. We can also think of those types of actions that more clearly convey the positive character of transgenerationality and are clearly committed to protecting it. In this sense, the preservation of cultural heritage and scientific progress are transgenerational actions. Likewise, money is also an eminently transgenerational instrument that functions as a store of value.

These considerations lead us to make two important observations. Firstly, it should be noted that transgenerationality cannot be acquired once and for all. It can be protected and strengthened or, vice versa, weakened – even severely. The second observation concerns the intrinsic transgenerational disposition of the human species. Our species, particularly in its need of care when compared to species, has been able to evolve precisely because of its disposition to transgenerationality. In other words, human beings are naturally inclined to be transgenerational, at least as far as family relationships are concerned (i.e., in the area of primary transgenerationality), while they develop secondary or social transgenerationality with greater difficulty.

However, when they succeed in adopting fully transgenerational practices and attitudes even in extra-family social environments, the quality and level of well-being of a society generally improves significantly. Through educational and caring relationships, parents give their children individual autonomy and a set of notions, knowledge and skills that enable them to navigate the world, while through secondary transgenerationality, social institutions and bodies enable societies to last.

IV. Transgenerational Images

In May 2019 I was in Nanjing, China for a series of conferences at Nanjing Normal University. Anyone who has some time to visit the city and wants to understand more about the ancient capital of China should visit The Nanjing Massacre Memorial Hall. This space is dedicated to the victims of the massacre perpetrated against its citizens by the Japanese army. In 1937, Japanese troops invaded Nanjing, the capital of the Republic of China, after the Japanese air force had severely weakened the resistance of the ground forces. The city was quickly taken. The massacre that followed and lasted for six weeks is considered one of the most horrific in human history. The city was sacked, set on fire and about 300,000 people, women, men, and children, were massacred. About 20,000 women were raped.

The memorial was built in 1985, with the design by two famous Chinese architects, Qi Kang and He Jintang (Figs. 1 and 2). The goal of a memorial is to make it impossible to forget what the memorial commemorates. Nanjing Massacre Memorial Hall is no exception. The names of the 300,000 victims of the Nanjing massacre are carved in marble and visually convey the idea of carnage. Behind the will to never forget, there is a strong bond between generations: those who have acted and those who keep the memory and reflect on it. The transgenerational bond kept alive by the memorial marks the memory of what some human beings have done. The warning never to do this again is crystallised in the ritual of symbolic and transfigured repetition that each visitor makes through the artistic and iconographic narration of that massacre. The memorial exhibits innocence and fury, two ways of life that often humankind expresses, and that art undertakes to reveal. The path inside the memorial unwinds through a wise selection of what ought to be remembered: on the one hand, the names of the 300,000 dead are carefully written to preserve their memory at least as long as human history lasts. On the other hand, what counts is clearly not their individuality, which is lost in the very long ranks of names that make up the list, but the number of deaths that made that tragedy so brutal.

Keeping a record of all the people killed recalls Arthur Danto's *Analytical Philosophy of History*, where the Ideal Chronicler takes note of everything that happens, at the exact moment it happens.[6] The idea of keeping track of every single name, indeed, resembles the Chronicler's constant recording. However, in this case the names were written *ex post*, due to the

6 Danto (1965).

will to remember only what was necessary not only, and perhaps not so much, to honour the dead, but to enable future generations to understand what the human being is capable of under certain circumstances. The memorial makes it impossible not so much to forget the names, which are lost in the countless number of traces, but also the actions carried out and their macabre cruelty. It is impossible not to face absolute horror when witnessing images like these.

Fig. 1: Qi Kang/He Jintang (Architects) and Wu Weishan (Sculpture) – Nanjing Massacre Memorial Hall

Fig. 2: Qi Kang/He Jintang (Architects) and Wu Weishan (Sculpture) – Nanjing Massacre Memorial Hall

These photographs portray the sculptures placed at the entrance and along the path of the memorial. Here the typification of the human beings involved in the massacre becomes a symbol. Now, it is clear that viewing a photograph or walking through the memorial are not the same kind of experience. Entering the memorial and walking through it is tantamount to somehow allow one to get closer to witnessing inescapable horror. The art in the memorial appears secondarily. The photos convey a different experience: we can look at them even without knowing much about the Nanjing massacre. For example, we may appreciate the technical qualities of the photographs, or the beauty of the sculptures that are captured in them. Or else, we may immerse ourselves in a more complete artistic experience if we have both knowledge of history (the facts about the Nanjing massacre) and understanding of the typical characteristics of digital media.

The photographs I took at the Nanjing Massacre Memorial Hall do not only capture images, but also produce a series of metadata that tell something about the world in which those photographs were taken. They reveal, for example, the author of the photo, the date it was taken, and its exact location. If I upload them to a digital platform – from Facebook or Instagram – to the "cloud" that contains my data – this metadata can be aggregated with other similar metadata produced by users who have been in the same or similar places (there are, unfortunately, many memorials around the world). This aggregation communicates something about, say, the type of people who tend to visit those places – for example, typifying them by age, gender, level of education, cultural background and so on. For example, one can discover to what extent visits to memorials are linked to memory preservation or, conversely, general tourism. And, again, one can find out how many children and adults visit them, how many visitors there are from year to year etc.

After all, this is not very different from what we do when we put our archives to work and make productive use of the information they store. What are photographic archives and artistic repertoires for, if not to preserve what (some thought) should be saved from the passing time and the oblivion that this inevitably entails? In the best case scenario, this allows us to creatively use the information we have decided to preserve. Uploading a digital image to an Internet platform means not only sharing the information conveyed by the image about the reproduced thing – possibly saving from oblivion something that, conveying certain properties, is seen as an art object. It also means making data available that allow us to process a rather precise description of the existing thing. Moreover, unlike paper archives, which also allow us to preserve considerable quantities of material and data, the web allows us to place the data in a network of incomparably finer, extended, and articulated relationships.

Not only is it possible to extract information from the images taken daily by visitors to memorials all over the world, but it also allows the images to be cross-referenced with information provided by visitors to museums, concentration camps, other mausoleums and so on. And, of course, it is possible to compare this mapping of reality with other mappings, which reflect other contexts. All this information serves at least three purposes. Firstly, to provide an accurate description of what surrounds us, at least with regard to the aspects that seem crucial to us. Secondly, to select and store this information with a view to forming what I would call "transgenerational capital". The transgenerational capital, alongside the "documedia capital"[7] and what economists call "social capital",[8] is one of the three capitals that we have at our disposal to work on the present without ceasing to guide the future.

Based on this description, it will probably be possible to plan for the future based on knowledge of what we are like, what interests we have, what we value most, what behaviours we share and what attitudes mark distinctions and differences between us. Basically, through backcasting – the planning method used to design a future that a given society considers desirable and work backwards to achieve it – we can acquire informed and detailed knowledge of the present, creating both a regulatory and axiological framework of reference and a future horizon to be reached through the design of the present.

Therefore, digital images, in our example, serve a twofold purpose. Firstly, the more obvious one of selecting and preserving memory, both personal and public. Secondly, a perhaps more hidden, but also more crucial purpose, which is to offer data that delivers a fine and uninterpreted description of the present, based on the idea that what we do describes and qualifies us. Digital images are a trace of what we do, what we value, what we despise and so on. All this, in perspective, can allow us to reconstruct the blueprint of the great soul of humanity with its many faces and infinite facets.

The crucial problem that arises at this point concerns boundaries. In other words, it makes sense to ask oneself how much space should and can be given to correct or regulate the implicit anthropology that all this data allows us to outline. Also, one can wonder to what extent it is possible to

---

7 For the notion of documedia capital, see Ferraris/Paini (2018); Ferraris (2022).

8 Bartolini/Bonatti (2002).

intervene to modify this anthropology. These questions, of course, go beyond the sphere of understanding the mere data, the digital object, or the trends that emerge from data aggregation or disaggregation. Rather, they relate to what we mean by freedom, the delimitation of its boundaries and a possible modelling of human societies. So, it is not so much about the ethics of images, but about the construction of an ethics for the world to which those images belong, in the awareness that the hidden information conveyed by those images can be more useful and more crucial than the manifest information they bear.

References

Andina, Tiziana (2006): *An Ontology for Social Reality* (translated by Sarah De Sanctis) (London: Palgrave Macmillan 2006)

Bartolini, Stefano/Luigi Bonatti (2002): 'Environmental and Social Degradation as the Engine of Economic Growth', 41 Ecological Economics, No. 1 (2002) 1–16 (online available at https://doi.org/10.1016/S0921-8009(02)00176-3)

Danto, Arthur C. (1965): *Analytical Philosophy of History* (Cambridge: Cambridge University Press 1965)

Dobson, Andrew (1999): *Fairness and Futurity – Essays on Environmental Sustainability and Social Justice* (Oxford/New York: Oxford University Press 1999)

Ferraris, Maurizio (2022): 'Who Cares About Privacy? – The Documedia Surplus Value', in: Dreier, Thomas/Andina, Tiziana: *Digital Ethics – The issue of images* (Baden-Baden: Nomos 2022) 81– 100

Ferraris, Maurizio/Paini, Germano (2018): *Scienza nuova – ontologia della trasformazione digitale* (Torino: Rosenberg & Sellier 2018)

Filippi, Elena (2020): 'Narciso nel Quattrocento – percezione, conoscenza, arte', Rivista di estetica (2020) 96–117

Gosseries, Axel/Meyer Lukas H. (2009): *Intergenerational Justice* (Oxford/New York: Oxford University Press 2009)

Hume, David (1994): 'Of the Original Contract', in: Haakonssen, Knud, *Hume – Political Essays* (Cambridge Texts in the History of Political Thought) (Cambridge: Cambridge University Press 1994) 186–201 (online available at https://doi.org/10.1017/CBO9781139170765.029)

Kant, Immanuel (2011): *Sette scritti politici liberi* (Firenze: Firenze University Press 2011)

Kohut, Heinz/Tatafiore, Adamo S. (1977): *Narcisismo e analisi del sé* (Torino: Bollati Boringhieri 1977)

Schützenberger, Anne Ancelin (1998): *The Ancestor Syndrome: Transgenerational Psychotherapy and the Hidden Links in the Family Tree* (London: Routledge 1998)

Tremmel, Jörg Chet (2006): *Handbook of Intergenerational Justice* (Cheltenham, UK/ Northampton, MA: Edward Elgar 2006)

Tremmel, Jörg Chet (2009): *A Theory of Intergenerational Justice* (Abingdon: Taylor&Francis Group 2009)

Westra, Laura (2006): *Environmental Justice and the Rights of Unborn and Future Generations: Law, Environmental Harm and the Right to Health* (London/Sterling, VA: Earthscan 2006)

Photo credits

Figs. 1 and 2: Artchitecture: Qi Kang/He Jintang; Sculpture: Wu Weishan; Photos: Author

Chapter 10
Iconoclasm and Iconoclash – The Digital Restoration of the Movement-Image

Cosetta Saba

I. Iconoclasm as a Means of Innovation and Reappraisal

According to Boris Groys, iconoclasm acts as a mechanism of historical innovation and a means of reappraisal through a process involving the constant destruction and replacement of old values with new ones.[1] Iconoclastic action would thus be directed not only at the past, but also – indeed above all – at the present. In any case, in the first two decades of the 2000s, in "discontinuous continuity" with the 20th century, we evidence destructive gestures that focus on art as a political and aesthetic field where socio-cultural and economic tensions are expressed. There are many cases and manifestations of destructive actions that concern the present. In 2015, we saw the destruction of the works of Kader Attia, Daniel Buren, Leandro Erlich, Moataz Nasr, Pascale Marthine Tayou in the Donetsk People's Republic (DPR). These works are examples of 'silent' destruction, in addition to the suppressed project "Where is the Time?" by the Izolyatsia Foundation[2] in collaboration with the Galleria Continua (Italy) initiated in 2012 in Donetsk (Ukraine). In radically different contexts and circumstances, the destructive gestures of artists Blu and Banksy provoke attentional upheavals and participatory behaviour. Blu, in disagreement with the museum exhibition programme "Street Art. Bansky & Co – Art in the Urban State", erased his works from the walls of Bologna in 2016.[3] Blu's gesture, on the one hand, opposes that of detaching, from an urban territorial context, a wall on which a work of street art is impermanently traced in order to re-territorialise it in a museum context and, on the other hand, raises conservation issues. In turn, Bansky acted during an auction at

1 Groys (2008).
2 https://izolyatsia.org/en/foundation.
3 The exhibition, curated by curators Luca Ciancabilla, Christian Omodeo and Sean Corcoran, ran at Palazzo Pepoli, Museum of the History of Bologna from 18 March to 26 June 2016.

Sothesby's in 2018, remotely activating an automatic device that, hidden in the casing/frame, dissected the hard copy of Girl with Balloon (2014) into vertical strips.[4] The work, a multiple, was one of the copies reproducing the mural created by Banksy in London in 2002. In both cases, the increase in cultural and economic valorisation triggers a crisis of the symbolic presence of the artistic sign in its visual evidence and in the materiality of its support and vector, making it necessary for the artists to make a destructive or, more precisely, an auto-destructive gesture.

Looking back at the 20th century, one can see how iconoclasm was brought *to* art and *into* art (in a trans-textual key through work on copies or reproductions). It is also clear that it was understood as a value/functional transformation that was an artistic practice. This was according to the *lignée L.H.O.O.Q.* "rectified ready-made", realised in 1919 by Marcel Duchamp, or according to that of the *tableau-piège* (trap painting) *Utiliser un Rembrandt comme planche à repasser (Marcel Duchamp)* realised by Daniel Spoerri in 1964 and referring to the Duchampian concept of "reciprocal ready-made". In other words, the aesthetic interference between the artistic and non-artistic dimensions of an object – natural or otherwise – stems from the practice of the artist who is capable of both changing the status of an ordinary object and of an artistic object. Thus, an ordinary object becomes a work of art and a work of art is transformed into an ordinary object that is usable, functionally adaptable, and exposed to destruction.

However, what is of interest here does not concern the repertoire of more or less contemporary iconoclasms, but rather the modulations of the iconoclastic gesture[5] in its *unconscious* variants, that is, the gesture that destroys not in its intent, but outcome.

One case among many is the work *Door: 11, rue Larrey Paris 1927* by Marcel Duchamp ("artistic regeneration" of a door of the flat where Duchamp had lived): during the preparation for the International Art Exhibition of the Venice Biennale in 1978,[6] the door was accidentally repainted by the painters of the Giorgione paint shop, who were maintaining the Italian Pavilion where the work was installed.[7] More recently, in

4 https://www.youtube.com/watch?v=vxkwRNIZgdY.

5 Birnbaum (1997).

6 The theme of this Biennale, "Dalla natura all'arte e dall'arte alla natura" ("From nature to art and from art to nature"), engaged the curators Achille Bonito Oliva, Antonio del Guercio, Filiberto Menna and Jean Christophe Amman.

7 The destruction of the original varnish as well as the partial abrasion of the signature and the date caused damage to the work, resulting in monetary and

the context of "Street Noise", an exhibition at P/O/S/T, a gallery in Seoul's Lotte Street Mall, two young visitors interpreted the performance/installation work *Untiled* by artist JonOne as a work with a participatory character and, consequently, used the paints and brushes, conceived by the artist as compositional elements of the work, as tools to intervene, tracing marks[8] on the work itself. These are cases where the focus should not be on the institutional theory of art – which holds that art is a kind of thing whose existence depends on theories[9] – but on the unconsciously iconoclastic act where, due to context and circumstance, the eventuality of the "reciprocal ready-made" is not allowed. In any case, these are unintentional acts that impact the works "destructively" with consequences on their cultural transmissibility.

The question we want to raise is the following: In the field of art, can an act be destructive, constructive, conservative in and of itself, or rather, does it become historically so in relation to someone and something? But *when*? *How*? *Why*? According to what conception, idea, theory of *history* and *art history*? "Art", as we understand it, thought of as an "extended field"[10] and referring both to the movement of images[11] and to the technologically based moving image.

II. Iconoclasm and Iconoclash

According to Bruno Latour, "Icono*clasm* is when we know what is going on at the moment of destroying something and we know the motivations behind what seems to be a clear project of destruction. [...] Icono*clash*, on the other hand, is when one does not know, or hesitates, or is at a loss when faced with an action for which there is no way of knowing, without further investigation, whether it is destructive or constructive."[12] Icono*clash* – a word composed of the two terms *icono* ("image", "icon")

compensable damages. A long legal dispute ensued, which was only concluded in 2011, between the Fondazione Biennale di Venezia, the insurance companies, the Giorgione company and the owner of the work, the gallery owner/collector Fabio Sargentini, who had exhibited it at the L'Attico Gallery in Rome in November 1973.

8 https://abcnews.go.com/International/young-couple-mistakenly-vandalizes-440000-painting-south-korea/story?id=76844914.

9 Dickie (1974) and (1997); Danto (1997); Genette (1994) and (1997).

10 Krauss (1979).

11 Michaud (2006) 26.

12 Latour (2002).

and *clash* – is the title of an exhibition curated by Bruno Latour and Peter Weibel, presented at the Center for Art and Media (ZKM) in Karlsruhe in 2002. The exhibition aimed to analyse "[...] only those places, objects or situations where there is an ambiguity, a hesitation, an iconoclash, about how to interpret the production and destruction of images". The intention was to "understand how the question of the construction/destruction of images is posed in the Western tradition"[13] by investigating, in the contemporary world, the *clash* on the status of images within the fields of art, science and religion. By "image", Latour means "[...] every sign, every work of art, inscription or material image [picture], which acts as a mediation to access something else".[14] And it is precisely the *image as mediation to access something else* that is the problem. On the other hand, from an anthropological perspective, Hans Belting believes that *mediation* implies a *medium* that is not immediately the image itself: "A medium is a form or transmits the very form in which we perceive the images. [...] The politics of image relies on their mediality [...]. The politics of images needs a medium to turn an image into a picture".[15] Belting therefore perceives the visibility of the image through a process of transformative mediation and transmission. The medium is the transmissive or host medium that images need for visibility.[16] According to Belting:

> "The link of physical images with the mental images into which we translate them may explain the zeal inherent in any iconoclasm to destroy physical images. The iconoclasts wanted to eliminate images in the collective imagination, but in fact they could destroy only their media. What the people could no longer see would, it was hoped, no longer live in their imagination. The violence against physical image served to extinguish mental images."[17]

This continues to apply to contemporary iconoclasm, which also aims to prevent the public "visibility" of images by activating a relationship between memory and the negation of the image. Think, for example, about the physical destruction of regimes' public sculptures in the former Soviet Union or Iraq. This use of visual media was designed to imprint themselves in the collective imagination. In this case we are faced with iconoclasm understood as a practice of symbolic liberation and as censor-

13 Ibid. 300.
14 Ibid. 290.
15 Ibid. 305.
16 Belting (2002).
17 Belting (2005).

ship/erasure. The aim is to hide or destroy certain images in order to protect others.[18] From this perspective, one can go into the "archaeology of hatred" expressed by Latour or observe the archive *at work* (*anarchive*) as defined by Jacques Derrida in *Mal d'archive*.[19] However, it is the icono*clash* that acts and reveals itself in the ambiguity between preservation and deletion, between preservation and loss, between protection and destruction of images on the levels of cataloguing/documentation/preservation/restoration after the "digital turn". While considering these plans in an interrelated way – a fortiori for technologically based complex works (installation, multichannel, environmental and interactive) – the focus will be on digitisation processes affecting preservation and restoration practices of non-native digital single-channel film and video works.

III. Digital Preservation and Restoration

Digital preservation and restoration attempt the impossible task of counteracting the physical and chemical degradation of media (film or magnetic tape) and the obsolescence of reproduction tools. Thus, to make cultural transmission possible, it is necessary to separate the image from its original support through the digital scanning of the film, the digital reception of the electronic signal, and the transfer and transformation of the analogue into the computer domain. From an anthropological and technological perspective, this process evidences the dynamics of "survival" of contemporary images.

From the study of the "archives" of moving images and the decision-making models underlying restoration programmes, a risk emerges that concerns not simply the selection and elimination method, termed "corruption", but the act which severs the relationship between the work and its historical-artistic context (*the relation between work and context*).[20] This is an iconoclash act because it implies the obliteration of the modes of reception and sensorium of a given historical moment. The emphasis on what becomes common in the modes of perception relates, in political and aesthetic terms, to the "medium" in Benjamin's sense. In the different versions of the essay *The Work of Art in the Age of its Technical Reproducibility* (1935–36), the focus is on the historical variability of collective sensory per-

18 Latour (2002) 328.
19 Derrida (1995).
20 Gamboni (1997).

ception. And what Walter Benjamin defines as medium is the place where the collective sensory perception historically finds organisation through a series of contingencies which, in modernity, concern technology, imply devices that function as instruments of mass communication.[21] This is the perceptive and constitutive dimension that history and time assign to a given work. However, it is not our time and history, but those in which the work was conceived/realised. In this sense, the work of preservation should include not only the preservation of the artistic *intentio* (the cardinal principle of restoration protocols), but also the forms of aesthetic experience and the modes of production/reception of the sensory context.

The current digital re-meditation of non-digital images in the social space occurs through multiple displays which are still experienceable, but also transformable.[22] This is because they imply the cancellation of the material and sensorial difference they carry.[23] Similarly, preservation and restoration interventions often remove differences (concerning materials, types of supports, formats and reproduction devices) since they support the digital "rebirth" of analogue images as "a reconfiguration of contemporary spectacular pleasure".[24] On the one hand, there is a colonisation process of the gaze and the "sensitive". On the other hand, there is an "iconoclash memory" justified by creative reuse, as a hypothetical valorisation of archive images. This is perhaps the case of the film *They Shall Not Grow Old* made in 2018 by Peter Jackson.

Evidently, there is not an awareness of acting on the concrete media historicity of moving images, invalidating them even in their quality of visual sources. In fact, they are historical sources which can be read from wide and multiple documentary perspectives.[25] Even the search for "original visual qualities" (an issue that would require new in-depth studies)[26] is likely to fall into the gravitational order of icono*clash* or the act of unconsciously destroying images in a sort of "benevolent vandalism". One thinks, for example, of the *effacing/embellishing* practices indulged in by certain digital

21 Benjamin (1935/36, 2008).
22 Groys (2008).
23 Bellour (2012) 50.
24 Catanese (2013) 76, 82.
25 Marcenò (2008).
26 The concept of "*originale*" defines a quality referring to being "compatible" and "not equivalent to" the "*originaria*" version. Also, with respect to media provenance, this has to do with the documentary "integrity" of the work and the preservation of the modes of reception of the era in which the work was produced, as well as its aesthetic and cultural history.

restoration operations or the interventions made on the form and matter of the analogue image that betray a positivist and evolutionary-deterministic idea of technologies that can be summarised as follows: "In the past, if one could have had them, one would have used contemporary technologies". With statements of this kind, it is unclear what is being said and, above all, what one is doing. This is even though it is clear that in the processes of *preservation* and *restoration*[27] the digital remediation system (hardware and software devices) implies, in all its levels of application, many levels of transformation.[28]

The software automation should be the subject of further investigation. This "automation", in fact, erases defects or mechanical corruptions (stains, dust, scratches on the emulsion), imperfections, dulling, physical-chemical deterioration of the film (decomposition of the emulsion) or drop out, "speakle", and create impulsive noises of the magnetic tape etc. However, in doing so, they produce "artefacts" in the image, modifying its configuration. How to restore the material dimension (without avoiding comparison with the practices of Glitch Art)?

How to handle colour interpretation? How to prevent the software from deleting – as it does for defects – what appears as a light effect (shimmers, reflections, rapid movements) on a single frame? The automatic process, in fact, "provides that all extraneous elements, present in a single frame or with abnormal movement behaviour, are eliminated".[29] These are techniques for translating "figures" and "figural" aspects of the image that involve interdisciplinary knowledge, research and study.

Certain digital restoration operations, therefore, intervene on the form as well as the material of the analogue image. The criteria guiding the automatic correction process (embellishing), those orienting the restorer's eye (the human eye) and implying the tendencies of the spectator's taste define the aesthetic *koinè* of contemporary audio-visual languages. This is based on the icono*clash* gesture exercised through the computer application, "the digital". This is both a (transient) device of preservation (preser-

27 A clarification of terminology: "Preservation" designates operations undertaken to protect the artifact that do not involve a "deliberate and radical" transformation of its "material appearance" and form (direct preservation; environmental preservation). The term "restoration", on the other hand, defines a type of programmatic intervention that introduces visible transformations. Preservation and restoration define the activity of conservation.

28 Saba (2013).

29 Catanese (2013) 98; Fossati (2018) 84.

vation and/or restoration) of delivery "to future memory", but also of re-programming[30] of the "digitised" works.

Evidently, direct conservation actions risk leading to a rather paradoxical situation whereby the digital restoration of the analogue moving image is pursued from an aesthetic point of view. Simultaneously, its historical dimension is systematically erased, as it is adapted (i.e., subjected to a principle of "assimilation") to the qualitative resolutions that are characteristic of contemporary digital images in the name of the "necessary" technological convergence of the media and the adaptive logic which convergence seems to require. On the one hand, the re-mediation system and protocols provide for the documentation of restoration processes and the reversibility and repeatability of the processes. On the other hand, however, computer tools automatically produce deletions or artefacts without a restorer's knowledge which results in consequences that are more destructive the more visually and sonically complex the moving image is.

For example, in the restored version of the film *Nostra Signora dei Turchi* (1968) by Carmelo Bene, the "black background" of some sequences, i.e., the black background that the actor's body emerges from, is an artefact of the re-editing system. Indeed, it erased the transparencies of the foreground/background relationship, the depth of field, the trajectories and the very dynamics of the camera movements. The results of the comparative tests for the definition of the digital restoration protocol of the film *We Can't Go Home Again* (1973) by Nicolas Ray[31] are differently exemplary (Figs. 1 and 2).

In these and other cases, in addition to defining the *text* of the *work*[32] to be preserved, restored and transmitted culturally (reference copy), the question of lost "information" produced through preservation and restoration practices arises. But how can analogue images be "saved" without indulging in the exhibition of the "patina", in the fetishism of the support – a support that cannot and must not be considered as *déchet*, an analogue waste – or, on the contrary, without exposing it to physical-chemical destruction?

30 N. Bourriaud, *Postproduction. Culture as Screenplay: How Art Reprograms the World*, Sternberg Press, London 2002.

31 Fossati (2018) 307–315.

32 The multidisciplinary methodology implies historical, semiotic, philological and analytical skills capable of restoring the "text" (*restitutio textus*) of the film work and, therefore, skills capable of reconstructing the production conditions (technological apparatus, executive techniques), the historical and cultural context, the modes of reception, the imaginaries, the ideologies, the optical unconscious.

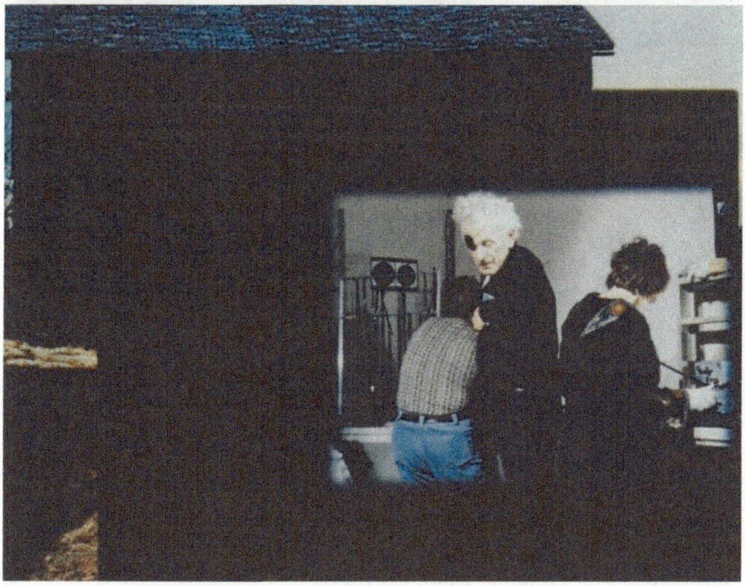

Figs. 1 and 2: Comparison of the test results of workflow for the restoration of the film We Can't Go Home Again (1973), Nicholas Ray

It is no coincidence that artistic practices are also concerned with these issues. The physical-chemical ruin can take on an ecstatic/spectacular register, as for example in the short film *Stadt in Flammen* (1984, Super8, col., 5') by Schmelzdahin (Jochen Lempert, Jochen Müller and Jürgen Reble),[33] or it can take on a *mnestic/archival* value as in *Trasparenze* (1998, Hi8 video, col., sound, 6') by Yervant Gianikian and Angela Ricci Lucchi. *Stadt in Flammen* is the outcome of a project in which a film (supporting a B-movie), unearthed from the garden after six months, was dissected into frames whose images, intensely attacked by bacteria, are assembled in a fractional montage (Fig. 3).

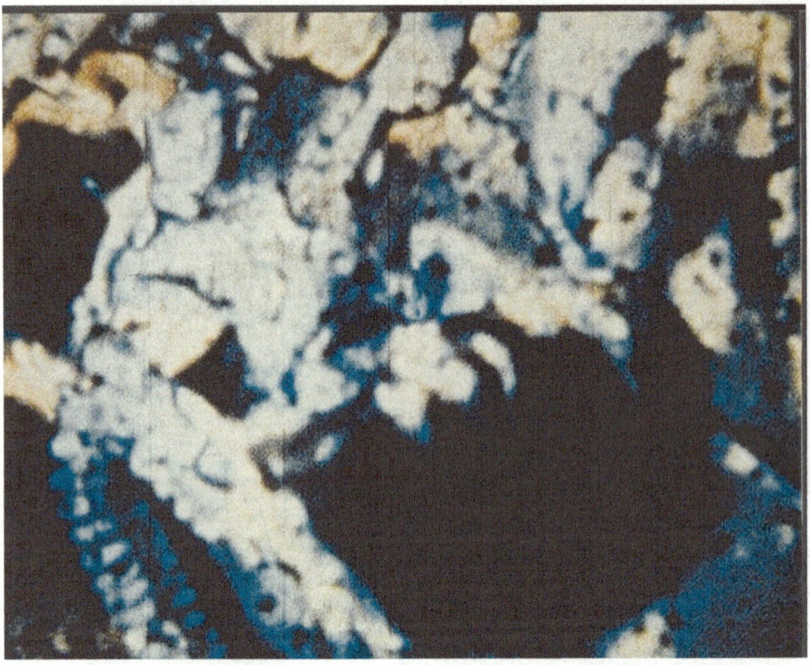

Fig. 3: Still of "Stadt in Flammen" (1984), Schmelzdahin

Trasparenze by Gianikian and Ricci Lucchi[34] began as a video letter (addressed to a friend) from the remains of a reel shot by Luca Comerio on Mount Adamello during World War I. It is a work about "self-deletion",

33 http://www.schmelzdahin.de/stadtinflammenfilm.htm.

34 https://www.pinterest.de/pin/743938432187616615/.

a reflection on the decomposition of nitrate film, the erasure of images, and the chemical and historical amnesia of the archive. About ten years earlier, in 1986, this film material and the images inscribed in it had been used by Gianikian and Ricci Lucchi to make the war part of their film *Dal Polo all'Equatore*.[35] In the process of decomposition, the film, which could no longer be unwound, was transformed into a single block. The torn support, the fluorescence and the faded colours remain transparent until the images shot by Comerio were completely erased (Figs. 4 to 7).

Figs. 4 to 7: Stills of Trasparenze (1998), Gianikian and Ricci Lucchi

IV. *Provisional Conclusion*

To conclude (on a provisional basis): What is no longer visible in the image and of the image is lost and erased. Our sensitivity to entropy attests to the fact that we cannot transform what is impermanent into something lasting. However, images never cease to bring out, aesthetically and histori-

35 Gianikian/Ricci Lucchi (2014) 36.

cally, how we think, look and feel them and what, through them, we do beyond and against all our intentions, whether conscious or unconscious.

References

Bellour, Raymond (2012): *La Querelle des dispositifs: Cinéma – Installations, Expositions* (Paris: P.O.L. 2012)

Belting, Hans (2002): *Bild-Anthropologie – Entwürfe für eine Bildwissenchaft* (Paderborn: Wilhelm Fink Verlag 2002)

Belting, Hans (2005): 'Image, Medium, Body: A New Approach to Iconology', 31 Critical Inquiry, No. 2 (Winter 2005) 308 – 319 (online available at https://culture.hse.ru/data/2013/12/10/1339178276/Hans%20Belting.%20Image,%20Medium,%20Body.pdf)

Benjamin, Walter (2008): *The Work of Art in the Age of Its Technological Reproducibility and other Writings on Media*, in: Jennings, Michael W./Doherty, Brigid/Levon, Thomas Y. (eds) (Cambridge/MA and London: The Belknap Press of Harvard University Press 2008)

Birnbaum, Daniel (1997): 'The Art of Destruction', Frieze Nr. 35 (June-August 1997) 37–38 (https://www.frieze.com/article/art-destruction)

Bourriaud, Nicolas (2002): *Postproduction – Culture as Screenplay: How Art Reprograms the World* (London: Sternberg Press 2002)

Brandi, Cesare (2005): *Theory of Restoration* (Firenze: Nardini 2005)

Catanese, Rossella (2013): *Lacune binarie – Il restauro dei film e le tecnologie digitali* (Rome: Bulzoni 2013)

Danto, Arthur C. (1997): *After the End of Art – Contemporary Art and the Pale of History* (Washington: Board of Trustees of the National Gallery of Art 1997)

Derrida, Jacques (1995): *Mal d'archive – Une impression freudienne* (Paris: Éditions Galiée 1995)

Dickie, George (1974): *Art and the Aestethic – An Istitutional Analysis* (Ithaka, N.Y.: Cornell University Press, 1974)

Dickie, George (1997): *The Art Circle – A Theory of Art* (Chicago: Chicago Spectrum Press 1997)

Didi-Huberman, Georges (1992): *Ce que nous voyons, ce qui nous regarde* (Paris: Éditions du Minuit 1992)

Fossati, Giovanna (2018): *From Grain to Pixel – The Archival Life of Film in Transition* (Amsterdam: Amsterdam University Press, 3rd edition 2018)

Gamboni, Dario (1997): *The Destruction of Art – Iconoclasm and Vandalism Since the French Revolution* (London: Reaktion Books 1997)

Genette, Gérard (1994): *L'Œuvre de l'art, 1 – Immanence et transcendance* (Paris: Éditions du Seuil 1994)

Genette, Gérard (1997): *L'Œuvre de l'art, 2 – La relation esthétique* (Paris: Éditions du Seuil 1997)

Gianikian, Yervant/Ricci Lucchi, Angela (2014): 'Secolo cane-lupo', in: Galasso, Elisabetta/Scotini, Marco: *Politiche della memoria – Documentario e archivio* (Rome: DerviceApprodi 2014)

Groys, Boris (2008): *The Art Power* (Cambridge/Ma.: The MIT Press 2008)

Kim, Hyun Soo (2021): 'Young couple mistakenly vandalizes $ 440,000 painting in South Korea' (3 April 2021, https://abcnews.go.com/International/young-couple-mistakenly-vandalizes-440000-painting-south-korea/story?id=76844914)

Krauss, Rosalind (1979): 'Sculpture in the Expanded Field', 8 October (Spring 1979) 30–44

Latour, Bruno (2002): 'What is Iconoclash?', in: Latour, Bruno/Weibel, Peter: *Iconoclash – Beyond the Image-Wars in Science, Religion and Art* (Karlsruhe/Cambridge, MA: MIT Press 2002)

Marcenò, Serena (2008): 'Metis e Penelope – Questioni di metodo tra scritture, pitture e discorsi', in: Carbone, Andrea L. (ed), *Iconografia e storia dei concetti* (Palermo: :duepunti edizioni 2008)

Michaud, Phillippe-Alain (2006): *Le Mouvement Des Images – The Movement of Images* (Paris: Editions du Centre Pompidou 2006)

Saba, Cosetta (2013): 'Media Art and Digital Archive', in: Noordegraaf, Julia/Saba, Cosetta/Le Maître, Barbara/Hediger, Vincenz (eds): *Preserving and Exhibiting Media Art – Challenges and Perspectives* (Amsterdam: Amsterdam University Press 2013) 101–120

Photo credits

Figs. 1–2: Courtesy of the Nicholas Ray Foundation and Eye Filmmuseum

Fig. 3: http://www.schmelzdahin.de/stadtinflammenfilm.htm

Figs. 4–7: https://www.pinterest.de/pin/743938432187616615/

Part 4
Binary Encoding, Artificial Intelligence and the Dissolution of the Visual Object

Chapter 11
Semioethics of the Visual Fake

Massimo Leone

Una de multis face nuptiali
digna periurum fuit in parentem
splendide mendax et in omne virgo
nobilis aevum.
(Horace, *Carmina*, III, 11)

I. The Intimate Nature of the Visual Fake

The ethics of images and fakes are intimately related. Through images, the human species can represent and evoke not only what is, but also what is not, giving rise to illusions. That is also the case for the verbal language, as words too allow human beings to describe what is not. Yet an essential semiotic difference subsists between the fakes found in images and those in words. It can be appropriately explained by Charles S. Peirce's semiotics theory. Images are predominantly iconic; their fabric can be in part conventional, yet the core of them is motivated. What they represent is recognized out of material similarity with how they represent it. Words, on the contrary, are largely symbolic: it is through a silent convention that they confer meaning. This difference lies in the foundation of language and is crucial regarding the fake in images. Albeit blatantly preposterous, images are inherently truthful, and this reverberates upon what they tell. For example, the counterfeited photograph of a political leader supposedly caught in obscene behavior could be recognized as farfetched, either because of its material qualities (when the forgery's quality is poor) or because of its genre (such as a caricature), yet it still confers meaning derived from its motivation. Thus, even a fake image of an event that has never taken place is a true image because it represents it through a materiality that follows the semiotic rules of iconicity.

The intrinsic motivation of an image also subsists when it lacks a proper figurative level. This occurs when the image fails to represent any recognizable objects through verbal language. Indeed, one can always recognize a shape, a topology, or a color (or even a component of it, like a hue, a level of brightness or saturation). An abstract painting, from this point of view, entails an ontology that an abstract word (a nonsensical neologism, for instance), does not. It consists of a materiality that always refers to the primary existence of shaped light, to a pre-existing matter. Words too, in both their written and oral expression, must rely on matter, such as the light contrasts of typography, or those of sound, yet this reference is already a symbolical one, not an iconic one like in images. The light patterns that underpin the shape, topology, and colors of an image already hold an iconic relation with what they might mean. This is because the human species perceives the world *inter alia* through images, though such characteristics are only partially matched by primitive image-making technologies such as drawing or painting (lack of color, lack of three dimensions, etc.). Even in the most extreme case, such as abstract paintings consisting of white canvases, the frame designates them as images by distinguishing them as signs from an external reality. Whereas the simple white color references the subjacent matter of light, the frame transforms the light into an image that resembles it.

II. The Visual Fake, Technology, and Evolution

It follows that the motivation of images is inevitably impacted by the evolution of technology. Today a prehistoric cave painting of a buffalo is still considered quite realistic as humans recognize a buffalo in the image and additionally, through its semiotic meaning. They are even surprised by the level of iconicity that the image displays. Yet, this surprise is always temporally qualified. Should a buffalo be drawn similarly today, it would be received as an expression of primitive art, not as a realistic representation. The reason is simple: image technology has evolved. Cave paintings may astonish for their primitive realism, yet 3D virtual moving images of buffalos are now marveled at for their *current* realism. Technological evolution can be seen through different semiotic ideologies. Humanities and social sciences, with notable exceptions, generally adopt an ideology of culturalization: phenomena involving human beings and their societies are such because of their contextual circumstances. From this perspective, digital virtual reality is no more realistic than cave paintings, but just differently so; cave paintings were, *mutatis mutandis*, the virtual reality of prehistorical times.

This view has an advantage. It helps contextualize and therefore, relativize the power of images. It underlines that, no matter how motivated they might look, their iconicity always at least partially results from language, from a convention. As the convention changes, the level of perceived realism of the image also changes. This phenomenon is evident especially in those epochs where the development of technology of representation is fast in relation to the average span of human life. The prehistorical human might have experienced this change too, for instance when first a certain pigment was used in cave paintings, yet it is unlikely that, in such a human's lifetime, this experience of radical technological change might have been encountered repeatedly. For the present-day human being, on the contrary, technology changes on a monthly, if not, daily basis. In the domain of representation, many of those who were born when color television had not yet been diffused are still alive, and in the meantime have experienced the advent of digital screens, flat screens, skyrocketing image resolution, virtual reality, augmented reality, and so on.

III. Conventionality and Motivation in the Technology of the Visual Fake

On the one hand, the increasing development of technology of representation seems to confirm the hypothesis of those who embrace a culturalist ideology: once a spectator is accustomed to the resolution of a 4K screen, setting the standard of ultimate realism, television watched with previous technology inevitably gives an impression of unrealism. This effect of 'vintage vision', however, is increasingly common. That means that, whereas conventionality has codetermined the reception of iconicity throughout the evolution of the species, the speed of its change has shown a tendency to increase along human history, probably out of cumulative impact: new technology begets newer technology, and so on and so forth. Thus far, in the domain of the technology of representation, this acceleration has been linear: the conventionality that frames the resemblance of images is changing at increasing pace. On the other hand, the alternative ideology considers that technology of representation does not only change but also evolves. It proposes that new representation and display technology allows one not simply to see differently, but also to see better. Improvement is generally defined in terms of realism: the less a gap is perceived between reality (or, rather, the non-technologically mediated perception of it) and representation (or, rather, the technologically mediated perception of reality), the better.

Supporters of the culturalist stance, traditionally including most semioticians, usually deconstruct this view. In their mind, there is not such a thing as a non-technologically mediated perception of reality. Reality is always perceived according to some habits, as the father of semiotics, Charles S. Peirce, would suggest. Further, these habits are shaped through social interactions within a community of interpreters, giving rise to a perceptual common sense. According to this view, we do not see better through new digital technology, but we get used to seeing better through it. There is no difference, then, between the realism of the cave painting and that of virtual reality since they both result from a cultural construction. Although there is some truth in this statement (iconicity always implies a frame of conventionality) and evidence tends to confirm it (perfectly realistic representation technology becomes vintage when supplanted by new devices), this view too, when expressed in extreme terms, becomes unreasonable. Denying any cultural conventionality in technological iconicity ultimately entails absurd consequences; but denying any natural iconicity in it also does. There is, indeed, a dimension of semiotic habit in perception, yet perception is not only that, for its conventionality must root itself in a neurophysiological ground shaped through natural evolution. On the one hand, it is true that humans get used to new representation technology, often yielding to the rhetoric of their perceptual proficiency. On the other hand, it is also true that they also get surprised by it, finding that novel devices for visual representation and display allow them, the human beings, to sensorially and mentally access images with unprecedented realism. The "reality effect" of representations is always a matter of conventions and habits, a symbolical matter; yet it is also a matter of material relations and prompts, an indexical matter.

The iconicity of images stems at the crossroad between these two dimensions: an image seems real because observers are used to its reality effect, but also because it matches the physiology of the human perception as resulting from a natural, biological evolution. History confirms it even better than anthropology. When the first Jesuits started proselytizing in 16th-century theretofore secluded Japan, they often displayed Christian paintings that shocked the audience. The reason, however, was not the content but the form. The Japanese were struck, and sometimes even converted, by Renaissance perspective, by the realism of its three-dimensional illusion. The reality effect of the representation relied on a convention, yet it did not solely rely on it. Even Japanese observers who had never been in contact with this optical and representative device could realize that it was able to construct images in an unprecedented way and impress the perception of the audience so that the realism of the representation could be transferred to the realism of the represented. In some cases, conversions took place because the Christian deities seemed to jump out of the canvases and share the same physical space of the observers.

IV. The Third Way of Semiotics

Between an ideology of radical cultural contextualization and one of radical naturality, semiotics proposes a reasonable midway, suggesting that iconicity is a cultural phenomenon, yet it is influenced by technological change, and in particular, by its speed and relation to the physiology of perception. Increasing pace in the advent of ever new technologies of representation and display implies a more rapid destabilization of perceptual habits, begetting in turn an effect of surprise and reality that is often naturalized also for commercial and persuasive purposes. Semiotics is called to debunk the pseudo-natural allure of new technology. It is also expected to somehow debunk the debunking. That means that, in certain circumstances, new technology actually increases the realism of representation not only in terms of cultural iconicity but also in those of indexical iconicity. Humans must certainly become accustomed to wearing a virtual reality helmet, yet what they are become familiarized to is the unprecedented representation of a three-dimensional, immersive space. Its persuasive power, in many cases, works exactly like it worked in the perspective of 16th-century Jesuit paintings in Japan: matching the physiology of perception, it induces a disrupting suspension of disbelief. On the one hand, semiotics must unveil the cultural conventions that underpin the reality effect of technology of representation and display. On the other hand, it should not overemphasize the rhetorical dimension of technology, either. The conclusion that observers do not actually see what they see is absurd and somewhat frustrating, and so is the hint that, if they were aware of the secret conventional roots of the lures of representation, they would see differently.

On the contrary, semiotics should encompass the idea that, if a community of perceivers, observers, and interpreters so promptly adopt a new representative convention, it is also the case because of the revolutionary way it interacts with the neurophysiology of perception in the species. This balanced approach entails important consequences as regards the ethics of images. It points at the necessity to develop a 'semioethics' of representation that is both culturally and biologically grounded. It considers, for instance, that images are what they are, and entail the potential ethical dangers that they entail, not only because of the symbolical conventions that underpin their iconicity, but also increasingly because of the impression of realism that they trigger in the human physiology of perception. Such composite reflection is urgent, especially regarding the persuasive effects that images can bring about. Considering images as exclusively based on cultural conventions is reductive, for it fails to explain both the persistence of their phenomenological power and the impact of new technology of visual representation in relation to human perception. Indeed, the power of images is based also on the fact that they interact with a specific innate feature of human physiology and cognition, as well as on the fact that the quality of such interaction is modified by the specific nature of the technology that is used for the production and display of images themselves.

A crucial issue in this domain is how images contribute to what is popularly called a "suspension of disbelief". That is, to obliterating the discrepancy between the representing image and the represented reality that the former signifies. When the represented image conveys stark realism, it replaces the same reality that they represent. Thus, the representing image appears as indistinguishable from the latter. Such is the case of every kind of trompe-l'oeil (a pictorial genre that seeks to give the illusion that a painting actually is what it represents): the reality effect of the image is such that iconicity is replaced by indexicality. What is seen does not only represent a signified reality, but *is* such reality, at least in the delusional observers' eyes. Mentioning such an extreme case of suspension of disbelief is important here because it could be hypothesized that much of the most recent technological change in the domain of visual representation and display aims to increase proficient trompe-l'oeil. More and more, the digital image aims at eliminating any 'uncanny valley' effect to develop a sort of semiotic autonomy from the represented reality. That leads to the ethical issue of the fake: the present-day hyper-realistic digital image presents itself not as a fiction but as a fact and, therefore, as a fake.

Yet technological advancement makes this fake more and more indistinguishable from the reality it represents, and increasingly able to aptly dissimulate its own nature of representation. If the history of representation technology is conceived not only in cultural, but evolutionary terms, it becomes important to distinguish between the different kinds of trompe-l'oeil that have emerged throughout history. On the one hand, it is true that the hyper-realistic image of a digital face fabricated through contemporary artificial intelligence is an instance of trompe-l'oeil as much as a Renaissance trompe-l'oeil painting. Yet the technological difference between the two instances cannot be ignored either: the latter would hardly present itself as a perfect fake, as a completely illusory replica of the reality it represented. Rather, its purpose was to trigger a temporary suspension of perceptual disbelief, to extoll the skilfulness of the painter rather than permanently deceive the spectator. Proper fake paintings, conversely, started to be produced and circulated because they had a market and they were sold and bought. Their aim, however, was not to attract admiration for the forger but to deceive the buyer. Giovanni Morelli's method of connoisseurship was specifically devised to unmask such forgeries and prevent buyers from acquiring fakes of great painters.

Yet in this case too, both a cultural and cognitive semiotics of the fake must emphasize not only similarities but also, and crucially, differences between the fake paintings of the pre-digital era and the fake images of the digital epoch. Advances in the digital technology of images has led to the creation of extreme trompe-l'oeil, to fakes that, unlike in the past, any human eye can no longer unmask. To detect the fake, the same machines that have contributed to create it must be invoked to unmask it. That leads to a whole new area of investigation, in the domain of the ethics of images, precisely concerning the ethics of digital fakes.

V. Semiotics as Discipline of the Fake

The fake is a key theme in several fields of investigation. In natural sciences, it defines the intentionally false: methodology and research must recognize it to gain a truthful understanding of reality. In the humanities, it is the counterpart of authenticity, the threatening shadow of western thought since its very onset: humanity should seek what is true and avoid falsity, treasure the authentic and ban the fake. Ethical doctrines and also religions emphasize the perniciousness of falsity and the dangerousness of forgery for social cohesion and harmony: Lies, that is, intentionally false but somehow believable representations of reality, must be avoided. Yet the possibility to represent, through language, not only what is, but also what is not, is a consubstantial feature of the human cognition. Humans are endowed with a unique capability for creating and using mendacious simulacra of the world, including the inner and invisible world of their emotions. After all, the human ability to create believable fictional representations of reality is parallel to the skill of creating believable fictional realities in the arts. Throughout history and across cultures, human communities have, therefore, devoted an immense amount of their energy to the central social issue of 'handling' the fake. Philosophers have sought to define falsity, stigmatizing it in most schools of thought. In some cases, however, they have also turned it into an element of philosophical speculation (from the Sophists to the Catholic casuistry, from Nietzsche to Derrida and Deconstructionism); ethical and religious leaders have also underlined the social hazard of systematic lying. Further, writers and artists have refined to the utmost the rhetoric of fictional storytelling and representation, and natural scientists have devised methods and procedures to recognize falsity and corroborate truth; social scientists have also sought to understand the motivations, processing, and effects of falsity; political thinkers and legal scholars have sought for the best strategies to limit and control the spreading of falsehood in social relations.

Yet there is only one discipline, in both natural sciences and humanities, where the fake is the primary object of investigation. That discipline is semiotics, the science of signification and communication. Umberto Eco, one of its founding fathers, defined it in his 1975 *Trattato di semiotica generale* ["Treatise of General Semiotics"] as "the discipline that studies everything that can be used to lie".[1] This definition can be taken as a point of departure. Indeed, although the fake is part of human cognition, and although practices and theories of the fake have characterized the entire history of humanity, technological change deeply impacts the human culture of forgery.

As it was suggested earlier, rock art in Lascaux or other prehistorical sites in the world were already a kind of fictional representation. The Palaeolithic man would already decorate caves with idealizing images of wild animals. Yet, the contemporary visitor can now explore a museum in Dordogne that is an exact replica of the authentic site, with no perceptible difference. 3D digital scanning and other advanced technologies have enabled the construction of a fake that can be experienced as authentic. Visitors are told that what they enter is a replica, of course. In an increasing number of circumstances, however, present-day individuals unknowingly interact with visual fakes without being given the opportunity to distinguish reality from fiction, truth from imposture. Techniques to produce an illusion of reality and truthfulness also have a long history. Virtuoso trompe-l'oeil paintings, for instance, are quite common in Western art history, and so is the manufacture of deceitful replicas. These have been paralleled, throughout Western art history, by an equally abundant amount of methods to unmask the fake. For instance, the fake unmasked by the already mentioned art connoisseur Giovanni Morelli.

Yet technological advances modify the relation between fake production and fake recognition. For instance, Apple currently invests enormous resources to ensure that facial recognition software on its devices is protected against fakes. Simultaneously, groups of hackers constantly try to overcome these security systems. Compared to the past, however, this race between fake makers and fake spotters is extremely fast, exceeding by far the skills of most present-day technology users. Advanced digital technolo-

1 Eco (1975) 18.

gy currently allows the fake to be more and more realistic, to transcend common skills for fake-detection, but also to be produced and circulated with unprecedented speed, beyond the reach of unspecialized fact-checking. New digital technologies for fake production (from deep fake to 3D-printed masks, from AI holograms to algorithmic trolls and other pseudo-users), together with new digital technologies for fake circulation (all kinds of social networks) are dangerously pushing the world toward the epistemic and social chaos that Western thought, over centuries, has seen as a threatening consequence of forgery and lies. These new technologies can be used to promote the formation of communities whose thoughts, emotions, and actions are manipulated through the rapid creation and frantic dissemination of false but credible digital representations of the world. This can lead to a gullible and impressionable society, conversely, a hyper-sceptical and cynical collective, or even political acquiescence or social polarization.

VI. The Background of Reflection: Advances and Lacunae

As a result of the troubling spread of the digital fake, an entirely new area of investigation has emerged at the crossroad of several social sciences and humanities. It is the area that inquires upon two key buzzwords of the last decade, that is, "fake news" and "post-truth". Literature on this area is abundant in several languages. Many recent studies concentrate on the ideological[2] or political[3] use of fake news, also with reference to specific geo-political contexts;[4] on its digital production,[5] with special emphasis on journalism;[6] on its viral diffusion,[7] especially through social networks;[8] on possible countering methods;[9] on the role of the fake in particularly sen-

2 Van Dijk/Hacker (2018); Fuchs (2020).
3 Farkas/Schou (2020).
4 On the USA, see Lockhart (2018); on Europe, see Eberwein/Fengler/Karmasin (2019); and on Russia, see Roudakova (2017) and Boyd-Barrett (2020).
5 Barnes/Barraclough (2019); Zimdars/McLeod (2020).
6 McNair (2018); Katz/Mays (2019).
7 Safieddine/Ibrahim (2020).
8 Sumpter (2018).
9 Dalkir/Katz (2020).

sitive domains, such as education,[10] food,[11] history,[12] medicine,[13] and sciences.[14] The philosophical issue of the post-truth has also been dealt with by several scholars,[15] from the point of view of the philosophy of communication,[16] moral philosophy,[17] ontology,[18] interdisciplinary thought,[19] as well as through relativistic approaches to the issue of "the genuine fake".[20] Historical perspectives have flourished too, seeking to nuance the novelty of the phenomenon.[21] Language sciences as well have a long tradition of dealing with lies, from the perspective of philosophy of language,[22] linguistics,[23] and semiotics.[24] Whereas for the analytic philosophy of language truth and falsity are logical attributions,[25] for the continental philosophy of language and semiotics are defined in relation to signification.[26]

All the founding fathers of semiotics have dealt with the topic:[27] 1) Charles S. Peirce in the US tradition;[28] 2) the main voices of structural semiotics, as early as a special issue of French key journal Communications devoted to the concept of "vraisemblable" (French for "plausible", "likely", "what seems true"), with essays by Tzvetan Todorov, Gérard Genette, Christian Metz, Julia Kristeva, Gérard Genot, Roland Barthes, and others;[29] Baudrillard famously returned on the topic,[30] and, more recently, a round table on "Post-vérité et démocratie" ("Post-Truth and Democracy") was

10 Peters (2018).
11 Schwarcz (2019).
12 De Baets (2018).
13 Fainzang (2016).
14 Arnold (2019); Jewett (2020).
15 See McIntyre (2018).
16 Robbito (2020).
17 Phillips (2019).
18 Condello/Andina (2019).
19 Duncan (2018).
20 Pyne (2019), focusing on art forgeries, fake fossils, nature documentaries, synthetic flavors, museum exhibits, Maya codices and Paleolithic replicas.
21 On the Middle Ages, Corran (2018); on the early modern period, Hadfield (2017); on Nazis, O'Shaughnessy (2017); in US history, Cortada/Aspray (2019); throughout western history, Denery (2015); Fraser (2020).
22 Michaelson/Stokke (2018).
23 Meibauer (2019).
24 Danesi (2019); Leone (2020); Violaris (2020).
25 Gorlée (2012).
26 Eco (1984).
27 Ousmanova (2004); Lorusso (2018).
28 See Cooke (2014).
29 For these authors, see Todorov (1968).
30 Baudrillard (1987) and (2000).

organized by Jacques Fontanille during the 2019 Congress of the French Association for Semiotics in Lyon, 11–14 June 2019;[31] Umberto Eco wrote extensively on the fake,[32] directed a special issue of the semiotic journal *Versus* on "Fakes, Identity, and the Real Thing",[33] and also dealt with the topic in numerous essays and novels (*Foucault's Pendulum*, *The Cemetery of Prague*, *Numero Zero*); finally, 3) Jurij M. Lotman on several occasions addressed the issue of the fake.[34]

Despite the abundance and variety of scholarly works dealing with the fake, the existent literature shows some conspicuous gaps: 1) a lack of inter-definition: scholars use abstract terms like "falsity", "untruth", "fake", "forgery", etc., as well as "fake news", "post-truth", "deep-fake", etc. in multifarious and, sometimes, contradictory ways; a theoretical and conceptual effort of semantic and pragmatic categorization and classification is in order; 2) a lack of interdisciplinarity: the themes of the construction, circulation, diffusion, and potential debunking of the fake are addressed from several perspectives, which nevertheless often fail to constructively complement each other; 3) a lack of cooperation between humanities and social sciences on the one hand and, on the other hand, natural sciences and engineering; the technology of the fake is currently so complex that it is exceedingly hard, for literati, to have a precise grasp of its generation and dissemination; and lastly 4) a lack of cross-fertilization between scholars and artists; the former have mostly tackled the fake as a problem, as a negative force that mars the waters of rational thinking in every domain of social life; yet, the fake is also the main resource of artistic creation; there is a close relation between the fake and fiction; artists can play a key role, therefore, in exploring the strategies of signification and communication through which a reality effect can be bestowed on a fake, concealing its content of falsity.

VII. The Tasks Ahead for a Semioethics of the Visual Fake

The main aim of a semioethics of fake images is filling these gaps and raising new social, academic, professional, and artistic awareness about the visual fake, its nature and evolution, its risks but also its opportunities,

31 Di Caterino (2020).

32 Eco (1986/1995).

33 Eco (1987), with essays by Eco, Prieto, Calabrese, and others.

34 Andrews (2003) 101; Makarychev/Yatsyk (2017).

its requirements for the citizens of the 21st-century world to fitly navigate through the complex digital representations of their technologically advanced societies. The challenges that lie ahead are related to these gaps, methods for gap-filling, but also to how societies and technologies of the visual fake might evolve in the future. The task ahead, in this domain, is not only philosophical or theoretical, but involves reaching an inter-disciplinary, operational, and proactive definition which can foster cooperation between humanities, social sciences, and natural sciences, scholars and engineers, the academe and non-academic stake holders between researchers and creators. Hence, disciplinary boundaries must be reconsidered to develop new theoretical creativity concerning the creation, circulation, and possible 'handling' of the fake in present-day technologically advanced societies. False representations of reality have accompanied the entire history of the human species and are probably consubstantial to its cognition; yet two new factors radically alter the presence of the visual fake in society. They are both inherent to digital and internet societies: on the one hand, the weight of big data; on the other hand, the new dimensions of digital realism.

A semioethics of the fake must, therefore, involve cross-interdisciplinary reconsideration of the new quantitative and sensorial trends of the fake, through crucial cooperation between heretofore separated approaches. Fake representations of reality gain unprecedented momentum through the social arena and impact with anomalous force on the formation of public opinion. Marginal distortions of truth acquire atypical visibility in social networks through a rhetoric of quantification. Their circulation is pervasive and accompanied by incessant and quantifiable relaying. Their diffusion, moreover, is increasingly fuelled by the adoption of multi-modal and multi-sensorial communication, which exploits the ancestral anthropological appeal of images and other visual artifacts but also enhances them through unmatched digital credibility. Investigation on this new level of fake-production and circulation in digital and internet societies now exceeds the epistemological and methodological framework of humanities alone. To understand the fake today, it is fundamental to come to terms with how machines more and more fabricate, spread, and promote the fake through automatic processes: fake news, post-truth, trolling, etc. are indeed unseizable without a deeply interdisciplinary consideration for 'the algorithms of the fake', that is, for the computational processes and devices of fake production.

Two usually diverging and mutually ignoring perspectives must, therefore, be knitted together: on the one hand, the academic reflection on the emergence of the fake in theoretical framing, social conversation, or scientific investigation; and on the other hand, the development of devices and algorithms to produce and diffuse false representations. Thus, awareness must be increased among technology creators about the social impact of digital advances. This will promote insights among researchers of the rule-changing potential of new digital technologies and the prospective opportunity to use them not only to create social misrepresentations, but also, conversely, to counter and debunk them. Synergy between theoretical and applied investigation is also key regarding the issue that the visual fake is not only a risky element in the formation of common sense, shared knowledge, and public opinion. It is also the basis for plans of action and pragmatic choices. Fake news encourages citizens to vote according to a distorted understanding of societies, as bots and other trolling algorithms influence international relations and can even be hijacked by disruptive political agencies. Thus, post-truth leads to unfounded economic attitudes and modifies the production and circulation of goods in-depth. Further, conspiracy theories condition the reception of science and the role of medicine in society. The visual fake, in other words, becomes a central social actor that mostly plays its role in an uncontrolled manner, altering social relations and trends based on counterfeited representations of reality.

Today, the visual fake is causing societies billions of damage in all sectors of social, economic, and political life. Simultaneously, it is becoming an evil industry for those who wish to profit by its diffusion in society. Instead, such a pernicious industry must be replaced with one that profits from the debunking of false representations of reality. This operation, however, will be impossible to accomplish without a deep knowledge of the 'grammar of figments', that is, the unwritten rules through which a false simulacrum is empowered with pragmatic force, with the ability to produce effects in its cultural and social environment. The rules of this grammar are not constant but vary across the historical epochs, the 'cultures of the visual fake', and depending on the technologies that are used to implement such rules. Yet a cross-cultural and trans-historical 'grammar of the figments' exists, giving rise to a deep-seated anthropology of the visual fake. Writers, painters, sculptors, and more recently also cinema directors and digital artists have long practiced the subtle art of simulacra in a masterly manner. Even without any formal awareness simulacra, they have created, for centuries, perfectly believable fictions, trustworthy figments. The time has come, therefore, to put this 'art of the fake' in dialogue with the 'science of the fake', with the aim of giving an incentive to societies where creativity can thrive, supported by a new digital and internet technology, but without begetting a domain of the fake over truth.

VIII. Conclusions: On Fakes and Viruses

In conclusion, the present essay will now propose a theoretical frame, based on semiotics, for the interdisciplinary study of the visual fake, having in mind the task of rebuilding semioethics. Although different branches of semiotics study language, meaning, signification, and communication with disparate slants, none of them more than Lotman's semiotics (and the "School of Moscow/Tartu") can rely on an extensive and stimulating array of concepts and theories as regards the structure of culture and its evolution. In Lotman's semiotics, the notion of "semiosphere" is key. The production, circulation, and diffusion of meaning in society is studied as though culture were a biosphere of meaning. In this semiosphere, texts and representations arise, are reproduced, proliferate, and spread around from the periphery to the center of the system or, conversely, dwindle, move to the margins, and fall into oblivion. Technology, in this metaphor, represents the infrastructure of devices and processes (from writing to algorithms) that ensures the reproduction of culture as non-genetic memory of the human species. Present-day cultural semiotics, inspired by Lotman as well as by other sources, adopts a systemic approach to culture but does not endorse mechanistic perspectives. Meme theory and socio-biology, indeed, are considered as relevant but not considerate enough of the role of subjects and their intention to shape the trajectories of meaning in society.

The present essay embraces, instead, a humanistic epidemiology of culture which treasures models of diffusion and contagion derived from natural sciences and biology, but considers the specific persuasive force of representations and texts. The increased importance of the quantitative aspect in the study of social networks as platforms for the diffusion of meaning bridges the gap between the natural science of epidemiology and the social science of cultural semiotics. If, in keeping with Lotman, culture is seen as a holistic system, that is as an entity that permeates its sinews according to structured patterns of diffusion, then false visual representations or, more generally, the visual fake, must also be considered in ecological terms. The core challenge ahead is therefore to find a place for the iconic fake in the human ecology of meaning. Would a semiosphere without any visual fake be ideal? This sentiment is more and more present in an epoch where distorted representations of reality mushroom in all domains of public life and hamper the correct course of human interactions. The comparison with the epidemiological framework, however, suggests a different angle.

While this essay is being written, the entire world is struck by the pandemic diffusion of a virus, "SARS-CoV-2". It is natural and understandable that in such circumstances, people start dreaming about a "world without viruses". Yet it is evident to specialists in virology that, despite advances in medicine and pharmaceutics, such expulsion of viruses from the world is not only impossible but also undesirable. Viruses have been always part of the natural environment, constantly contributing to its ecological equilibrium. What is to be dreamt about, then, is not a world without viruses but a world in which humans can coexist with viruses in an acceptable equilibrium. As scientific literature in the field emphasizes, however, such an equilibrium, which has been lasting for millennia, is now being broken by the new technological advances that grant the human species an unprecedented expansion throughout the biosphere. The fake is the cultural equivalent of a virus. Indeed, during the pandemic, many commentators have started to use the word "infodemic" to refer to the uncontrolled and disconcerting diffusion of unreliable, unascertainable, and even, bluntly fake representation of the epidemic.

Nevertheless, dreaming of a world without fakes, where all false representations would be miraculously banned by a superior ethics of language, political control, or technological devices (from truth serums to polygraphs, from captcha tests to automatic fact checking) is as unrealistic as dreaming of nature without viruses. Nobody understood it better than Jonathan Swift in Book IV of *Gulliver's Travels* (1726), which describes the fictional race of the Houyhnhnms, a breed of intelligent horses whose perfect rationality starkly contrasts with the beastly manners of the humanoid Yahoos. Houyhnhnms are endowed with a philosophy and, above all, with a language that is completely void of any political and ethical nonsense. Their language, for instance, does not contain any word for "lie" to the extent that, in order to refer to it, Houyhnhnms must use a circumlocution: "to say a thing that is not". Eliminating all imperfection from thought and all ambiguity from language has long been a human dream. Umberto Eco and other scholars have retraced and analyzed this quest for the perfect language. Yet linguists, semioticians, and philosophers of language know that humans are capable of fake because they are capable of meaning. Only a meaningless society would eliminate any trace of the fake in the world.

Yet, here too, the analogy between fakes and viruses, between pandemics and infodemics, is useful again: rapid advances in the technology of digital and internet communication have enlarged the domain of the visual fake and altered its equilibrium with the areas of controllable, trustworthy meaning. The comparison between proper epidemiology and viral diffusion of the fake can be extended even farther. As it is suggested by scientific investigation, which is now part of common knowledge, most recent pandemics have resulted from a biological process known as "zoonosis". This refers to the aggressive expansion of the human species throughout the planet, leading to atypical contact with other animal species that are hosts and vectors of viruses. Indeed, increased opportunities for "spillover" towards the human species ensue. Mutatis mutandis, it could be said that proliferation of meaning through new digital and internet communication technologies also produces a particular kind of spillover. Discursive domains that were heretofore separated come into close contact and blur, resulting in a "semionosis", that is, the passage of the visual fake from the discursive domain of fiction to that of non-fictional communicative interaction. Science fiction directors have been imagining dystopic scenarios for decades; that has not jeopardized the functionality of the political arena but, on the contrary, has allowed citizens to comprehend even more vividly the social scenarios that they would prefer to avoid. The visual fake in this case, through fiction, is a helpful and effective communication about reality. In the post-truth world, however, fictions do not limit themselves to prefigure scenarios of what human beings might or might not wish for their future, but blur with non-fictional discursive genres, induce adhesion to their representation of reality and, consequently, contribute to the true realization of their imaginary prospects. Conspiracy theories, for instance, do not announce themselves as fictions about the possible dangers of a society that loses control over its pharmaceutical industry, but as accounts of these dangers in a society that already lost it. As subtle as the distinction might seem, its political effects are disruptive: It is one thing to subject such industry to opportune societal control, but another to consider all vaccinations as harmful products of speculation.

A new systemic understanding of the ecology of the visual fake in present-day technologically advanced societies can only be gained through an equally systemic approach, involving the cooperation among sciences, between sciences and humanities, with engineers, and with artists. State of the art gaps and even more importantly, lacunae in the current societal 'handling' of the visual fake, can only be filled through a comprehensive effort to fully understand the role of false representations in human cultures and their interaction with technological progress. On the one hand, that will be conducive to finding new 'cultural vaccinations', that is, short-term remedies that might be engineered through the targeted usage of artificial intelligence (for instance, new devices, apps, and algorithms for fact-checking). On the other hand, such short-term cures deal only with the symptoms, not the underpinning pathogens of the proliferation of the visual fake in society. In the long term, it will be crucial to understand how the technological development in digital and internet communication has coalesced with other economic, infrastructural, and socio-cultural factors to progressively alter the human ecology of the visual fake, leading to uncontrollable spillovers of fictional depictions of reality into non-fictional visual genres.

References

Andrews, Edna (2003): *Conversations with Lotman – Cultural Semiotics in Language, Literature, and Cognition* (Toronto/Buffalo/London: University of Toronto Press 2003)

Arnold, Rolf (2019): *Fake News in Science and Education – Leaving Weak Thinking Behind* (Lanham, MD: Rowman & Littlefield 2019)

Barnes, Curtis Reid/Barraclough, Tom (2019): *Perception Inception – Preparing for Deepfakes and the Synthetic Media of Tomorrow* (Auckland, New Zealand: Brainbox 2019)

Baudrillard, Jean (1987): 'Au-delà du vrai et du faux, ou le malin génie de l'image', 82 Cahiers internationaux de sociologie, nouvelle série, (January-June 1987) 139–145

Baudrillard, Jean (2000): *The Vital Illusion* (New York: The Wellek Library Lectures 2000)

Boyd-Barrett, Oliver (2020): *Russia Gate and Propaganda – Disinformation in the Age of Social Media* (Abingdon/New York: Routledge 2020)

Condello, Angela/Andina, Tiziana (2019): *Post-Truth, Philosophy and Law* (London/New York: Routledge 2019)

Cooke, Elizabeth F. (2014): 'Peirce and the "Flood of False Notions"', in: Thellefsen, Torkild/Sørensen, Bernt/De Waal, Cornelis: *Charles Sanders Peirce in His Own Words – 100 Years of Semiotics, Communication and Cognition* (Boston: De Gruyter Mouton 2014) 325–331

Corran, Emily (2018): *Lying and Perjury in Medieval Practical Thought – A Study in the History of Casuistry* (Oxford: Oxford University Press 2018)

Cortada, James W./Aspray, William (2019): *Fake News Nation – The Long History of Lies and Misinterpretations in America* (Lanham, MD: Rowman & Littlefield 2019)

Dalkir, Kimiz/Katz, Rebecca (2020): *Navigating Fake News, Alternative Facts, and Misinformation in a Post-Truth World* (Hershey, PA: Information Science Reference 2020)

Danesi, Marcel (2019): *The Art of the Lie – How the Manipulation of Language Affects Our Mind* (Guilford, CT: Prometheus Books 2019)

De Baets, Antoon (2018): *Crimes against History* (London/New York: Taylor and Francis 2018)

Denery, Dallas G. (2015): *The Devil Wins – A History of Lying from the Garden of Eden to the Enlightenment* (Princeton, NJ: PUP 2015)

Di Caterino, Angelo (2020): 'Fake News – Une mise au point sémiotique', 123 Actes Sémiotiques (2020) 1–8 (online available at https://www.unilim.fr/actes-semiotiques/6445)

Duncan, Grant (2018): *The Problem of Political Trust – A Conceptual Reformulation* (London/New York: Routledge 2018)

Eberwein, Tobias/Fengler, Susanne/Karmasin, Matthias (2019): *Media Accountability in the Era of Post-truth Politics – European Challenges and Perspectives* (Abingdon/New York: Routledge 2019)

Eco, Umberto (1975): *Trattato di semiotica generale* (Milan: Bompiani 1975)

Eco, Umberto (1984): 'On Fish and Buttons – Semiotics and Philosophy of Language', 48 Semiotica (1984) 97–118

Eco, Umberto (1987): 'Fakes, Identity and the Real Thing', special issue of Versus 46 (Milan: Bompiani 1987)

Eco, Umberto (1995): *Faith in Fakes – Travels in Hyperreality* (first published 1986; cited after London: Minerva 1995)

Fainzang, Sylvie (2016): *An Anthropology of Lying – Information in the Doctor-patient Relationship* (Abingdon/New York: Routledge 2016)

Farkas, Johan/Schou, Jannick (2020): *Post-truth, Fake News and Democracy – Mapping the Politics of Falsehood* (Abingdon/New York: Routledge 2020)

Fraser, Matthew (2020): *In Truth – A History of Lies from Ancient Rome to Modern America* (Guilford, CT: Prometheus Books 2020)

Fuchs, Christian (2020): *Nationalism on the Internet – Critical Theory and Ideology in the Age of Social Media and Fake News* (London/New York: Routledge 2020)

Gorlée, Dinda L. (2012): *Wittgenstein in Translation – Exploring Semiotic Signatures* (Berlin: De Gruyter Mouton, 2012)

Hadfield, Andrew (2017): *Lying in Early Modern English Culture – From the Oath of Supremacy to the Oath of Allegiance* (Oxford: Oxford University Press 2017)

Jewett, Andrew (2020): *Science under Fire – Challenges to Scientific Authority in Modern America* (Cambridge, MA: Harvard University Press 2020)

Katz, James Everett/Mays, Kate K. (2019): *Journalism and Truth in an Age of Social Media* (Oxford/New York: Oxford University Press 2019)

Leone, Massimo (2020): 'Mona Lisa's Emoji – Digital Civilization and Its Discontents', 30 Social Semiotics (2020) 312–327

Lockhart, Michele (2018): *President Donald Trump and His Political Discourse – Ramifications of Rhetoric via Twitter* (New York and London: Routledge 2018)

Lorusso, Anna Maria (2018): *Postverità – Fra Reality Tv, Social Media e Storytelling* (Bari: GLF Editori Laterza 2018)

Makarychev, Andrey S./Yatsyk, Alexandra (2017): *Lotman's Cultural Semiotics and the Political – Reframing the Boundaries* (London: Rowman & Littlefield International 2017)

McIntyre, Lee C. (2018): *Post-truth* (Cambridge, MA: MIT Press 2018)

McNair, Brian (2018): *Fake News – Falsehood, Fabrication and Fantasy in Journalism* (Abingdon/New York: Routledge 2018)

Meibauer, Jörg (2019): *The Oxford Handbook of Lying* (Oxford and New York: Oxford University Press 2019)

Michaelson, Eliot/Stokke, Andreas (2017): *Lying – Language, Knowledge, Ethics, and Politics* (Oxford: Oxford University Press 2017)

Nicholas O'Shaughnessy (2017): *Marketing the Third Reich – Persuasion, Packaging and Propaganda* (London/New York: Taylor and Francis 2017)

Ousmanova, Almira (2004): 'Fake at Stake – Semiotics and the Problem of Authenticity', 66 Problemos (2004) 80–101

Peters, Michael A. (2018): *Post-Truth, Fake News – Viral Modernity and Higher Education* (Singapore: Springer 2018)

Phillips, Paul T. (2019): *Truth, Reality, and Meaning in History* (Toronto: University of Toronto Press 2019)

Pyne, Lydia (2019): *Genuine Fakes – How Phony Things Teach Us About Real Stuff* (London: Bloomsbury Sigma 2019)

Rabbito, Andrea (2020): *La cultura del falso – Inganni, illusioni e fake news* (Milan: Meltemi 2020)

Roudakova, Natalia (2017): *Losing Pravda – Ethics and the Press in Post-Truth Russia* (Cambridge/New York: Cambridge University Press 2017)

Safieddine, Fadi/Ibrahim, Yasim (2020): *Fake News in an Era of Social Media – Tracking Viral Contagion* (London/Lanham, MA: Rowman & Littlefield International 2020)

Schwarcz, Joseph A. (2019): *A Grain of Salt – The Science and Pseudoscience of What We Eat* (Toronto: ECW Press 2019)

Sumpter, David (2018): *Outnumbered: From Facebook and Google to Fake News and Filter-bubbles – The Algorithms That Control Our Lives* (London: Bloomsbury Sigma 2018)

Todorov, Tzvetan (1968): 'Recherches sémiologiques le vraisemblable', special issue of Communications 11 (1968)

Van Dijk, Jan A.G.M./Hacker, Kenneth L. (2018): *Internet and Democracy in the Network Society* (London/New York: Taylor and Francis 2018)

Violaris, Elena (2020): 'The Semiotics of Emoji – Infinite Jest and the Yellow Smiley Face', 61 Critique: Studies in Contemporary Fiction (2020) 193–205

Zimdars, Melissa/McLeod, Kembrew (2020): *Fake News – Understanding Media and Misinformation in the Digital Age* (Cambridge, MA: MIT Press, 2020)

Chapter 12
From Copy & Paste to Deep Fakes – Digital Collaging and Image Manipulation

Olivia Hägle

I. Introduction

Binary encoding, the basic principle of digital information processing, delivers access to a variety of new possibilities for the manipulation of visual objects. By dissolving images into their components, reducing them to their essential characteristics and recomposing visual objects, it is not only possible to manipulate existing visual objects. Rather, one may create entirely new visual objects in a deceptively realistic manner. In the context of these deceptions, not only do legal and technical questions arise but, increasingly, ethical ones too.

Of course, the fact that some people try to deceive other people by using deliberately manipulated words or images is not a new phenomenon. However, two remarkable changes can be observed in this context.

Especially in the field of image manipulation, there are new developments in the means used. Whereas for a long time persons manipulating images were constrained to their own manual, still widely primitive forms of manipulation or to extensive and expensive forms of manipulation executed by specialists, modern technologies now allow almost fully automated manipulations of still and moving images. Moreover, the results of these automated operations already exhibit a persuasiveness that can hardly be dispelled by the human eye.[1] Despite these technical advances, the claim of authenticity that images still enjoy goes far beyond what "simple" text-based disinformation can achieve.[2]

Apart from the methods used, the effects of such fakes are also new. Due to the increasing global interconnectivity in the information age, the consequences of such deceptions are both increasing in scale and impact. With a single manipulated item, it is possible to reach an almost infinite

---

1 Maras/Alexandrou (2019) 257 et seq.

2 Sherwin/Feigenson/Spiesel (2006) 241 et seq.

number of people without significant effort. This fact does not only intensify the consequences for those directly affected, but also paves the way for a variety of other consequences that additionally impact a wider public. One could observe the consequences of such information manipulation, for example, in the US election campaign in 2016. Today it is assumed to have been deliberately manipulated by a Russian campaign of disinformation.[3] And in times of the Covid-19 pandemic, one also observes the effects of such targeted disinformation campaigns.[4]

In the following, the path from other forms of pictorial manipulations to deep fakes will be outlined first, to later identify the particularities of deep fakes in the field of image manipulation (II.). Subsequently, an overview of currently possible application scenarios, the consequences for the affected individuals and the general public, as well as the rights potentially affected by deep fakes will be outlined (III. 1. and 2.). Finally, conceivable approaches to solving the problem of deep fakes will be described (III.3.).

II. From Copy & Paste to Deep Fakes – The Origins of Image Manipulation

Deep fakes are based on new technological developments and are still a relatively new phenomenon. For this reason, there are no rules that are specifically designed to solve the problems arising in this context, but similar phenomena, like other forms of image manipulation, and conflicts of interests are long known and have already been regulated and could therefore help to respond to this new phenomenon.

1. A brief history of image manipulation

a) Starting point: art forgery

Before the invention of photography and the resulting possibility of simple and numerous duplication of images, pictorial representations were

---

3 DiResta et al. (2019); Timberg/Romm (2018).

4 See for example the refurbishment of a German research network *CORRECTIV*, Coronavirus-Faktenchecks: Diese Behauptungen hat CORRECTIV geprüft, https://correctiv.org/alle-corona-faktenchecks.

basically unique.[5] Since a small number of highly appreciated pieces of art have always been met by a far greater number of wealthy people, the demand on the market could often only be satisfied by means of copies and counterfeits.[6] The origins of image manipulation lead therefore back to the beginnings of art forgery.

Painters have always copied the greatest artists to learn their style of painting. Such copies are not problematic as such. In addition, it is noteworthy that especially artists themselves often even appreciate good fakes.[7] Duplicates have only become problematic when they were used to deceive third parties. In antiquity, this fraudulent intent cannot generally be assumed, since it was common practice at that time for masters to maintain an entire atelier in which work was done in the style of the masters and from which all works were considered to be those of the masters, even if only a fraction of the manufacturing steps had been carried out by themselves.[8] In those days this practice was generally known and therefore not deceptive. In addition, people had a completely different conception of originality back then, but it has changed over the centuries. All too often, originality is now measured by the artist's own execution rather than the independent conception of a work.[9] Especially in the 20th century, the demand on the art market was so high that this century produced a large number of so-called master forgers.[10] Those forgers took advantage from the fact that the market craved for pictures from certain artists and if fakes of highly demanded pictures then appeared, they would subsequently be only superficially examined to see if they were real or faked.[11]

---

5 See Deussen (2007) 30. This development was reinforced even further by the transition from analogue to digital photography.
6 Ibid.
7 Hebborn (2011) 9. For different forms of copies from forgeries to artifacts created as homages, see Brinkmann (2020).
8 Partsch (2010) 30.
9 See Butin (2020) 38.
10 See Partsch (2010) 115 et seq.
11 For example, Han van Meegeren profited from the fact that the market craved for pictures by Jan Vermeer, see ibid. 122.

b) Making history with fake photographs

With the invention of photography, unexpected possibilities for the editing[12] and duplication of pictorial representations were developed.[13] This is accompanied by the potential to use images as a tool to influence numerous of people.[14] Long before the term "fake news" went viral in social media, the governments of totalitarian regimes already used this circumstance to their own advantage by distributing propaganda in the form of manipulated images to deliberately influence their population.[15] In particular, the former Soviet Union made extensive use of such manipulated photographs. These manipulations started with minor retouching such as the removal of a cigarette butt,[16] but also included the retouching of individual persons,[17] and went up to *damnatio memoriae*, the attempt to erase a particular person from collective memory.[18] The manipulations actually extended to a level where certain scenes were recreated for the photographs,[19] other representations were even completely staged.[20] Recently, manipulated images have also repeatedly appeared in the media (including those of non-totalitarian states).[21] And all these pictorial manipulations for the purpose of deception are enabled by an asymmetry concerning the information about the context in which photographs were being taken.[22]

---

12 The possibilities of editing range from subtle manipulations such as retouching of minor blemishes to complete photomontages.

13 Cf. Deussen (2007) 30.

14 Ibid.

15 Cf. Schuster (2020) 192.

16 Further information in Jaubert (1989) 110.

17 For some examples from Stalinism, see Stiftung Haus der Geschichte der Bundesrepublik Deutschland (2000) 82 et seq; King (1997).

18 For, e.g., the complete erasure of Trotzki see Jaubert (1989) 32; King (1997) 66 et seq.

19 One famous case of reconstruction was the image of the hoisting of the Soviet flag on the Reichstag in 1945, see Stiftung Haus der Geschichte der Bundesrepublik Deutschland (2000) 44 et seq.

20 See especially for the staged images of the leaders of totalitarian regimes Jaubert (1989) 53 et seq., 63 et seq., 79 et seq., and 99 et seq.

21 See the examples in: Stiftung Haus der Geschichte der Bundesrepublik Deutschland (2000).

22 Usually only the photographer has all the background information on how an image was taken, in contrast, the viewer only gets to see the final image; Boehme-Neßler (2010) 86.

c) "Face swap" as preliminary stage

For a while now, phenomena could be observed that come even closer to the conception of deep fakes. Parts of pictures in the form of faces have been cut out and integrated into other pictures. This was first done manually and later automatically.[23] The progression from these "face swaps" to deep fakes is not so remote. The sole difference is that with the deep fake technology, it is now possible to transfer facial expressions and gestures from one person to another and let the static "face swaps" turn into dynamic deep fakes.

2. The Technology behind: deep fake algorithms

A few years ago, this new phenomenon called deep fakes caused a worldwide wave of attention.[24] These are images[25] created with the help of artificial intelligence, which give the impression of authenticity.

a) Deep learning

The basic technology behind the current developments in artificial intelligence is deep learning.[26] Deep learning algorithms can solve a variety of problems. They work within an artificial neural network, which is a special form of an algorithm that is loosely based on the information processing in the human brain.[27]

---

23 For this approach see, e.g., Mallick (2016).

24 After a Reddit user published a number of pornographic videos, in which various female celebrities were seen, under the pseudonym Deepfakes at the end of 2017, this phenomenon was first reported on Vice in December 2017; see Cole (2017). Subsequently, worldwide reports about this phenomenon appeared; see, e.g., Roose (2018); FAZ Redaktion (2018).

25 Besides images and videos, voices are now also generated with the help of such "deep fake algorithms", see Chesney/Citron (2019) 1753 et seq. and, in particular, 1761 et seq.; Greengard (2020) 18.

26 On the use of deep learning technology in the context of deep fakes see further Nguyen et al. (2019).

27 Further on the information processing in an artificial neural network see Alpaydin (2020) 271 et seq.; especially on learning in an artificial neural network Russell/Norvig (2016) 694 et seq.

The term "deep fake" combines a variety of technologies based on deep learning algorithms. Autoencoders and Generative Adversarial Networks, are two applications that should be emphasised in the following discussion. Both these technologies offer the tools to create deep fakes with only a few images – as a matter of fact, even a single image of the targeted person is sufficient for some algorithms –[28] and a few hours of training with a sufficient processor.[29] Those deep fake algorithms permit the transfer of facial expressions and gestures from one person to another. And these technologies are already freely available to the public on the internet.

b) *Autoencoder*

One way to create convincing deep fakes is to use a so-called autoencoder. An autoencoder is a special form of an artificial neural network that consists of two nets: an encoder and a decoder. For creating a deep fake, in which person A's face should be exchanged by person B's face, data material of these two different persons is necessary to train the nets. For each of the faces, one encoder-decoder-pair is required. The encoders try to reduce the images to their substantial attributes and the decoders, to reconstruct the respective images from their substantial attributes received from the encoders to create a counterpart of the image.[30] The trick of this technology is that, after the weights have been memorised, decoder A is replaced by decoder B, so that the facial expressions of person A are reconstructed with the face of person B.[31] This process is enabled by the fact that the two encoders share their weights which means that the encoders have learned the common features of these two faces.[32] The decoders can therefore easily be exchanged and yet reconstruct the respective face from the reduced data.

---

28 See, e.g., the proposal of Siarohin et al. (2019).

29 See, e.g., the attempt to create one's own deep fake as an AI-layman by Schreiner (2019).

30 Nguyen et al. (2019) 2.

31 Ibid.

32 Ibid.

c) Generative adversarial network

Another way to create deep fakes is by way of a so-called generative adversarial network (GAN) which also consists of two different nets: a generator and a discriminator.[33] The learning process here runs in cycles. Imagine an art forger who wants to fool a gallery with his fake paintings.[34] Transferred to an artificial neural network, this art forger is the generator, and therefore receives some original paintings as input and must reproduce them. Now the faked pictures are sent to the gallery with several real pictures. There, a trainee should determine whether it is an original or a fake. After completion of the classification, both the trainee and art forger receive feedback to improve their results in the next learning cycle.

The final result is a picture of a person that was either never taken this way or has no real counterpart at all.

3. The power of images: why images are more than simple information media

These deep fakes are particularly effective when used to deceive other people, as they have the special power of images. Years ago, as the possibilities of digital image manipulation increased, similar problems were faced. Images, especially in the form of photographs, largely claim for authenticity in our society.[35] Therefore, viewers of an image, manipulated in a way that is unrecognisable at first glance, tend to assume that this picture is a representation of reality.[36] This seems surprising, at least on closer inspection, since in pictures in general, and photographs in particular, certain forms of manipulation are already immanent. After all, pictures always only show a part of the whole, a perspective, and are therefore not free of any external influences and thus not purely objective.[37] But why, given this background, do images – especially photographs – continue to have a largely unquestioned power of persuasion?

The outstanding persuasiveness of pictures may be based on the fact that pictures make a certain circumstance generally perceivable and thus

33 Goodfellow et al. (2014) 1.

34 Example based on Sabsch (2018).

35 See Schwarte (2015) 27 et seq.

36 See, e.g., the argument of the German Federal Constitutional Court (Bundesverfassungsgericht, BverfG), 1 BvR 240/04 of 14 February 2005.

37 Similarly Deussen (2007) 32 et seq.; Schürmann (2013) 17 et seq.

accessible to a general evaluation.[38] Conversely, this persuasiveness may also be due to the special way that the human eye and brain perceive an image.[39] The visual perception is the most important source of knowledge for the human mind,[40] therefore we prefer to rely upon the things we can see with our own eyes. However, continuing to refer to images without reflecting seems dangerous, as the meaning of images is already in a process of change which is (also) due to the developments in the field of pictorial illusion. Based on this pictorial power of persuasion, deep fakes can cause a lot of harm.

III. Deceptions Through Image Manipulation in the Information Age

1. State of the art: what AI is already capable of

The origins of deep fakes date back to pornography.[41] And even after several years of using this technology, by far most deep fakes still contain pornographic content.[42] These pornographic videos usually feature female celebrities as actresses and musicians.[43] And in the case of these pornographic deep fakes, the defamation of the person (especially females[44]) is still the main focus. But it is to be expected that the creators and users of such fakes will increasingly pursue additional purposes, especially in the economic and political field. In the political field, currently far more primitive forms of pictorial manipulation are still sufficient to deceive the observers (so-called "cheap fakes" or "shallow fakes").[45] However, the situation is slightly different in the economic field, where there have been

---

38 Schwarte (2015) 9.

39 This is what already happened in the context of image manipulation; see Deussen (2007).

40 See also, e.g., Anderson (2020) 1 et seq.

41 For the first report on deep fakes see Cole (2017).

42 E.g., for about thousands of deep faked nude pictures of women that appeared on Telegram see Möller (2020). For more information on deep fake sex videos see Citron (2019) 1921 et seq.

43 Ajder/Patrini/Cavalli/Cullen (2019) 2.

44 According to the study by Deeptrace, deep fake pornography even exclusively affects women; see ibid.

45 E.g., on various social media platforms manipulated videos were circulating, showing Nancy Pelosi, the US Democrat and House Speaker, in a slowed down way to give the impression that the politician was drunk; see Harwell (2019); O'Sullivan (2020).

cases of cyber criminals using audio deep fakes to obtain high amounts of money.[46]

Besides all these negative (potential) application scenarios, this technology can also be used in other areas in a meaningful way. Such positive fields of application can, for example, be found in art[47], the economy[48] and entertainment[49], especially in the form of satirical deep fakes[50]. It is even possible to give people who have lost their voices a chance to have them back.[51] Although these fields of application are generally positive and should not be obstructed by excessively strict regulatory measures, ethical principles must also be considered. Here too, the basically desirable end does not justify every means.

2. *Deep learning technology and its consequences*

But every technology has an inherent potential for damage to a certain extent. This also applies to the technology behind deep fakes. And depending on the use of deep fakes, they can have a multitude of direct consequences for the individual as well as further and indirect consequences for our society as a whole. For this reason, not everything that is technically possible using the means available to us is also reasonable from an ethical perspective. A distinction must therefore be made between what is technically possible, what is legally legitimised, and, within these limits, which also appears to be ethically acceptable.[52]

---

46 Stupp (2019).

47 Probably the most famous AI artwork and at the same time a deep fake in a broader sense is the "Portrait of Edmond Belamy", which was auctioned in 2018 at Christie's auction house; see Christie's (2018). In the meantime, however, a whole community of AI artists has already formed, see AIArtists.org, https://aiartists.org.

48 For example, this technology has been used to synthetically create a large number of artificial faces for stock photos, Berger (2019).

49 In the film industry, for example, this technology can be used to bring actors who have already passed away back onto the screen; see Chesney/Citron (2019) 1770 et seq.

50 See, e.g., the satirical video in which Barack Obama seems to give an opinion on his successor Donald Trump to warn of the dangers of deep fakes, BuzzFeedVideo (2018).

51 See for example the Project Revoice of the ALS Association, https://www.projectrevoice.org, in the context of which the technology of Lyrebird is used; see Lyrebird AI, https://www.descript.com/lyrebird.

52 These ethical questions do not only affect creators, but also intermediaries.

a) *Consequences for the individual as a social being*

In addition to the potential infringements, which will have to be addressed immediately, further consequences for the affected individuals must be feared. Even if the creator of the deep fake did not have fundamentally malicious intentions, such deep fakes can have various consequences for the personal integrity and social behaviour of the affected persons.[53] Those effects do not simply result from the mere creation of the deep fakes, but in particular, from the disclosure and dissemination of such images. For this reason, it is necessary to address these activities in the context of regulation.

b) *Potentially affected rights*

The most obvious right that could potentially be affected in the context of deep fakes is the right of publicity. This right protects, inter alia, the right to self-determination, including the right to decide if and how to present oneself in public and the right to one's own image. Because one's appearance is a, if not the most, significant aspect of one's personality, special effects on the right of publicity can be observed when images of one's appearance are involved. But does the infringement worsen if manipulations improve? In some contexts, the manipulations even profit from the fact that the final image (the output of the algorithm in form of the deep fake) is blurred or imperfect, because it seems more authentic. Currently, even the most primitive forms of manipulation seem to be sufficient to deceive a large portion of the recipients.[54] Therefore, it is often not necessary to have particularly good manipulations to cause serious harm.

Additionally, deep fakes require at least a few images, so there are also copyright issues to discuss. During the process of creating, the original images or at least parts of them need to be copied and one could argue that also the finished fake is a duplication of the original image or the original images.

---

53 For the story of Indian journalist Rana Ayyub, who had been a victim of a deep fake, see Citron (2019); see also Chesney/Citron (2019) 1773.

54 See above the examples of the Nancy Pelosi Cheap Fake videos.

c) Indirect consequences: disinformation

From an external point of view, the indirect consequences of this phenomenon, which will be addressed hereafter under the term disinformation, are potentially even more severe than the direct consequences for the individual. The persuasive power of images in combination with deep fake technologies, which enable the automated and uncomplicated creation of a multitude of manipulations, is a dangerous mixture because it can be used for targeted deceptions in sensitive sectors (such as in the political context). Another problem arising from deep fakes is that, at the moment, images have a very high level of credibility, e.g., as evidence in court, and important decisions are based on them. But in times of deep fakes, authenticity can't be guaranteed anymore. If we cannot trust our own eyes and ears anymore, the consequence is a general uncertainty, that can easily be exploited by perpetrators.[55]

With this multitude of potential risks that is intensified by our handling of images, it is necessary to find solutions to address these different aspects.

3. Regulating the consequences: possible solutions for this problem

a) Legal mechanisms

One way of regulating deep fakes is to use legal mechanisms. In law, basically a choice between three courses of action exists. One may completely prohibit, partly prohibit or fully permit.

Full permission is not an option regarding the issues linked to deep fakes, as the technology has an inherent potential for too much damage. A complete ban does not seem appropriate either, as there are certainly positive applications.[56] This points towards a partial ban, to be supplemented by duties of care and supervision for intermediaries.

Legal systems constantly lag behind the technological reality. Currently, there are no[57] provisions specifically designed to address the issue of deep fakes. But to implement some kind of partial ban, there already are regula-

---

55 Chesney and Citron have described the consequences of this general uncertainty about what is real and what is fake under the term "the liar's dividend"; for further details see Chesney/Citron (2019) 1785 et seq.

56 See above III.1.

57 For a few exceptional cases there already exist regulations, see immediately below.

tions that could be formulated in a way that is sufficiently general to cover new situations and could therefore also be applied to deep fakes. Such general provisions could especially be found in the regulations concerning copyright and the right of publicity (in particular the right to one's own image) and its non-constitutional manifestations.[58] These regulations on the special forms of the right of publicity were basically created with regard to the simple possibility of reproduction of certain personality describing attributes, such as the German Kunsturhebergesetz (KUG) with regard to the invention of photography[59] or the General Data Protection Regulation for the protection of personal data regarding the recent technological developments in connection with globalisation.[60] Since the right of publicity and copyright are open for development and depend on the technological progress,[61] they could provide for appropriate compensation in the context of deep fakes.

Through the mechanisms of the right of personality and copyright, the affected persons are particularly entitled to claim injunctive relief and compensation for damages.[62] In addition, there are also criminal law mechanisms: Defamatory deep fakes may be subject to offences against the personal sphere[63] and against honour, and if further goals are pursued, such as self-enrichment (as in the well-known CEO-fraud cases[64]), offences

---

58 In Germany, in particular the peronality rights' protection of one's own image provided for by the Kunsturhebergesetz (KUG) may be applied to deep fakes; see, e.g., Hartmann (2019) and (2020). – For constitutional aspects of the protection of one's own image see Eichenhofer (2022). In addition, at European level applying the regulations of the General Data Protection Regulation may also be considered, since pictures are also personal data; see Müller-Tamm (2022).

59 German Reichstag, Reichstagsprotokolle 11. Legislatur-Periode, 1530.

60 Recital 6, Regulation (EU) 2016/679 of the European Parliament and of the Council of 27 April 2016 on the protection of natural persons with regard to the processing of personal data and on the free movement of such data, and repealing Directive 95/46/EC (General Data Protection Regulation), Official Journal of the EU L 119 of 4 May 2016, corrected Official Journal L 127 of 23 May 2018.

61 Regarding the right of publicity see Götting (2019) § 2 note 1. Regarding copyright see Specht (2019) 253 et seq. and Hofmann (2016) 482 et seq.

62 In German law, this is enabled by Section 823 (1) and Section 1004 (1) of the German Civil Code in connection with the general right of personality and by Section 97 et seq. of the German copyright law. Moreover, the General Data Protection Regulation provides further claims for deletion and compensation resulting from the protection of personal data.

63 See, e.g., Section 201a (2) of the German Criminal Code, which deals with the protection of the personal sphere from images.

64 See already above III. 1.

against assets may apply.[65] Moreover, in a few cases, special regulations regarding deep fakes have recently been created.[66]

The affected individuals are therefore already protected by the legal system. However, it might be difficult to enforce their rights against the infringers. This is partly due to the fact that anonymity still prevails on the Internet to a large extent. In addition, information – and in particular, manipulated information[67] – spreads rapidly on social media platforms, reaching a wide range of people within a very short time.[68] Further, the effectiveness of countermeasures is controversial, at any rate it is difficult to stop disinformation once in circulation.[69]

In order to improve law enforcement, additional options are available, for example in intellectual property, one could claim the right to information against intermediaries.[70] In the context of the right of publicity, however, such explicit supplementary options are missing, which creates an imbalance in the enforcement of different rights[71] on the internet. For

---

65 Besides, there are further special criminal law regulations, for example in Section 33 of the German KUG and in Sections 106, 108 of the German copyright law.

66 In some US states, for example, it is illegal to create and spread deep fakes featuring politicians in temporal connection with elections (California Assembly Bill No. 730, Texas Senate Bill No. 751). In 2019 the state of Virginia extended the existing prohibition of non-consensual pornography to deep fake pornography (House Bill No. 2678). Also, China recently announced new regulations concerning deep fakes, Reuters (2019). In addition, the new Proposal for a Regulation of the European Parliament and of the Council laying down harmonized Rules on Artificial Intelligence (Artificial Intelligence Act) should be mentioned in this context, which contains a labeling requirement for users of AI systems that generate or manipulate media, see Art. 52 (3) of the Proposal of an Artificial Intelligence Act.

67 See, e.g., Vosoughi/Roy/Aral (2018).

68 See Paschke/Halder (2016) 726.

69 See further Del Vicario et al. (2016); Zollo et al. (2015).

70 See Article 8 of Directive 2004/48/EC of the European Parliament and of the Council of 29 April 2004 on the enforcement of intellectual property rights (Official Journal of the EU L 157 of 30 April 2004), based upon Article 47 of the Agreement on trade-related aspects of intellectual property rights (TRIPS-Agreement), as well as Article 8 of Directive 2001/29/EC of the European Parliament and the Council of 22 May 2001 on the harmonisation of certain aspects of copyright and related rights in the information society (Official Journal of the EU L 167 of 22 June 2001), and Articles 15 (2) and 18 of Directive 2000/31/EC of the European Parliament and of the Council of 8 June 2000 on certain legal aspects of information society services, in particular electronic commerce, in the Internal Market (Official Journal of the EU L 178 of 17 July 2000); Dreier (2022), § 101 note 1a.

71 For the different layers of legal rights with regard to encoded and materially stored information see Raue (2022).

this reason, there are considerations about creating instruments to improve law enforcement on the internet in the context of violations of personal rights. The German *Netzwerkdurchsetzungsgesetz* (NetzDG), for example, can at least partially be traced back to these considerations.[72]

As already seen in the context of law enforcement, information intermediaries play a key role in the regulation of deep fakes because they significantly contribute to the intensification of infringements by spreading disinformation on the internet. Conversely, they are able to combat infringements more effectively through the measures they take. However, these obligations cannot be unlimited, since, after all, Art. 15 of the eCommerce Directive stipulates a prohibition of a general duty of monitoring. Whereas previous attempts have been made to limit the liability of intermediaries, recently an opposing tendency seems to be observed on a European level. The European Court of Justice seems to be increasingly expanding intermediaries' duties of supervision in recent decisions by extending Art. 3 (1) Information Society Directive to secondary liability.[73] This development, which is also reflected in the introduction of the new Art. 17 of the DSM-Directive,[74] is likewise to be appreciated against the background of deep fakes and disinformation.

However, these legal mechanisms are by no means a complete solution, since they are at least partially powerless in relation to the indirect consequences of disinformation. Once in circulation, the manipulated information and its further implications can hardly be stopped by legal measures alone. Consequently, other mechanisms are needed to additionally address this problem.

---

72 See the explanatory memorandum of the Entwurf eines Gesetzes zur Verbesserung der Rechtsdurchsetzung in sozialen Netzwerken (NetzDG), German parliament (Deutscher Bundestag), BT-Drucksache 18/12356, 2. At the European level, the Proposal for a Regulation of the European Parliament and of the Council on a Single Market For Digital Services (Digital Services Act) was recently published (Doc. COM(2020) 825 final of 15 December 2020) that is also intended to address this issue.

73 See, e.g., ECJ Judgements C-682/18 and C-683/18, ECLI:EU:C:2021:503 – YouTube and Cyando; C-160/15, ECLI:EU:C:2016:644 – GS Media; C-527/15, ECLI:EU:C:2017:300 – Stichting Brein (Filmspeler) and C-610/15, ECLI:EU:C:2017:456 – Stichting Brein (Pirate Bay); Spindler (2019), 285.

74 In this context, the Proposal for a Digital Services Act (Doc. COM(2020) 825 final of 15 December 2020) should also be mentioned. According to the Proposal, the privileged position of the intermediaries should not be rejected entirely but replaced by a tiered liability system.

b) Technical solutions

In computer science, two potential ways of addressing the problem can be identified. Firstly, special techniques could be used to detect manipulated images. And why not fight fire with fire?[75] One could use AI technologies – more precisely a binary classifier – to distinguish real and manipulated images. These technologies have drastically improved recently, but so have the manipulations. It is only a matter of time before the manipulations overtake the detection methods again. Additionally, the deceivers benefit from data compression which often occurs when generated data needs to be transferred (for instance when images are shared on the web or audio is transmitted over a phone line). The resulting incompleteness and imperfection of information lead to traces left by the algorithms during generation becoming blurred and thus, detection is hampered which further strengthens the deception.[76] Irrespective of this, such methods are not effective in every respect. Especially for the disabled individual, they only offer a subsidiary benefit since the infringement has already occurred. The infringement can no longer be undone, and detection methods can therefore only help in the context of law enforcement. In contrast, those detection methods could help to reveal disinformation. In general, however, one must ask how effective purely subsequent measures could be, especially in the context of disinformation.

Secondly, for this reason, it is obvious to consider preventive technical protection measurements. There are various ways to protect the original pictures against manipulation. In contrast to those detection methods mentioned above, these protection mechanisms have the advantage that they address the real problem and do not merely intervene afterwards. But are such methods really more effective? The "problem" – or at the same time the advantage – of any technical protection mechanism is that they are constantly being developed. Technology becomes better by breaking or circumventing it, as this is the only way to identify the weak points. It is therefore not surprising that every technical protection measure has been broken so far. In the end, in all likelihood, technical protection measures will only be able to increase the threshold for counterfeiting and manipulation. However, even if such protective mechanisms might not

75 See, e.g., already Clark (1996): "The answer to the machine is in the machine".

76 See Unterrichtung der Enquete-Kommission Künstliche Intelligenz – Gesellschaftliche Verantwortung und wirtschaftliche, soziale und ökologische Potenziale, German parliament (Deutscher Bundestag), BT-Drucksache 19/23700, 464.

completely prevent manipulations, they can at least help to prove existing manipulation.

c) Social measures

In addition to legal and technical measures, society should be considered as a third dimension. At the moment, people still believe what they see. So, it is much easier to deceive people by using images than with simple disinformation. This is the starting point for change. Society needs to be more aware of this issue. All the other possible solutions will remain ineffective or even be taken *ad absurdum* if everyone does not become aware of this problem. For example, legal measures seem meaningless if the enforcement of rights in court is based on "false facts". And classification algorithms become useless if AI is trained to detect fake images with undetected deep fakes.[77] It is therefore necessary to question the authenticity of images.

d) Combination

The effects of this problem will soon also appear in sensitive sectors, as in court where important decisions are made and where images have developed into an important source of knowledge. For this reason, it is necessary that the handling of images is amended, particularly in key positions. Images should no longer be granted unlimited significance in court proceedings. This can be legally implemented by reversing the burden of proof; i.e., it should be assumed that any picture presented as evidence to a trial court is fake unless it is explicitly marked or can be proven beyond reasonable doubt as authentic.[78] Reversing the burden of proof also seems appropriate against the background of the asymmetry of information with regard to photographs.[79] If an image is not verifiably authentic, the technical detection mechanisms described above could help to prove or exclude manipulation.[80] Simultaneously, this provides an incentive for journalists,

---

77 For the consequences false information can have for the training of AI, see Hurtz (2020).

78 See Deussen (2007) 145 et seq.

79 See above I. 2.

80 To this effect cf. Leone (2022).

photographers and increasingly also for information intermediaries (who all occupy key positions) to work diligently and ethically in order to regain the meaningfulness that images once enjoyed. Such an approach also facilitates the handling of images for everyone.[81]

For this purpose, consistent principles will have to be formulated that regulate the handing of (potentially manipulated) information in general and images in particular, by these key operators. These ethical questions raised by deep learning-technologies are not entirely novel. But, they have become considerably more intense in the context of automated and highly convincing visual deceptions in the form of deep fakes. It is therefore possible to rely on the familiar ethical principles in connection with images, deceptions and disinformation, which will have to be applied and adapted to the particularities of the new phenomenon.

IV. Conclusion

In fact, there already are measures that are – if used properly, combined and adapted selectively – able to adequately, still not extensively, regulate the phenomenon of deep fakes. However, it is neither possible, nor reasonable to regulate deep fakes extensively by using the strict measures of law and technology, since on the one hand, the phenomenon of deep fakes is constantly developing, and on the other hand, a single technology can be used equally for positive and negative purpose.[82] This "gap" can and should be filled by ethical rules, seeking a responsible and transparent handling of this technology.

References

Ajder, Henry/Patrini, Giorgio/Cavalli, Francesco/Cullen, Laurence (2019): *The State of Deepfakes: Landscape, Threats, and Impact* (2019, https://regmedia.co.uk/2019/10/08/deepfake_report.pdf)

Alpaydin, Ethem (2020): *Introduction to machine learning* (4th ed., Cambridge/MA.: MIT Press 2020)

Anderson, John R. (2020): *Cognitive psychology and its implications* (9th ed., New York: Worth Publishers 2020)

81 Similarly, Deussen (2007) 147.

82 See, e.g., the different possible applications of audio deep fakes, above III.1.

Berger, Daniel (2019): 'Stockfoto-Firma veröffentlicht 100.000 KI-Gesichter' (2019, https://www.heise.de/newsticker/meldung/Stockfoto-Firma-veroeffentlicht-100-000-KI-Gesichter-4537889.html)

Boehme-Neßler, Volker (2010): *BilderRecht – Die Macht der Bilder und die Ohnmacht des Rechts* (Berlin/Heidelberg: Springer 2010)

Brinkmann, Franziska (2020): 'Formen der Kopie von der Fälschung bis zur Hommage – Eine Begriffsbestimmung und ihre Grenzen', in: Dreier, Thomas/Jehle, Oliver: *Original – Kopie – Fälschung* (Baden-Baden: Nomos 2020) 57–104

Butin, Hubertus (2020): 'Die Crux mit dem Original – ein Begriff und seine Grauzonen in der Kunstgeschichte und im Rechtswesen', in: Dreier, Thomas/Jehle, Oliver: *Original – Kopie – Fälschung* (Baden-Baden: Nomos 2020) 37–55

BuzzFeedVideo (2018): 'You Won't Believe What Obama Says In This Video!' (2018, https://www.youtube.com/watch?v=cQ54GDm1eL0)

Chesney, Robert/Citron, Danielle (2019): 'Deep Fakes – A Looming Challenge for Privacy, Democracy, and National Security', 107 California Law Review (2019) 1753–1819

Christie's (2018): 'Is artificial intelligence set to become art's next medium?' (2018, https://www.christies.com/features/A-collaboration-between-two-artists-one-human-one-a-machine-9332-1.aspx)

Citron, Danielle (2019): 'How deep fakes undermine truth and threaten democracy', TEDSummit 2019 (2019, https://www.ted.com/talks/danielle_citron_how_deepfakes_undermine_truth_and_threaten_democracy/transcript)

Citron, Danielle Keats (2019): 'Sexual Privacy', 128 Yale Law Journal (2019) 1870–1960

Clark, Charles (1996): 'The Answer to the Machine is in the Machine', in: P. Bernt Hugenholtz (ed), *The Future of Copyright in a Digital Environment* (The Hague/London/Boston: Kluwer Law International 1996) 139–145

Cole, Samantha (2017): 'AI-Assisted Fake Porn Is Here and We're All Fucked' (2017, https://www.vice.com/en_us/article/gydydm/gal-gadot-fake-ai-porn)

CORRECTIV (2020): 'Coronavirus-Faktenchecks – Diese Behauptungen hat CORRECTIV geprüft' (2020, https://correctiv.org/alle-corona-faktenchecks)

Del Vicario, Michela/Bessi, Alessandro/Zollo, Fabiana/Petroni, Fabio/Scala, Antonio/Caldarelli, Guido/Stanley, Eugene H./ Quattrociocchi, Walter (2016): 'The spreading of misinformation online', 113 Proceedings of the National Academy of Science of the USA (2016) 554–559

Deussen, Oliver (2007): *Bildmanipulation – Wie Computer unsere Wirklichkeit verzerren* (Berlin/Heidelberg: Springer 2007)

DiResta, Renee/Shaffer, Kris/Ruppel, Becky/Sullivan, David/Matney, Robert/Fox, Ryan/Albright, Jonathan/Johnson, Ben (2019): 'The Tactics & Tropes of the Internet Research Agency' (2019, https://disinformationreport.blob.core.windows.net/disinformation-report/NewKnowledge-Disinformation-Report-Whitepaper.pdf)

Dreier, Thomas (2022): 'Commentary on § 101 of the German Copyright Act', in: Dreier, Thomas/Schulze, Gernot: *Urheberrechtsgesetz* (München: C.H. Beck 7th ed. 2022)

Eichenhofer, Johannes (2022): 'The Constitutional Protection of Images', in: Dreier, Thomas/Andina, Tiziana: *Digital Ethics – The issue of images* (Baden-Baden: Nomos 2022) 357 – 385

Enquete-Kommission Künstliche Intelligenz – Gesellschaftliche Verantwortung und wirtschaftliche, soziale und ökologische Potenziale (2020): 'Bericht der Enquete-Kommission Künstliche Intelligenz – Gesellschaftliche Verantwortung und wirtschaftliche, soziale und ökologische Potenziale' (2020, https://dip21.bundestag.de/dip21/btd/19/237/1923700.pdf)

FAZ Redaktion (2018): 'Jetzt also "Fake Porn"' (2018, https://www.faz.net/aktuell/wirtschaft/kuenstliche-intelligenz/fake-porns-mit-ki-werden-promis-in-pornos-eingebaut-15419920.html)

Götting, Horst-Peter (2019): 'Geschichte des Persönlichkeitsrechts', in: Götting, Horst-Peter/Schertz, Christian/Seitz, Walter: *Handbuch Persönlichkeitsrecht* (München: C.H.Beck 2nd ed. 2019)

Goodfellow, Ian J./Pouget-Abadie, Jean/Mirza, Mehdi/Xu, Bing/Warde-Farley, David/Ozair, Sherjil/Courville, Aaron/Bengio, Yoshua (2014): 'Generative Adversarial Networks' (2014, https://arxiv.org/abs/1406.2661)

Greengard, Samuel (2020): 'Will Deepfakes Do Deep Damage?', 63 Communications of the ACM (2020) 17–19

Hartmann, Frank (2019): 'Der Schutz vor Deepfakes durch das Kunsturhebergesetz', in: Taeger, Jürgen: *Die Macht der Daten und der Algorithmen – Regulierung von IT, IoT und KI* (Edewecht: Oldenburger Verlag für Wirtschaft, Informatik und Recht 2019) 563–579

Hartmann, Frank (2020): 'Der persönlichkeitsrechtliche Schutz vor Deepfakes', Kommunikation und Recht (2020) 350–357

Harwell, Drew (2019): 'Faked Pelosi videos, slowed to make her appear drunk, spread across social media' (2019; https://www.washingtonpost.com/technology/2019/05/23/faked-pelosi-videos-slowed-make-her-appear-drunk-spread-across-social-media)

Hebborn, Eric (1997): *Der Kunstfälscher* (3rd ed., Cologne: DuMont 2011; original ed.: Hebborn, Eric: *The Art Forger's Handbook*, London: Cassell 1997)

Hofmann, Franz (2016): 'Grundsatz der Technikneutralität im Urheberrecht? – Zugleich Gedanken zu einem more technological approach', Zeitschrift für geistiges Eigentum (2016) 482–512

Hurtz, Simon (2020): 'Wikipedia auf Scots – Hälfte der Artikel ist gefälscht' (2020, https://www.sueddeutsche.de/digital/wikipedia-scots-uebersetzung-englisch-1.5030086)

Jaubert, Alain (1989): *Fotos, die lügen – Politik mit gefälschten Bildern* (Frankfurt am Main: Athenäum 1989)

King, David (1997): *Stalins Retuschen – Foto- und Kunstmanipulation in der Sowjetunion* (Hamburg: Hamburger Edition 1997)

Leone, Massimo (2022): 'Semioethics of the Visual Fake', in: Dreier, Thomas/Andina, Tiziana: *Digital Ethics – The issue of images* (Baden-Baden: Nomos 2022) 187–205

Mallick, Satya (2016): 'Face Swap using OpenCV (C++/Python)', (2016, https://www.learnopencv.com/face-swap-using-opencv-c-python)

Maras, Marie-Helen/Alexandrou, Alex (2019): 'Determining authenticity of video evidence in the age of artificial intelligence and in the wake of Deepfake videos', 23 The International Journal of Evidence & Proof (2019) 255–262

Möller, Malin (2020): 'Telegram – Mehr als 100.000 Deepfake-Nacktbilder von Frauen öffentlich geteilt' (2020, https://www.spiegel.de/netzwelt/web/telegram-mehr-als-100-000-deepfake-nacktbilder-von-frauen-oeffentlich-geteilt-a-4b34eeef-43d8-4c90-ba43-8dff569edc09)

Müller-Tamm, Lorenz (2022): 'Portrait or Personal Data – The Rivalry of Image and Data Protection Legislation', in: Dreier, Thomas/Andina, Tiziana: *Digital Ethics – The issue of images* (Baden-Baden: Nomos 2022) 239–252

Nguyen, Thanh Thi/Nguyen, Cuong M./Nguyen, Dung Tien/Nguyen, Duc Thanh/Nahavandi, Saeid (2019): 'Deep Learning for Deepfakes Creation and Detection' (2019, https://arxiv.org/abs/1909.11573)

O'Sullivan, Donie (2020): 'Another fake Pelosi video goes viral on Facebook' (2020, https://edition.cnn.com/2020/08/02/politics/fake-nancy-pelosi-video-facebook/index.html)

Partsch, Susanna (2010): *Tatort Kunst – Über Fälschungen, Betrüger und Betrogene* (München: C.H.Beck 2010)

Paschke, Anne/Halder, Christoph (2016): 'Auskunftsansprüche bei digitalen Persönlichkeitsrechtsverletzungen', Multimedia und Recht (2016) 723–727.

Raue, Benjamin (2022): 'The Multi-Layered Information in a Digital Image', in: Dreier, Thomas/Andina, Tiziana: *Digital Ethics – The issue of images* (Baden-Baden: Nomos 2022) 229–237

Reuters Staff (2019): 'China seeks to root out fake news and deepfakes with new online content rules' (2019, https://www.reuters.com/article/us-china-technology/china-seeks-to-root-out-fake-news-and-deepfakes-with-new-online-content-rules-idUSKBN1Y30VU)

Roose, Kevin (2018): 'Here Come the Fake Videos, Too' (2018, https://www.nytimes.com/2018/03/04/technology/fake-videos-deepfakes.html)

Russell, Stuart J./Norvig, Peter (2016): *Artificial intelligence – A modern approach* (3rd ed., Boston/Columbus/Indianapolis: Pearson 2016)

Sabsch, Tim (2018): 'Eine kurze Einführung in Generative Adversarial Networks' (2018, https://blog.codecentric.de/2018/11/eine-kurze-einfuehrung-in-generative-adversarial-networks)

Schreiner, Maximilian (2019): 'KI –Deepfake selbst erstellen – so geht es, so lange dauert es' (2019, https://mixed.de/ki-deepfake-selbst-erstellen-so-geht-es-so-lange-dauert-es)

Schürmann, Eva (2013): 'Erscheinen als Ereignis – Zeittheoretische Überlegungen zur Fotografie', in: Alloa, Emmanuel: *Erscheinung und Ereignis – Zur Zeitlichkeit des Bildes* (München/Paderborn: Fink 2013) 17–38

Schuster, Martin (2020): *Fotopsychologie – Fotos sehen, verstehen, gestalten* (Berlin/ Heidelberg: Springer 3rd edition 2020)

Schwarte, Ludger (2015): *Pikturale Evidenz – Zur Wahrheitsfähigkeit der Bilder* (Paderborn: Wilhelm Fink 2015)

Sherwin, Richard K./Feingenson, Neal/Spiesel, Christina (2006): 'Law in the Digital Age – How Visual Communication Technologies are Transforming the Practice, Theory, and Teaching of Law', 12 Boston University Journal of Science and Technology (2006) 227–270

Siarohin, Aliaksandr/Lathuilière, Stéphane/Tulyakov, Sergey/Ricci, Elisa/Sebe, Nicu (2019): *First Order Motion Model for Image Animation*, 33rd Conference on Neural Information Processing Systems (NeurIPS) (2019, http://papers.nips.cc/paper/8935-first-order-motion-model-for-image-animation.pdf)

Specht, Louisa (2019): 'Zum Verhältnis von (Urheber-)Recht und Technik', Gewerblicher Rechtsschutz und Urheberrecht (2019) 253–259

Spindler, Gerald (2019): 'Die neue Urheberrechts-Richtlinie der EU, insbesondere "Upload-Filter" – Bittersweet? Analyse der Änderungen beim Text- und Datamining, Leistungsschutz für Presseerzeugnisse und Pflichtenkreis für Hostprovider', Computer und Recht (2019) 277–291

Stiftung Haus der Geschichte der Bundesrepublik Deutschland (2000): *Bilder, die lügen* (Bonn: Bouvier Verlag 2nd edition 2000)

Stupp, Catherine (2019): 'Fraudsters Used AI to Mimic CEO's Voice in Unusual Cybercrime Case' (2019, https://www.wsj.com/articles/fraudsters-use-ai-to-mimic-ceos-voice-in-unusual-cybercrime-case-11567157402)

Timberg, Craig/Romm, Tony (2018): *New report on Russian disinformation, prepared for the Senate, shows the operation's scale and sweep* (2018, https://www.washingtonpost.com/technology/2018/12/16/new-report-russian-disinformation-prepared-senate-shows-operations-scale-sweep)

Vosoughi, Soroush/Roy, Deb/Aral, Sinan (2018: 'The spread of true and false news online', 359 Science (2018) 1146–1151

Zollo, Fabiana/Novak, Petra Kralj/Del Vicario, Michela/Bessi, Alessandro/Mozetič, Igor/Scala, Antonio/Caldarelli, Guido/Quattrociocchi, Walter (2015): 'Emotional Dynamics in the Age of Misinformation', 10 PLoS ONE (2015) 1–22

Chapter 13
The Multi-Layered Information in a Digital Image

Benjamin Raue

An image, especially a digital image, is a complex entity comprised of a variety of information. You can think of it as a Russian matryoshka doll — behind each piece of information awaits another piece of information, followed by yet another piece of information. The same is true for the various stakeholders whose interests are affected by an image. There is a stakeholder behind a stakeholder behind a stakeholder.

An image may reveal personal or confidential information about a person or object depicted, or a viewer might be offended by an image's content. Other interests might be affected by the creation and distribution of the image. A photographer or painter wants protection against the appropriation, alteration or destruction of his or her images, and is entitled to a share of revenue generated by the image. Other artists and "prosumers" seek to use existing images in their creative or communicative process. These instances highlight only a small fraction of the potential conflicts of interest in the creation or use of an image.

In this article, I would like to demonstrate how those different conflicts of interest and respective stakeholders might be structured in an information layer model. This information layer model was introduced by *Herbert Zech* in his habilitation thesis "Information als Schutzgegenstand"[1] (the verbatim translation would be "Information as an Object of (legal) Protection"), and builds on concepts of *Benkler*[2] and *Lessig*[3] as pointed out by *Zech* himself as well as by those reviewing his work.[4] The information model does not provide definitive answers on how to mediate the aforementioned conflicts. However, it is a helpful tool for analysing and structuring the multitude of information and thus interests in an image, as well as the different legal instruments upon which solutions may be based.

---

1 Zech (2012).
2 Benkler (2000) 562.
3 Lessig (2001) 23.
4 Zech (2012) 43; see also Dreier (2013) para.4.

According to *Zech*, information can be divided into three different dimensions: structural information, syntactic information, and semantic information.[5] In order to address further relevant legal issues of a digital image, I propose adding the context of image creation as a fourth dimension. While the context of image creation is not information stored in a digital image, it is, at least from the perspective of German law, a context that requires consideration for a comprehensive analysis of an image's opposing interests.

I. Semantic Information

The semantic layer of information is characterised by the meaning that a recipient of the information attributes to the data with which she is provided.[6] For example, a picture's pixel arrangement conveys the semantic information that a certain person, object or landscape is depicted (e.g., the picture from this volume's cover provides the semantic information of a certain view of Lake Como). If the semantic information relates to a person, it may infringe upon personality rights or data protection law. If an image depicts objects, for example paintings, sculptures, buildings, machines, cars or other individually designed objects, then this information might incite conflict with copyright law, the protection of trade secrets, or, in rare cases with patent law, and even property law, in some jurisdictions.[7]

Although semantic information may be subject to the individual rights mentioned, this does not necessarily mean that protected semantic information may not be included in an image. When applying the conflicting rights, it must be taken into account that any legal restriction on the use of semantic information severely affects individuals' freedoms of communication, the freedom of expression and information (Art. 11 Charter of Funda-

5 Zech (2012) 35 et seq.

6 Ibid. 37 et seq.

7 For example in France where the *Cour de Cassation* decided that "l'exploitation du bien sous la forme de photographies porte atteinte au droit de jouissance du propriétaire" (Cour de Cassation, Chambre civile 1, of 10 March 1999, 96–18.699, Bulletin 1999 I N° 87 p. 58 – Café Gondrée), which the Court later restricted to photographs causing "trouble anormal" (Cour de Cassation, Assemblée plénière, of 7 May.2004, 02–10.450, Bulletin 1999 I N° 87 p. 58 – l'Hôtel de Girancourt). See also Schack (2006) 149.

mental Rights of The European Union), and the freedom of the arts and sciences (Art. 13 Charter of Fundamental Rights of The European Union).

The restriction necessary to protect individual rights or public interests must be balanced with and be proportionate to the restriction of fundamental freedoms. Consequently, the use of semantic information should only be restricted when necessary for the protection of other rights, which cannot be achieved by less intrusive means. In this respect, the information level model can be of assistance. Restricting the use of *semantic* information has usually a much stronger impact on the aforementioned freedoms than restrictions on the other information levels, e.g., restricting the use of syntactic information or restricting the access to structural information.

Figs. 1 and 2: Shapard Fairey, Hope (left), and Mannie Garcia, Obama (right)

This can be illustrated by the following example. The iconic blue and red Barack Obama "Hope" poster, created by *Shepard Fairey*, which became a key symbol during Obama's 2008 presidential campaign (Fig. 1).[8] The

8 https://en.wikipedia.org/wiki/Barack_Obama_%22Hope%22_poster#Origin_and_copyright_issues.

poster was based on a photograph taken by *Mannie Garcia* (Fig. 2).[9] When balancing the interest of the original photo's photographer with that of the poster designer, it would be very far-reaching if the poster designer were prohibited from using the pose featured in the original photo and thus a *semantic piece of information* about Barack Obama.[10] On the other hand, requiring the poster designer to compensate the photographer of the original photo for the use of the original photo's syntactical information might be a fair balance of interests. The photographer has invested time and money to create this *syntactical information* and saves the poster designer the effort of creating an identical or similar image himself or herself (or obtaining permission from another photographer).

Another, separate question is whether Barack Obama would have the right to restrict the use of his portrait (*semantic information*), or whether he must have a share of the revenue from merchandise (sweatshirts, t-shirts, coffee mugs) bearing that image.

II. Syntactic Information

The syntactic layer of information categorises information in coded form, such as a photograph or a computer file.[11] Semantic information needs to be fixed in syntactic form (on at least one structural layer, see below III.) in order to be stored, processed and re-used.[12] The person or entity responsible for creating syntactic information, e.g., a painter or a photographer, may hold rights in the coded information, but not necessarily in the semantic information contained in the coded information.

In the example above, *Mannie Garcia* owns the copyright of the original *Barack Obama* photograph that was later transformed into the iconic poster. That copyright entitles him to control the copying, distribution

9 The factual and legal background can be found in the paper of Fisher et al. (2012).

10 It is therefore disputed whether and to what extent the copyright or the ancillary right in a picture extends to the pose of the pictured person(s) or objects, see OLG Köln, 6 U 189/97 of 5 March 1999, Gewerblicher Rechtsschutz und Urheberrecht (GRUR) 2000, 43 – Klammerpose; OLG Hamburg, 3 U 302/94 of 29 June 1995, Zeitschrift für Urheber- und Medienrecht-Rechtsprechungsdienst (ZUM-RD) 1997, 217 – Troades-Inszenierung; Rogers vs. Koons, 960 F.2d 301 (2nd Cir. 1992); Schulze (2018) para. 36; Schack (2017) para. 875.

11 Zech (2012) 38 et seq.

12 Even if information is memorised by a human, it is stored by structural changes in brain synapses.

and making available of the specific photograph, meaning the specific syntactic information he created by taking and storing that photograph. That protection is extended, at least in principle, to the use in modified form as long as the syntactic information is still recognisable.[13] However, *Garcia* does not necessarily "own" *Barack Obama's* pose featured in the photo.[14] That means, *Garcia* cannot forbid any other photographer to take very similar or virtually identical pictures of *Barack Obama*, thus creating a new syntactic code of the picture. A different result is only justified if the creation (and not only the depiction) of the pose itself is considered a personal, individual creation, leading to a copyright in the pose. This is not the case in our example, as *Garcia* only depicted a scene from a reality unaltered by *Garcia* when he captured the photograph.

Still, the owner of syntactic information may have a certain influence on the use of semantic information stored therein. The photographer of a unique moment in time, such as humankind's first steps on the moon, can control the use, distribution and availability of that information as long as there are no other photographs of that particular scene. Although he or she does not have a subjective right in the semantic information itself, the right holder can control the *access* to and the *distribution* of that information.

The same applies to information stored in (copyrighted) photographs that depict works of visual arts that are in the public domain. Although works in the public domain can be used by anyone without permission from the original creator, a different copyright regime protects the photographs syntactic information. Consequently, art works in the public domain are, *de facto*, not in the public domain as long as the syntactic information about the art work is still protected by a copyright or ancillary right (and the owner of the unique physical embodiment of the work restricts access to the structural information, see below III.). The European legislator has addressed the problem in Art. 14 Directive 2019/790 on copyright and related rights in the Digital Single Market. The directive obliges Member States to end copyright or related right protections of any material resulting from an act of reproduction when a work of visual art's term of protection has expired, unless the material resulting from that act of reproduction is original in the sense that it is the author's own intellectual creation.

---

13 For the recognisability test, cf. CJEU, C-476/17 of 29 July 2019, ECLI: EU:C:2019:624 para. 31 – Pelham.

14 See above footnote 10.

Nonetheless, this freedom of information for existing reproductions, and according syntactic information of works of visual arts, comes at a price. It is unlikely that costly high-quality reproductions of works of visual arts will continue to be made in the future, unless the creation of the public goods is subsidised by third parties.

III. Structural Information

Structural information is information stored on a physical medium, such as a hard drive, flash drive, a cloud server, or, in a non-digital context, a photographic print, painting, or drawing.[15] Even in a digital context, structural information is still of great importance. Although information as such is an immaterial good and may be used by many different users simultaneously, it must be materialised for permanent use (e.g., stored on computer discs or paper). Information cannot be stored in a completely matterless way.

The owner of the structural information controls access to the syntactic and semantic information stored on his or her property. However, legal control does not extend to the syntactic or semantic information as such, as long as the property owner does not fulfil the independent criteria for the creation of rights in syntactic or semantic information. If a photographer sells a print of a self-portrait, the purchaser acquires ownership of the print but neither copyrights in the photograph nor personality rights in the self-portrait.[16] On the other hand, by transferring the ownership of the print, the photographer loses control over the print and the new owner might block access to it. If the photographer loses his or her remaining copy of the syntactic information, she needs the consent of the print's owner to restore her own syntactic information via a new copy of the photograph. Consequently, German copyright law provides the author with a right to access the original or a copy of a work if necessary to make further copies of the work.[17]

15 Zech (2012) 41 et seq.

16 Cf. sec. 44 para. 1 UrhG: "(1) If the author sells the original work, in case of doubt he does not grant the right of use to the acquirer."

17 Cf. sec. 25 UrhG: "(1) The author may require the owner of the original or a copy of his work to make the original or the copy accessible to him, to the extent that this is necessary for the production of copies or adaptations of the work and does not conflict with legitimate interests of the owner. (2) The owner shall not be obliged to surrender the original or the copy to the author".

If a digital image is stored on a hard drive and then altered or destroyed, it is, again, necessary to distinguish between the different layers of information. The owner of the hard drive is entitled to damages in any case, as this alteration or destruction mainly concerns physical property and consequently the structural layer. As the syntactic information is usually stored in many different places, the interests of the creator as owner of the syntactic information are unharmed. This may only be the case if the last remaining structural information storing the syntactical information is destroyed. This is unusual in a digital context and therefore more of a problem for architectural works or site-specific art. The German Federal Supreme Court has decided in a recent case concerning the "HHole for Mannheim" that the author's moral rights might be infringed if site-specific art in a museum is permanently destroyed.[18]

IV. Context of Creation

At least in Germany, the context in which a photograph is taken may impose restrictions on the photographer. A property owner may restrict the act of taking a photograph based on his or her ownership of a building or land. For example, a photo taken in the garden of Castle Sanssoucis in Potsdam could infringe upon the property right of the *Stiftung Preußischer Kulturbesitz* (Prussian Cultural Heritage Foundation), the owner of the castle and surrounding gardens. While German jurisprudence recognises that the owner of real property does not have the right to prohibit photography of his or her property *per se*,[19] the owner does have the right to control access to the property and to restrict the taking of photographs on his or her property.[20] It is therefore a question of legal remedies whether the infringement of the property right by unlawful photography extends to

---

18 BGH, I ZR 98/17 of 21 February 2019, Zeitschrift für Urheber- und Medienrecht (ZUM) 2019, 508 – HHole (for Mannheim). See also BGH, I ZR 99/17 of 21 February 2019, ZUM 2019, 521 – PHaradise; BGH, I ZR 15/18 of 21 February, ZUM 2019, 528 – Minigolfanlage, and the commentary by Schulze (2019).

19 BGH, I b ZR 111/63 of 13 October 1965, Neue Juristische Wochenschrift (NJW) 1966, 542 (543 et seq.) – Apfel-Madonna; BGH, V ZR 45/10 of 17 December 2010, NJW 2011, 749 para. 15 – Preußische Gärten und Parkanlagen I; BGH, V ZR 14/12 of 1 March 2013, NJW 2013, 1809 para. 15 – Preußische Gärten und Parkanlagen II. – For the different approach of the French Cour de Cassation, see above footnote 7.

20 BGH, V ZR 324/13 of 19 December 2014, Neue Juristische Wochenschrift (NJW) 2015, 2037 para. 10 – Preußische Kunstwerke.

the product of this infringement – the photograph itself.[21] The German Federal Supreme Court has affirmed the latter in highly controversial decisions.[22] The same reasoning may apply in certain areas where photography is prohibited by law, such as in the case of photographs taken of military installations.

V. Conclusion

The information layer model is a tool to structure and analyse the varying interests that may exist within a digital image. While the model does not provide definitive answers, it does allow the identification of the appropriate layer of information for mediating the different interests. Accordingly, the regulation can be limited to specific aspects of information and, consequently, restricting the conflicting interests as little as possible.

References:

Benkler, Yochai (2000): 'From Consumers to Users: Shifting the Deeper Structures of Regulation Toward Sustainable Commons and User Access', 52 Federal Communications Law Journal (2000) 561–579 (online at https://www.repository.law.indiana.edu/cgi/viewcontent.cgi?article=1242&context=fclj)

Dreier, Thomas (2013): 'Book Review of Zech, Information als Schutzgegenstand', 4 Journal of Intellectual Property, Information Technology and E-Commerce Law (2013) 66–67

Fisher, William W. III/Cost, Frank/Fairey, Shepard/Feder, Meir/Fountain, Edwin/Stewart, Geoffrey/Sturken, Marita (2012): 'Reflections on the Hope Poster Case', 25 Harvard Journal of Law and Technology (2012) 244–338 (online available at http://jolt.law.harvard.edu/articles/pdf/v25/25HarvJLTech243.pdf)

Lessig, Lawrence (2001): *The Future of Ideas – The Fate of the Commons in a Connected World* (New York: Vintage Books, 2001)

Raue, Benjamin (2012): 'Einschränkung der Filmfreiheit durch Eigentum?', Kunst und Recht (2012) 166–169

21 See BGH, V ZR 14/12 of 1 March 2013, Neue Juristische Wochenschrift (NJW) 2013, 1809 para. 12 – Preußische Gärten und Parkanlagen II; Raue (2017) 573 et seq.; dissenting Schack (2011) 376.

22 BGH, V ZR 14/12 of 1 March 2013, Neue Juristische Wochenschrift (NJW) 2013, 1809 para. 12 – Preußische Gärten und Parkanlagen II.

Raue, Benjamin (2017): *Die dreifache Schadensberechnung – Eine Untersuchung zum deutschen und europäischen Immaterialgüter-, Lauterkeits- und Bürgerlichen Recht* (Tübingen: Mohr Siebeck 2017)

Raue, Benjamin (2019): 'Die Rechte des Sacheigentümers bei der Erhebung von Daten', Neue Juristische Wochenschrift (2019) 2425–2430

Schack, Haimo (2006): 'Comment on the decision of the Cour de cassation, Assemblée plénière, of 7 May 2004', Zeitschrift für Europäisches Privatrecht (2006) 150–157

Schack, Haimo (2010): 'Comment on the decision of the German Federal Supreme Court, V ZR 45/10 of 7 December 2010', Juristenzeitung (2011) 375–376

Schack, Haimo (2017): *Kunst und Recht* (Tübingen: Mohr Siebeck 3rd edition 2017)

Schulze, Gernot (2018): 'Commentary on § 24 of the German Copright Act', in: Dreier, Thomas/Schulze, Gernot: *Urheberrechtsgesetz – Kommentar* (München: C.H. Beck 6th edition 2018)

Schulze, Gernot (2019): 'Comment on the decision of the German Federal Supreme Court, I ZR 98/17, of 21 February 2019', Gewerblicher Rechtsschutz und Urheberrecht (2019) 617–619

Zech, Herbert (2012): *Information als Schutzgegenstand* (Tübingen: Mohr Siebeck 2012; online available: DOI 10.1628/978-3-16-152162-1)

Photo credits

Fig. 1: Shepard Fairey; https://en.wikipedia.org/wiki/File:Barack_Obama_Hope_poster.jpg

Fig. 2: Mannie Garcia/Associated Press

Chapter 14
Portrait or Personal Data – The Rivalry of Image and Data Protection Legislation

Lorenz Müller-Tamm

I. Introduction

Until the 1990s, photography was largely based on analog methods.[1] However, advancements in technology led to its almost complete digitalization. Today, most photographs are produced, stored, and sent electronically. They are viewed using electronic display devices such as computer screens or smartphones. A photograph is no longer simply a picture, a print, a material entity, but consists of a multitude of electronic data. At the same time, technical development has also impacted the view of images on an immaterial level. This is because the image seems to dissolve and disintegrate into pixels and countless single pieces of information including image data, location data and data on the time of capture.

As it is often the case, technical and social developments impact law. In the days of analog photography, the law was mostly settled: the person depicted in a picture was affected in his or her right to one's image and could assert rights from this protection against the photographer or publisher in case of an infringement.[2] However, the increasing regulation of data processing has resulted in an area of law that also covers images. This has ignited a rivalry between the two regulatory regimes and led to the question of which regime should photographing and publishing personal portraits be assigned to – does it belong to the protection of images, data protection, or both? In the following chapter, this question will first be approached with a brief overview of German image protection law and European data protection law (II.). Then the relationship between the

---

1 Analog photography encompasses all camera techniques not using a digital storage medium, but chemical processes such as exposing photographic films or hard plates.

2 This applies, of course, only to countries that have provided a protection of images, e.g., Germany (§§ 22, 23 Kunsturhebergesetz), Italy (Legge n. 633/1941, Art. 96, 97) or France (Code Civil Art. 9, via the right to privacy).

two regulatory regimes, which is subject to ongoing legal debates, will be outlined (III.). Irrespective of this specific, detailed legal dispute on a methodical level, the more general question of whether the protection of images is still necessary regarding data protection law will be addressed in the final remarks (IV.).

II. The Collision of Regulatory Regimes in German Law

German law protects the right to one's own image with a specific parliamentary act, the *Kunsturhebergesetz* (German Art Copyright Act, KUG) of 1907. For more than 100 years, it has provided the regulations for the protection of images. Even though the European Data Protection Directive 95/46/EC came into force as early as 1995 and was transposed into national law,[3] there was broad agreement among German courts that the KUG took precedence over data protection law.[4] It was not until the European General Data Protection Regulation (GDPR) entered into force in 2016 that the debate on the relationship between the two regulatory regimes arose again and the precedence of the protection of images was widely questioned.[5]

1. The codification of the right to one's own image in the KUG: an overview

§ 22 KUG requires the consent of the person depicted in an image when the image is distributed or publicly displayed.[6] An image in the sense of this legal provision is a depiction of a person, i.e., the representation of the person in his or her real appearance corresponding to life.[7] Usually, an image is a photograph and includes both analog and digital photographs.[8]

---

3 In Germany, the Directive was implemented within the scope of the *Bundesdatenschutzgesetz* (German Federal Data Protection Act, BDSG).

4 See, e.g., BGH VI ZR 9/14 of 11.11.2014 = Gewerblicher Rechtsschutz und Urheberrecht (GRUR) 2015, 295; Lauber-Rönsberg/Hartlaub (2017) 1058 with further references.

5 Raji (2019) 64–65; Klein (2017) 152.

6 The stage of taking pictures is not regulated in the KUG, but only subject to judge-made law; see also below III.3.

7 Specht-Riemenschneider (2022) § 22 KUG note 1.

8 Further examples of images are drawings or paintings of persons; see, e.g., Fricke (2019) § 22 KUG note 5.

Since the scope of application is very broad according to the wording of § 22 KUG, the courts have attempted to narrow the scope of the act.[9] As an unwritten requirement, the person depicted must be recognizable, which is mainly determined by the fact that the portrait shows the facial features or other personal attributes of the person.[10] The circle of persons relevant for the assessment of recognizability is the wider circle of acquaintances of the person depicted.[11]

Exceptions to the consent requirement are granted, inter alia, for contemporary historical images and for those used for artistic purposes (§ 23 KUG). However, this does not apply if the portrait harms a legitimate interest of the person depicted which requires a balanced assessment of the conflicting positions.[12] If the interest of the person depicted in the image prevails, he or she is entitled to cease-and-desist claims and damage claims.[13]

2. *Images in the scope of European data protection law*

The central regulatory subject matter of the GDPR is the "processing of personal data". Art. 4 No. 1 GDPR defines personal data as "any information relating to an identified or identifiable natural person". When a picture is taken with a digital camera, image data and so-called "Exchangeable Image File Format" data (EXIF data) are stored. The image data records exterior (physical) characteristics of the person pictured[14] and depending on the image, information about his or her economic circumstances, cultural and ethnic origin, religious affiliation or sexual orientation.[15] In addition, the EXIF data capture recording parameters such as the date, the time and – if the camera has a GPS module – the location. Based on the data created

9 Tausch (2016) 68 with further references.

10 BGH I ZR 151/56 of 14.02.1958 = Gewerblicher Rechtsschutz und Urheberrecht (GRUR) 1958, 458; I b ZR 126/63 of 09.06.1965 = Neue Juristische Wochenschrift (NJW) 1965, 2148 (2148–2149); Tausch (2016) 69.

11 Dreyer (2018) § 22 KUG note 6; Specht-Riemenschneider (2022) § 22 KUG note 4; OLG Köln, 15 U 133/13 of 06.03.2014 = Gewerblicher Rechtsschutz und Urheberrecht – Rechtsprechungs-Report (GRUR-RR) 2015, 318.

12 See, e.g., Eichenhofer (2022).

13 For further details, see Fricke (2019) § 22 KUG notes 23–39.

14 Sundermann (2018) 439.

15 Cf. Herbort (2017) 101; Schnabel (2008) 660.

by means of a photograph, a person can be identified or identifiable.[16] Images can therefore qualify as personal data.[17] However, the GDPR also partially narrows its scope of application by excluding activities for family or personal purposes, such as taking pictures in the context of leisure, holiday or hobby.[18]

The lawfulness of processing image data is based on art. 6 GDPR and the grounds for lawfulness listed which include, inter alia, the consent of the data subject (art. 6 (1) a) GDPR) or the exercise of legitimate interests pursued by the controller[19] of the data (art. 6 (1) f) GDPR). The interests of the controller must be balanced against the interests or fundamental rights and freedoms of the data subject – an assessment which is similar to the one in § 23 of the German KUG. If the data processing is found unlawful, the data subject has, inter alia, the right to erasure (art. 17 GDPR) and to compensation (art. 82 GDPR). Furthermore, administrative fines can be imposed by the authorities (art. 83–84 GDPR). Irrespective of the lawfulness, the controller must provide the data subject with all relevant information about the data processing (art. 12–15 GDPR).

III. The Relationship Between the GDPR and the KUG

The GDPR and the KUG regulate the same factual situation, i.e., the protection of people being depicted in images, but to some extent, they result in contradictory legal consequences.[20] In general, a European regulation such as the GDPR is directly applicable in all Member States pursuant to

16 The question of when a person can be considered identifiable by means of data has not yet been definitively settled. It could be required that the data controller himself is able to identify the person concerned, or it could suffice if anybody can identify the person concerned. The CJEU seems to take a compromise position. In the Breyer decision, it declared that additional knowledge of third parties can be taken into account if this knowledge is likely to be used to identify the data subject (CJEU, case C-582/14 of 19.10.2016, ECLI:EU:C:2016:779 – Breyer).

17 Specht-Riemenschneider/Jennessen (2019) 114; Dregelies (2019) 299.

18 Cf. Ernst (2021) Art. 2 DSGVO note 18.

19 Art. 4 No. 7 GDPR defines “controller” as the natural or legal person, public authority, agency or other body which determines the purposes and means of the processing of personal data. The controller is the addressee of the obligations and liabilities of the GDPR; see Raschauer (2018) Art. 4 DSGVO note 120.

20 This concerns, e.g., information requirements, conditions for a consent to data processing and damage claims. For further details, see Bienemann (2021) 15.

art. 288 (2) TFEU and, if a collision of two provisions occurs, as is the case here, European law takes precedence over national law.[21]

1. *Opening clauses in the GDPR*

However, the GDPR contains special provisions that further define its relationship with the national law of the Member States and allow them, in limited ways, to establish their own standards that deviate from the GDPR (so-called opening clauses). The most important of these special provisions is stipulated in art. 85 GDPR, although the relationship between the first two paragraphs of art. 85 GDPR has not yet been clarified. Pursuant to art. 85 (1) GDPR, Member States shall, via legislation, reconcile the right to protection of personal data under the GDPR with the right to freedom of expression and information, including processing for journalistic purposes and for scientific, artistic, or literary purposes. According to art. 85 (2) GDPR, Member States shall provide for derogations or exemptions from the main chapters of the GDPR for processing carried out for journalistic, scientific, artistic or literary purposes, if they are necessary to reconcile the right to the protection of personal data with the freedom of expression and information.

There appears to be general consent that art. 85 (2) GDPR provides for an opening clause for national law.[22] In contrast, it is disputed whether art. 85 (1) GDPR also contains such an opening clause.[23] Since the wording is not clear in this respect, the first paragraph could also be understood as a mere general adaptation mandate and the second paragraph could provide for the only opening clause in art. 85 GDPR.[24] The answer to this

---

21 ECJ, case 6/64 of 15.07.1964, ECLI:EU:C:1964:66 – Costa/E.N.E.L.; case 106/77 of 09.03.1978, ECLI:EU:C:1978:49 – Simmenthal; see also Kruis (2013) 98 with further references.

22 Pauly (2021) Art. 85 note 5; Pötters (2018) Art. 85 note 4; Lauber-Rönsberg/Hartlaub (2017) 1060.

23 In favor of qualifying Art. 85 (1) GDPR as an opening clause see, e.g., Bienemann (2021) 58; Lauber-Rönsberg (2019) 377; Cornils (2018) 64; Ziebarth/Elsaß (2018) 583; Frey (2018) Art. 85 note 2; Schulz/Heilmann (2018) Art. 85 note 7; Michel (2018) 842.

24 In favor of classifying Art. 85 (1) GDPR only as a general adaptation mandate to balance data protection rights and freedom of expression and information Pauly (2021) Art. 85 DSGVO notes 4–5; Buchner/Tinnefeld (2020) Art. 85 DSGVO note 12; Pötters (2018) Art. 85 notes 2 and 14; Klein (2017) 209; Kühling/Martini et al. (2016) 286.

question directly impacts the applicability of national law because art. 85 (1) GDPR – unlike art. 85 (2) GDPR – does not know any limitation to journalistic, scientific, artistic and literary purposes of processing and to specific chapters of the GDPR.

Three main arguments are submitted to classify paragraph 1 of art. 85 GDPR as a general regulatory mandate without an opening clause. However, all these arguments can be refuted with good reasons, especially when considering the history of the drafting of the GDPR. The first argument refers to the duty of the Member States to notify the Commission pursuant to art. 85 (3) GDPR if they have adopted legal provisions based on art. 85 (2) GDPR. Art. 85 (1) GDPR, on the contrary, is not mentioned here.[25] Although this appears to be a substantial systematic argument against the qualification of paragraph 1 as an opening clause, it is probable that an extension of the notification obligation under paragraph 3 to the first paragraph was simply missed in the urgency of the last weeks of the legislative process.[26]

Moreover, this oversight would not be the only one in the GDPR, as for example, the GDPR had originally referred to the non-existent art. 15 (1)(b) GDPR in art. 15 (4) GDPR.[27]

Secondly, it is argued that only art. 85 (2) GDPR contains detailed provisions on the conditions under which Member States may derogate from the GDPR by national law. Art. 85 (1) of the GDPR would therefore be too far-reaching if it were understood as an opening clause for member state regulations.[28] However, this objection can be countered with a restrictive interpretation of the opening clause.[29] Together with an increased burden of justification in the event of the enactment of national legislation, this opening clause can be limited so that there is no risk of the GDPR regulations being undermined. Thirdly, it is argued that art. 85(2) GDPR would be redundant if all cases were already covered by the broad scope of art. 85 (1) GDPR.[30] However, art. 85 (2) GDPR will not become obsolete if the first paragraph is also interpreted as an opening clause. This is at least true if the second paragraph is understood as a mini-

25 Kühling/Martini et al. (2016) 288.

26 Cornils (2018) 53–54; Lauber-Rönsberg (2018) 419.

27 Specht-Riemenschneider/Jennessen (2019) 116.

28 Buchner/Tinnefeld (2020) Art. 85 DSGVO note 12; Kühling/Martini et al. (2016) 287; see also Lauber-Rönsberg/Hartlaub (2017) 1061.

29 Specht-Riemenschneider/Jennessen (2019) 117.

30 Raji (2019) 65.

mum standard for particularly important purposes, such as the freedom of communication and art.[31]

Moreover, classifying art. 85 (1) GDPR as a general adaptation mandate without an opening clause would be pointless. Without an opening clause, Member States could not bring communication rights in line with data protection rights as required by art. 85 (1) GDPR since the GDPR would take precedence over any national law.[32] This outcome would also be contrary to the objective pursued by the Member States with the insertion of a more general opening clause. In the context of the Council Presidency's GDPR proposal, the Member States feared that an overly narrow opening clause such as art. 85 (2) GDPR would create the false impression that fundamental communication rights rank below data protection law.[33] It is therefore more convincing to additionally qualify art. 85 (1) GDPR as an opening clause for national law. However, definitive legal certainty will only be reached with a decision by the Court of Justice of the European Union (CJEU).

2. *The KUG and the opening clauses of the GDPR*

The conclusion that both paragraphs (1) and (2) of art. 85 GDPR provide for opening clauses leads to the follow-up question of whether the KUG fulfils the conditions of these clauses.

a) *Journalistic and artistic purposes*

As art. 85 (2) GDPR requires, §§ 22 and 23 KUG deviate from the GDPR regarding, inter alia, the lawfulness of data processing. Also, the KUG creates a reasonable balance between the freedoms of communication and art

---

31 Cornils (2018) 60–61.

32 Lauber-Rönsberg (2018) 420.

33 Council of the European Union, 24/04/2013, Doc. Nr. 8825/13 (p. 11). Similarly, the European Parliament had expressed its view that a restriction of Art. 85 GDPR to journalistic, artistic and literary purposes would not do justice to the right of freedom of expression (European Parliament, Draft Report on the proposal for a regulation of the European Parliament and of the Council on the protection of individual with regard to the processing of personal data and on the free movement of such data (General Data Protection Regulation), 16/01/2013, p. 196).

and the right to protection of personal data.[34] This is because § 23 KUG provides exceptions to the consent requirement of the person depicted unless the interests and rights of the person depicted take precedence. Therefore, it may be argued that §§ 22 and 23 KUG fulfil the requirements of art. 85 (2) GDPR in principle.[35] However, the opening clause in art. 85 (2) GDPR is restricted to data processing for journalistic and artistic purposes.[36] Thus, only § 23 (1) no. 1 KUG which provides an exemption for images portraying an aspect of contemporary history[37] and § 23 (1) no. 4 KUG which stipulates an exemption for images for artistic purposes, are covered by the opening clause. In contrast, § 23 (1) no. 2 and no. 3 KUG do not usually fall within the scope of art. 85 (2) GDPR.

It might appear problematic that the KUG not only covers the purposes mentioned in art. 85 (2) of the GDPR – in particular journalistic and artistic purposes – but also applies to images for other purposes. It is occasionally argued that a restriction of the respective norm, in this case the KUG, to journalistic and artistic purposes is required to effectively comply with the opening clause of art. 85 (2) of the GDPR.[38] As such a limitation has not yet been undertaken, it might be inferred that the opening clause does not apply at all and that the GDPR takes precedence over the KUG in its application. However, it seems more convincing to conclude that the KUG, although not applicable in its entirety, does apply in cases of privileged purposes.[39] If a part of a law does not fall under art. 85 (2) GDPR, the GDPR does not state at any point that a precedence of application is not possible for other parts. This also complies with the regulatory purpose of art. 85 GDPR which aims at protecting and strengthening the freedom of expression and art, as underlined by recital 153 of the GDPR. Besides, even if one still considers this result as problematic,

---

34 OLG Köln I-15 W 27/18 of 18.06.2018 = Zeitschrift für Datenschutz (ZD) 2018, 434 (435).

35 Lauber-Rönsberg/Hartlaub (2017) 1060–1061; Fricke (2019) § 22 KUG note 3; Dregelies (2019) 302–303; Ziebarth/Elsaß (2018) 583; BGH VI ZR 250/19 of 07.07.2020, para. 10; OLG Köln I-15 W 27/18 of 18.06.2018 = Zeitschrift für Datenschutz (ZD) 2018, 434 (both court decisions with regard to journalistic purposes). Disagreeing, however, *Klein* (2017) 152; Raji (2019) 64–65.

36 The other two purposes mentioned in Art. 85 (2) GDPR are not relevant with regard to the application of the KUG.

37 Images of contemporary history will usually fall within the term "journalistic purposes", which is to be interpreted broadly, as recital 153 GDPR states. See also CJEU, case C-345/17 of 14.02.2019, ECLI:EU:C:2019:122 – Buivids.

38 Klein (2017) 223–225.

39 Lauber-Rönsberg/Hartlaub (2017) 1061.

a continuing application of the KUG – regardless of the purpose – would then still be possible via art. 85 (1) GDPR.[40]

b) Other purposes

As explained, the use of personal images for certain purposes, such as photographs in the area of private individual communication or in social networks, are not covered by art. 85 (2) GDPR.[41] Therefore, the application of the KUG to the processing of images for other purposes is only possible if one classifies art. 85 (1) GDPR as an opening clause, as it is assumed in this article.[42]

c) Opening clauses and already existing laws

One question that arises for both opening clauses of art. 85 GDPR is whether they require newly enacted legislation. It might be argued that only new or at least amended laws could restrict the GDPR through the opening clauses in art. 85 GDPR.[43] Indeed, the KUG, which has remained practically unchanged for more than 100 years, can hardly be described as an adaptation and reaction to the GDPR. Nevertheless, the objection can be countered by the fact that the GDPR does not explicitly require a newly created law at any point. A parallel can be drawn with the implementation of European secondary law into national law. Here, it is possible that a (national) law that has already entered into force can also act as an implementing statute.[44] Besides, it can be beneficial for the purpose of legal certainty that an already existing, functioning regulatory system, which has also been developed by case law over the decades, can continue to remain in force.[45] Therefore, it should be irrelevant whether the scope granted to

40 This is, of course, only possible if Art. 85 (1) GDPR is considered as an opening clause.
41 Cf. Specht-Riemenschneider/Jennessen (2019) 125–126.
42 Cf. Lauber-Rönsberg (2018) 430–431; see above III.1.
43 Klein (2017) 182.
44 Benedikt/Kranig (2019) 5.
45 Ziebarth/Elsaß (2018) 580; Lauber-Rösberg/Hartlaub (2017) 1061; Roßnagel (2017) 279.

the Member States is filled by newly created or – as in this case – already existing regulations.[46]

3. *The (legal) discrepancy between capturing images and their publication*

The KUG regulates the distribution and public display of images. Regarding the act of photography, German image law offers protection only based on case law through the general right of personality (*allgemeines Persönlichkeitsrecht*). Therefore, in the absence of sufficient codification, it can be argued that no opening clause is fulfilled and that the GDPR takes precedence. The taking of images and their further processing would then be covered by two different regulatory regimes.

The precedence of the GDPR when capturing images could lead to unreasonable results if their publication is permitted under the KUG – which is not superseded by the GDPR –, whereas the taking of a picture would be unlawful under the GDPR. Taking a picture can be usually classified as the lesser infringement of the right of personality in comparison to its publication or distribution. Such a contradiction could be partly avoided by basing the balancing of interests according to art. 6 (1) f) GDPR on the same principles as they were already applied by courts in the context of the general right of personality and the KUG. However, this approach remains without a legal basis, finds no support in the GDPR, and does not resolve the dichotomy of image protection. Against this background, it would therefore only be sensible and legally certain to resort to a legislative intervention.[47]

IV. Concluding Remarks: The Future of Image Protection Law

The analysis of legal details in the relationship between the GDPR and national protection of images such as the KUG is important, but it also obscures the view of fundamental questions. Regardless of the specific controversial legal points, the more general and abstract question of how to regulate images, i.e., the depiction of persons in photographs, arises. Is

46 Krüger/Wiencke (2019) 77; Roßnagel (2017) 278 (with regard to Art. 6 (2) GDPR); a more critical view is taken by Hildebrand (2018) 589.

47 Ziebarth/Elsaß (2018) 584; see below IV.

the right to one's own image obsolete? Are all images just data, and thus should be regulated under data protection law?

On the one hand, today's photography is indeed very similar to other forms of extensive data processing. Most people always have a device capable of taking pictures at their disposal, such as smartphones or digital cameras, and use them very frequently.[48] In this regard, the reason why data protection law was established – the increasing use of automated data processing and enormous data volumes[49] – also applies in principle to the processing of images. Moreover, the proximity of taking pictures of peoples' faces and data processing is most obvious in the cases of both biometric passport photographs[50] and video surveillance.

On the other hand, merely because an area such as the right to one's own image falls under a broader legal framework does not mean that it is a perfect fit. For example, information requirements of data protection laws such as the GDPR often cannot be fulfilled in a sensible way for photographers and the threat of administrative fines in case of GDPR infringements could have chilling effects on photographic activities. Also, the reasons for lawfulness in processing image data depend on vague and undefined requirements ("legitimate interests of the controller"). This is an even bigger problem when considering that there is no extensive case law for the assessment of image data. Even the GDPR recognizes that there are areas, especially including journalism, communication, science, and art, which should be regulated in special (non-data) laws. These laws can take the special characteristics and particularities of the nature of image protection into account and offer protection to persons depicted in images when it is really needed.

What does this mean for the legal framework in Germany? A legal intervention by the German parliament appears to be advisable to clarify the relationship between the KUG and the GDPR. Here, it would seem reasonable to regulate the right to one's own image in special legislation and to adapt it to technical developments. Further, the stage of taking a picture could also be regulated to prevent a divergence of the legal frameworks for images.

---

48 A striking example for the use of cameras and the inflation of images nowadays is the current number of 995 pictures uploaded on the social network Instagram per second, which totals up to 86 million pictures per day (https://www.omnicoreagency.com/instagram-statistics/).

49 Cf. BT-Drucksache 7/1027, pp. 1 and 17.

50 Dreier (2019) 71 et seq.

References

Benedikt, Kristin/Kranig, Thomas (2019): 'DS-GVO und KUG – ein gespanntes Verhältnis', Zeitschrift für Datenschutz (2019) 4–7

Bienemann, Linda (2021): *Reformbedarf des Kunsturhebergesetzes im digitalen Zeitalter – Eine rechtsdogmatische Untersuchung unter besonderer Berücksichtigung der Einflüsse von DSGVO und InfoSoc-RL* (Baden-Baden: Nomos 2021)

Buchner, Benedikt/Tinnefeld, Marie-Theres (2020): 'Commentary on Art. 85 DSG-VO', in: Kühling, Jürgen/Buchner, Benedikt: *Datenschutz-Grundverordnung – BDSG* (München: C.H. Beck 3rd edition 2020)

Cornils, Matthias (2018): *Das datenschutzrechtliche Medienprivileg unter Behördenaufsicht?* (Tübingen: Mohr Siebeck 2018)

Dregelies, Max (2019): 'Fotografieren in der Öffentlichkeit und Datenschutz', Zeitschrift für das gesamte Medienrecht (2019) 298–303

Dreier, Thomas (2019): *Law and Images*, Art and Law 3.1 (Leiden/Boston: Brill 2019)

Dreyer, Gunda (2018): 'Commentary on § 22 KUG', in: Dreyer, Gunda/Kotthof, Jost/Meckel, Astrid/Hentsch, Christian-Henner: *Urheberrecht, Urheberrechtsgesetz, Verwertungsgesellschaftsgesetz, Kunsturhebergesetz* (Heidelberg: C.F. Müller 4th edition 2018)

Eichenhofer, Johannes (2022): 'The Constitutional Protection of Images', in: Dreier, Thomas/Andina, Tiziana: *Digital Ethics – The issue of images* (Baden-Baden: Nomos 2022) 357–385

Ernst, Stefan (2021): 'Commentary on Art. 2 DSGVO', in: Paal, Boris/Pauly, Daniel: *Datenschutz-Grundverordnung – Bundesdatenschutzgesetz* (München: C.H. Beck 3rd edition 2021)

Frey, Dieter (2018): 'Commentary on Art. 85 DSGVO', in: Schwartmann, Rolf/Jaspers, Andreas/Thüsing, Gregor/Kugelmann, Dieter: *DS-GVO/BDSG – Datenschutz-Grundverordnung und Bundesdatenschutzgesetz* (Heidelberg: C.F. Müller 2018)

Fricke, Michael (2019): 'Commentary of § 22 KUG', in: Wandtke, Artur-Axel/Bullinger, Winfried: *Praxiskommentar Urheberrecht* (München: C.H. Beck 5th edition 2019)

Herbort, Nina (2017): *Digitale Bildnisse* (Tübingen: Mohr Siebeck 2017)

Hildebrand, Angela (2018): 'Künstlerische Straßenfotografie ohne Einwilligung der abgebildeten Person', Zeitschrift für Urheber- und Medienrecht (2018) 585–590

Klein, Florian (2017): *Personenbilder im Spannungsfeld von Datenschutzgrundverordnung und Kunsturhebergesetz* (Frankfurt: Peter Lang 2017)

Krüger, Stefan/Wiencke, Julia (2019): 'Bitte recht freundlich – Verhältnis zwischen KUG und DS-GVO', Multimedia und Recht (2019) 76–80

Kruis, Tobias (2013): *Der Anwendungsvorrang des EU-Rechts in Theorie und Praxis* (Tübingen: Mohr Siebeck 2013)

Kühling, Jürgen/Martini, Mario/Heberlein, Johanna/Kühl, Benjamin/Nink, David/ Weinzierl, Quirin/Wenzel, Michael (2016): *Die Datenschutzgrundverordnung und das nationale Recht – Erste Überlegungen zum innerstaatlichen Regelungsbedarf* (Münster: Monsenstein und Vannerdat 2016)

Lauber-Rönsberg, Anne (2018): 'Die Auswirkungen der DSGVO auf das zivilrechtliche Äußerungsrecht', UFITA – Archiv für Medienrecht und Medienwissenschaft (2018) 398–435

Lauber-Rönsberg, Anne (2019): 'Zum Verhältnis von Datenschutzrecht und zivilrechtlichem Äußerungsrecht', Zeitschrift für das gesamte Medienrecht (2019) 373–383

Lauber-Rönsberg, Anne/Hartlaub, Anneliese (2017): 'Personenbildnisse im Spannungsfeld zwischen Äußerungs- und Datenschutzrecht', Neue Juristische Wochenschrift (2017) 1057–1062

Michel, Stefan (2018): 'Bewertungsportale und das Medienprivileg – Neue Impulse durch Art. 85 DSGVO', Zeitschrift für Urheber- und Medienrecht (2018) 836–843

Pauly, Danie (2021): 'Commentary on Art. 85 DSGVO', in: Paal, Boris/Pauly, Daniel: *Datenschutz-Grundverordnung – Bundesdatenschutzgesetz* (München: C.H. Beck 3rd edition 2021)

Pötters, Stephan (2018): 'Commentary on Art. 85 DSGVO', in: Gola, Peter: *Datenschutzgrundverordnung – Kommentar* (München: C.H. Beck 2nd edition 2018)

Raji, Behrang (2019): 'Auswirkungen der DS-GVO auf nationales Fotorecht', Zeitschrift für Urheber- und Medienrecht (2019) 61–66

Raschauer, Nicolas (2018): 'Commentary on Art. 4 DSGVO', in: Sydow, Gernot: *Europäische Datenschutzgrundverordnung – Handkommentar* (Baden-Baden: Nomos 2nd edition 2018)

Roßnagel, Alexander (2017): 'Gesetzgebung im Rahmen der Datenschutz-Grundverordnung. Aufgaben und Spielräume des deutschen Gesetzgebers?', Datenschutz und Datensicherheit (2017) 277–281

Schnabel, Christoph (2008): 'Das Recht am eigenen Bild und der Datenschutz', Zeitschrift für Urheber- und Medienrecht (2008) 657–662

Schulz, Sebastian/Heilmann, Stefan (2018): 'Commentary on Art. 85 DSGVO', in: Gierschmann, Sibylle/Schlender, Katharina/Stenzel, Rainer/Veil, Winfried: *Kommentar Datenschutzgrundverordnung* (Cologne: Reguvis 2018)

Specht-Riemenschneider, Louisa (2022): 'Commentary of the German KUG', in: Dreier, Thomas/Schulze, Gernot: *Urheberrechtsgesetz*, (München: C.H. Beck 7th edition 2022)

Specht-Riemenschneider, Louisa/Jennessen, Dennis (2019): 'Persönlichkeitsschutz im digitalen Umfeld in Zeiten der Mehrebenenregulierung', in: Aldenhoff, Christian/Edeler, Lukas/Hennig, Martin/Kelsch, Jakob/Raabe, Lea/Sobala, Felix: *Digitalität und Privatheit – Kulturelle, politisch-rechtliche und soziale Perspektiven* (Bielefeld: transcript 2019) 111–128

Sundermann, Steffen (2018): 'Fotografien von Menschenansammlungen nach der DSGVO', Kommunikation und Recht (2018) 438–445

Tausch, Sebastian (2016): *Persönlichkeitsrechtsverletzungen durch die Veröffentlichung von Fotos im Internet* (Baden-Baden: Nomos 2016)

Ziebart, Lennart/Elsaß, Lennart (2018): 'Neue Maßstäbe für die Rechtmäßigkeit der Nutzung von Personenbildnissen in der Unternehmenskommunikation?', Zeitschrift für Urheber- und Medienrecht (2018) 578–585

Chapter 15
Human Authorship and Art Created by Artificial Intelligence – Where Do We Stand?

Gianmaria Ajani

> "We must expect great innovations to transform the entire technique of the arts, thereby affecting artistic invention itself and perhaps even bringing about an amazing change in our very notion of art".[1]

I. Introductory Note

Art as an expression of technique, art as a display of sentiment: there is no need to be an art connoisseur to evoke how often these two descriptions have been opposed. Law as culture and law as a tool for social engineering: these two narratives partake, as well, in a long intellectual history, although less known to the wider public. Those more focused on tools and techniques share an aspiration for global uniform regulations, while those keen on cultures and emotions manifest a preference for *ad hoc* local regulations. This tension between a favour for a global harmonization of rules and a deference to cultural diversities also affects copyright laws. As is well known, an age-old cultural and political difference between the French inspired and Anglo-American copyright laws has not completely been understood. Authors and their works still receive, in some regards, and despite international conventions, different treatment depending on the jurisdiction.

Today, we observe new regulatory approaches arising from technology such as the emergent Artificial Intelligence (AI)-generated art. Since the 70s, computers have been used to create imaginative works such as poetry, paintings, and musical compositions. Most of those computer-made *oeuvres* derived from the programmer's inputs, while the machine was simply an instrument, like a brush or a camera. While this perception persists

---

1 Paul Valéry, *Pièces Sur L'art. La Conquête de l'ubiquité* (1928), quoted by Walter Benjamin as epigraph to his *The Work of Art in the Age of Mechanical Reproduction*, 1935.

today, we are also facing a dramatic technological change which grants us the opportunity to re-evaluate the role played by processors in the creative course.

When computers were considered as nothing more than a tool, legal provisions were applied accordingly. Most of today's AI-driven mechanisms however, develop algorithms through machine learning. The incremental separation of machines from humans brings a new challenge to an established set of provisions of law and arts. When confronted with new challenges brought in by AI-generated works, the law appears wanting. Globally, most commentators refer to the letter of the law, where a "human factor" seems to be an inescapable requirement of copyright authorship. Others minimise the matter, noting the scarcity of judicial cases where AI-generated art is at stake.

In my opinion, the debate on the impact of AI on copyright laws is significant and should not be postponed, based on a pretext of immaturity, if not irrelevance, of the topic. It is significant at least for the following reasons: AI-driven systems and the artworks that they produce nurture policy issues that affect copyright ownership entitlements and legal protection of artists, researchers, engineers who are experimenting in the field. Also, AI-generated creations question the dynamics among art producers, artworks, and the public. The aim of this essay is to indicate that this matter is incumbent and relevant for both international and national legal regimes of regulating art production.

II. A New Agenda for Copyright Laws

Imagination, creativity, and therefore, the making of art are abilities peculiar to human intelligence, and vibrant marks of humankind. Among the three, imagination precedes creativity in the development of human consciousness, while creativity may, but not necessarily does, reflects itself in a product. A product can be a tool, a tale, and even, an artwork. Initially, the law paid little attention to such creativity. Indeed, both the production and trade of its results were regulated by two main areas of private law: property and contract. Eventually, creativity was perceived as an important driver of human progress. This perception led to the first copyright regimes being established in the 18th century.

Today, the so-called 4th revolution[2] is boosted by the development of machine learning[3] and deep learning software which allows autonomous systems to learn and execute outputs without being explicitly instructed by human beings. While arguing that the traditional copyright laws are inadequate to cope with new technology involved in creating artworks, Shlomit Yanisky-Ravid contends that *oeuvres* autonomously generated by machines challenge a basic tenet of copyright law, namely that only humans can create works: "Copyright laws are simply ill-equipped to accommodate this tech-revolution and are therefore unlikely to survive in their current form. In order to address the change in the way art is being created, we must either rethink these laws, give them new meaning, or be ready to replace them".[4] Clearly, AI-generated creations raise a number of copyright questions.

Firstly, the development outlined above has occurred in parallel with a continuous evolution of data mining technology. Further, widened access to all types of data also represents a set of multiple challenges to "classic copyright regulations"[5]. Training an algorithm may require the use of images, texts, or other data. Artworks used to train can be in open source, in the public domain, or protected. While it would not be easy to determine which works have been effectively used in the training process, one wonders whether a claim for copyright infringement of protected works would be successful. Secondly, the programmer could sell the algorithm's code as a work in itself. Thirdly, from a different, but altogether relevant, perspective, AI-generated art raises the issue of preserving algorithms.[6] Their fast deprecation has even encouraged some artists to qualify their output as temporary performances rather than paintings or videos.[7] Fourthly, authorship is concerned whenever an AI system, being dependent on the

---

2 See Floridi (2014).

3 "Machine learning" is a branch of artificial intelligence based on the idea that systems can learn from data, identify patterns and make decisions with minimal human intervention. "Deep learning" is a type of machine learning that trains a computer to perform human-like tasks, such as recognizing speech, identifying images or making predictions. See Thoma (2016).

4 Yanisky-Ravid (2017); see also Bridy (2012) 5.

5 When using the expression "classic copyright regulations", I refer to the body of enactments adopted in the course of the 19th and the 20th century, both at the level of national and supranational law. Being "classic", these enactments are, at times, challenged by new artistic actions.

6 The business practice of recurrently updating software frameworks can make trained neural network models obsolete over time.

7 Gaskin (2018), quoting artist Harshit Agrawal.

learning algorithm, is capable of making combinations that are increasingly autonomous from the original set of materials provided by the programmer. When the deterministic nature of software becomes a probabilistic process, we observe a qualitative leap that cannot be explained by the metaphor of the "brush and tool". All these issues have legal implications that are not clearly covered by current copyright regulations.

In this work I explore the fourth issue which deals with the ontological nature of AI-generated creations which challenge classical copyright law concepts, namely authorship and originality.

Today, computers produce artistic or innovative outputs. These programs, however, should not be considered as either "able" or "not able" to autonomously produce works.[8] Rather, there is a continuum linking, at one extreme, 'computer-assisted' works and, at the other extreme, autonomously generated works. The middle of the continuum is broad and includes methods with varying grades of human intervention. Depending on the degree of human intervention, the form of the output may be minimally, significantly, or substantially determined by software. And while for computer-assisted works the software is a production device, for *autonomously generated works* the outcome may be unpredictable.[9]

These outcomes become an epistemological case. Their legal status is uncertain and depends on our attitude towards the degree of autonomy from humans that machines "enjoy".[10] Already, we appreciate "e-David" and "Paul," robots capable of drawing portraits in the inventive style of Patrick Tresset, their artist programmer.[11] More than merely copying machines, Tresset's robots are fitted with an "autonomous artistic creativity" that makes them capable of producing "objects that are considered as artworks".[12] Indeed, those following contemporary art updates know that a "generative adversarial network" (GAN)[13], having ref-

8 See: Sawyer (2012) 143 et seq.

9 For an early account see Dreier (1992).

10 See Thaler (1996).

11 E-David takes pictures autonomously with its camera and draws original paintings from the snapshots. By using different techniques, it makes "autonomous and unpredictable decisions about the image, the shapes and colors, the match of lights and shadows"; see Yanisky-Ravid (2017) 669.

12 See Hodgkins (2016).

13 A generative adversarial network (GAN) is a machine learning model, invented by Ian Goodfellow in 2014, in which two neural networks compete with each other to become more accurate in their predictions. GANs typically run unsupervised. See Gatys/Ecker/Bethge (2015) 2.

erenced 15,000 portraits from various centuries, had painted on canvas a *Portrait of Edmond Belamy*.[14] The work, signed at the bottom right with $\min_{G} \max_{D} E_x\left[\log\left(D\left(x\right)\right)\right] + E_z\left[\log\left(1 - D\left(G\left(z\right)\right)\right)\right]$, namely part of the algorithm code that produced it, was presented at a Christie's auction.

The *Paul*-originated paintings have been exhibited in major art museums and acquired by galleries, museums, and art fairs for display, while the *Edmond Belamy* portrait was sold for 432.000 USD.

These examples, among others, evidence that questioning the nature of an artwork produced by automatic systems is not a pursuit confined within a purely theoretical debate. The existence of these works, and in particular, their appearance in the art world, forces us to understand their place within copyright regulation, as well as the art world.

III. AI-Generated Art and Creativity

Countless descriptions have been associated with the concept of "creativity". It can be "weak" or "strong", "exploratory" or "transformational", and additionally, "4th dimensional". A model of creativity devised by Mihály Csikszentmihályi[15] includes three interrelated elements:

- an accepted, and agreed upon, domain of current knowledge;
- an agent who alters a component of the domain to produce something novel; and
- a field of experts that ultimately decide whether the novelty will be accepted into the existing domain.

Kyle Jennings has identified three criteria for an agent to qualify a system featuring creative autonomy:

- autonomous evaluation (the system can evaluate its acceptance of a creation without seeking opinions from an outside source);[16]

---

14 Christie's (2018).

15 Csikszentmihályi (1988).

16 The following definitions are provided by Jennings (2010): "autonomous evaluation requires that the system be able to issue opinions without consulting an outside human or machine intelligence. However, the system is free to ask for or observe others' opinions at other times, and to store this information".

- autonomous change (the system initiates and guides variation to its standards without being explicitly directed when and how to do so); and
- non-randomness (the system's evaluations and standard changes are not purely random).[17]

Applying these criteria to AI means that "[...] progress[ing] from a capable apprentice to a creator in its own right, an AI system must be able to both independently apply and independently change the standards it uses. This ideal will be called 'creative autonomy,' and represents the system's freedom to pursue a course independent of its programmer's or operator's intentions".[18] Following these approaches, an author is not the lone component of the creative process. Nor does creativity exist independently in any of the listed elements. Rather, creativity depends on individual capacity, acquisition of information and judgment by experts.

This perspective can free AI-systems from the identification of "autonomy" as a state of complete segregation. Kyle Jennings' argument logically supports the recognition of a truly independent AI system as one where transformational (and not pure exploratory) creativity emerges out of interactions among many different agents. In such an environment, machine learning may enable an AI system to change its preferences not randomly, but as a reaction to continuously collected evaluations and opinions.[19] Also, an AI system may attain experience from the senses. For example, AI painters have shown that AI paintings can be influenced by sounds, lights and temperature in the environment, or even keywords that the system autonomously chooses.[20]

In its purest appearance, creativity may lead to ingenious works which challenge standards and canons and ultimately produce unconventional art. "Unconventional" is the appropriate word, as it means deviating from conventional canons. But is AI-generated art unconventional? Indeed, it is one thing to reproduce a painting from the digestion of thousands of similar artworks, and it is another to produce unusual works, marked by a new style.

Ahmed Elgammal, the director of the Art and Artificial Intelligence Laboratory at Rutgers University, built upon the development of GAN

17 Jennings (2010) 490.
18 Ibid. 491.
19 Ibid. 499.
20 Moss (2015).

systems to establish the creative adversarial network (CAN).[21] This system is specifically programmed to produce originality and creates images which differ from those collected. In this case, the images consisted of paintings from the 14th century onwards in all styles. Generally, works produced through a CAN system have received appreciation in the art world. Important auction houses in particular, have introduced these *oeuvres* into international visual art markets. CAN systems stretch across two extremes: the innovative capacity of AI-made works to depart from established canons, and the ability to produce *oeuvres* that are not foreseeable by the algorithm's designer. One algorithm creates a solution, the other judges it, and the system loops back and forth until the intended result is reached. The innovative aspect is that the generator is informed to produce an image that the discriminator recognises as "art", but which does not fall into any of the existing styles.

If humans do not trigger the action taken by an automatic system, nor partake at the end of the process by supplying sufficient "intellectual creation" to match the minimum standard of authorship requested by the Berne Convention for the Protection of Literary and Artistic Works, one might well consider these outputs to be "autonomously computer-generated".

IV. AI-Made Art and the Law

Let us assume, then, that an *oeuvre* is produced via an independent AI process, free from human intervention in the making. What would its legal status be?

According to most authors, copyright law is not currently structured to accommodate the innovative authorship frame of "people-who-write-programs-that-make-art".[22] This position can be read in two different ways. Firstly, whether innovative authorship leads to the recognition of authorship for programs-that make-art. Secondly, whether a conservative approach would be adopted to maintain that copyright should only grant "human authorial rights".

The latest generation of AI systems makes it difficult to understand where the programmer's contribution ends and the user's role begins. This becomes even more confusing when the program is coded to produce

21 Elgammal (2017).
22 See Zemer (2006) and (2016).

expressive choices independent of both the programmer and user. Indeed, perhaps the challenge AI brings to copyright law is so robust it necessitates a change of perspective regarding authorship requirements.

Such a change would undoubtedly challenge classic copyright law which focuses on the position of the author. Despite numerous position papers, white papers, governmental reports and recommendations,[23] national lawmakers have not yet addressed the subject. This is unsurprising, as most policymakers view such regulation as premature. In their opinion, existing copyright laws can respond, at both national and international level, to the challenges brought into the system by AI-generated artworks.

In my view, this position holds so long as one maintains that artworks produced by machines are *derived* from human action. Until recently, it was a common belief that a machine, though defined as "intelligent", lacked the "creative aptitude" to produce artworks. Indeed, it is well known that the law in many countries only protects "original" works created by human intelligence. "Until recently", I said. However, today many new projects attest that it is not worth condemning the matter as simply irrelevant.

The 1886 Berne Convention failed to define authorship because it was generally acknowledged thatthe term "author" implies a human element. In the United States it is more explicit as the Federal Copyright Office declared that it will "register an original work of authorship, provided that the work was created by a human being".[24] This statement originates from Feist Publications vs. Rural Telephone Service Company Inc.[25] In this case, the court ruled that copyright law only protects "the fruits of intellectual labour" that "are founded in the creative powers of the mind." Within the European Union, the Court of Justice has ruled several times that copyright only applies to *original* works, and that originality must reflect the "author's own intellectual creation".[26] Likewise, EU Member States national laws imply, more or less explicitly, that the "human factor" is the prerequisite to provide copyright protection to authors.

UK law deserves a special note, as its copyright legislation contains specific provisions dealing with computer-generated works. According to

---

23 See, e.g., French Ministère de l'enseignement supérieur (2017); UK Science and Technology Committee of the House of Commons (2016); U.S. National Science and Technology Council-Subcommittee on Machine Learning and Artificial Intelligence (2016).

24 U.S. Copyright Office (2017) § 306.

25 499 U.S. 340 (1991).

26 ECJ, case C-5/08 of 16 July 2009 – Infopaq.

Sec. 178 of the UK Copyright Designs and Patent Act (CDPA, 1988), a computer-generated work is defined as "a work that is generated by a computer such that there is no human author". Under s. 9.3 of the same CDPA authorship of such work is "given to the person by whom the arrangements necessary for the creation of the work are undertaken". However, this legislation is a legal fiction set to solve the authorship dilemma of AI works on the belief that the computer is merely a tool. Clearly, "the person responsible for making such arrangements is not the true author under copyright law, as evidenced by s. 9.1 CDPA".[27] The more removed AI is from human interference, the less likely authorship will be granted due to the lack of human intervention. British and similar legislation adopted in other common law jurisdictions do not seem to be a workable solution to this dilemma. Even if it is viable for AI systems which are not autonomous, the identity of the "person responsible for the arrangements" remains unclear.

The problem compounds when the automatically generated output cannot be traced back to any human action or interference. According to existent copyright regulations, an AI independently generated work will not be recognized as an "artwork" in the sense of copyright law and, therefore, will not be subject to the legal protection provided by copyright privileges. In other words, so long as the process is recognised by the law as driven by a human agent and the result of a human mind, the law will be adapted to follow suit and grant humans copyright. However, when technology advances to the extent that it is difficult to recognize the "person making the arrangements for the work", there is a legal vacuum. The challenge cannot be solved by implementing minimal amendments to copyright law. Rather, we should understand that inertia or minimal adjustment will not make up for the uncertainties originated in the copyright systems by AI. This vacuum will generate confusion and judicial irresolution.

In fact, this legal dilemma revolves around two options:

- a strict reading of copyright law: if there is no way to provide protection, then the law does not intend to protect AI generated works. This option will result in leaving AI generated artworks in the public domain;[28] or

27 Denicola (2016).
28 See Ramalho (2017).

- assigning the title and related protections by choosing one or more privileged holders, such as the *programmer*[29] or the *user*.[30]

The "human factor", then, remains the centre of the analysis.

Its permanence, however, has not prevented a flourishing of proposals to find a way out of the maze of lacking legal regulations and outdated normative theories, to adjust copyright laws to the advancement of technology. Among those proposals, the most challenging are the ones addressed to consider "AI-driven non-human agents" as potential subjects of law, as well as those developing new theories within the law of robots.[31] Colin Davies contends that "a corporate body has under UK law legal recognition as an individual." Therefore, "a computer which is more akin to a true person, more particularly with the new generation of artificial intelligent computers, should be accorded the same status. This will enable us to attribute authorship of computer-generated works/inventions to the body best entitled to them, the computer, and allow the respective claims of interested parties to be determined not by arbitrary rules of law, but by the parties themselves, through negotiated contractual terms. Revolutionary this may be, but no more so than granting intellectual property rights, as we currently do, to a body corporate".[32]

V. AI-Made Art and the Art World

So far, I have looked at the law. A restrictive reading suggests that whenever there is not a human author, there is no copyright protection. Therefore, whenever new generation AI-machines autonomously produce *oeuvres* without human interference, these works are in the public domain. Lacking a clear identification of an author, copyright law excludes these works from protection.

Let us now shift our attention from the *subject* to the *object*. Non-human intelligent agents, not qualified by the law as "authors", can independently produce works remarkable by their aesthetical impact. Whether those works can be qualified as "artworks" depends, sometimes, on the law,

29 A *programmer* (also called *coder*) is an individual that writes computer software or applications by giving the computer specific programming instructions.
30 *Users* are the people (or other systems) for whom the software is written.
31 See Pagallo (2013) 155–181.
32 Davies (2011) 618.

but particularly on the *art world*.[33] In fact, an artwork is not only what is defined by the law.[34] As art historians have repeatedly proven, the art world is able to recognize works that escape any legal classification. AI undeniably pushes to the forefront an understanding of art where the social network[35] related to the artistic practice does not involve an author in a traditional, human sense. The outputs of AI may very well be of such a quality that they can sustain enjoyable appreciation in ways that are not dissimilar from those found in more traditional art *genres*.

This happens despite the inability of copyright law to resolve the authorship dilemma. The structure of traditional copyright law, from its property law origins, is not designed to trace situations where authors, artworks, and users blur. This has already been proven by contemporary visual arts, which brought quite several challenges to copyright law.

Views differ on the relationship between human and not-human agents. This stems from a discussion emerging in the literature on the identification of an AI-operated machines as "owners" of generated works. This option – supported by some scholars – grants an artificial intelligent agent legal personhood but does not necessarily imply a recognition of authorship. This view has been developed most clearly by Gabriel Hallevy who advocates the recognition of legal personality for AI operated machines.[36] Recent literature suggests that autonomy, creativity, and advancement of AI systems should lead to their recognition as independent subjects vested with limited patrimonial rights and duties.[37] As stated by Yanisky-Ravid, "the corporation as a legal entity can serve as a basis for imposing rights and duties on AI systems. Corporations are legal entities subject to a legal regime, including corporate, labor, and even criminal law. Therefore, the question relating to AI entities has become 'does the growing intelligence of AI entities subject them, as any other legal entity, to legal social control?'".[38]

However, advocating a legal status for intelligent machines – although discussed at both the *political* and *legal* level – remains a proposal confined within a limited circle of proponents. The main counterargument is well known: the law acknowledges personality for corporations in all legal systems, but corporations are constituted by human beings. The traditional

33 On Arthur Danto and the art world see Andina (2017).

34 Duboff (1990).

35 See McIver Lopes (2017) and (2009).

36 Hallevy (2012) 211.

37 Chopra/White (2011) 1–3.

38 Yanisky-Ravid (2017) 670; see also Weaver (2014) 3 et seq.

paradigm is based on the idea that humans are "behind" legal entities and corporations. This criticism still holds true, at least for EU institutions where no reform agenda is clear. On 12 February 2019 the European Parliament adopted a Resolution on a comprehensive European industrial policy on artificial intelligence (AI) and robotics.[39] After describing AI as "one of the strategic technologies of the 21st century", the European Parliament presented several recommendations to the Member States, advocating "human-centric technology," to avoid the possible misuse of AI technologies to the detriment of fundamental human rights. The European Parliament insisted on the predominance of the human factor over computer systems based on "the 'man operates machine' principle of responsibility," and recommend[ed] that "humans must always be ultimately responsible for decision-making".[40]

As a set of Russian dolls, the human factor re-emerges from every notion, be it authorship, originality, or creativity. As the human factor is founded in classical copyright law, the latter influences any possible interpretation internal to the legal discourse. We must, therefore, accept that the legal interpretation is not ready to abandon its classical foundation. At the same time, we should also acknowledge that classical law is crippled by the advancement of new technologies, and in particular by the newly AI-autonomously generated *oeuvres*.

VI. Concluding Remarks

Advancements in technology and the last generation of autonomous AI systems are posing a new challenge to the legal regime of authorship. Neither interpretation nor simple adjustments of existing laws seem to be a proper response. For the first, time we experience a manner of making art which assumes the non-existence of a human author. Lacking an adequate understanding of the scale and perspectives of these advancements, it is likely that, while the art world is embracing AI-generated artworks, its legal counterpart remains unresponsive.

This contribution aimed to offer a view on the phenomenon of AI-made art, and to observe how it can be accommodated within copyright law. I have distinguished between different kinds of AI-generated *oeuvres*. Some cases, to be accurate, do not really challenge current laws. Whenever a

39 2018/2088 (INI).
40 Ibid.

human intervention can be detected in the creative process, an AI system remains a tool, a sophisticated tool, but a tool, nonetheless. And according to existing copyright laws, even a modest contribution is sufficient to recognize originality. An analogous solution applies whenever the artwork is independently created by the AI, but the human intervention consists in a selection of what has been made. In such cases the law is clear in recognizing human authorship as the act of selecting and choosing is traditionally viewed as subsisting of copyright. Beyond those instances, a remaining issue is whether a work *autonomously* generated and selected by an AI program, absent whatsoever human involvement, can subsist of copyright. In this case, different arguments lead to the conclusion that the current law is not helpful. Yet, the lack of regulation does not necessarily mean that such works lack qualification as an artwork. It rather means there is an absence of legal protection.

To make up for this deficiency, several authors from different research fields have elaborated a great array of proposals.

As we have seen, the first of these solutions follows the logic of the structure of copyright law. According to this approach, works without protection would simply fall into the public domain. AI-independently-made works in the public domain would be free to be used by everyone. However, identifying authorship in the case of works crafted by an indistinct merging of human and machine contributions may be problematic. This would lead to a detrimental uncertainty in the legal protection of those instances. Also, one can imagine potential conflicts between individuals claiming authorial rights on the artwork and other parties interested in upholding the public domain. Moreover, while the default solution based on public domain is possible in civil law countries, it would be difficult in common law jurisdictions where regulations are based on the legal fiction of "the person making the arrangements for the work". This would result in a divergent approach between civil and common law jurisdictions regarding the treatment of AI-made works. Additionally, there could be a conflict regarding authorship based on the principle of non-discrimination when a person with an interest in an AI-generated artwork contends that a work of art created by an AI system should receive protection despite not being made by a human. The decision of a court in such a case would depend on the approach to the concept of originality adopted. The supposed simplicity of the public domain option would not stand up to those reservations.

Other legal mechanisms devised by some commentators, such as the extension of the "work made for hire" doctrine, or the extension of the norms on protection of "previously unpublished works", share, in my opinion, a critical point. They are all based on fragile legal fictions which were intended for completely different circumstances. Also, they cannot be easily transferred from a common law environment into a civil law legal order.

Those who are not persuaded by the public domain option, nor by thorny adjustments of current regulations, could consider solutions which reflect the allocation of rights to individual(s) playing a role in the AI process, such as the programmer and/or the user. As mentioned previously, those solutions suffer from serious uncertainties on the actual determination of personal contributions.

We are finally left with the most radical option, to recognize AI-generative systems as such entitlement to their autonomously produced artworks *de lege ferenda*. While this would correspond with some projects already developed and accepted by the art world, from a purely legal perspective it would entail not only a technical, but also a "cultural revolution" within classical copyright law. This is not to deny that the time to rethink classical copyright law is here. Rather, that we should recognize that vesting AI systems with legal personhood is not a minimal action to be taken, as it infers legal changes in other areas of the law and not only in copyright regulations.

The existence of autonomous AI processes is today, a fact. As such, it deserves focused attention and should, in my opinion, to be treated in the framework of the wider debate on a future "law of robots".

Art production is not detached from the technological process.[41] It has never been, from painters developing new ways to make pastels, to the invention of cameras and videos. The advent of AI driven agents cannot be treated as a simple quantitative upgrade in technology, as it affects the core of the relationship between art and law: authorship and originality. This is the message sent by the art world sent to legislators and policy makers. It is apparent that policy makers responded to the invitation from the EU Parliament to the Commission to design a legal frame for assigning a limited personhood to AI systems poorly. The lack of success of this response reveals that, at least within Europe, policy makers are far from convinced from legislating a functional and adaptive legal framework for the various types of artificial intelligence. Still, the case should be reconsidered at the EU level, to prevent further divergence among national legislation.

In my view, the case of authorship in AI autonomously generated art – already considered by the art world – should find its way within the wider framework of the law of (and for) robots.

41 See Ferraris (2019) 5 et seq.

In the meantime, rather than developing fragile legal fictions built on elements of company or copyright law designed with differing aims, the legal world should develop contractual models. Whenever the current law does not fit the needs of our human communities, contracts have proved to be the best adaptable, flexible, and specific remedy to gaps in legislation. Agreements could determine, case by case, how to allocate privileges and rights, and how to distinguish the contribution of every participant. Additionally, whenever human involvement is not detectable, contracts could grant legal significance to the inventiveness of the AI designers. Within Europe, scholars and experts, judicial courts, EU institutions have already begun adapting the law of contracts to resolve this lacuna. As a result, new areas of conventional relationships have been established, mostly based on agreed commitments to share rights, and allocate privileges, to increase information for the benefit of the parties and the general public. However, it is said that the art world does not warm to the idea of contracting as a remedy.[42] This is certainly true. AI-generated art, however, occurs within a different environment, where know-how and financial investments in technology favour the recourse to voluntary agreements. Contracts and agreements among "non-authors" could provide some predictability while waiting for law to regulate the creative works produced by the art world.

To reach that point, however, a cultural change is needed: a change that innovators in art-generating AI cannot attain on their own, but that will be eventually caused by more robust policy concerns prompted by advancements in robots' capacity to sense, to think, and to act.

References

Andina, Tiziana (2017): 'What is Art? The Question of Definition Reloaded', 1 Art and Law, Issue 2 (2017) 1–88

Bridy, Annemarie (2012): 'Coding Creativity: Copyright and the Artificially Intelligent Author', 5 Stanford Technology Law Review (2012) 1–28 (https://papers.ssrn.com/sol3/papers.cfm?abstract_id=1888622)

Chopra, Samir/White, Laurence F. (2011): *A Legal Theory for Autonomous Artificial Agents* (Ann Arbor: Michigan University Press 2011)

42 John Merryman rightly noted: "In the artworld, the word 'contract' is a red flag. People react emotionally and irrationally to it"; Merryman/Elsen/Urice (2007) 852.

Christie's (2018): 'Is artificial intelligence set to become art's next medium?' (2018, www.christies.com/features/A-collaboration-between-two-artists-one-human-one-a-machine-9332-1.aspx)

Csikszentmihályi, Mihály (1988): 'Society, culture, and person: A systems view of creativity', in: Sternberg, Robert: *The Nature of Creativity – Contemporary Psychological Perspectives* (Cambridge: Cambridge University Press 1988) 325–339

Davies, Colin R. (2011): 'An Evolutionary Step in Intellectual Property Rights. Artificial Intelligence and Intellectual Property', 27 Computer Law & Security Review (2011) 601–619

Denicola, Robert C. (2016): 'Ex Machina – Copyright Protection for Computer-Generated Works', 69 Rutgers University Law Review (2016) 251–287 (https://papers.ssrn.com/sol3/papers.cfm?abstract_id=3007842)

Dreier, Thomas (1992): 'Creation and Investment: Artistic and Legal Implications of Computer-generated Works, in: Leser, Hans G./Isomura, Tamotsu, *Wege zum japanischen Recht – Festschrift für Zentaro Kitagawa zum 60. Geburtstag* (Berlin: Duncker & Humblot 1992) 869–888

Duboff, Leonard D. (1990): 'Toward a Legal Definition of Art', 12 Hastings Communications & Entertainment L.J. (1990) 303–351 (https://repository.uchastings.edu/hastings_comm_ent_law_journal/vol12/iss3/3)

Elgammal, Ahmed et al. (2017): 'Creative Adversarial Networks Generating "Art" by Learning About Stuyles and Deviating from Style Norms', arXiv: 1706.07068v1 [cs.AI] (2017) 1–22

Ferraris, Maurizio (2019): 'From Fountain to Moleskine – The Work of Art in the Age of Its Technological Producibility', 2 Art and Law, Issue 4 (2019)

Floridi, Luciano (2014): *The Fourth Revolution – How the Infosphere is Reshaping Human Reality* (Oxford: Oxford University Press 2014)

French Ministère de l'enseignement supérieur (2017): 'La Stratégie France I.A: soutenir la dynamique française autour de l'intelligence artificielle' (2017, https://www.enseignementsup-recherche.gouv.fr/cid116143/la-strategie-france-i.a.-soutenir-la-dynamique-francaise-autour-de-l-intelligence-artificielle.html)

Gaskin, Sam (2018): 'When Art Created by Artificial Intelligence Sells, Who Gets Paid?', Art Market, September 17, 2018 (https://www.artsy.net/article/artsy-editorial-art-created-artificial-intelligence-sells-paid)

Gatys, Leon A./Ecker, Alexander S./Bethge, Matthias (2015): 'A Neural Algorithm of Artistic Style', arXiv: 1508.06576v2 [cs.CV] (2 September 2015) 1–16 (https://arxiv.org/pdf/1508.06576.pdf)

Hallevy, Gabriel (2012): 'Unmanned vehicles – Subordination to criminal law under the modern concept of criminal liability', 21 Journal of Law, Information and Science (2012) 200–211 (http://www8.austlii.edu.au/au/journals/JlLawInfoSci/2012/12.pdf)

Hodgkins, Kelly (2016): 'A British artist spent 10 years teaching this robot how to draw, and it totally shows', Digital Trends (2016, https://www.digitaltrends.com/cool-tech/robotic-artist)

Jennings, Kyle E. (2010): 'Developing Creativity – Artificial Barriers in Artificial Intelligence', 20 Minds & Machines (2010) 489–501 (https://link.springer.com/content/pdf/10.1007/s11023-010-9206-y.pdf)

McIver Lopes, Dominic (2017): 'Beauty – The Social Network', 47 Canadian Journal of Philosophy (2017) 437–453

McIver Lopes, Dominic (2009): *A Philosophy of Computer Art* (London/New York: Routledge 2009)

Merryman, John Henry/Elsen, Albert E./Urice, Stephen K. (2007): *Law, Ethics and the Visual Arts* (Alphen aan den Rijn: Kluwer 5th edition 2007)

Moss, Richard (2015): 'Creative AI: the robots that would be painters' (2015, https://newatlas.com/creative-ai-algorithmic-art-painting-fool-aaron/36106/)

Pagallo, Ugo (2013): *The Law of Robots – Crime, Contracts and Torts* (Dordrecht: Springer 2013)

Ramalho, Ana (2017): 'Will robots rule the (artistic) world? A proposed model for the legal status of creations by artificial intelligence systems' (2017, https://papers.ssrn.com/sol3/papers.cfm?abstract_id=2987757)

Sawyer, Robert Keith (2012): *Explaining Creativity – The Science of Human Innovation* (Oxford: Oxford University Press 2012)

Thaler, Stephen (1996): 'Neural Networks that Autonomously Create and Discover' (1996, https://imagination-engines.com/pcai-cm.html [https://perma.cc/52TZ-GPNB]).

Thoma, Martin (2016): 'Creativity in Machine Learning', arXiv: 1601.03642v1 [cs.CV] (2016, https://arxiv.org/pdf/1601.03642.pdf)

UK Science and Technology Committee of the House of Commons (2016): 'Robotics and Artificial Intelligence' (2016, https://publications.parliament.uk/pa/cm201617/cmselect/cmsctech/145/14502.htm)

U.S. Copyright Office (2017): *Compendium of U.S. Copyright Office Practices* (3rd ed. 2017, https://copyright.gov/comp3/)

U.S. National Science and Technology Council-Subcommittee on Machine Learning and Artificial Intelligence (2016): 'Preparing for the future of AI' (2016, https://obamawhitehouse.archives.gov/sites/default/files/whitehouse_files/microsites/ostp/NSTC/preparing_for_the_future_of_ai.pdf)

Weaver, John Frank (2014): *Robots are people too – How Siri, Google Car and Artificial Intelligence Will Force Us to Change our Laws* (Santa Barbara: Praeger 2014)

Yanisky-Ravid, Shlomit (2017): 'Generating Rembrandt – Artificial Intelligence, Copyright, and Accountability in the 3d Era. The Human-Like Authors Are Already Here', 90 Michigan State Law Review (2017) 659–726 (https://ir.lawnet.fordham.edu/cgi/viewcontent.cgi?article=1955&context=faculty_scholarship)

Zemer, Lior (2016): *The Idea of Authorship in Copyright* (London: Routledge 2016)

Zemer, Lior (2006): 'Rethinking Copyright Alternatives', 14 International Journal of Law and Information Technology (2006) 137–145 (https://doi.org/10.1093/ijlit/eai024)

Part 5
Technology, Ethics and Legal Norms

Chapter 16
A Face in the Cloud? – Identifying Moral Issues and Constraints in Cloud-Based Image Storage

Wybo Houkes

Our lives are rapidly becoming more digitized. Focusing only on entertainment: many people still buy paperback crime novels, some might still buy newly released music on CD, and a rare few might even buy movie DVDs. Yet many of these purchases will be made online; and for all these goods there are now alternatives or 'substitutes' that offer the same content in a digital, often more easily accessible format. The recent pandemic, the most disruptive global event in decades, has only accelerated the pace of digitization and extended it to more domains. Reflection on any aspect of the wide-ranging, varied, and most likely fundamental repercussions of digitization is therefore urgently needed, from the broadest possible variety of disciplinary perspectives.

In line with the theme of this volume, this chapter considers how digitization affects our involvement with images. These effects are again wide-ranging. Here, I focus on the increasing use of what I label 'cloud-based image storage': cloud-based services to store, organize and share images, such as Amazon Prime Photos, Apple Photos, Flickr, Instagram, or Google Photos. More specifically, I will investigate the increasing use of such services for personal images, such as family photos. This trend has economic and legal aspects and has been studied from – to name but a few – a design perspective (focusing on user-friendliness or effectiveness of the technology), a business perspective (focusing on commercial viability), or a sociological perspective (focusing on changes in practices of use). This chapter will touch upon all these aspects and perspectives, but primarily explore the use of photo cloud storage from a *moral* perspective. I will focus on actions associated with personal images and cloud storage, such as curating collections of images, sharing them with others, and removing them from storage. My guiding questions will be: which actions should users be entitled to perform? Which actions should others (such as service providers) not be entitled to perform? How should services be organized to ensure basic user/consumer rights? I seek general answers to these questions which will provide guidelines for evaluating services without evaluating a specific service. Because of the explorative character of the chapter, there will be no more than a passing reference to existing services. My primary aim is to show that there are genuine and relatively pressing ethical issues concerning photo cloud storage, and to demonstrate how such issues can be discussed while taking into account some of the economic, sociological and legal complexities involved.

The chapter is organized as follows. After making some necessary preliminary distinctions concerning digitization (I.) and describing photo cloud storage in general terms (II.), I turn to moral analysis of these services. A first step is to apply a continuity heuristic to balance the rights between the parties involved (III.). This continuity is attractive from a usability perspective and may also be factored into ethical and legal rules concerning the rights of providers and users. Yet it leads to conceptual difficulties in specifying what continuity involves. After proposing a specification at the level of basic user activities, in a second step (IV.), I develop a set of moral constraints on cloud-based image storage, resulting from the function of collections of personal images as 'technologies of memory',[1] supporting formation of and reflection on individual and collective identity. I identify such constraints for the basic activities of accumulating, accessing, curating, and deleting personal images in cloud-based storage. Some conclusions are to be found in V.

I. Digitization in Economic Transactions

Before discussing photo cloud storage, some preliminary distinctions regarding the phenomenon of digitization are needed. Precisely because of its wide-ranging and complex nature, it is important to differentiate its many aspects and instances. Without doing so, there is a risk that discussions of salient aspects of digitization become side-tracked and evolve into discussions of related phenomena, ideological trends, or historical continuities. I want to focus on aspects of digitization that make specific moral differences, rather than on their relation to globalization or capitalism and consumerism.

Rather than attempting to find a comprehensive definition or set of characteristics, I focus on the digitization of simple economic transactions, such as purchasing a crime novel, ordering food or subscribing to a streaming service. At least three distinctions can be made here, all which contrast

1 Van House/Churchill (2008).

'digitized' transactions with 'non-digitized' ones and are orthogonal to each other. These three distinctions are also orthogonal to the more standard economic distinction between *goods* – transferable items that provide utility, produced by some and consumed by others – and *services* – non-transferable items used by some and provided by others.

One distinction, which concerns the environment, is that between *online* and *offline* transactions. One might purchase goods in an online environment such as eBay rather than at a local bookstore. Another distinction concerns the goods or, more broadly, items involved in the transaction: they may be *digital* or physical, e.g., the e-book version of Colin Dexter's *The Daughters of Cain* and a paperback print version, respectively. Thirdly, and perhaps least conspicuously, there is a distinction that has become an integral part of the transition to a digital economy, although it has much older roots. This concerns the format of the transaction itself: rather than a one-off or *singular* transaction, these are *subscription-based*, i.e., involve a recurring fee rather than a single payment. These transactions may involve regular deliverance of goods (say, fresh pairs of socks every month) or unlimited access to a repository of products, such as that offered by Netflix. Moreover, fees may be a flat-rate or proportional to usage, or subscription-based transactions may be free of charge to the user (initially, to some extent, or entirely).

The table below (Table 1) illustrates these distinctions and shows that they are to some extent independent of each other, by identifying a transaction that is an example of each possible type.

Another useful notion when analysing digitization of transactions is *substitutivity*. This is often applied to goods, such as brands of coffee, but I will use it to include services. Substitutive digitized transactions compete directly with (some set of) non-digitized transactions. Indeed, engaging in the former makes it far less likely that one will engage in the latter. The substitutive effects of digitization are well-known (go ask at your local record store if you are not convinced); a point of contention, to be discussed in the next section, is to what extent digitization leads to overall added value for the parties involved.

Type	Environment	Item	Transaction	Example
1	Offline	Physical	Singular	Purchasing a *Brothers in Arms* CD at the record store two blocks away
2	Offline	Physical	Subscription	Purchasing a subscription to the paper version of *Anglers Journal*
3	Offline	Digital	Singular	Purchasing *The Daughters of Cain* and uploading it to your e-reader at the local bookstore
4	Offline	Digital	Subscription	Purchasing a gift card for access to Spotify Premium at the local supermarket
5	Online	Physical	Singular	Purchasing sheep on AliBaba
6	Online	Physical	Subscription	Purchasing a subscription for printer paper on Amazon
7	Online	Digital	Singular	Purchasing a pdf of Houkes (2018) at the publisher's website
8	Online	Digital	Subscription	Purchasing a subscription to Apple Music

Table 1: A typology of transactions

II. 'Servitization' and Cloud-Based Image Storage

With the distinctions of the previous section in place, this section highlights some aspects of cloud-based image storage that might make a moral difference. In a nutshell: the transactions involved in cloud-based image storage involve digital items, an online environment, and are subscription-based. They are thus, examples of what are labelled *'Type-8' transactions* in Table 1. As such, they are maximally different from transactions that were once central to our involvement with personal images, which involved physical goods such as printed photos, purchased at photographers' stores or drugstores in singular transactions – *Type-1 transactions* in Table 1. Moreover, Type-8 transactions have to a large – and still growing – extent replaced Type-1 transactions. This section will schematically describe how this replacement occurred and highlights the evolving nature of transactions.

Some readers may, like the author, be old enough to remember home slide shows. Other than contemporary events that go by the same name (e.g., in PowerPoint), these involved mechanical projectors, stacks of small, framed transparencies and portable projection screens. Interestingly, in their basic set-up – the arrangement of equipment, the presence of an audience – there are strong continuities with the magic-lantern demonstrations used for entirely different purposes by Athanasius Kircher in the 17th

century[2] or the Royal Geographical Society in the late 19th century.[3] By contrast, nowadays, sharing a set of images with one's family might be as simple as sending them a link to a selection of cloud-stored images. This allows them to browse through the images whenever (if ever) they like, using any equipment that provides access to the digitized images, at any location where such equipment may be used. Leaving aside the user experience and practice of viewing, comparing the home slide show and the cloud-stored album highlight all three aspects of the taxonomy presented in section I., as well as the (highly schematized) stages of digitization.

In terms of the product, the slide show featured transparencies, high-resolution positive photographs with a standard size of 35 millimetres held inside a plastic frame. Most consumers of these goods obtained them from specialized photography shops or drugstores, where rolls of photographic film could be bought and processed, producing the transparencies. These would be returned to the owner of the film roll, together with the roll itself. Transparencies could then be framed at home using specialized equipment. An image – say, of a five-year-old building a sandcastle on a Normandy beach – would thus be processed into a physical good, purchased in a singular transaction in a local shop and then owned by the producer of the image – say, your mother. Some enthusiasts (like the author's father) could do the processing at home, so that the production of individual transparencies did not require any singular transactions at all: only the equipment and raw materials (such as funny-smelling chemical baths) needed to be bought.

Digital photography changed all of this, but not all at once. At least initially, only the production of the image and its processing changed. Transparencies could still be purchased from local shops and drugstores, in singular transactions. Initially, the images would however be in a digital format (say, a JPEG file) and could conceivably be transferred to the shop on a memory stick.

At a later stage, this transaction was transferred to a digital environment. Images, in a suitable digital format, could be uploaded on the website of a local shop or drugstore, and payment for further processing and perhaps delivery of the transparencies to one's home could proceed digitally. By the time of this stage, framed transparencies and home slide shows were things of the past; but, for instance, family albums with printed photographs were not. Importantly, moreover, consumers would still

2 Vermeir (2005).

3 Hayes (2018).

own physical goods after completion of the transaction. In terms of Table 1, a *Type-1* transaction has changed into a *Type-5* transaction at this point in the narrative.

Storing and sharing images via Google Photos or Flickr is different again from this transaction – the similarities might end in it occurring in a digital environment. Firstly, *only* digital items need to be involved. Granting access to images merely requires sending a link: no physical good, such as a transparency or printed photo, needs to be produced. Rather, the transaction involves storage of digital items (say, uploaded jpg images) in a digital environment that may also facilitate this exchange. Secondly, central to the transaction is access to sets of digital items, including the option to add and remove items and share the access with others. Further, this access is provided *as a service* by those in charge of the digital environment – acting as a provider, not as a producer in the transaction. In terms of the typology, this constitutes a *Type-8* transaction.

This means that sharing access to one's vacation photos is different from treating one's guests to a home slide show. Previously, the slide show involved the use of equipment, transparencies and other physical goods that were owned by the slide-show enthusiast, after several singular Type-1 transactions. Now, it is as if a third party grants you unlimited access for private showings in *their* home, perhaps for a fee.

This explains why the provider may charge you or otherwise seek compensation for this form of access – one would not expect free access to a stranger's home cinema or jacuzzi, after all. It also becomes clear how overseeing this environment can be the basis of a successful business model. In fact, this subscription model of providing access to digital content or otherwise providing services in a digital environment is one of *the* success stories of 21st century capitalism.[4] It forms the basis of the storage services discussed here, but is also the driving force behind Spotify, Netflix, and – outside the domain of entertainment – Windows 365.

Subscription-based transactions have been around for centuries, for instance in selling newspapers and magazines. Its recent widespread adoption, by the entertainment and software industries among others, is, in part, a response to the perceived threat posed by digitization and global access to digital environments – namely the free sharing of copyrighted materials on platforms such as Napster and the Pirate Bay. This sharing involved digital items such as mp3 or mp4 files purchased by some consumers in *Type-7* (or perhaps *Type-3*) transactions prior to sharing.

4 See, e.g., Johnson/Christensen/Kagermann (2008).

Anti-'piracy' campaigns, lawsuits and other countermeasures have been far less effective in preventing consumers from engaging in this form of sharing than the shift to flat-rate subscription-based *Type-8* transactions. Offering unlimited access to high-quality, legal copyrighted materials for a low recurring fee has, it appears, strongly disincentivized consumers from downloading files illegally.

The subscription model has, however, proliferated to all kinds of transactions. Some of these transactions involve physical goods (*Type-1* transactions substituted with *Type-6* transactions if the latter proceed online). In the Netherlands, one can buy a subscription to a "circular mattress"[5] or socks. Other transactions are arguably additive: firms, for instance in manufacturing industries, seek financial or strategic benefits through what has been called a shift from "manufactured goods to integrated solutions",[6] "service growth"[7] or, perhaps most evocatively, "servitization".[8] Examples include elevators and medical equipment, durable tangible goods that are typically bought together with maintenance contracts (i.e., services). Although the term 'servitization' suggests otherwise, the trend is largely regarded as a positive one in the management and marketing literature: the focus in the literature is on identifying ways to facilitate the process and to aid firms in developing servitization capabilities and overcoming market challenges – all to capture *extra* value and gain competitive advantage.

In combination, we see a trend towards ever more transactions that offer services – in particular, forms of access – for a subscription fee, substituting for transactions that end in transfer of ownership. Cloud-image image storage is just one example of what has been called an 'Age of Access'[9] and of what I will call servitization here; just as it is an example of digitization. There is, once again, no necessary connection between digitization, subscription business models, and servitization – but in practice they form an extremely powerful tandem, with clear incentives and success stories.

---

5 https://www.auping.com/nl/news/koninklijke-auping-versnelt-circulaire-ambities-met-start-bedzzzy (in Dutch).

6 Windahl/ Andersson/Berggren/Nehler (2004).

7 Kowalkowski/Gebauer/Oliva (2017).

8 Vandermerwe/Rada (1988). This source, broadly acknowledged as coining the term in this context, shows that "servitization" as a growth strategy precedes widespread digitization. See also Baines/Lightfoot/Benedettini/Kay (2009); Zhang/Banerji (2017).

9 Rifkin (2000).

Yet, this brief discussion has looked at the phenomenon and motivations for servitization almost exclusively from the business perspective. In what follows, I examine the moral issues in these entangled phenomena, focusing on a specific case and the user perspective.

III. Seeking Moral and Practical Continuity

The previous section described the trend towards servitizing transactions, shifting them from *Type-1* to *Type-8*, and it provided some background to understand and analyse this trend from a business perspective. In this section, I will turn to a moral analysis. I will argue that despite the fundamental differences between the transactions involved, there are good reasons to seek continuity with non-digitized practices, both from an ethical and from a practical perspective.

First, we should note that there is no general moral wrong-doing in servitizing transactions. Servitization might provide benefits (financial or otherwise) to producers-turned-service-providers as well as to consumers-turned-end-users, e.g., in terms of extra convenience (as for the socks) or contributing to a circular economy in one's sleep (as for the mattress). Under some conditions, servitization and other access-based schemes may be the only way to create a sufficient incentive to produce or maintain some goods (so-called 'club goods').[10] Cinemas and swimming pools provide cases in point.

Yet what is at stake here is not (only) offering new goods, but *changes* in the types of transactions used and associated changes in people's actions involving the goods. Digitization, as outlined above, comprises many such *substitutive* changes. Digital music services such as Apple Music and Spotify – to give one quick example – provide audio content through a *Type-8* transaction, substituting for most consumers the purchase and subsequent ownership of CDs through *Type-1* transactions. Subscription-based licensed access, however, no longer allows some forms of sharing audio content that were allowed upon purchase (i.e., borrowing one's CD to a friend). Arguably, this may disincentivize users from engaging in illegal downloading and thus preserve producers' incentives to offer the good. Yet, it *does* constrain users' actions, meaning that transaction servitization entails certain forms of interference that need moral justification.

10 Cornes/Sandler (1996).

Elsewhere, I have shown that these changes can be analysed through considering *bundles of rights* rather than through using monolithic and contested concepts such as "ownership".[11] Here, I want to use a differentiated conception of such rights. This draws on the so-called incidents that were proposed by Hohfeld in an analysis of legal rights,[12] and that were also used to substantially develop moral rights.[13] This distinguishes, among others, *permissions* or *privileges* from *claim-rights*, and analyses moral rights as combinations of these basic incidents. Moreover, it makes these concepts relative to agents – labelled *A* and *B* – and actions.

To introduce each of these, with a simple example, consider a person's right to write notes in a copy of *The Daughters of Cain*. The *permission* to do this is the absence of a duty to refrain from it – or, put differently, the absence of a right for others to interfere with this type of action. A *claim-right*, by contrast, means that *B* has a duty not to interfere with *A*'s action. Now suppose that *A* obtained the copy from a Little Free Library. Then, arguably, *A* does not have a duty not to write notes in it – and thus a permission to do so; still, others (e.g., the volunteer steward of the library) may seek to prevent *A* from the note-writing. In case *A* purchased the copy, however, others (e.g., the owner of the bookstore) have a duty not to interfere, i.e., *A* has a claim-right rather than a 'mere' permission with respect to other agents *B*. Finally, prior to purchasing the copy, *A* has a duty not to write notes in it: the owner of the bookstore has a right to interfere. Here, *A* has neither a permission nor a claim-right.

As this example makes clear, *Type-1* transactions – such as purchasing transparencies of images at a photographer's store – traditionally come with various claim-rights, e.g., to display the transparencies; to borrow them to others; or to destroy them at will. More specifically, such rights were originally held by the producer of the goods (i.e., the transparencies, not the images) and these producer rights are traditionally exhausted after the transaction.[14] The production of transparencies requires handling the film roll (a tangible good) and processing the images (an intangible good). However, in the typical *Type-1* transaction involving transparencies, none of the rights over the film roll or the images are exhausted; buying transparencies at a store does not give the store owner the claim-right or even the permission to, say, display the images.

---

11 Houkes (2018).

12 Hohfeld (1917).

13 As reviewed in, e.g., Edmundson (2012); Wenar (2021).

14 This "bundles of rights" approach is developed in much greater depth in, e.g., Perzanowski/Schultz (2015).

Analysing in some detail which incidents are involved in various transactions highlights how the interests involved are balanced, and which – if any – forms of interference are warranted. Ideally, transactions are structured in such a way that legal and moral rights are protected, and economic incentives for producing and using goods and services are maintained. In practice, this is a complicated and continuous balancing act: changes in consumer needs, but also in the actions afforded by items have economic effects (say, on the commercial viability of certain goods). However, these may also trigger legal and moral disputes. Technological change also has great potential to disturb any previous balance, especially if it is a non-incremental change.

In some cases, digitization triggers a need for fine-tuning or adjusting an existing balance because of the increased potential for actions. One example is the use of digitally manipulated images of deceased celebrities for commercial purposes, which triggers fine-tuning of the right of publicity to safeguard the interests of heirs, fans and the general public.[15] In other cases, the changes wrought by digitization are too large and trigger a need to *recreate* the balance. This, I submit, is true for servitization: the shift from *Type-1* transactions, with singular purchases of physical goods in offline environments, to *Type-8* transactions, which are subscription-based and service-oriented, is too large to address through fine-tuning of one or two claim-rights.[16]

The comprehensive assessment required to recreate a balance from scratch may well be unfeasible, given the many interests and contextual details at stake. Even the simple purchase of a paperback novel, as in the example above, involves a bewildering variety of claim-rights and permissions with respect to multiple agents. For this very reason, a sensible approach for the moral component of this task – applicable before any further fine-tuning or more comprehensive assessment – is to *seek as much continuity as possible* on the level of permissions and claim-rights. If agents had permissions or claim-rights regarding certain actions after some transactions, then they had no duties to refrain from these actions and others might have duties not to interfere. If any known transaction is then substituted by another transaction, the very same permissions and claim-rights may pertain, unless there is some compelling reason why there are now

15 Petty/D'Rozario (2009).

16 The size of the difference is described by others as "a bifurcated universe" (Perzanowski/Schultz (2005)) or "worlds apart" (Wendehorst (2016)). Although this might overstate the case (Houkes 2018), it indicates the difficulties experienced in addressing the shift.

duties to refrain from actions or interference. On this basis, one may argue that purchasing access to digital content should, just as purchasing paperback novels, come with a right to share them with persons of one's own choice.[17] Conversely, any *new* opportunities for action that arise for some parties in the new transaction need to be justified before they ground new permissions or claim-rights. Thus, Apple should arguably not have presented all iTunes subscribers with U2's album *Songs of Innocence* without their (the subscribers) explicit consent. That the subscription-based transaction gave Apple this opportunity did not automatically give them permission to do so.[18]

This 'continuity heuristic' is rich in assumptions: from an economic perspective, it assumes substitutivity; and from a moral perspective, it assumes prior permissions and claim-rights without identifying any morally relevant interests at stake. Still, before turning to problems of implementing the heuristic, there are reasons to think that continuity will be sought also from a practical perspective, and this provides indirect support for seeking moral continuity.

The practical reasons for continuities concern the design and usability of the items involved in the transaction. Following Norman's seminal work on user-centred design,[19] it is widely considered a precondition for adoption and usability that there is a match between its features and the mental models of its prospective users – where the model is a representation of a good's features and of the actions that may be taken with it. Mental models, in turn, are based to some extent on perceptible features of the item (called 'use cues' by Norman), but to a far larger extent on previous experience with successful use with items in the same broad functional category. To give a simple household example: it is possible to design a toaster with features and affordances that have little in common with those of toasters familiar to users, but this will seriously impede usability, adoption and thus ultimately commercial success of even 'technologically' superior toasters. This insight holds true for digital items as well as for physical ones and for physical items that become digitized. In all cases, continuities in functionalities and user interfaces increase adoption and usability, and strong discontinuities are a major cause of market failure.

17 Houkes (2018).

18 https://appleinsider.com/articles/18/09/09/the-free-u2-album-songs-of-innocence-was-a-debacle-for-apple-fans-on-september-9-2018.

19 Norman (1988).

There is already some research on the mental models of cloud-based image storage. One recent study[20] focuses on the generational differences in perceptions, to identify ways to improve usability and overcome adoption barriers for older users. It finds that mental models of older users vary considerably and often poorly reflect the actual functionalities and affordances of photo storage services. It concludes that more should be done to make digital photo tools resemble physical photo albums, an approach that is sometimes labelled "familiarity design".[21]

This and other studies into mental models show that, from a usability or commercial perspective, it is best to maximize mental-model or cognitive continuities. Such continuities would carry over into the legal realm because they create *reasonable expectations*[22] regarding what may and may not be done with the items based on the transactions. Finally, the desirability of mental-model continuity from a commercial and usability perspective and consequent legal continuity aligns with the earlier plea for *moral* continuity, i.e., preserving the existing balance of rights between parties. Traditional *Type-1* transactions then serve as a benchmark for digitized, servitized transactions: tradition exerts a cognitive, commercial, legal, and moral pull.

Yet can such continuity be achieved, given the fundamental differences between physical goods and their digitized mentioned above, regarding subscription-based, service-oriented counterparts? Granting users the exact same rights over their images in *Type-8* transactions as they had in *Type-1* transactions may well upset any prior balance. After all, business models adapted because of digitization: it may just not be commercially viable to offer users all their traditional rights without some extra compensation for the producer-turned-provider. Furthermore, it may be difficult to specify the rights for which continuity is sought. Claim-rights and permissions concern actions that may be taken with the item, based on the transaction, e.g., "to look at one's stored images at will" or "to share images with people of one's choice". Yet many actions associated with physical photos or albums – such as "to tear up all photos showing one's partner after a break-up" – are simply impossible. Digital 'counterparts' of such actions can be imagined, but these are strictly speaking not identical; and calling them 'counterparts' or 'equivalents' risks begging the question. Conversely, digital environments afford many actions – such as "to remove red-eye

20 Axtell/Munteanu (2019).

21 E.g., Zhang/Banerji et al. (2016).

22 See, e.g., Helberger (2011); Helberger/Loos/Guibault/Mak/Pessers (2013).

effects in images with a few mouse-clicks" – that were, again strictly speaking, previously impossible. Furthermore, following a basic insight from philosophical action theory, any action can be described at multiple levels. Actions that are equivalent under one description may be very different under others: "to look at pictures" is a high-level description of sequences of radically different actions in a physical and digital environment. Even for cloud-based image storage itself, research has shown that users typically have very different mental models of the constitutive actions in relatively basic processes for cloud-based storage, such as "uploading and viewing pictures".[23]

This suggests that complete continuity does not make sense as a practical or moral aspiration. The discontinuity is so obvious, and a new balance so much still in the making, that protecting user rights in servitized transactions should be mostly a matter of due diligence on the part of those users. After all, even if digital photo storage is organized in 'photo albums' placed on a 'shelf', users should know – among many other things – that they have not purchased pictures or an album that they own and may dispose of as they wish; that they may lose access to their albums once they stop paying the subscription fee; and, in case they are not paying a monetary fee, that you are paying with personal data.

This response overshoots its mark in ignoring both that producers and service providers have a responsibility to respect basic consumer rights and – more importantly – that many digital services are presented in such a way that they resemble familiar transactions. As much as this improves usability and lowers adoption barriers, benefiting the provider, it *also* creates reasonable expectations about the rights involved and the transaction. Making maximal use of familiarity design to create 'cosmetic' similarities, deliberately highlighting superficial continuities, while capturing maximal value from the underlying discontinuities, is a slippery slope to manipulating and deceiving users into commercially desirable behaviour.

The right conclusion to draw is therefore that, wherever continuity is highlighted, in presentation or description, expectations are also created about permissions and claim-rights. These expectations need to be actively corrected or endorsed by whoever highlighted the continuity. Conversely, any discontinuities that might be reasonably overlooked by users should be deliberately highlighted (in a more accessible form than in most terms of service). Here, entirely new action potentials on the part of service

23 Axtell/Munteanu (2019) Section 4.

providers (e.g., inspecting images purely for their own benefit) should be made explicit or not result in any new claim-rights or permissions.

Continuity might only be found in relatively coarse-grained descriptions of actions (e.g., "to organize images" or "to edit images"), but such descriptions are also typically found in user interfaces, users' mental models and, importantly, in specifications of legal rights. These all refer to actions such as "to display" or "to share" rather than "to upload a jpg to a server" or "to project a transparency for Uncle Kees's entertainment". Counterparts of such actions involved in servitized goods and transactions are the loci of reasonable user expectations and should be accepted as such by providers or – alternatively – very explicitly dismissed.[24] According to the continuity heuristic, providers should either accept the adoption barriers resulting from the latter or the loss of captured rights and value resulting from the former.

IV. Moral Constraints on Cloud-Based Image Storage

In this section, I identify several provisional constraints concerning cloud-based image storage, the transactions involved, and the information provided. These constraints are considered for both the users and the providers of these digital services. In line with the results of III., most constraints concern reasonable expectations regarding claim-rights and permissions. These are organized by four high-level actions that have been distinguished – under slightly varying headings – in the literature on the use of photo cloud storage, especially in studies that compare it to or otherwise discuss it in continuity with the use of traditional photo albums.[25]

For these actions, I focus on rights and permissions that would be equivalent to those associated with traditional photo albums – in line with the continuity approach outlined in the previous section. Moreover,

---

24 This aligns with a statement by Maciej Szpunar, advocate general to the Court of Justice of the European Union, regarding the lending of e-books by public libraries: if lending e-books is arranged in a similar way as lending physical books, some coarse-grained action descriptions such as "to share" or "to borrow" still apply. Consequently, the existing exception for public lending as its "modern equivalent" may be applied; see Advocate General's Opinion in Case C-174/15 – Vereniging Openbare Bibliotheken v Stichting Leenrecht, 16 June 2016, https://curia.europa.eu/jcms/upload/docs/application/pdf/2016-06/cp160064en.pdf.

25 E.g., Keightley/Pickering (2014); Broekhuijsen/van den Hoven/Markopoulos (2017); Axtell/Munteanu (2019).

I highlight those that are mostly closely connected to the exercise of individual autonomy. This reflects what some have identified as the primary function of rights, namely, to serve the interest of right holders in exercising autonomous choice.[26] Photo albums and their digital equivalents are not merely repositories of information, although they may also serve as such. They are also instruments of identity or what some have called 'technologies of memory'.[27] This is the same for traditional photo albums[28] as well as for digital ones;[29] these continuities persist despite any differences.[30] Images, either tangible or digital, serve as memory cues,[31] and organizing and displaying images supports the formation and maintenance of narrative identity, both individual and collective (e.g., as a family or group of friends). Interference with actions that involve (self- or collective) identity formation and expression thereof does more than merely upset some vested interests that came with a now outdated technology. Thus, the constraints discussed in this section do more than assume that there were claim-rights and permissions associated with physical photo albums: they are based on reasons that there should (or should not) have been such claim-rights and permissions – and that the same should apply after digitization. In this section, it is assumed that the transactions involved in cloud-based image storage are substitutive for those involved in physical photo albums. I will return to this assumption in the concluding section.

1. *Accumulating*

Accumulating images includes creating them and uploading or transferring them into cloud storage. Not all the images in one's storage may be one's own creation; most people also store images that were created by others, such as their family and friends.

As an activity, this creates an aggregate or repository of images without any narrative structure. Still, these images serve as memory cues or, more broadly, resources for identity formation and self-expression. As such, it is important to have a large measure of control over which images may and may not be stored. This leads to two constraints.

---

26 Edmundson (2012) Chapter 7.
27 Van House/Churchill (2008).
28 Hirsch (1997).
29 Van Dijck (2008).
30 Frohlich/Kuchinsky/Pering/Don/Ariss (2002); Keightley/Pickering (2014).
31 Broekhuijsen/van den Hoven/Markopoulos (2017).

One is that accumulating personal images is best done deliberately. Many cloud storage services offer automatic uploading options or 'passive storage', by which any image created by a user is stored by default. Furthermore, the ubiquity of smartphones has radically increased our opportunities for creating images, and people's individual photo collections have grown from hundreds to often tens of thousands[32] – many of which are automatically uploaded. Consequently, many users are surprised by the sheer number of images in their storage, many of which they did not even remember creating.[33] For the purpose of identity formation, unintentional accumulation creates a need for more extensive curation and deletion.[34] Otherwise, it may lead to 'mnemonic noise' that only interferes with processes of reminiscence and storytelling rather than facilitating it. This is not only a privacy concern that leads to constraints on provider's terms of service, but it should give users pause in opting for comfort or completeness at the price of undermining the value of their collection as a technology of memory. This may be expressed in terms of duties that users have to themselves or, alternatively, in terms of a lack of permission on the provider's part to activate automatic uploading without the user's consent.

A second constraint more exclusively targets the service provider. There are recurring concerns that people use cloud storage services to collect (and share) materials that they did not create themselves and over which they consequently do not have authorship rights.[35] Providers vary in their policies regarding such copyright infringements. Currently, most only respond to complaints by copyright-holders, but conceivably content could be actively monitored, and any content to which the user has no legal rights could be removed (or fail to upload in the first place). Such policies would interfere with private use of copyrighted materials that, in some cases, may be owned by those who uploaded the images and, in other cases, freely shared by their creators with those who stored them. Interfering with such practices would not have been acceptable (or possible) for traditional photography, and increased possibilities for monitoring and

---

32 Broekhuijsen/van den Hoven/Markopoulos (2017).

33 Clark/Snyder/McCoy/Kanich (2015).

34 See below, IV. 3 and 4.

35 A more trivial constraint is that users retain any authorship rights that they have over the images; storage should not come with transfer of intellectual property rights.

checking cloud-stored images or applying upload filters do not make it any more acceptable (or necessary for the case of personal use).[36]

2. Accessing

This activity involves all kinds of access to the images for its owner/creator and others. It includes viewing them, navigating through collections, and sharing them with others – either deliberately or not. Displaying in a digital environment is partly equivalent to browsing through a physical photo album or attending a slide show, but without the narrative element, which will be discussed below under 'curating'. Facilitating various kinds of display has been called the 'database' or 'storage' functionality.[37]

A first access-related constraint, echoing well-rehearsed privacy concerns, is that a user should have full control over who has access to which images. Sharing images fosters social connections and prevents social isolation, as has been found in various studies.[38] Many users share images mainly with friends and family, and express worries about unauthorized access, or accidentally giving someone access to too many materials. Service providers should therefore impose no restrictions on whom a user wants to give access, but without making full access the default option. Furthermore, sharing access rights with others should not automatically give them a license to use these images for their own purposes – just as showing others your physical photo albums does not give them the rights to change them or take pictures of them. Some providers offer users the option to specify the license for each stored image, such as 'All rights reserved' or 'Public Domain Dedication (CC0)'.

Second, access by the service provider should be kept to the minimum needed to operate the service or any additional value captured through access should be made fully explicit to the users. It is now sufficiently well known that the business models of many providers allow access in order to personalize advertisements, or otherwise collect data on users. Users

---

36 For the new European legislative framework see Article 17 of Directive (EU) 2019/790 of the European Parliament and of the Council of 17 April 2019 on copyright and related rights in the Digital Single Market and amending Directives 96/9/EC and 2001/29/EC (OJEU L 130 of 17 May 2019, 92), defining the legal duties of online content-sharing service providers vis-à-vis rightholders and its users.

37 E.g., Axtell/Manteanu (2019).

38 See earlier references.

should not need to read the terms of service to find out, but the contrast with access to traditional photo albums is so stark that close monitoring of business practices or even more explicit warnings to users – rather than relatively neutral descriptions of 'legitimate uses' by providers – are called for.

Thirdly, and perhaps most contentiously, users should not become too dependent on particular service providers for access to their stored images. Servitization is attractive from a business perspective because it enables capturing value over a longer time, and disincentivizing transactions with business rivals. Adding ever more services for customers, at relatively low subscription fees (or partly/initially free of charge), is a very powerful growth engine for big tech companies, also because many such services show high 'customer loyalty'. This loyalty – more appropriately called 'retention' – may be fostered through positive incentives, such as making the service attractive and easy to use, but also by making it difficult for users to transfer their stored content or to retain access after cancelling their subscription. This is the same for services with database functionalities, and more strongly for those that allow elaborate curation (see below, IV.3). What users stand to lose is not just the time invested, but also the resulting narrative. To put it dramatically, if one's personal or family history is documented through photo cloud storage, this aspect of one's identity is being made hostage to payment of a subscription fee, as well as continued existence of the service provider, including file formats etc. It is worth studying how incentives for cancelling subscriptions or transferring to another service provider are best safeguarded, e.g., by stimulating or requiring interoperability of storage services. This would serve to protect the rights of users over these technologies of memory, as well as to prevent virtual monopolies over communities of users.

3. Curating

Curating images comprises several activities, all aimed at preserving, organizing, editing, tagging and sorting the content of one's photo storage, deciding what to keep, and in which structures and formats. Arranging printed pictures in a photo album or preparing a slide show of one's transparencies were traditional forms of this activity. The number of images produced and stored nowadays produces a far greater need for curation, to prevent databases filled with "faceless stuff".[39] In line with this, when

39 Van House/Churchill (2008).

comparing digital storage to physical photo collections, users report that curation activities have become more important in digital storage to create and preserve a valuable collection of images, and that these activities have become more demanding and time-consuming. This goes for providing an explicit narrative structure (e.g., by organizing images and writing captions), but also for more rudimentary forms of curating, such as tagging images with metadata or simply organizing them in sub-collections.

This creates opportunities for providers to make their photo-storage services more attractive to users, viz., by making curation easier or less strenuous. Usability studies have identified both the need and opportunities for storage services to enhance their narrative functionality,[40] and many providers have indeed done so. However, these opportunities come with constraints.

One constraint are features of cloud-based storage services that allow users to curate digital images much like they would curate physical photo albums. This familiarity design would on the one hand greatly improve usability, especially for older users who have experience with physical albums. On the other hand, this approach would be susceptible to the argument presented in section III. that users may reasonably expect to have the same rights and permissions over the resulting digital albums as they did over the physical albums – or it should be made very clear to them that they do not, on pain of lowering adoption barriers through manipulative presentation of the service.

Another, perhaps obvious constraint is on the access to curated collections. Such collections have a better claim on being technologies of memory and identity formation than mere image databases, and therefore giving users full control over who can and cannot access curated collections is even more important. Options to customize sharing settings on social media such as Facebook – in response to demands for more transparency to and control for users – are a case in point.

Thirdly, providers might offer (automated) suggestions that support or partly replace curating activities by users. Examples are suggested collections of 'related' pictures or automated tagging. As useful and attractive as these might be, they require more extensive access to and processing of images than users would – or should – want. For one thing, these suggestions indicate the activity of pattern-recognition algorithms or other forms of data mining. In particular, images in cloud storage are likely to contain

40 E.g., Keightley/Pickering (2014); Broekhuijsen/van den Hoven/Markopoulos (2017).

many faces of the same or closely related people, with a multitude of expressions. This makes such collections invaluable resources for developing facial-recognition technologies – which providers often describe at best indirectly and abstractly in the terms of service (e.g., as "our products"). The ethical problems of such technologies cannot be spelled out here,[41] but are substantial. This means that users should at least be made aware of this usage of their collections, so that they can consider these potentially negative side-effects of a slight reduction of their workload in curating.

Another aspect of automated curation is that there is value in performing curating activities.[42] Organizing pictures and writing captions are themselves techniques of storytelling, which trigger memories, and facilitate reflection on one's identity. Users need to consider carefully whether the ease of (partly) outsourcing such activities outweighs the value of engaging in them. This may not lead to rejecting the outsourcing: given the workload involved in curating, some automated assistance might be needed to engage in these activities in the first place.

Finally, on a related note, automated curation may reduce options for tailor-made curated collections. Identity and personal narratives are to some extent specific to social situations and interactions: one does not show the same 'face' to one's grandmother and one's colleagues, for instance. Users of photo services would indeed prefer (in principle) to express themselves differently to different social relations, and this contributes substantially to the workload. Automation may again reduce this, but at the price of either giving an even richer source of resources for alternative applications (i.e., pattern recognition algorithms could also be trained for images associated with particular social situations) or sharing only marginally different versions of oneself with different social relations (in case the options for automated fine-tuning are limited).

4. Deleting

A final set of activities is the removal of images, curated or not. Users tend to overlook these activities in their mental models of cloud photo storage,[43] although when prompted, they identify the risks that come with inadequate or incomplete opportunities to delete images.

---

41 See, e.g., Selinger/Leong (2021) for a thorough review.

42 E.g., Stevens/Abowd/Truong/Vollmer (2003).

43 Axtell/Munteanu (2019).

Constraints on these activities are closely associated with those on accumulating or accessing. As said above, there may be too much accumulation from the user's perspective because of automatic uploading from various devices or apps. If accumulating is not constrained directly, users should have ample options to delete images: they have claim-rights on doing so. Furthermore, deleting trivially leads to lack of access, but the latter should not be mistaken for the former. Although losing or accidentally deleting images is mentioned by many users as the primary risk of storage services, they also express scepticism about the completeness of deletion.[44] The difficulties people encounter in making sure that their images can no longer be accessed by anyone, are well-documented. But where this may concern proliferation of images over websites and repositories, 'deleted' is also a flexible notion when it comes to single files. Many apps contain paradoxically named 'Deleted items' folders, and even items that have been 'permanently deleted' from such folders can still be retrieved with some effort by many users. Mistrust whether service providers have 'permanently' deleted items once they can no longer be accessed by the user therefore seem well-grounded. And providers should do more to ensure deletion and assure users of it: making it difficult for users to verify whether images have been deleted constitutes interference with an action to which they are entitled. In the past, one would have been outraged if a photographer had retained images that she had processed for her clients, and worried if it were unclear whether she had retained the images. Here, the argument of section III. applies in full force: users have a right to have their images be deleted without a trace from storage services.

V. Conclusions

In this chapter, I have discussed cloud-based image storage from a moral perspective. After proposing a continuity heuristic for moral assessment and discussing some conceptual difficulties in its implementation, I derived a set of provisional moral constraints on cloud-based image storage, associated with the function of collections of personal images to support the formation and reflection of individual and collective identity.

This discussion does little more than scratch the surface. More systematic and specific analyses are needed to spell out the claim-rights and permissions that users and providers should and should not have. Some,

44 Keightley/Pickering (2014).

but not all of the constraints in section IV. have been explicitly formulated in these terms. This also shows that more may be at stake than these Hohfeldian incidents: I have used a partial analysis at best to analyse basic rights in servitized transactions, which can and should be supplemented in many respects. Furthermore, moral constraints have been identified based on cloud-based services being 'technologies of memory' that substitute for physical photo albums. This ignores the many other functions – new or old – that such services might have for users. Such functions may give rise to constraints of their own.

Despite these limitations, I hope to have shown that there are genuine moral issues to be resolved concerning cloud-based image storage, and illustrated, at the very least, one way to address these issues. Furthermore, and more importantly, I hope to have conveyed some of the urgency of engaging with these issues – not only because of the growing importance of cloud-based services in maintaining collections of personal images, but also because the servitization and digitization of this aspect of our lives is only one instance of an ever more encompassing trend.

References

Axtell, Benett/Munteanu, Cosmin (2019): 'Back to real pictures – A cross-generational understanding of users' mental models of photo cloud storage', Proceedings of the ACM on Interactive, Mobile, Wearable and Ubiquitous Technologies 3, Article 74 (2019, available at https://dl.acm.org/doi/10.1145/3351232)

Baines, Tim S./Lightfoot, Howard W./Benedettini, Ornella/Kay, John M. (2009): 'The servitization of manufacturing – A review of literature and reflection on future challenges', Journal of Manufacturing Technology Management (2009) 547–567

Broekhuijsen, Mendel/van den Hoven, Elise/Markopoulos, Panos (2017): 'From PhotoWork to PhotoUse – Exploring personal digital photo activities', Behavior & Information Technology (2017) 754–767

Clark, Jason W./Snyder, Peter/McCoy, Damon/Kanich, Chris (2015): '"I saw images I didn't even know I had" – Understanding user perceptions of cloud storage privacy', CHI'15: Proceedings of the 33rd Annual ACM Conference on Human Factors in Computing Systems (2015; https://doi.org/10.1145/2702123.2702535) 1641–1644

Cornes, Richard/Sandler, Todd (1996): *The Theory of Externalities – Public Goods and Club Goods* (Cambridge: Cambridge University Press 1996)

Edmundson, William A. (2012): *An Introduction to Rights* (Cambridge: Cambridge University Press 2nd edition 2012)

Frohlich, David M./Kuchinsky, Allan/Pering, Celine/Don, Abbe/Ariss, Steven (2002): 'Requirements for Photoware', Proceedings of the 2002 ACM Conference on Computer-Supported Cooperative Work (New York: ACM Press) 166–175

Hayes, Emily (2018): 'Geographical light – the magic lantern, the reform of the Royal Geographical Society and the professionalization of geography c. 1885–1894', Journal of Historical Geography (2018) 24–36

Helberger, Natali (2011): 'Standardizing consumer expectations in digital content', Info (2011) 69–79

Helberger, Natali/Loos, Marco B.M./Guibault, Lucie/Mak, Chantal/Pessers, Lodewijk (2013): 'Digital content contracts for consumers', Journal of Consumer Policy (2013) 37–57

Hirsch, Marianne (1997): *Family Frames – Photography, Narrative and Postmemory* (Cambridge, MA: Harvard University Press 1997)

Hohfeld, Wesley N. (1917): 'Fundamental Legal Conceptions as Applied in Judicial Reasoning', The Yale Law Journal (1917) 710–770

Houkes, Wybo (2018): 'Licensed to share?' in: Joerden, Jan.C./Schmücker, Reinold/Ortland, Eberhard (eds), Jahrbuch für Recht und Ethik (2018) 209–223

Johnson, Mark W./Christensen, Clayton M./Kagermann, Henning (2008): 'Reinventing your business model', Harvard Business Review (2008) 58–67

Keightley, Emily/Pickering, Michael (2014): 'Technologies of memory: Practices of remembering in analogue and digital photography', new media & society (2014) 576–593

Kowalkowski, Christian/Gebauer, Heiko/Oliva, Rogelio (2017): 'Service growth in product firms – Past, present and future', Industrial Marketing Management (2017) 82–88

Norman, Donald A. (1988): *The Design of Everyday Things* (New York: Basic Books 1988; original title: *The Psychology of Everyday Things*)

Perzanowski, Aaron K/Schultz, Jason (2015): 'Digital exhaustion', UCLA Law Review (2015) 889–946

Petty, Ross/D'Rozario, Denver (2009): 'The use of dead celebrities in advertising and marketing: Balancing interests in the right of publicity', Journal of Advertising (2009) 37–49

Rifkin, Jeremy (2000): *The Age of Access* (New York: Tarcher/Putnam 2000)

Selinger, Evan/Leong, Brenda (2021): 'The ethics of facial recognition technology' in: Véliz, Carissa (ed): *The Oxford Handbook of Digital Ethics* (Oxford: Oxford University Press, 2021, http://dx.doi.org/10.2139/ssrn.3762185)

Stevens, Molly M./Abowd, Gregory D./Truong, Khai N./Vollmer, Florian (2003): 'Getting into the living memory box: Family archives & holistic design', Personal and Ubiquitous Computing 7 (2003) 210–216

van Dijck, José (2008): 'Digital photography: Communication, identity, memory', Visual Communication 7 (2008) 57–76

Van House, Nancy A./Churchill, Elizabeth F. (2008): 'Technologies of memory: Key issues and critical perspectives', Memory Studies 1 (2008) 295–310

Vermeir, Koen (2005): 'The Magic of the Magic Lantern (1660–1700): On analogical demonstration and the visualization of the invisible', The British Journal for the History of Science (2005) 127–159

Wenar, Leif (2021): 'Rights', in: Zalta, Edward N. (ed): *The Stanford Encyclopedia of Philosophy* (Spring 2021 edition, https://plato.stanford.edu/archives/spr2021/entries/rights/)

Wendehorst, Christiane (2016): *Sale of Goods and Supply of Digital Content – Two Worlds Apart?* European Parliament, Directorate General for Internal Policies, Policy Department C In-Depth Analysis PE 556.928 (2016, https://www.europarl.europa.eu/cmsdata/98774/pe%20556%20928%20EN_final.pdf)

Windahl, Charlotta/Andersson, Pierre/Berggren, Christian/Nehler, Camilla (2004): 'Manufacturing firms and integrated solutions: Characteristics and implications', European Journal of Innovation Management 7 (2004) 218–228

Zhang, Wanrong/Banerji, Sujit (2017): 'Challenges of servitization – A systematic literature review', Industrial Marketing Management (2017) 217–227

Chapter 17
The Deontic Power of the Internet – Access Controls and the Obsolescence of Legal Norms

Thomas Dreier

I. What It's All About and what Consequences Does it Entail?

By now, it is common knowledge that the Internet[1] is not a legal vacuum. If, despite this generally shared conviction, it is felt that law has no or only limited validity on the Internet, this feeling has less to do with a lack of Internet-related legal regulation. Rather, it relates to a lack of adequate or at least sufficient enforcement.

But this is not all that can be said about the relationship between digital technology and the law. Generally, technology not only extends the scope of action, but it also defines and sets limits to what can be done by using it. Of course, the freedom-enhancing and, simultaneously, freedom-limiting effect of technology is not limited to digital technology and the Internet. Already analogue tools, such as a hammer, enable certain uses (such as driving nails) and they do not allow other uses (such as pulling out screws). However, when it comes to accessing digital content via the Internet, the layer of legal rules which regulate what is permitted, is super-imposed by the second layer of technology. This layer determines the limits and the extent to which content – and therefore also images – can be viewed and used. Moreover, assuming that law and ethics are not necessarily congruent, ethical rules provide a third layer to the relationship between law and technology.

To avoid falling into an abstract discussion of the two or even, three layers of regulation, this chapter will begin with only two scenarios as examples.[2] The first example involves private copying of copyrighted works and the second relates to the freedom to make quotations and parodies of copyrighted material in view of filtering technologies used by content

---

1 The term "Internet" is used in this chapter in a general manner, referring to both technical means of digital communication (such as LAN, WLAN etc.), and distribution tools (such as content sharing platforms, social media etc.).

2 Additional examples are discussed below, II.2.c.

sharing platforms. In both examples, the starting point is that copyright laws reserve, for authors and rightsholders, the exclusive right to make copies of works subject to copyright. However, to enable communication and benefit users, the reproduction right of authors and rightsholders is limited by several exceptions. Amongst these exceptions one finds the right to make private copies and the right to cite from copyrighted works or use copyrighted works for purposes of parody. The problem to be discussed in this chapter, evident in the first example, arises if technological copy protection prevents a user from making private copies as permitted by the law. In the second example, filtering technology used by content sharing platforms might prevent the upload of an otherwise legitimate citation or parody of copyrighted material.

It is submitted that technical access controls and technical configuration regulate how users can use content. It follows that to the extent code assumes the function of law, code replaces law as the traditional regulatory instrument. Already two decades ago, Harvard law professor Lawrence Lessig described the first effect by the catchword of "code as law".[3] The second effect is what I term the deontic power of technology. In other words, whereas the law defines what we *may* do, technology defines what we *can* do. The sphere of what is allowed is overlaid by the sphere of what can be done. This entails several consequences.

First, the additional technical layer does not seem to pose a problem if the technology applied to provide and communicate content enables the users to access, consume and redistribute content to the extent permitted by law. Also, those who make use of the potentially access blocking technology may decide to grant the users greater access and use possibilities than the minimum allowed for by law. To cite just one example, a technical device might allow for the making of a greater number of private copies of copyrighted works than is permitted by copyright law. From a legal point of view this is perfectly acceptable if the permission to engage in such uses is granted by the rightsholder. The possibility to make use of copyrighted works becomes, however, problematic, if the technology enables uses, e.g., of copyrighted works for which the respective rightsholder has not given his or her consent, such as in the case of illegal file sharing, including the use and marketing of tools for illegal file sharing (e.g., BitTorrent software, but also online content-sharing service providers such as YouTube, to the extent that they allow the publicly making available of copyrighted material without the consent of the respective rightsholder).

3 Lessig (1999).

This becomes a problem when legal regulation allows users to engage in acts which technology deliberately makes impossible to perform. In these cases, users are prevented from taking advantage of the freedom to act as granted by the law. In this respect, quite practically, the law loses its regulatory function which is replaced by technology. However, this reality is not only practical, but it also has theoretical consequences. As a norm presupposes the ability of the norm addressee to decide against the fulfilment of the command contained in the norm (after all, legal norms are only "ought"-norms),[4] technical limitations deplete the legal norm of its normative content. Moreover, the use of such technology results in a "technically configured self-execution" of the rules defined not by the legislator but by those who use the technology. Simultaneously, the decision-making power to define the limits of the freedom to act thus shifts from the public lawmaker to private providers of products and services.

This shift tends to occur outside the institutional framework of democratic decision-making, bypassing it. Thus, the use of digital access-regulating devices by those who offer digital products and services to users not only entails consequences within rather limited and specialized areas of law such as, e.g., copyright. Rather, it affects the very structure of the organization of public life within societies, threatens its democratic structures and leads to a shift in the power relation between State authorities and private players. It is this shift which brought Pamela Samuelson from Berkeley University to speak of "private legislation"[5] and other authors such as Yochai Benkler from the New York University of "private ordering".[6]

The notion of private parties performing legislative tasks is problematic in the following two scenarios. Firstly, when the legislature allows private legislation – e.g., the application of technical protection measures to control access and prevent unauthorized copying of copyrighted material – on a voluntary basis. In addition, in such cases the legislature has flanked this way of private legislation with the legal means of copyright circumvention protection, which in turn tends to curtail the use freedoms the legislature had initially granted himself (Section II.). Secondly, it is problematic when the legislature expressly and obligatorily transfers the power to decide disputes about the legality or illegality of posts on social media – at least at a first stage – to private platform operators. Examples are Article 17 Para-

4 Möllers (2015/2020); for the freedom to act in an illegal way see also Becker (2019).
5 Samuelson (2003).
6 Benkler (2000).

graph 9 of the DSM-Directive,[7] § 3 of the German "Netzwerkdurchsetzungsgesetz",[8] and at times by order of the courts, which mandate platform operators to judge the legality or illegality of posts made by users on their respective platforms (Section III.).

II. Voluntary Application of Technical Measures Restricting Legal Freedoms Supported by Anti-Circumvention Legislation

1. From public goods to technical protection measures

The question becomes how did the law react to this discrepancy between what is permitted by law and what is technologically possible? What mechanisms has the legislature created to eliminate, or at least counter this discrepancy?

Examining the area of copyright – an area where this discrepancy plays a role in the case of communication via images – one must step back in time and briefly recall why exclusive copyright protection exists in the first place. From a European-centred author's rights point of view, copyright is designed with the aim of recognizing creative works as emanations from their authors and protects the author's financial interest in the proceeds generated by the exploitation of their works. Conversely, Anglo-American copyright law focuses almost exclusively on the economic aspect of providing incentives to authors and publishers for investment in creative works.[9] Hence, from an economic point of view, intellectual property law is the answer to what has been called the "tragedy of the commons", i.e., to the undesirable results of inefficient under-investment in and over-consumption of the scarce resource of intellectual creations.[10] By creating an artificial, legal exclusivity, intellectual property rights turn the public good of intellectual creations into a commercially tradeable object.

7 Directive (EU) 2019/790 of the European Parliament and of the Council 17 April 2019 on copyright and related rights in the Digital Single Market and amending Directives 96/9/EC and 2001/29/EC (OJ EU L 130 of 17 May 2019, 92 et seq.).

8 Gesetz zur Verbesserung der Rechtsdurchsetzung in sozialen Netzwerken (Netzwerkdurchsetzungsgesetz, NetzDG) of 1 September 2017 (German OJ BGBl I 3352), as last modifed by article 1 of the law of 3 June 2021 (BGBl. I p. 1436).

9 For a more detailed comparison see, e.g., Baldwin (2014); Strowel (1993).

10 See only the fundamental works by Hardin/Baden (eds) (1977); Ostrom (1990).

The problem described above that digital and networking technologies create for the exclusive intellectual property rights' system results from the ease of copying copyrighted material at marginal cost without loss of quality, as well as from the possibility of unlimited communication via the Internet. These effects which are a direct consequence of digital and networking technologies undermine the participation of authors in the proceeds which result from the use value of their intellectual creations as well as the return of the publishers' investment. When copyrighted content in digitized form was still distributed using a material carrier, the problem was that such acts of unpaid copying undertaken by users was beyond the rightsholders' control of the content copied. This eroded the rightsholder's revenue-stream which no longer corresponded to the aggregate use value users derive from using the copyrighted subject matter.

Hence, the idea was formulated to use technology to prevent this outcome unwanted by the rightsholders, or, as Charles Clark, then advisor to the UK publishers' association, once formulated: "The answer to the machine is in the machine".[11] According to this strategy, the legal exclusivity disturbed by digital and networking technology should be re-established by protecting the otherwise defenceless copyrighted intellectual creations through the application of technological protection measures (TPMs). Typically, TPMs block access to copyrighted material or regulate use intensities such as, e.g., copy protection attached to a musical CD, which does not dis-enable the possibility to listen to the music, but dis-enables the possibility to make copies.

However, from the rightsholders' perspective, the problem remained unresolved. Although TPMs might prove successful in practice, at least in theory they could almost always be circumvented. Moreover, once a circumventing tool is designed it can easily be distributed via the Internet, thus undermining the very protection the application of a TPM was supposed to provide. It comes therefore not as a surprise that the legislature succumbed to the pressure of rightsholders, adding yet another layer of protection by way of a legal anti-circumvention protection. This legislation, first introduced by two international Treaties adopted as early as 1996 on a global level in a top-down approach,[12] deems the "manufacture,

11 Clark (1996).

12 Article 11 of the WIPO Copyright Treaty (WCT) and Article 18 of the WIPO Performances and Phonograms Treaty (WPPT). For the justification of anti-circumvention protection in the field of copyright, see, in particular, Marks/Turnbull (1999); Gasser (2006). – The international rules were followed, on the level of the EU, by Article 6 of the InfoSoc-Directive 2001/29/EC (Directive 2001/29/EC of the

import, distribution, sale, rental, advertisement for sale or rental, or possession for commercial purposes of devices, products or components or the provision of services which: (a) are promoted, advertised or marketed for the purpose of circumvention of, or (b) have only a limited commercially significant purpose or use other than to circumvent, or (c) are primarily designed, produced, adapted or performed for the purpose of enabling or facilitating the circumvention of, any effective technological measures" as illegal according to EU law.[13]

2. *Technical protection measures and copyright exceptions and limitations*

However, generally, TPMs are rather "stupid". Implemented like any other piece of software by means of informatics, TPMs work based on zeros and ones. They only "know" "black" and "white", "current" and "no current", and their output reads either "pass" or "block", i.e., "do not pass". It follows that as long as TPMs are not able to arrive at a decision on the semantic level of information,[14] they are unable to recognise on a discrete yes/no-basis. This is particularly troubling when deciding whether a portion of the text or image copied is used as an illegal reproduction or as a legal citation, satire, parody or pastiche.[15] In other words, as long as TPMs are not "smart" enough to make decisions on the basis of a semantic understanding of both the content they judge and the context in which the content in questions is used in a given case, TPMs inevitably tend to block uses of copyrighted content which are perfectly legal.

The question becomes how did the legislature, the courts and legal literature react to this problem of technological over-protection?

European Parliament and of the Council of 22 May 2001 on the harmonisation of certain aspects of copyright and related rights in the information society, OJ EU L 167 of 22 June 2001, 10 et seq.), which was subsequently implemented into EU Member States' national copyright laws. – An earlier rudimentary anti-circumvention protection regulation was at the European level already contained in Article 7 (1) (c) of the Computer Program Directive (Council Directive 91/250/EEC of 14 May 1991 on the legal protection of computer programs, OJ EU L 122 of 17 May 1991, 42 et seq.).

13 Art. 6 (2) of the InfoSoc-Directive 2001/29/EC.

14 For the distinction between the structural, syntactic and semantic layers see Raue (2022).

15 For these exceptions to the exclusive reproduction and public communication rights of copyright see Art. 5 (3) (d) and (k) of the InfoSoc-Directive 2001/29/EC.

a) Legislative solutions

When adopting the InfoSoc-Directive in 2001,[16] the legislature was aware of the discrepancy between the legal freedom to act and the freedom to act allowed by technology. As a result, it was stated in Art. 6 (4) (1) of the InfoSoc-Directive that rightsholders should make available to users whose use of copyrighted material is covered by a copyright exception "the means of benefiting from that exception ..., to the extent necessary to benefit from that exception". Although this legal provision seems to arrange for the primacy of law over technology, it does have several limitations.

Firstly, it only applies when the user has legal access to the protected work in question.

Secondly, and more importantly however, it does not apply to all, but only to a limited number of existing copyright exceptions. These exceptions concern (1) paper reproductions, (2) non-commercial reproductions made by publicly accessible libraries, educational establishments or museums as well as by archives, (3) certain ephemeral recordings of works made by broadcasting organisations, (4) reproductions of broadcasts made by social institutions pursuing non-commercial purposes, as well as reproductions and public communications (5) for the purpose of illustration for teaching or scientific research, (6) for persons with a disability as well as (7) for the purposes of public security or to ensure the proper performance or reporting of administrative, parliamentary or judicial proceedings.[17] To apply the preference of the law over technology likewise to the exception allowing private copying is, however, optional.[18] It is interesting to note that in the InfoSoc-Directive, neither the exception allowing for quotations nor the one for the purpose of caricature, parody, or pastiche are listed as receiving such preferrential treatment. This may sound more disquieting than it actually is, since in practice, beneficiaries of these latter exceptions can make use of protected works at least in those cases in which they have legitimate access to the works quoted, criticized or humourized via parody and satire.

Thirdly, it seems to be generally accepted in EU Member States that the legal provision cited does not establish a right to self-help of the user. Rather, rightsholders are only obliged to provide the necessary means to

16 Directive 2001/29/EC of the European Parliament and of the Council of 22 May 2001 on the harmonisation of certain aspects of copyright and related rights in the information society, OJ EU L 167, 10 et seq. of 22 June 2001.

17 Article 5(2)(a), (c), (d), (e), (3)(a), (b) and (e) of the InfoSoc-Directive.

18 Article 5(2)(b) of the InfoSoc-Directive.

the beneficiaries of the exceptions listed.[19] Most importantly, however, according to Art. 6 (4) (4) of the InfoSoc-Directive, the rules just described do not apply in an online environment. In other words, if a rightsholder and a user are directly linked with each other via the Internet, the rightsholder is legally allowed to block the use covered by any statutory exception by way of technological means. It appears that this provision was motivated by the – neo-liberal – consideration that once two parties are in direct contact, they can freely negotiate and mutually agree upon the terms and conditions of their transaction.

However, despite the criticism which Article 6 (4) (4) of the InfoSoc-Directive attracted,[20] recently the pendulum appears to have slightly swung back. Firstly, when enacting the DSM-Directive,[21] Art. 6 (4) (4) of the InfoSoc-Directive was declared inapplicable to the new exceptions contained in the DSM-Directive for text and data mining, cross-border online teaching and reproductions made for the preservation of cultural heritage.[22] Secondly, the EU legislature recognized the importance of the exceptions for quotation, criticism, review as well as for uses for the purpose of caricature, parody or pastiche, especially in the online environment of content-sharing platforms used as social media. These exceptions, which were not included in the list of exceptions that may trump TPMs in the InfoSoc-Directive, have now been strengthened at least vis-à-vis technical filtering systems used by online content-sharing platforms so that they ultimately prevail over any technical blocking.[23] Even if details are left to the stage of national implementation and negotiations between rightsholders and operators of content-sharing platforms, this new regulation is definitively a step forward.

19 See also recitals 51 and 52 of the InfoSoc-Directive, and for an overview of the situation in several Member States von Lewinski (2010) para. 11.6.13.
20 See, e.g., Dusollier (2003); Koelman (2000); Koelman/Helberger (2000).
21 Directive (EU) 2019/790 of the European Parliament and of the Council of 17 April 2019 on copyright and related rights in the Digital Single Market and amending Directives 96/9/EC and 2001/29/EC, OJ EU L 130 of 17 May 2019, 92 et seq.
22 Articles 7 (2) sentence 2 and 3 to 6 of the DSM-Directive.
23 Article 17 (7) of the DSM-Directive.

b) *Reactions of the courts*

In the beginning, the courts dealt less with the scope of legal anti-circumvention protection, but rather with to what extent the scope of the exclusive right of making copyrighted works publicly available via the Internet depended on the application of TPMs. In this regard, initially the Courts did not seem very sensitized to the problem of technology overriding legal freedoms. On several occasions, when holding that certain acts committed on the Internet were copyright-free, the courts in their decisions added that this applies as long as there are no TPMs in place.[24] By way of *argumentum e contrario*, already such formulations suggested the inverse conclusion that the very same acts with regard to technologically protected copyrighted material are as such subject to copyright, and this in addition to the infringement of the legal prohibition of circumventing TPMs.

Indeed, in the meantime – in which the CJEU declared both the acts of hyperlinking and framing/embedding falling outside of the public communication right in case no TPMs are applied,[25] encompassing framing of works that are protected by copyright which were made, with the authorisation of the copyright holder, freely accessible to the public on another website – the CJEU[26] concluded that the author's exclusive public communication right is infringed by embedding in cases in which "that embedding circumvents measures adopted or imposed by that copyright holder to provide protection from framing". Already before, some national courts of the EU Member States had arrived at similar conclusions.[27]

---

24 See only, e.g., for the case of simple hyperlinking CJEU, case C-466/12 of 13 February 2014, para. 26, ECLI:EU:C:2014:76 – Svensson (the copyrighted material linked to "was not subject to any restrictive measures"); similarly the German Federal Supreme Court (Bundesgerichtshof, BGH), case I ZR 259/00 of 17 July 2003, Gewerblicher Rechtsschutz und Urheberrecht (GRUR) 2003, 959 (961) – Paperboy ("Ein Berechtigter, der ein urheberrechtlich geschütztes Werk ohne technische Schutzmaßnahmen im Internet öffentlich zugänglich macht").

25 CJEU, case C-466/12 of 13 February 2014, ECLI:EU:C:2014:76 – Svensson (hyperlinking); case C-348/13 of 21 October 2014, ECLI:EU:C:2014:2315 – BestWater International (embedding). For the boundaries between copyright-relevant and not copyright-relevant linking to copyrighted content which was illegally posted, see CJEU case C-160/15 of 8 September 2016, ECLI:EU:C:2016:644 – GS Media.

26 CJEU case C-392/19 of 9 March 2021, ECLI:EU:C:2021:181 – VG Bild-Kunst.

27 See, e.g., for Germany BGH, case I ZR 39/08 of 29 April 2010, Gewerblicher Rechtsschutz und Urheberrecht (GRUR) 2011, 56 – Session-ID. – Similarly in Germany also BGH, case I ZR 178/08 of 11 February 2010, Gewerblicher Rechtsschutz und Urheberrecht (GRUR) 2010, 822 (824) – Half-Life 2 (concluding that legal exhaustion of the distribution right was excluded in the case of a computer

However, regarding the potentially overreaching effect of TPMs, the CJEU seems to follow a somewhat less strict line. At least in one case, the CJEU required that legal protection against anti-circumvention requires that "other measures ... which ... could cause less interference with the activities of third parties or limitations to those activities, while still providing comparable protection of the rightsholder's rights" are not available.[28] This decision subjects legal anti-circumventing legislation to the principle of proportionality.[29] Hence, in order to define in practice, which TPMs are protected against circumvention, a complex balancing of many factors such as "inter alia, of the relative costs of different types of technological measures, of technological and practical aspects of their implementation, and of a comparison of the effectiveness of those different types of technological measures as regards the protection of the rightsholder's rights, that effectiveness however not having to be absolute" must be taken into account. Additionally, "the purpose of devices, products or components, which are capable of circumventing those technological measures" must also be examined.

In that regard, "the evidence of use which third parties actually make of them will, in the light of the circumstances at issue" be particularly relevant. And in particular, it should be examined "how often those devices, products or components are in fact used in disregard of copyright and how often they are used for purposes which do not infringe copyright."[30] It is needless to state, on the one hand, that this balancing undertaken by the CJEU leaves a relatively large margin of discretion to the national courts of the Member States. On the other hand, by focusing solely on the configuration and use of TPMs and their primary use for copyright protection, the CJEU does not even address the core issue discussed in this chapter. Of course, firstly, the problem of a possible overreaching and over blocking was at best indirectly at issue in the case referred to the CJEU. Secondly, it can be said that in line with the separation of powers the CJEU respects

---

game which was protected by a technical program key); it is, however, at least questionable whether this holding can still be upheld after the decision of the CJEU in case C-128/11 of 3 July 2012, ECLI:EU:C:2012:407 – UsedSoft.

28 CJEU, case C-355/12 of 23 January 2014, ECLI:EU:C:2014:25, paras. 29 et seq. – Nintendo.

29 Article 6 (2) of the InfoSoc-Directive 2001/29/EC, as interpreted in the light of its Recital 48, which states that in order to enjoy anti-circumvention protection, TPMs "should not ... have a commercially significant purpose or use other than to circumvent the technical protection"; CJEU, case C-355/12 of 23 January 2014, ECLI:EU:C:2014:25, para. 30 – Nintendo.

30 Ibid., para. 38.

the decision of the EU legislature which, with the InfoSoc-Directive has opted for strong and far-reaching copyright protection.[31]

c) *Additional issues described in legal literature*

It shall only briefly be mentioned here that the problem of technological configurations blocking actions by users which are as such permitted by law, is not limited to the limitations of copyright and access and/or reproduction-controlling TPMs. In legal literature, several other situations have been identified in which the same problem arises.[32]

One such constellation concerns the question whether the principle of EU-wide exhaustion of the national distribution rights can be eliminated by technical dispositives.[33] According to the principle of EU-wide exhaustion,[34] once an object protected by an intellectual property right has been put on the market by the rightsholder or with his or her consent, this object can freely circulate within the Single Market, without being hindered by national distribution rights. This principle was established by the ECJ at an early stage of the European integration process with the aim of preventing the principle of free movement of goods from being undermined by the exercise of nationally split distribution rights.[35] With the advent of technology, however, it became possible to resort to market segmentation within the EU both for digital goods and services. The resulting question is whether it is legally permissible, under EU law, to separate national markets within the EU by way of technology in cases in which EU law forbids market segmentation.[36]

31 See Recital 9 of the InfoSoc-Directive ("Any harmonisation of copyright and related rights must take as a basis a high level of protection". – For criticism, favouring a balanced approach of legitimate protection interests and freedom of expression see, e.g., Dreier (2016); Geiger (2021).

32 For both an overview and extensive discussion see Specht (2019).

33 Other cases are the factual extension of statutory terms of IP protection, the de facto reservation of legal prerogatives not provided by law, and territorial limitations of use possibilities; see Specht (2019), pp. 353 et seq.

34 In the US, the principle of exhaustion is discussed under the name of "first sale doctrine" (17 U.S.C. § 109(a)).

35 ECJ, case 78/70 of 8 January 1971, ECLI:EU:C:1971:59 – Deutsche Grammophon.

36 It should be noted, however, that so far, in view of the absence of an obligation to deliver goods and services in all of the EU-Member States, such prohibitions exist above all, if not exclusively, in intellectual property law.

In this respect, the so-called Portability Regulation[37] sticks out. This Regulation requires providers of an online content service provided against payment of money to enable subscribers who are "temporarily present in a Member State to access and use the online content service in the same manner as in the Member State of residence".[38] The example of the Portability Regulation is interesting for two reasons. On the one hand, it prohibits technical configurations on a strictly territorial basis which would block access of legitimate users to the service once they are temporarily abroad. And in imposing this duty on the providers of online-musical services, the EU legislature is not concerned with how providers would comply with this legal obligation. On the other hand, by limiting this duty of providing access to national users who are temporarily abroad, the EU legislature accepts the general validity of the principle of territoriality and the otherwise unhindered freedom of online-music providers to restrict access to their service on a territorial basis. Of course, it might be argued that providing online-music is in essence a service to which the principle of exhaustion – which is generally limited to the resale of physical copyrighted objects but doesn't extend to public communications – doesn't apply.[39] Also, economic concerns point to the direction of keeping the internal market territorially segmented, since deciding otherwise might eventually prevent the emergence of music services. However, the problem of tension between mandatory effects of exhaustion on the one

37 Regulation (EU) 2017/1128 of the European Parliament and of the Council of 14 June 2017 on cross-border portability of online content services in the internal market, OJ EU L 168, 1 et seq. of 30 June 2017.

38 Ibid., Article 3 (1).

39 This is explicitly stated in Article 4 (2) as further interpreted by Recital 29 of the InfoSoc-Directive. – It should be noted, however, that when the ECJ, in case 62/79 of 18 March 1980, ECLI:EU:C:1980:84 – Coditel v. Ciné Vog firstly made the distinction between the distribution of physical goods (exhaustion) and the public communication of protected works in immaterial form (no exhaustion), it didn't argue on the basis of strict principles, but, but rather examined whether rightsholders have obtained, when authorizing the first public communication of their works also for subsequent acts of public communication such as a cable retransmission of an initial over the air-tv program signal. Secondly, in its Used-Soft-decision, case C-128/11 of 3 July 2012, ECLI:EU:C:2012:407, the CJEU has adopted a different approach at least for the exhaustion of computer programmes which were transmitted online to both the first and the second acquirer. However, in its subsequent Tom Kabinet-Decision, case C-263/18 of 19 December 2019, ECLI:EU:C:2019:1111, the CJEU refuted this approach for works covered by the InfoSoc-Directive.

hand, and the hindrance of these effects by way of technology remains worth being discussed.

Another major area where legal freedoms can be eliminated by technology is technologically implemented end-user license agreements (EULAs). Generally, in countries, such as Germany, that provide for court control of unfair standard terms and conditions,[40] certain conditions can be declared null and void, thus losing their binding force. In other words, the end-user who is not bound by such illegal clauses, can access and use the content by disregarding the non-binding restrictions. The situation, of course, differs when the restrictive conditions are technologically implemented. A user wanting to use digital content has no choice but to agree to the pre-formulated and non-negotiated terms and conditions. If the user does not agree, he or she cannot access the content in question at all. This is a typical "love it or leave it"-situation, which severely limits the end-users' room for action. Of course, the user might give his or her consent and, after being granted access, use the content disregarding any illegal standard term which limits his or her freedom to make use of the digital content. However, even this leeway may easily be blocked by the person offering the service. All that is necessary is to implement the restrictive clauses not merely in writing, but through self-executing technology which makes it impossible to use the product or service in a way that disregards the otherwise illegal standard use terms.

3. *Some thoughts for discussion*

a) *Is there really a problem?*

However, when making an ethical judgment about such technical configurations that overstep, restrict, or even eliminate legally guaranteed freedoms to act, some additional thoughts must be considered.

To begin with, it should be recalled that every technology has in-built restrictions on the freedom to act. While enabling certain actions, technological devices never enable all of them. Therefore, already by definition, when using a particular technical device or technology, users are unable to perform certain acts one might think of. In ethical terms, it follows that non-enabling features of technology and technological devices cannot as such be considered as being ethically objectionable. On a psychological

---

40 Sections 305 et seq. of the German Civil Code (Bürgerliches Gesetzbuch, BGB).

level, users are well aware of this phenomenon. In the analogue environment, it is clear to users that not obtaining the full potential of a given technology is justified when it would require additional investment from the person offering the technology. In the digital environment, however, artificial use restrictions are less well received by users, since offering the full technological potential often does not require additional investment. Quite to the contrary, it is the technology which restricts per se existing possibilities of use which calls for additional investment on the part of those who offer such use-restricted digital devices or services. It follows that an ethical problem is evident when a given technology or technical device might enable its users to a greater extent, if it were not for its technological use-restricting features which have been built in by its designer. In such cases, the artificially built-in limitation of otherwise technically possible uses appears to need justification.

Before examining such possible justifications,[41] one might ask why not simply let the free will of the users – and by their aggregate the market – decide? Indeed, one might argue that no ethical problem exists with in-built technological restrictions if the consumers are content with them, do not feel unduly burdened and do not complain. After all, technical use restrictions notwithstanding, users may view and experience such devices as enlarging – rather than as restricting – their freedom to act. If this were not so, the long queues in front of branded IT stores could not be explained, whenever a new device containing certain deliberately in-built technical restrictions is put to the market. Moreover, as Lawrence Lessig has pointed out, whether a user considers a particular technical device as enhancing or restricting his or her freedom to act, depends on the point of reference. For children, e.g., a smartphone is a tremendous enlargement of their possibilities to communicate, whereas for adults, who were already used to portable telephones, any possible advantages of a smartphone might be offset by perceived disadvantages because of a lack of expected data and privacy protection.

Similarly, regarding the intervention of the law, it can be argued that legal regulation is not an end in and of itself, but rather a means to guarantee citizens' freedom to choose. From this perspective, whenever users are content with the restrictions of a particular technical device, a legal norm that prohibits such restrictions would be difficult to legitimize. Of course, the situation is different when the consumer is happy with a particular technical device and the price paid because he or she hasn't been properly

41 See below, II.3.b.

informed about the scope and effects of the built-in technical restrictions. Since withholding the information affects the basis for the formation of the user's free will, what has been said above therefore only holds true if users are sufficiently informed about the technical restrictions in place. Hence, legitimizing built-in technological use restrictions therefore presupposes that the user will be duly informed about such restrictions. In legal – and most likely also in ethical – terms, this points into the direction of adopting obligations to make the restrictions transparent, rather than to ban them completely. In addition, even if users are sufficiently informed in order to form a free will of their own, they can only exercise their free will if they have a real choice. However, there is no such possibility to choose in cases where the technical configuration only allows for the binary decision of obtaining "access" or "not obtaining access". To be more precise, in such cases the freedom to choose is affected to the extent that other competing offers of goods and services are not available, which provide for less restrictive – or at least different – technical restrictions. The latter is, of course, questionable in view of the present oligopolistic situations regarding the "big five".[42]

At any rate, it becomes clear that an ethical – and legal – judgement of whether built-in technological restrictions should be banned at all, the extent they should be banned, if a transparency obligation is required, or whether anti-monopolistic measures should be taken can only be made on a case-to-case basis.

b) Advantages of technological restrictions

Apart from the possible in-built technological restriction justifications based on the individual user's free will, her or his personal choices on the micro level and the market as arbiter discussed above,[43] there are also justifications on the macro level of the economy at large.

According to economists, technical configurations which artificially restrict use possibilities of a technical device allow for what is called product and service diversification together with price differentiation. What is meant by these terms is that by applying technological devices which regulate access and use possibilities of a given content, one and the same

42 "Big Five", or GAFAM, relates to Google (Alphabet), Amazon, Facebook (Meta), Apple and Microsoft.

43 See above, II.3.a.

content can be offered to consumers in various forms, each allowing for different use possibilities. In addition, these different use possibilities could then be offered by way of price differentiation, i.e., by asking a different price for each of them. An example might be movies which can be sold in the form of DVDs without or with copy protection, in the form of streaming which can be recorded or only be viewed once. Each of these different versions of one and the same movie can be offered on the market for a different price.

In general economic terms, product diversification and price differentiation are said to make sense – and hence, could be said to be ethically justified. This is because the availability of cheaper versions allows for more consumers to view the content made available (in the example cited the movie), thus leading to a better consumer supply. At the same time, over-payments by those consumers who only intend to make restricted use of the content offered are avoided. Further, as more users will pay for cheaper – albeit use-restricted – versions, producers can better skim the users' overall willingness to pay and hence, increase their income. In sum, from the point of view of an overall welfare analysis, this is what economists call a "win-win situation". If this analysis proves to be true,[44] then it is evident that leverage on the part of users must be excluded. In other words, it must be guaranteed that users do not buy a cheap use-restricted version and then remove the restriction to obtain greater use-possibilities than they paid for. In view of this, legal anti-circumvention protection would seem to be justified as well, as the essential building block of such an environment of optimal distribution of digital content.

It is, of course, another matter to then justify any overshooting tendency of the TPMs used to achieve the desired product differentiation. In this regard, a proper balance will have to be found between the actual and consequential costs of tailormade technical solutions on the one hand, and the desire to retain the possibility to undertake acts permitted by law on the other hand, especially if these acts contribute to the freedom of information and the freedom of speech. In this regard, a balancing which only would look at dollars and cents would be inappropriate, considering that the two freedoms just mentioned are the most fundamental values in democratic systems.[45]

44 For a critical account of anti-circumvention protection applied to music which can be shared via peer-to-peer filesharing networks, see, however, Benkler (2000).

45 For further general discussion of those fundamental freedoms see, e.g., Eichenhofer (2022) and Geiger (2022).

III. Mandatory Decision-Making Power by Private Parties

1. Case scenarios

It is one thing that the legislature leaves it to the *discretion* of private parties to decide whether they want to affix technological access-restricting devices to their digital technological products and services, and if they do so, to provide legal anti-circumvention protection. However, it is yet another thing if the legislature itself *mandates* private parties, i.e., platform providers, to decide the legality of content posted which leads to blocking or even deletion of the content that is considered, by the platform operators, as illegal. The latter scenarios are found both on the European and – depending on the individual states' laws – national level. Only three such scenarios shall be briefly presented here to illustrate the ethical and legal problems that are linked to them.

At the European level, Article 17 (7) (1) of the DSM-Directive[46] obliges EU Member states to provide legislation which imposes the burden on content-sharing service providers to ensure "the availability of works or other subject matter uploaded by users, which does not infringe copyright and related rights, including where such works or other subject matter are covered by an exception or limitation". This particularly applies to the now EU-wide mandatory exceptions concerning "quotation, criticism, review" and "use for the purpose of caricature, parody or pastiche" (Article 17 (7) (2) (a) and (b) of the DSM-Directive). According to this mechanism, content-sharing service providers will decide whether an individual upload of third parties' copyrighted content by a platform user is covered by a copyright exception or not. In addition, Article 17 (4) obliges online content-sharing platform providers to ensure that users do not post copyrighted material for which no consent has been given by the rightsholder. In case of an unauthorised posting, the platform provider is burdened with the duty to pay damages to the respective rightsholder, unless he or she can demonstrate that he or she has "(a) made best efforts to obtain an authorisation, and (b) made, in accordance with high industry standards of professional diligence, best efforts to ensure the unavailability of specific works and other subject matter for which the rightsholders have provided the service providers with the relevant and necessary information; and in any event (c) acted expeditiously, upon receiving a sufficiently substantiated notice from the rightsholders, to disable access to, or to remove

46 See footnote 22.

from their websites, the notified works or other subject matter, and made best efforts to prevent their future uploads in accordance with point (b)." In other words, platform providers are obligated to decide themselves whether a posting by one of its users occurs with or without the consent of the rightsholder's consent.

At the national level, a similar scenario arises whenever national legislation provides for a ban on certain speech acts, such as incitations to hate or even war, denial of the holocaust, etc.,[47] and, at the same time, obliges the providers of platforms on which users can post comments to delete, or block access to, illegal postings.[48] Here too, the legislature has mandated the platform operators to make a first judgement regarding the legality or illegality of the postings before the issue is eventually forwarded to a reviewing body and, in the event of a continuing dispute, decided by the courts.

Finally, also at the national level, a similarly structured scenario is to be found when the platform operator, rather than being obliged to remove certain speech acts which are explicitly forbidden by law, is called upon to delete or block access to posts made by one user which the person targeted by the comment considers the post in question as offensive and insulting, if not as outright libellous and slanderous. In Germany, e.g., such a duty of platform providers to become active once they receive a complaint by an allegedly aggrieved party, has been developed by the courts with the aim of providing effective protection to personality rights' infringements.[49]

---

47 In Germany, such restrictions are indeed quite numerous, see sections 86, 86a, 89a, 91, 100a, 111, 126, 129–129b, 130, 131, 140, 166, 184b, 185–187, 201a, 241 and 269 of the German penal Code (Strafgesetzbuch, StGB).

48 See, e.g., the German law on the enforcement of rights in social networks (Gesetz zur Verbesserung der Rechtsdurchsetzung in sozialen Netzwerken; Netzwerkdurchsetzungsgesetz, NetzDG) of 1 September 2017 (BGBl. I p. 3352), last amended by Article 1 of the law of 3 June 2021 (BGBl. I p. 1436). The law imposes a duty on platform operators to delete or block access to "obviously illegal" content within 24 hours, and other illegal content within 7 days after a complaint has been filed.

49 For the duty to remove or delete upon fulfilment of the corresponding duties to examine the posts, and the procedure of giving each of the two parties concerned the possibility to be sufficiently heard, see, e.g., BGH VI ZR 93/10 of 25 October 2011, Gewerblicher Rechtsschutz und Urheberrecht (GRUR) 2012, 311 – Blog-Eintrag, and VI ZR 34/15 of 1 March 2016, Gewerblicher Rechtsschutz und Urheberrecht (GRUR) 2016, 855 – www.jameda.de.

2. Structural issues

In all three scenarios mentioned, the issue discussed in this chapter of technology not permitting (speech) acts which otherwise are permitted by law,[50] is a direct consequence of the sheer number of uploads.

Traditionally, in the analogue world, the number of actionable infringements remained by and large manageable.[51] In the digital world of platforms, however, individual control of each single out of the millions of posting is clearly no longer possible. Moreover, digital technology allows for a far wider and quicker spreading of illegal postings than in the analogue world. Hence, leaving illegal postings accessible until redress by the courts – even if only by way of interim relief – has been obtained, is likewise no longer an option. Rather, immediate action is required, if the harm resulting from illegal postings is to be limited to a tolerable extent.

Inevitably, this finding entails two consequences. Firstly, it leads to the legal involvement of intermediaries, i.e., in the cases discussed here, the providers of content-sharing platforms and platforms where opinions can be posted by individual users. It is these platform providers who are entrusted by the lawmaker with a first-sight control since they are the only actors able to speedily enforce the law by way of blocking access to – if not even outrightly deleting – illegal postings. Secondly, even if automated filtering-technology is nowhere mentioned in the DSM-Directive,[52] there is almost general agreement that the mass of uploads can only be effectively controlled by rather elaborate upload-filters.[53] However, with filtering inevitably comes the danger – if ineffective under-blocking is to be avoided – of over-blocking, i.e., the blocking of so-called false positives. In the area of copyright, the task of the platform providers is not made any easier by the fact that due to the need to safeguard users' human rights as per the Charter of Human Rights of the EU, Article 17 (8) of the DSM-Directive

50 For private legislation under the German NetzDG Tschorr (2021).

51 Of course, even in the analogue world, certain mass transactions required some bundling of individual means of legal redress, such as, e.g., the control of commonly used standard terms and conditions by way of judicial test cases and forms of collective or class actions, which shall, however, not be discussed here in detail.

52 Article 17 (4) (b) of the DSM-Directive only speaks of "best efforts to ensure the unavailability of specific works and other subject matter", and only mandates platform providers "in accordance with high industry standards of professional diligence".

53 This is notwithstanding the somewhat sybilline statement by the German Government to the contrary; see German Government (2019), para. 4 ("Upload filters should be prevented if possible").

explicitly prohibits – in line with prior CJEU decisions[54] – that monitoring for unlawfully uploaded content on a content-sharing platform by the platform provider results in a "general monitoring obligation".

Therefore, in all three scenarios discussed, platform providers are intermediaries legally responsible to first decide the legality or illegality of content posted. The question is how the number of false positives can be minimized. It should be noted that it is not always easy to judge whether a given speech act is illegal or whether it can be said to be legal. The reason simply is that on the one hand, the semantic meaning of speech acts is to a large degree context dependent. On the other hand, the courts have developed an elaborate system of balancing a variety of different criteria, which cannot be easily replicated by filters, nor by the hundreds of platform provider employees whose task it is to minimize the number of false positives after the stage of filtering.

But even if the law provides for complaint procedures,[55] asymmetries exist between the default setting of blocking and non-blocking on the one hand, and the number of complaints filed against false positives and false negatives by the parties concerned. If "blocking" is the default setting of the filtering systems used, there will be a tendency of over blocking and hence an infringement of the fundamental right of free speech, since most of those whose posts have been *blocked* will not complain. However, choosing "not-blocking" by the platform provider as the default setting will invariably lead to under blocking, since many of those who consider themselves *infringed* by the postings, will not complain.[56] This, however, results in an increased number of infringements of personality rights or copyrights. In addition, if platform providers are threatened by the possibility of paying damages in the event of an incorrect judgement,[57] this

54 See CJEU Cases C-70/10, Slg. 2011, I-11959 – Scarlet Extended; C-360/10, ECLI:EU:C:2012:85 – SABAM; and again C-314/12, ECLI:EU:C:2014:192 – UPC Telekabel Wien. – Whether Article 17 of the DSM-Directive complies with these requirements is the subject of the proceedings before the CJEU in case C-401/19 – Poland./.Parliament and Council. Answering this question negatively, e.g., Spindler (2019) and Reda/Selinger/Servatius (2020), whereas Specht-Riemenschneider (2020) arrives at a positive conclusion under the condition that certain safeguards in favour of freedom of expression are provided for.

55 See, e.g., Article 17 (9) of the DSM-Directive; Section 3 of the German NetzDG; and the decisions by the German BGH (footnote 51).

56 For the German NetzDG see the empirical findings by Liesching (2021).

57 For a detailed analysis of the multiple duties of online content-sharing platform providers see, e.g., Conrad/Nolte (2021).

is an incentive for platform providers to block more rather than less and hence to exercise some form of censorship.[58]

And, finally, the problem with private legislation enabled by entrusting providers with decision-making powers is that the providers' own private preferences decide what can be said and/or found on the Internet. Thus, on the Internet, these private preferences at least partially replace, and in some cases threaten to undermine the legal rules and the values underlying the fundamental rights guarantee of freedom of expression. In other words, in many cases the platform's community standards decide the limits of freedom of expression and no longer the legislator or, within the framework of fundamental rights control, the courts.

3. *Ethical considerations*

From an ethical point of view, one might, of course, argue in all three cases that the legislature should not mandate private platform providers neither with such potentially far-reaching powers to formulate binding rules nor with the authority to make final decisions in individual cases in the first place. However, as has been described above, due to the incredibly large number of conflicts enabled by digital communication technology between freedom of expression on the one hand and personality as well as copyrights on the other hand, such a solution is no more a viable option than banning digital platforms altogether. Quite to the contrary, the state legislator must ensure that the fundamental freedoms of its citizens are protected and balanced in a way which limits the individual fundamental freedoms as little as possible. Thus, the state most likely has a duty to involve private platform providers in the prevention of infringements and the enforcement of its citizens' fundamental rights.

Hence, to reconcile automated mass examination of huge amounts of images with a legal assessment in each individual case in an ethically founded way, the task of the legislature must – and can only – be to strike a proper, albeit delicate, balance between restrictions on the right of free speech on the one hand, and copyrights and personality rights on the other hand. Moreover, since part of this task is delegated to internet platform providers, their rights must be safeguarded as well.

---

58 For detailed reasoning see Ortland (2022).

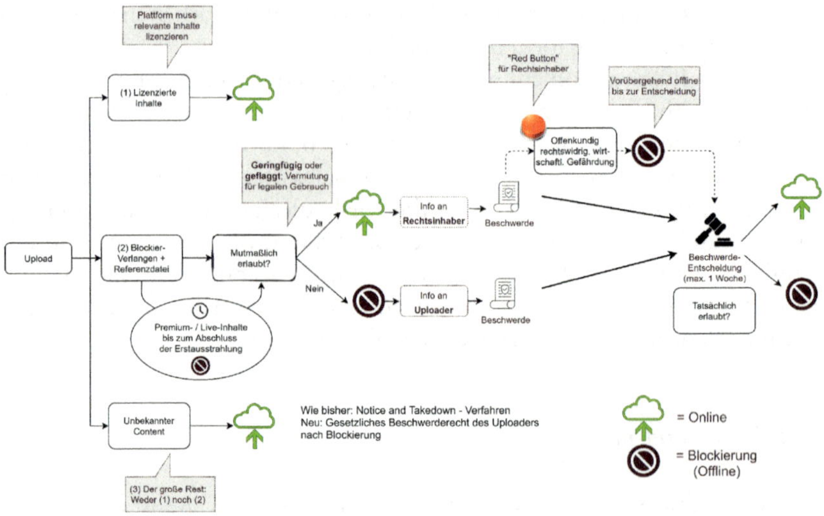

Fig. 1: German Ministry of Justice: Flowchart of uploading, checking, blocking, and allowing of third party copyrighted content to be posted by the users of content-sharing platforms, implementing Art. 17 of the DSM-Directive[59]

There are several options available to the legislature to accomplish this task. First, the legislator can exert influence by fine-tuning the content and scope of the control obligations imposed on platform operators. Another possibility is to create a carefully differentiated and balanced mechanism of posting, objection, removal, objection and renewed posting or final blocking, an example of which has been proposed by the German Ministry of Justice and Consumer Protection in the wake of the implementation of Article 17 of the DSM Directive (Fig. 1). A complimentary tool is to design efficient and fast-working complaint mechanisms and to ensure that remaining disputes are resolved without undue delay by the courts, and eventually under state control.[60] Of course, just decisions in individual cases are only possible at the cost of the complexity of the relevant procedures. However, this phenomenon is neither a new one, nor is it

59 https://www.bmj.de/SharedDocs/Gesetzgebungsverfahren/Dokumente/RegE_Gesetz_Anpassung_Urheberrecht_digitaler_Binnenmarkt_FAQ.pdf?__blob=publicationFile&v=4.

60 Postulating such an at least partial regaining of state control see, e.g., the Recommendation of the 2nd Chamber of Parliament, the German Bundesrat (2021) 19 (at para. 24).

limited to solving the problem of separating legal from illegal postings via content-sharing platforms on the Internet. Rather, it is also well known from other conflicts of interest in which the legislator is called upon to act.

At least it can be said that in respect of providers of online content-sharing services who make use of filtering technology, the legislature has put themselves back into the driver's seat by setting a particular goal to be achieved while leaving it to the platform operators to decide how this result is to be achieved by technical means.

Finally, the legislature is well advised to limit the freedom of platform providers to draft their community guidelines to make sure that such internal regulations and standards do not conflict with and undermine essential fundamental freedoms guaranteed by law.

IV. Concluding Remarks

It is of course true that regarding both the voluntary application of access blocking or use-restricting devices to digital content, and the mandatory decision making by intermediaries, the legislator establishes the legal framework of general rights and obligations, compliance with which is ultimately reviewed by the courts. However, in both cases, the legislature enables private parties to further define the limits of what users of digital technical devices can do effectively. Moreover, asymmetries in the use of the complaint mechanisms provided for by law and, not least, in the use of recourse to the courts, result in private providers of products and services ultimately deciding what is considered permissible. This can include what is considered an appropriate technical access or use restriction in the one case and an impermissible expression in the other case. Consequently, the ethical question is in which cases this result appears to be ethically justified in the light of the necessary balance of conflicting freedom rights (right of property, right of expression, freedom of market formation and decision making on markets etc.). As has become apparent, there is no easy answer to this question. Most importantly, however, as it appears there also is no one-size-fits-all answer. Rather, individual answers will have to be found for each individual case scenario, based on what appears to be ethically appropriate. This might, in turn, instruct the lawmaker when regulating the limits of permissible private legislation by technological means as described in this chapter.

Finally, one might ask whether the issue described in this chapter is – on a general level – not just another variant of the opposition of *ex ante* paternalistic protection on the one hand, and *ex post* correction by legal action on the other hand. Thus, such solutions may already be found in other such constellations with similar dilemmas. Indeed, regulation theory has developed and provides a greater array of regulatory mechanisms than the mere alternative of an ex-ante approach of prohibiting on the one hand and an ex-post approach of assessing whether damage is done on the other. A promising solution to this dilemma might be to aim at increased transparency and greater information of users about the existence and properties of technology.

And yet, for the time being, when trying to find an appropriate answer, the ethical compass does not always point to a clear direction. It seems that appropriate ethical and legal rules will still have to be formulated.

References

Baldwin, Peter (2014): *The Copyright Wars – Three Centuries of Trans-Atlantic Battle* (Princeton: Princeton University Press 2014; online available at https://www.jstor.org/stable/j.ctt6wq0z2)

Becker, Maximilian (2019): 'Von der Freiheit, rechtswidrig handeln zu können', Zeitschrift für Urheber- und Medienrecht (2019) 636–648

Benkler, Yochai (2000): 'An Unhurried View of Private Ordering in Information Transactions', 53 Vand. L. Rev. (2000) 2063–2080

Clark, Charles (1996): 'The Answer to the Machine is in the Machine', in: P. Bernt Hugenholtz (ed), *The Future of Copyright in a Digital Environment* (The Hague/London/Boston: Kluwer Law International 1996) 139–145

Conrad, Albrecht/Nolte, Georg (2021): 'Schrankenbestimmungen im Anwendungsbereich des UrhDaG – Zu viele Rollen der Diensteanbieter beim urheberrechtlichen Interessenausgleich?', Zeitschrift für Urheber- und Medienrecht (2021) 111–124

Dreier, Thomas (2016): 'Thoughts on revising the limitations on copyright under Directive 2001/29', Journal of Intellectual Property Law & Practice (2016) 138–146

Dusollier, Séverine (2003): 'Tipping the Scale in Favour of the Right Holders – The European Anti-Circumvention Provisions', in: Becker, Eberhard/Buhse, Willms/Günnewig, Dirk/Rump, Nils (eds): *Digital Rights Management – Technological, Economic, Legal and Political Aspects* (Berlin: Springer Verlag 2003) 462–478

Eichenhofer, Johannes (2022): 'The Constitutional Protection of Images', in: Dreier, Thomas/Andina, Tiziana (eds), *Digital Ethics – The issue of images* (Baden-Baden: Nomos 2022) 357–385

Gasser, Urs (2006): 'Legal Frameworks and Technological Protection of Digital Content – Moving Forward towards a Best Practice Model', Fordham Intellectual Property, Media & Entertainment Law Journal (2006) 39–113

Geiger, Christophe (2022): 'Contemporary Art on Trial – The Fundamental Right to Free Artistic Expression and the Regulation of the Use of Images by Copyright Law', in: Dreier, Thomas/Andina, Tiziana (eds), *Digital Ethics – The issue of images* (Baden-Baden: Nomos 2022) 387–415

German Bundesrat (2021): 'Stellungnahme des Bundesrates zum Entwurf eines Gesetzes zur Anpassung des Urheberrechts an die Erfordernisse des digitalen Binnenmarktes', Bundesrats-Drucksache 142/21B of 26 March 2021

German Government (2019): 'Erklärung der Bundesrepublik Deutschland zur Richtlinie über das Urheberrecht und verwandte Schutzrechte im Digitalen Binnenmarkt; insbesondere zu Artikel 17 der Richtlinie' (Berlin: Federal Ministry of Justice and Consumer Protection 2019; https://www.bmj.de/SharedDocs/Downloads/DE/News/PM/041519_Erklaerung_Richtlinie_Urheberrecht.pdf)

Hardin, Garrett /Baden, John (eds) (1977): *Managing the Commons* (San Francisco: W. H. Freeman 1977)

Koelman, Kamiel J. (2000): 'A Hard Nut to Crack – The Protection of Technological Measures', European intellectual Property Review (2000) 272–288

Koelman, Kamiel J./Helberger, Natali (2000): 'Protection of Technological Measures', in: P. Bernt Hugenholtz (ed): *Copyright and Electronic Commerce*, (Alphen aan den Rijn: Kluwer Law International 2000), 165–227

Lessig, Lawrence (1999): *Code and other laws of cyberspace* (New York: Basic Books 1999)

Liesching, Marc (ed) (2021): *Das NetzDG in der praktischen Anwendung – Eine Teilevaluation des Netzwerkdurchsetzungsgesetzes* (Berlin: Carl Grossmann 2021; https://carlgrossmann.com/?ddownload=12203)

Marks, Dean S./Turnbull, Bruce H. (1999): 'Technical Protection Measures – The Intersection of Technology, Law and Commercial Licences', WIPO Document WCT-WPPT/IMP/3 (Geneva: WIPO 1999; https://www.wipo.int/edocs/mdocs/copyright/en/wct_wppt_imp/wct_wppt_imp_3.pdf)

Möllers, Christoph (2015): *The Possibility of Norms – Social Practice beyond Morals and Causes* (Oxford: Oxford University Press 2020; first published as *Die Möglichkeit der Normen – Über eine Praxis jenseits von Moralität und Kausalität*, Berlin: Suhrkamp Verlag 2015)

Ortland, Eberhard: 'Algorithmic Censorship of Online Visual Contents – Ethical, Political, and Economic Rationales', in: Dreier, Thomas/Andina, Tiziana (eds), *Digital Ethics – The issue of images* (Baden-Baden: Nomos 2022) 323–334

Ostrom, Elinor (1990): *Governing the Commons – The evolution of institutions for collective action* (Cambridge/New York/Victoria: Cambridge University Press 1990)

Raue, Benjamin (2022): 'The Multi-Layered Information in a Digital Image', in: Dreier, Thomas/Andina, Tiziana (eds), *Digital Ethics – The issue of images* (Baden-Baden: Nomos 2022) 229–237

Reda, Julia/Selinger, Joschka/Servatius, Michael (2020): *Article 17 of the Directive on Copyright in the Digital Single Market – A Fundamental Rights Assessment* (2020, https://freiheitsrechte.org/home/wp-content/uploads/2020/11/GFF_Article17_Fundamental_Rights.pdf)

Samuelson, Pamela (2003): 'DRM {and, or, vs.} the Law', 46 Communications of the ACM, Issue 4 (2003) 4–45

Specht, Louisa (2019): *Diktat der Technik – Regulierungskonzepte technischer Vertragsinhaltsgestaltung am Beispiel von Bürgerlichem Recht und Urheberrecht* (Baden-Baden: Nomos 2019)

Specht-Riemenschneider (2020): *Leitlinien zur nationalen Umsetzung des Art. 17 DSM-RL aus Verbrauchersicht* (Berlin: Verbraucherzentrale Bundesverband e.V. 2020; https://www.vzbv.de/sites/default/files/downloads/2020/06/23/2020-06-12-specht-final-art_17.pdf)

Spindler, Gerald (2019): *Gutachten zur Urheberrechtsrichtlinie (DSM-RL) – Europarechtliche Vereinbarkeit (Artikel 17), Vorschläge zur nationalen Umsetzung und zur Stärkung der Urheberinnen und Urheber* (2019; https://www.gruene-bundestag.de/fileadmin/media/gruenebundestag_de/themen_az/netzpolitik/pdf/Gutachten_Urheberrechtsrichtlinie_01.pdf)

Strowel, Alain (1993): *Droit d'auteur et copyright* (Brussels: Bruylant 1993)

Tschorr, Sophie (2021): 'Privatisierung der Rechtsdurchsetzung in der digitalen Welt – Ist Unionsrecht der Motor?', Kommunikation und Recht (2021) 82–86

von Lewinski, Silke (2010): 'Information Society Directive', in: Michel M. Walter/Silke von Lewinski (eds), *European Copyright Law – A Commentary* (Oxford: Oxford University Press 2010)

Photo credits

Fig. 1: German Ministry of Justice and Consumer Protection; https://www.bmj.de/SharedDocs/Gesetzgebungsverfahren/Dokumente/RegE_Gesetz_Anpassung_Urheberrecht_digitaler_Binnenmarkt_FAQ.pdf?__blob=publicationFile&v=4

Chapter 18
Algorithmic Censorship of Online Visual Content – Ethical, Political, and Economic Rationales

Eberhard Ortland

I. Introduction

Images can be powerful, exciting or incisive, appealing or appalling and therefore, sometimes controversial. Some images move us to act, some call for comments, and some leave us speechless. But some images can also be harmful. An encounter with certain images may disturb some or most of the people who see them. What has been seen cannot be unseen again. The circulation and accessibility of certain images may also be offensive to people who do not even feel offended themselves, but who, for certain reasons, do not want others to see those images, at least not unless they meet certain conditions. The accessibility of some images may violate legitimate interests – of the persons depicted in the image or of people who are not even depicted in the image but whose relatives, friends, idols or belongings are shown in a way they would not like to share with others, or in a way they find objectionable for some reason. There may also be economic or political reasons why some people do not want certain images to be freely accessible to anybody, or why they want to subject the availability of certain images to certain conditions.

Arguably, some of these reasons can be regarded as legitimate, while some may be contested. But how and according to which sets of criteria can we decide which of the reasons cited for limiting the production, distribution or accessibility of certain images ought to be accepted as legitimate and which should be rejected – either in general, or at least under certain circumstances – to preserve some generally recognized, superior good? And how should we deal with conflicts about the circulation and accessibility of certain images that cannot be resolved on common grounds?

Conflicts about the circulation and accessibility of certain images increase considerably with the spreading of digital media and communication technologies, for obvious reasons: There are now exponentially more, and more diverse, images than ever before in human history. The number of people involved in making or taking images as well as the number of automatically operating cameras have likewise increased in totally unprecedented ways. Digital computer networks allow images to circulate around the world in light speed on countless channels. Thus, they are now accessible to unprecedented audiences from most heterogeneous cultural backgrounds. The global circulation of images brings about countless occasions of cross-cultural short circuit experiences, when certain audiences take offence at images that were considered completely innocent, rather funny, or maybe daring, but definitively legal by those who produced them or by those who liked them and distributed them online because they wanted to share them with others.

The central question is: Who shall decide, according to which criteria, under which circumstances which images may or may not be shown? While it is certainly true that these issues are at the centre of any debate on the ethics of images, it is, however, rather surprising that it is hardly ever made explicit that all the activities deemed necessary to avoid or reduce conflicts about images – such as content moderation or some sort of regulation – inevitably involve some form of censorship.

II. Censorship

Censorship is a highly contentious issue. It has been contentious for centuries. It was officially abolished in most European states and in the so-called free world since the American and the French Revolution. However, the process was lengthy and included severe set-backs and was not accomplished in most countries before the middle or even the end of the twentieth century. Yet, some sort of censorship was and continues to be executed in many countries most of the time.

I have previously argued that censorship "is not only the suppression of speech, public communication, or other kinds of expression or information … by the government or church authorities". Rather, "censorship occurs whenever people, institutions or organizations succeed in imposing their political or moral values or particular interests on others by suppressing the circulation of certain words, images, or ideas that they find offensive or otherwise objectionable".[1] Such a broad definition of censorship is useful and necessary given today's fragmented and multi-layered political, sectarian and corporate powers.

1 Ortland (2018) 129.

Of course, it is important that state authorities do not directly and officially control the mass media in countries where democracy and the freedom of the press flourish. However, direct intervention by state authorities is not the only kind of censorship to be concerned about. It does not help us very much if we may trust that the government will refrain from censoring the mass media, as long as other actors or agencies are legally entitled or even obliged to control and restrict the public circulation of certain types of information or expression, words, images or sound recordings. I think it is time that we face the reality of censorship and start a realistic discussion about the various types of censorship as well as the reasons why certain kinds of censorship are regarded as desirable and legitimate, at least under certain circumstances, while others are not.[2]

Most discussions about censorship focus primarily or exclusively on the interruption and suppression of communication, and on the prohibition of certain words, signs or images. These are the cases when conflicts about the right to communicate or to express oneself become most strikingly apparent. However, as we have learned from Foucault,[3] it is important to understand that power is not necessarily and not even primarily repressive, but that it is always directed at certain positive goals: at influencing the way people behave, how they see things and what they regard as desirable or detestable. To understand the impact of censorship, we must be aware that in most cases the intervention of the censor does not lead to the suppression of objectionable content, but rather to the approval of all kinds of expression deemed acceptable.

Censorship is a filter. The purpose of any filtering is to separate the filtrate that can pass from the residue that is retained or extracted from the filtered mixture. Sometimes we filter because we are interested in the residue, usually we want the filtrate to be clear of certain stuff. Censorship is driven by a strong negative interest in certain types of expression that the censor – or those who have installed the censor – do not want to circulate in public. Yet the aim of censorship is not to retain large chunks of ongoing communication, but rather to direct people to use only expressions which can be expected to be acceptable under the censors' critical eyes.

Thus, censorship can be regarded, in a way, as a special type of co-authorship imposed on the primary author by a co-author who is typically

2 For a discussion of different types of censorship see Jones (2001); Green/Karolides (2005); Mathiesen (2008); Ortland (2018) 129–136; Heldt (2019) §§ 9–12 and 19–24.

3 Foucault (1975).

absent and is perhaps not even a fellow human being but rather the anonymous and elusive "powers that be". The censor rarely discusses the wanted results with the primary author, but silently demands that the expression submitted by the author meets certain expectations to be approved.[4] Under a censorship regime, authorship becomes shady and the expression, corrupt. People must learn to read, whatever they get to read, with double vision. They distrust the surface, search for hidden meanings, try to guess what the author might have wanted to say but had to avoid or camouflage to pass the censorship filter.

III. Reasons for Censorship

Censorship is deeply ambivalent, neither always bad nor simply good. Obviously, censorship stifles free speech. It distorts the way we express ourselves (or whatever). It creates or reinforces power imbalances. And it channels, in often problematic ways, the stream of communication that is vital for each of us. We may be appalled by such distortions and power imbalances, and often rightly so. But then we must ask if we could really imagine a society that allows all kinds of expression – words, images, sounds and information about anything and anybody that anybody wants to share with others, or to throw at others – to circulate without any restrictions.

There are reasons why some kind of censorship is deemed necessary under certain circumstances. Some of these reasons are political and will always be controversial. As the saying goes, one person's or state's terrorist is another person's or state's freedom fighter.[5] Other reasons are mainly economic, for example concerning the enforcement of copyright claims or trademarks.[6] But there are, I think, also serious ethical or moral concerns, rooted in normative ideas about rights we think we have or ought to have, and in ideas about what is relevant for a good life, for men, women and children, living together more or less closely but not always peacefully. We must recognise and analyse these reasons,[7] and figure out how they relate to the political and economic rationales that are also relevant for both the legitimacy, and the limits of legitimacy, of certain kinds of censorship.

4 Steinhauer (forthcoming).
5 Ganor (2002).
6 Aufderheide (2020).
7 Ortland (2018).

Even fervent advocates of free speech[8] had to concede that some kinds of images, texts or other kinds of content that can be easily uploaded and thus made accessible to the public by virtually anybody at any time, can, indeed cause serious harm.[9] Typical examples include depictions of or incitement to child abuse, graphic violence or cruelty, terrorist propaganda videos, hate speech and harassment.[10] More controversial is whether state authorities or internet service providers should be entitled or even obliged to protect users from unwanted exposition to pornography, explicit adult content or other kinds of unwanted content regarded as spam.[11] Furthermore, online content moderation is already applied to large extents,[12] and will undoubtedly be applied in the foreseeable future,[13] not only to block or delete obviously illegal content of the types just mentioned, but likewise for primarily economic reasons, in order to enforce copyright and other types of intellectual property claims.[14]

All major social media platforms have developed so called "community standards" or "guidelines" that rule out making available any material that falls under these categories, and many have some other more specific rules. Platform operators may be quite optimistically assuming that a considerable overlap exists between the policies of the large platforms and the applicable laws in the countries where these platforms offer their services, and also with our widely held ethical views. Besides broad areas of overlap, however, there are still relevant points where our ethical views might diverge. There are still differences between the applicable laws of different countries. Furthermore, there are differences between the laws of several countries and particular ethical claims either against or in favour of the public accessibility of certain kinds of images, and also between those particular laws and particular ethical convictions and the more or less uniform, "global" approach of the platform policies.

Indeed, we can no longer ignore that there are profound cross-cultural differences that make it very difficult to find a balance that will be acceptable in most societies. The question, then, is, of course, of how we are going to deal with such differences. Must we learn to avoid certain words

---

8 Garton Ash (2016).

9 Waldron (2012).

10 Kabasfrooshan (2019).

11 Cf. e.g., Cambridge Consultants (2019) 31; see also Ortland (2018) 136–161 (with further references).

12 Gillespie (2018).

13 Sartor/Loreggia 2020.

14 Valais (2015); Bar-Ziv/Elkin-Koren (2017); Husovec (2018).

and images that, for example, Muslims or Christian fundamentalists may find offensive? Or should they instead learn to respect, if not to embrace, liberal ideas about free speech?

IV. Algorithmic Judgment and the Pragmatics of Pictorial Speech Acts

Even if we might someday, hopefully, arrive at widely shared criteria for legitimate and necessary distinctions between acceptable and unacceptable images, there will still be the problem of how these criteria should be applied to the vast amount of information and misinformation circulating on the internet. Three or four years ago, there were broad discussions in the news media about overburdened content moderators at Facebook and other social media platforms and the law enforcement officers who must watch hours of sickening material, mostly images or videos, every day. "As the amount of user-generated content that platform users upload continues to accelerate, it has become impossible to identify and remove harmful content using traditional human-led moderation approaches at the speed and scale necessary".[15]

Will Artificial Intelligence sooner or later be able to solve this problem? Perhaps it might cause even more severe problems than those it is supposed to solve. Obviously, there are serious problems concerning the accountability of anonymous and non-transparent algorithms making decisions that may affect people's freedom of expression or other fundamental rights.[16] In order to sustain the rule of law, there will always be a need for human review and due process.[17]

But there are also considerable technical limits that need to be addressed. With automated hash-matching, further advances in deep neural network computing, machine learning and artificial intelligence technology, algorithms can now perform certain pre-moderation tasks in sifting large amounts of data. In other words, they can significantly improve the training data and assist human moderation.[18] It is important to note, however, that the classification of images according to the applicable criteria for blocking as well as for unblocking certain kinds of content poses con-

15 Cambridge Consultants (2019) 4.

16 Perel/Elkin-Koren (2017); Sinnreich (2018); Senftleben (2020).

17 Reinhardt (2020) 260–62.

18 For a brief summary of the technological development, see Cambridge Consultants (2019) 16–22; Jani/Chaudhuri/Patel/Shah (2020); Llansó/van Hoboken/Leerssen/Harambam (2020).

siderable challenges that no automated algorithm so far can overcome, and there are reasons why this problem cannot be solved by simply improving the approaches to AI that have so far been developed.[19]

Whether we like it or not – and whether we like to call it 'censorship'[20] or not – I am afraid, algorithmic content moderation is here to stay. It has only evolved in recent years, but we may – and must – expect it to further increase and literally become pervasive.

Still, the automatic, algorithmic application of the criteria we (or whoever gets to decide) want to see applied on the vast stream of images and other forms of content circulating online is a huge problem and will probably remain a huge problem for any currently foreseeable future. Basically, this is the problem of judgment.[21] Of course, there are many kinds of decisions, i.e., determining judgments in Kant's sense,[22] which do *not* pose any particularly difficult problems of judgment, and which can be delegated to more or less automatic algorithms. By now, automatic pattern recognition software can determine incredibly complex and subtle patterns in images, surfaces, 3D physical bodies, environments or continuous temporal forms better than human observers could. We rely on such algorithms every day in many ways.

Facial recognition is still a huge challenge. But then we are told that some algorithms are now much better at it than even the most attentive humans.[23] Indeed, it is often difficult for most of us to recognize strangers merely from a photograph. Sometimes we won't recognise even our close acquaintances if we encounter them in places where we did not expect them, or we mistake strangers for friends.

What is really difficult for pattern recognition algorithms to figure out, however, is the distinction between relevant and irrelevant context. Such distinctions require a different type of judgment than the simple 'match' or 'no match' distinction. Regarding images, the question of context goes beyond the problem of framing — what is or ought to be regarded as part of the picture, and what ought to be distinguished from the picture as belonging to its background or surroundings. We have probabilistic

---

19 See Gorwa/Binns/Katzenbach (2020); Gillespie (2020); Castets-Renard (2020); Elkin-Koren (2020), from a constitutional law perspective and with an interesting suggestion for an "adversarial approach" by implementing "contesting algorithms"; Käde (2022).

20 Sirichit (2015); Cobbe (2019); Armijo (2020).

21 Cf. Kant (1790) A vii = AA V, 169.

22 Kant (1790) AA V, 179; Hanna (2017) suppl. 4.

23 Babcock (2015); Klosowski (2020); MacCarthy (2020).

algorithms that can deal with such questions in many cases quite successfully, and we are, indeed, so used to expecting the algorithms to work that we find it startling to see them fail. But artificial intelligence algorithms so far have not been particularly successful in cases that require reflective judgment in Kant's terms,[24] or sound inductive generalisations from very limited data.

With regard to images, the main difficulty for algorithms that are expected to decide which images ought to be blocked or deleted concerns the pragmatics of "pictorial speech acts",[25] rather than the syntactics of visual configurations or typical forms of depiction. People can do very different kinds of things with the same or quite similar pictures. And pictures that can be used to do the same or similar things may look totally different from one another.

From the Google *Transparency Report*, we can see that algorithms for "automated flagging" have been relevant for 95 % of the removal or blocking decisions. Apparently, "automated flagging" does not yet mean automated blocking or deletion, at least not at Google. Rather, a workforce of some 10,000 employees occupied with censorship tasks at Google account for these decisions.[26] Now, what kind of content can these automated flagging algorithms recognise as probably illegal? Does this recognition work only with the help of a huge database of material marked for blocking for various reasons, from criminal law or hate speech regulations to the enforcement of copyright claims? Or can the algorithm recognize, for example, on a probabilistic account previously unknown images that should be blocked because they fall under one of the categories like child pornography, incitement to violence or terrorism? Other questions that are going to remain relevant, as far as we can see, include: How much time would an average content moderator usually have to decide about a video? How often does the judgement of human moderators differ from the preliminary assessment provided by the algorithm? And to what degree is the judgment process accelerated with the help of the automated flagging algorithms? These are only some of the questions that will obviously need to be discussed when formulating an ethics of images in the light of censorship that invariably comes with it.

24 Kant (1790) AA V, 179–181.

25 Kjørup (1978), see also Scholz (1991) 123–130; Bredekamp (2015) 58–59.

26 Google (2020).

References

Armijo, Enrique (2020): 'Reasonableness as Censorship – Algorithmic Content Moderation, The First Amendment, and Section 230 Reform', CSAS Working Paper 20–10 Fairfax, VA: George Mason University, Antonin Scalia Law School, Gray Center for the Study of the Administrative State, Spring 2020) (online available at https://administrativestate.gmu.edu/wp-content/uploads/sites/29/2020/03/Armijo-Reasonableness-As-Censorship.pdf)

Aufderheide, Patricia (2020): 'How much copyright censorship is OK?' American University, Center for Media and Social Impact, Fair Use Blog, May 30, 2020, https://cmsimpact.org/fair-use-blog/much-copyright-censorship-ok/

Babcock, Ernest J. (2015): *Privacy Impact Assessment for the Facial Analysis, Comparison, and Evaluation (FACE) Services Unit* (Washington D.C.: FBI Services, Information Management, May 1, 2015, https://www.fbi.gov/services/information-management/foipa/privacy-impact-assessments/facial-analysis-comparison-and-evaluation-face-services-unit)

Bar-Ziv, Sharon/Elkin-Koren, Niva (2018): 'Behind the Scenes of Online Copyright Enforcement – Empirical Evidence on Notice & Takedown', 50 Connecticut Law Review, No. 2 (2018) 339–385 (online available at https://opencommons.uconn.edu/cgi/viewcontent.cgi?article=1395&context=law_review)

Bredekamp, Horst (2015): *Der Bildakt* (Berlin: Wagenbach, 2015)

Cambridge Consultants (2019): *Use of AI in Online Content Moderation – Report on behalf of Ofcom* (Cambridge: Cambridge Consultants, 2019) (online available at https://www.ofcom.org.uk/__data/assets/pdf_file/0028/157249/cambridge-consultants-ai-content-moderation.pdf)

Castets-Renard, Céline (2020): 'Algorithmic Content Moderation on Social Media in EU Law: Illusion of Perfect Enforcement', 20 Illinois Journal of Law, Technology & Policy, No. 2 (2020) 283–323 (online available at http://illinoisjltp.com/journal/wp-content/uploads/2020/12/Castets-Renard_Final (1).pdf)

Cobbe, Jennifer (2020): 'Algorithmic Censorship by Social Platforms – Power and Resistance', 34 Philosophy & Technology (2020) 739–766 (online available at https://doi.org/10.1007/s13347-020-00429-0)

Elkin-Koren, Niva (2020): 'Contesting algorithms – Restoring the public interest in content filtering by artificial intelligence', Big Data & Society (July-December 2020) 1–13 (online available at https://doi.org/10.1177/2053951720932296

Foucault, Michel (1975): *Surveiller et punir – Naissance de la prison* (Paris: Gallimard, 1975)

Ganor, Boaz (2002): 'Defining Terrorism', 29 Media Asia, No. 3 (2002) 123–133 (online available at https://doi.org/10.1080/01296612.2002.11726675)

Garton Ash, Timothy (2016): *Free Speech – Ten Principles for a Connected World* (New Haven, CT/London: Yale University Press, 2016)

Gillespie, Tarleton (2018): *Custodians of the Internet: Platforms, Content Moderation, and the Hidden Decisions that Shape Social Media* (New Haven and London: Yale University Press, 2018)

Gillespie, Tarleton (2020): 'Content moderation, AI, and the question of scale', Big Data & Society (2020), https://doi.org/10.1177/2053951720943234

Google (2020): *Transparency Report*, https://transparencyreport.google.com/ and https://transparencyreport.google.com/copyright/overview (quoted data from 18 Sept. 2020)

Gorwa, Robert/Binns, Reuben/Katzenbach, Christian (2020): 'Algorithmic content moderation – Technical and political challenges in the automation of platform governance', Big Data & Society (February 28, 2020) (online available at https://doi.org/10.1177/2053951719897945)

Green, Jonathan/Karolides, Nicholas J. (2005): *Encyclopedia of Censorship* (New York: Facts on File, 2005)

Hanna, Robert (2004): 'Kant's Theory of Judgment', in: Zalta, E.N.: *Stanford Encyclopedia of Philosophy* (first published Wed Jul 28, 2004; substantive revision Mon Oct 23, 2017, https://plato.stanford.edu/archives/win2018/entries/kant-judgment/)

Heldt, Amélie Pia (2019): 'Upload-Filters: Bypassing Classical Concepts of Censorship?', 10 JIPITEC, No. 2 (2019) 57–65, https://www.jipitec.eu/issues/jipitec-10-1-2019/4877/JIPITEC_10_1_2019_57_Heldt-JIPITEC_10_1_2019_57_Heldt-Upload-Filters

Husovec, Martin (2018): 'The Promises of Algorithmic Copyright Enforcement – Takedown or Staydown? Which is Superior? And Why?', 42 Columbia Journal of Law & the Arts (2018) 53–84 (online available at https://journals.library.columbia.edu/index.php/lawandarts/article/view/2009/971)

Jani, Kunal/Chaudhuri, Mainak/Patel, Hrishitva/Shah, Manan (2020): 'Machine learning in films – An approach towards automation in film censoring', 2 Journal of Data, Information and Management, No. 2 (2020) 55–64 (https://doi.org/10.1007/s42488-019-00016-9)

Jones, Derek (2001): *Censorship – A World Encyclopedia* (London/New York: Routledge 2001)

Kabasfrooshan, Ashkan (2019): 'Counter Strike – Exposing Worst ContentID Abusers', Context TV, Business Battleground (2019), https://www.youtube.com/watch?v=-e59ApQino

Käde, Lisa (2022): 'The Issue of the Image of Algorithms', in: Dreier, Thomas/Andina, Tiziana (eds), *Digital Ethics – The Issue of Images* (Baden-Baden: Nomos 2022) 335–353

Kant, Immanuel (1790): *Kritik der Urtheilskraft* (1790), in: Windelband, Wilhelm (ed), *Kants gesammelte Schriften*, Akademie-Ausgabe, Vol. V (Berlin: de Gruyter 1908) 165–485

Kjørup, Søren (1978): 'Pictorial Speech Acts', 12 Erkenntnis, No. 1 (1978) 55–71

Klosowski, Thorin (2020): 'Facial Recognition Is Everywhere. Here's What We Can Do About It', The New York Times, July 15, 2020 (online available at https://www.nytimes.com/wirecutter/blog/how-facial-recognition-works/)

Llansó, Emma/van Hoboken, Joris/Leerssen, Paddy/Harambam, Jaron (2020): *Artificial Intelligence, Content Moderation, and Freedom of Expression – A working paper of the Transatlantic Working Group on Content Moderation Online and Freedom of Expression* (2020) (online available at https://www.ivir.nl/publicaties/download/AI-Llanso-Van-Hoboken-Feb-2020.pdf)

Matthiesen, Kay (2008): 'Censorship and Access to Information', in: Himma, Kenneth E./Tavani, Herman T. (eds), *Handbook of Information and Computer Ethics* (Hoboken, NJ: J. Wiley & Sons 2008) 573–587

MacCarthy, Mark (2020): 'Who thought it was a good idea to have facial recognition software?', Brookings, August 20, 2020 (online available at https://www.brookings.edu/research/who-thought-it-was-a-good-idea-to-have-facial-recognition-software/)

Ortland, Eberhard (2018): 'A Moral Need for Censorship, Access Restrictions, and Surveillance? The Ethics of Copying and the Freedom of Communication', 26 Jahrbuch für Recht und Ethik/Annual Review of Law and Ethics (2018) 125–180

Perel, Maayan/Elkin-Koren, Niva (2017): 'Black Box Tinkering – Beyond Disclosure in Algorithmic Enforcement', 69 Florida Law Review (2017) 181–221

Reinhardt, Jörn (2020): 'Algorithmizität und Sichtbarkeit – Konflikte um Bilder in den sozialen Medien', in: E. Schürmann, Eva/von Plato, Levno (eds), *Rechtsästhetik in rechtsphilosophischer Absicht – Untersuchungen zu Formen und Wahrnehmungen des Rechts* (Baden-Baden: Nomos 2020) 249–262

Sartor, Giovanni/Loreggia, Andrea (2020): *The impact of algorithms for online content filtering or moderation – Study, requested by the JURI committee, PE 657.101* (Brussels: European Parliament, Policy Department for Citizens' Rights and Constitutional Affairs 2020) (online available at https://www.europarl.europa.eu/RegData/etudes/STUD/2020/657101/IPOL_STU(2020)657101_EN.pdf)

Scholz, Oliver R. (1991): *Bild, Darstellung, Zeichen – Philosophische Theorien bildhafter Darstellung*, (Freiburg/München: Alber 1991)

Senftleben, Martin (2020): 'Institutionalized Algorithmic Enforcement – The Pros and Cons of the EU Approach to UGC Platform Liability', Florida International University Law Review (2020) 299–328 (online available at https://ecollections.law.fiu.edu/lawreview/vol14/iss2/11/)

Sinnreich, Aram (2018): 'Four Crises in Algorithmic Governance', 26 Jahrbuch für Recht und Ethik/Annual Review of Law and Ethics (2018) 181–190

Sirichit, Methaya (2015): 'Censorship by Intermediary and Moral Rights – Strengthening Authors' Control Over Online Expressions Through the Right of Respect and Integrity', 3 Journal of Law, Technology and Public Policy (2015) 54–159

Steinhauer, Eric (forthcoming): 'Zensur', in: Ortland, Eberhard/Dreier, Thomas/Schmücker, Reinold (eds), *Original und Kopie – Ein Sachlexikon* (Hamburg: F. Meiner forthcoming)

Valais, Sophie (2015): 'Copyright enforcement online: policies and mechanisms', IRIS-plus (Strasbourg: European Audiovisual Observatory, 2015–3) (online available at https://rm.coe.int/1680783480)

Waldron, Jeremy (2012): *The Harm in Hate Speech* (Cambridge, MA: Harvard University Press, 2012)

Zuckerberg, Mark (2018): Facebook CEO Mark Zuckerberg Hearing on Data Privacy and Protection, *C-SPAN* (10 April, 2018, https://www.c-span.org/video/?443543-1/facebook-ceo-mark-zuckerberg-testifies-dataprotection)

Chapter 19
The Issue of the Image of Algorithms

Lisa Käde

Algorithms have been a part of our daily lives for a long time. This paper will consider the need for a regulation of algorithms from three different perspectives of images.

Firstly, while they are usually associated with controlling machines, especially computers, algorithms are increasingly well suited to deal with images. In that capability, computers – enabled by algorithms – can help analyze large amounts of images at a time, generate entirely new images, sort them, and augment the human ability to perform tasks which require a great attention to detail. Secondly, images can also be used to label algorithms according to their functionality and impact. Visual representations of complex concepts can be an effective way to increase the transparency of algorithms and related processes. Thirdly, looking beyond the intuitive meaning of the word "image" as a visual representation, "image" also describes a mental impression or conception of something.[1] Appreciating how frequently humans are confronted with algorithms without knowing what exactly they are dealing with, it seems worth considering how the imagination influences the image of algorithms.

Still, when talking about algorithms and how to deal with them, dystopian – mostly science-fiction related – scenarios come to mind. We remember armies of supposedly friendly robots suddenly going awry, turning against humankind. We remember "PRECRIME" and its way to predict crimes before the culprits even conceive them.[2] And – above all – we think of artificial intelligence (AI) as an autonomous construct overcoming restrictions and surpassing human intelligence, killing everything that stands in its way.

However, people are not only concerned with robots in sci-fi movies. A very recent example of a seemingly discriminative algorithm, which

---

1 "Image", *Merriam-Webster.com Dictionary*, Merriam-Webster, https://www.merriam-webster.com/dictionary/image.

2 Referring to the movie "Minority Report", Twentieth Century Fox Film Corporation 2002.

selects thumbnail previews of pictures users post on *Twitter*, suggested unconscious racism on the platform. Thumbnail selections occur when an image is too large to be displayed in the respective context. Instead, a part of the picture is selected which seems to be representative of the picture. In this example, each image consisted of various pictures of different people. The algorithm seemed to prefer such parts of these pictures providing images of white people over such parts which depict people of color. Plenty of examples appeared to support this theory.[3] Still, it might not be just as bad as it seems, since such algorithms evaluate many factors in pictures to provide a satisfying result such as contrast, brightness, image quality etc. These are also factored into the Twitter algorithm's preview selection of images. If the images which display previously "discriminated" people are of better quality and contrast than the images of those people which the algorithm seemingly favoured before, suddenly the algorithm seems to neglect the latter while selecting the former as a thumbnail.

Another algorithm displaying discriminative behaviour made the news in 2015, when the Google Photo app introduced a feature which automatically labelled photos according to the content the algorithm recognized. A user posted a screenshot of how one of their friends was labeled as a gorilla.[4] While the problem probably lies in training data bias or imperfect automatic labelling of training data,[5] Google "resolved" this issue by simply removing the label "gorilla" altogether.[6] Moreover, Italy is considering using facial recognition and sound observation technologies in football stadiums to tackle issues of actual racism – leading to high-resolution images and sound recordings of conversations of visitors.[7] There was also intense discussion regarding the different COVID-19 contact tracing apps and data protection issues related to their use. These cases also highlight potential conflicts of interest and are therefore worth recalling when regulating algorithms.

3 Impressive examples are available at https://www.theguardian.com/technology/2020/sep/21/twitter-apologises-for-racist-image-cropping-algorithm. Meanwhile, Twitter reacted to this issue and promised to give users more control, see https://blog.twitter.com/en_us/topics/product/2020/transparency-image-cropping.

4 See, e.g., https://www.bbc.com/news/technology-33347866.

5 The algorithm might not have been presented with enough photos of people of colour, for example.

6 Rendering the program unable to detect actual gorillas, as well, see, e.g., https://www.wired.com/story/when-it-comes-to-gorillas-google-photos-remains-blind/.

7 See https://algorithmenethik.de/2020/09/23/italien-in-echtzeit-gegen-rassistische-fussballfans.

The bad associations triggered by algorithms are some of the reasons why people may be cautious to implement algorithms more widely. One could say the (mental) *image* people have of algorithms seems to be an *issue*. Even though most of the truly terrifying scenarios are pure science-fiction (at least for now), they can still be overwhelming. "We cannot change what we do not understand"[8], says a character in a recent book by the author Schätzing, referring to the source code of a super intelligent system that evolved to a point at which humans could no longer control its actions. Most of the time we also avoid what we do not understand. A lack of understanding suggests a lack of control. And we don't like being out of control, it makes us feel helpless and fear sets in. Even though not all uses of algorithms might appear as drastic as the ones depicted in these scenarios, imposing regulation on supposedly dangerous subject matter seems to give us peace of mind.

It is therefore more than ever important to understand why – and how – those algorithms do what they do, to both improve them and calm down the discussing masses, and to prevent jumping to conclusions. To contribute to this understanding, this chapter will first analyze the need for algorithms to be regulated, taking into account the impact they have on society (I). After some remarks concerning terminology (of both algorithms as well as regulation) to limit the scope of this paper (II), existing approaches to regulation (of algorithms) are presented (III). Additionally, practical approaches to foster transparency and trust in algorithms will be briefly introduced (IV).

I. The Need for Regulating Algorithms

So, why do we need to regulate algorithms? Before answering this question, it should be noted that so far, it has not yet been specified what exactly is to be understood by an "algorithm". The reason is that the image of the abstract concept of "algorithms" is a very strong one and might give rise to a highly subjective understanding by different audiences. The meaning of the term will therefore be discussed only at a later stage. For now, this section will continue to embrace all different forms of algorithms.

The desire to regulate algorithms stems from various domains, including fear of algorithms or technology in general, biased data or algorithmic decision making, as well as the potential to improve software and interdis-

8 Schätzing (2018) 602 et seq.

ciplinary communication, and the awareness that algorithms are already impacting our everyday lives.

1. Fear of algorithms and technology

One might fear algorithms because of their opacity. The concept of the so-called "black box" – an algorithm which has input and output interfaces for interacting with a user, but does not offer insight into the inner workings, usually in the context of machine learning and AI – is often used to highlight algorithmic opacity. To many people, all kinds of algorithms are black boxes, simply because they cannot read code or understand how the program works. Artificial Intelligence is often referred to as a "black box"[9] which might fuel the apparent opacity of AI in general. Moreover, people might fear biased data, meaning machine learning algorithms trained on data selected by humans might inherently be subconsciously biased or discriminative.[10] In addition, some people are afraid of technology in general,[11] and fear that there is no way to ask a machine for clarification in the same way one could interact with a person.[12] The latter concerns especially decision-making systems when the decision made by the algorithm affects an individual's life.

2. Improvements through regulation

At the same time, regulation might present a chance to improve algorithms. Industry standards – which may result from regulation[13] – could guide developers to produce better code, and more thorough testing could potentially prevent damage once an algorithm is implemented and put to action. Regulation will also bring together people from many disciplines to come to acceptable terms for all parties.

---

9 De Streel et al. (2020) 3 et seq.; Pasquale (2015); Data Ethics Commission (2019) 189; German AI Strategy (2018) 16; European Commission (2018) 13.

10 See, e.g., Hajian/Bonchi/Castillo (2016); German AI Strategy (2018) 37; European Commission (2019) 18; Data Ethics Commission (2019) 167 et seq.

11 For research on "technophobia" see, e.g., Brosnan (2002) 10 et seq.

12 See results of representative phone interviews conducted by Kolany-Raiser/Heil/Orwat/Hoeren (2019) 15.

13 E.g. AlgoRules, https://algorules.org; industry standards already exist, e.g., for encryption, see Smid/Branstad (1988); Heron (2009).

3. *Present impact of algorithms*

Regulation is also not restricted to algorithms which might exist in the near or far future. Algorithms are already part of our daily lives. Users could encounter individual – possibly unfair – pricing in online shops or insurance rates,[14] there might be automated decision-making in the public administration for simple administrative acts,[15] recommendation systems already guide users through online shops and social media, possibly unconsciously affecting their behaviour. Others might be subject to an automated grant decision.[16] Many companies have algorithms pre-select their applicants, and some countries use software such as COMPAS to get recommendations for the early release of prisoners.[17]

As discussed at the beginning of this paper, the great power of AI in the context of image analysis also potentially poses risks of discrimination which should be addressed by regulation – both for prevention and mitigating effects on society.

All things considered, the topic of the regulation of algorithms seems like something that should have been dealt with a while ago. But, like most technology related aspects of regulation, the law is more reactive than anticipative of developments.

II. *Some Remarks Concerning Terminology*

Before one can dive into the discussion of regulating algorithms, some common ground should be found to clarify the basic terms. Even though there are many (abstract) ways to define both algorithms and regulation, no consensus seems to exist on a general definition on the term "algorithm",[18] while the definition of "regulation" merely seems to be depending on the context it is used in.

---

14 Paal (2019) 43 et seq.; Simon/Butscher (2001); Thomas (2012); see also the findings by the European Consumer Organisation (BEUC) in BEUC (2020).

15 Luthe (2017); Malgieri (2019).

16 On the issue of using algorithms to assess creditworthiness see, e.g., Data Ethics Commission (2019) 231.

17 See https://www.equivant.com/northpointe-risk-need-assessments; Brennan/Dieterich/Ehret (2009).

18 Künstner (2019) 36.

1. Regulation

According to *Wikipedia*, regulation is the "management of complex systems according to a set of rules and trends". Others define regulation as a means to "govern or direct according to rule" or "to bring order, method or uniformity".[19] In the legal context, regulation is usually used as a way to describe the process of imposing legal restrictions upon a subject matter. In EU law, "regulation" could be contrasted with the term "directive": while the former has binding legal force throughout EU member states, the latter needs to be implemented by national law.

2. Algorithm

The term "algorithm" could describe a "set of rules that precisely defines a sequence of operations"[20] or – in other words – an unambiguous instruction for the solution of a pre-defined problem. Notably, most definitions of algorithms steer clear of referencing specific *types* of algorithms, such as "machine learning algorithms" or "decision-making algorithms". The number of different algorithm species seems to be infinite.

Sometimes, in common language, computer programs in general are referred to as algorithms, whereas the term could also be used as an abstract description of a computer program and its underlying concepts (e.g., "the Google Search algorithm", "the Facebook newsfeed algorithm").[21] In the context of the regulation of algorithms, the term encompasses the abstract concept of automated processes as well as the specific issues of self-learning and self-improving systems.

The discussion on the regulation of algorithms seems to have received increasing attention over the past two to three years.[22] This is because research and applications of machine learning and AI are flourishing due to technical progress in hardware development and data availability. These kinds of algorithms are present in most of the above examples and are symptomatic for the "black box" discussion. Since the most recent publications of the EU and the German Federal Government on the regulation of

---

19 https://www.merriam-webster.com/dictionary/regulate.

20 Stone (1971) 4.

21 See also https://www.merriam-webster.com/dictionary/algorithm.

22 See GoogleTrends on "machine learning" and "artificial intelligence", https://trends.google.com/trends/explore?date=all&q=machine%20learning,artificial%20intelligence.

algorithms refer to AI and machine learning, this paper as well will focus on machine learning (ML) algorithms and AI.

3. *Regulating algorithms*

In a nutshell, one could describe the regulation of algorithms as *providing a legal framework for the development and use of algorithms.* But, as indicated before, the term "algorithm" is extremely broad. Even if it were restricted to computer programs, recurring to this definition would treat all algorithms equally, regardless of their complexity and purpose. While this might seem beneficial, the simple text editor "Notepad" does not need the same restrictions as complex systems like "COMPAS"[23] which eventually have legal effects on individuals. It should also be noted that developers could refrain from innovating and investors could stop providing funding simply because they fear contravening laws if regulation is too restrictive. Additionally, as fast as technology advances, there is no way to tell what kinds of algorithms we will encounter in the near future. A legal framework to regulate algorithms should therefore be flexible so that it only restricts those algorithms which need to be controlled in a way that is open to future developments. It should also, as precisely as possible, define which class of algorithms it strives to regulate, both because different algorithms pose different issues and to not inadvertently affect "innocent" algorithms.

Finally, it should be noted that regulation by way of a "legal framework" does not necessarily have to be comprised of formal laws. It could also include mandatory certifications, industry guidelines, EU directives and regulations. Self-regulation could also be factored in.[24]

III. *Examples of Existing Approaches to Regulation*

One way to respond to the issue of regulating algorithms is to consider the classification of algorithms: those which make up what is called "AI", for example, versus those implemented in domains such as online platforms like social media websites. The latter needs to regulate any kind of algo-

23 See footnote 16.

24 Künstner (2019) 40.; German AI Strategy (2018) 29; Data Ethics Commission (2019) 70 et seq. and 201 et seq.

rithm while considering the disparities of the platform and the users. The former deals with the specificities of a certain type of algorithm irrespective of its application, such as facial recognition, automatic thumbnail selection or deep fake image generation.

1. *Initiating regulation through algorithm type-specific guidelines*

In 2019, the EU High Level Expert Group (HLEG) on AI published its "Ethics Guidelines for Trustworthy AI".[25] Even though that does not sound like "regulating algorithms", a second – deeper – examination reveals some quite relevant thoughts which should at least guide the regulation of algorithms.

The aim of these guidelines is not to explicitly regulate, but to somehow encourage *trust* in algorithms – regulation might be one way of fostering such human trust. The HLEG identified four main ethical pillars which need to be addressed when dealing with AI (or algorithms in general):[26]

1) AI needs to always respect human autonomy
2) AI needs to always prevent harm
3) AI needs to be fair
4) AI needs to be explicable.

In a next step, the HLEG AI Guidelines drew up a non-exhaustive list of requirements for trustworthy AI which are in line with those ethical principles. This list includes human agency and oversight, technical robustness and safety, privacy and data governance, transparency, diversity, non-discrimination and fairness, societal and environmental wellbeing, and accountability. Of course, these requirements and guidelines may sound convincing, but they are in no way binding for any programmer, company, or authority. They are also very abstract, and as such make no suggestions on how they could be incorporated into AI.

In a similar fashion, the German Commission on Data Ethics issued a report discussing data and algorithms, their impact on society and suggested ways of regulation.[27] The German Commission placed a great emphasis on human dignity, human autonomy as an expression of freedom, privacy, security (of privacy, goods, physical and emotional safety, environment),

25 European Commission (2018).
26 Ibid., 11 et seq.
27 Data Ethics Commission (2019).

democracy (digital technologies impact freedom of expression and freedom of information, among others), justice and solidarity, and sustainability (referring to the UN Sustainable Development Goals).[28]

The HLEG then elaborated on technical and non-technical methods to implement these requirements in practice, as did the German Commission on Data Ethics. This is an essential step towards an *actual* regulation that leaves the confinement of lengthy documents and is received by those individuals shaping and using the algorithms addressed by the regulation. Those suggestions include the establishment of certification mechanisms, standardisations, codes of conduct, thorough testing and validation, among others. However, one question remains: How can regulators reach the people designing and implementing AI and other algorithms?

2. *Regulating with respect to the domain of application*

Another approach of regulation does not address the supposed dangers of specific algorithms, but assesses the issues stemming from the situation where the algorithm is applied. An example would be the regulation of internet platforms, where users are dealing with an internet website interface, possibly providing personal or business data – either for delivery purposes, product display in online shops or even as payment, like in the case of ad-based services – without having any means of knowing what the algorithm will do with their data, or why they are shown the content they get to see. The issues of voter manipulation by means of tailored and manipulated (fake) news delivery come to mind.[29] TikTok users might wonder why they are presented with videos on specific topics, and some people of colour might question why automated towel or soap dispensers won't react to their activation gesture[30] or why virtual backgrounds in online conferencing tools do not recognize their faces.[31]

It is not as if the topic was a blank slate. There already are different kinds of statutes and EU directives and regulation pointing towards a regulation of algorithms, some of which will be discussed in this section.

---

28 Data Ethics Commission (2019) 43 et seq.

29 Referring to the *Cambridge Analytica* incident, see, e.g., https://www.theguardian.com/news/2018/mar/17/cambridge-analytica-facebook-influence-us-election.

30 See, e.g., https://metro.co.uk/2017/07/13/racist-soap-dispensers-dont-work-for-black-people-6775909/.

31 https://twitter.com/colinmadland/status/1307111818981146626.

a) EU General Data Protection Regulation (GDPR)

Even though the GDPR does not contain the word "algorithm" or "computer program", it still deals with many topics and situations related to algorithms. A search for the word "automated" will lead to several recitals and provisions which are dealing with the issue of regulating algorithms – including, but not limited to, recitals 15, 67, 68 and 79 as well as articles 2, 20, 21 and 22.

Prima facie, data protection seems to be a topic of static information which might be stored digitally. But – obviously – data protection nowadays is above all concerned with *algorithms* that store data, considering that data subjects do not have full access to the algorithms involved, transparency is usually difficult to provide, and algorithms make it easy to deal with great amounts of data at very low cost. Thus, at the very beginning of the regulation, in Article 2.1, the GDPR limits its scope to the "processing of personal data wholly or partly by automated means and to the processing other than by automated means [...] which form part of a filing system or are intended to form part of a filing system."

Article 22 deals with the issue of automated individual decision-making, even though the topic is not necessarily data protection related. It reads: "The data subject shall have the *right* not to be subject to a decision based *solely* on *automated processing*, including profiling, *which produces legal effects* concerning him or her or similarly significantly affects him or her" (emphasis added). This section provides succinct criteria which – if fulfilled – not only afford the data subject with a right not to be subject to such a decision (except for the cases stated in paragraph 2, which include situations in which the decision is necessary for entering into or performing a contract between the data subject and the data controller), but also poses a duty to "implement suitable measures to safeguard the data subject's rights and freedoms and legitimate interests" in paragraph 3. Of course, there are many ways to circumvent this provision, by having humans confirm the automated decision, for example. Moreover, it indicates what the EU deems worthy of regulating: The focus is not on a certain algorithm, but specific real-life situations.

When the GDPR was first introduced, due to the high fines imposed by it, many companies (and individuals, as well) invested time and money to ensure that their data processing was transparent (e.g., by providing data privacy statements on their websites). As a regulation with direct impact on the EU member countries, the GDPR at least achieved some degree of transparency of data processing. Technically, it does not regulate *algorithms* but those who apply algorithms in their processing of personal data. It does therefore not try to influence the structure or development of algorithms, but manage the effect on those affected by the algorithms – it could be regarded as a regulation of the *use of algorithms*.

b) Ranking: regulation in a B2B context

Algorithms are also widely used to rank goods and services on online platforms and search engines. Since these platforms are the basis of many marketing and sales concepts and algorithms used in that context have the potential to influence competition to a great degree, regulation seems appropriate and necessary to provide transparency. One approach regarding the issue of ranking goods or services online in a B2B context has recently been published in the "Guidelines on ranking transparency" by the EU, pursuant *to* Regulation (EU) 2019/1150[32], aiming to protect not consumers but providers of goods and services which rely on online intermediate providers to present their products for sale.

The regulation as well as the guidelines take into account the power and visibility of high-ranked goods and services in search engines and other online platforms, such as online warehouses, and require those intermediate providers to transparently explain their ranking mechanisms. These include the parameters used to rank entries, and the guidelines explicitly state that they apply irrespective of the technologies used for ranking.[33] The guidelines were published to support providers of online intermediation services and search engines in being compliant with Regulation 2019/1150. The regulation itself is legally binding in the EU member states, therefore – contrary to the guidelines on AI – these guidelines are less abstract and (probably) more relevant to those implementing and using algorithms for their purposes.

32 Regulation (EU) 2019/1150 of the European Parliament and of the Council of 20 June 2019 on promoting fairness and transparency for business users of online intermediation services, O.J. EU L 186, 57 et seq.

33 "Individual assessment and technologically neutral approach", section 1.3.2 of the Guidelines.

c) *Automated administrative acts in Germany*

In an entirely different area of law, Germany has a provision on "entirely automated acts of administration" (in the context of social administration). § 31a Social Code (SGB) Book X reads: "An administrative act can be entirely produced by automated facilities, as long as there is no need to have the individual case processed by an official. If the authority uses automated facilities to produce administrative acts, it has to appreciate such actual information relevant to the individual case provided by the person concerned which would not be determined in the automated process".[34]

Like the GDPR, the section does not regulate a specific algorithm, but rather uses the more general term "automated facilities" and thereby regulates any administrative act which is not produced by a human being. Notably, the provision does not require any kind of outward transparency. § 31a SGB X aims at providing technology-neutral electronic administrative services.[35] It does not alter the existing provisions on administrative acts but aims at ensuring that subjects of administrative acts are not disadvantaged by the automation of said acts.[36]

A similar provision exists for administrative acts in general, see § 35a Administrative Procedures Act (VwVfG). It restricts the use of automation to situations where there is no room for evaluation regarding the decision of the respective administrative act. § 35a VwVfG also requires that such automated decision be allowed by an applicable law, to ensure that only suitable procedures are making use of automation.[37] This could include the images taken by automated speed cameras which result in speeding tickets being automatically sent to the respective individuals. This is not yet being practiced in Germany.

3. *Summary*

These were only a few examples of laws which are already regulating (the use of) algorithms. More can be found in the regulation of algorithmic trading in the German Securities Trading Act (§ 80 II ff.) or article 18 of

---

34 Translation by the author.

35 Heße, Sabine, 'Commentary on § 31a SGB X', in: BeckOK Sozialrecht, note 2.

36 Ibid. note 5.

37 Luthe (2017).

the EU Directive on markets in financial instruments, for example,[38] and even more are in the making.[39]

There are many different legal areas trying to address the issue of automation and algorithmic involvement. Each of them deals with different issues and treats them in different ways. For developers and those responsible for IT-systems and applications, this would mean that they must be aware of all laws possibly applicable to an algorithm they are developing to be compliant. This becomes more complicated if multi-purpose algorithms are involved, meaning that upon creation, it is unclear how those algorithms will be deployed (such as many machine learning algorithms).

Discussions in Germany frequently address the idea of creating an "Algorithmen-TÜV", which means creating an institution responsible for testing algorithms.[40] However, this idea doesn't seem promising for several reasons. Firstly, it would be a German solution to an international problem. After all, algorithms are created everywhere and in uncountable numbers. There is no way a single national institution could thoroughly check all of them in a timely manner. While one could claim that such an institution could either only check algorithms used by the national administration or provide a general list of approved algorithms, this approach does not seem to be able to keep pace with the speed of algorithm development and could hinder innovation and digitalisation. Secondly, a certification like a TÜV-seal could suggest false confidence in new technology to the likes of the Diesel Scandal. How would one define which algorithms need to be certified? Also, the certification would most likely require companies to provide their source codes for the certifiers to "look into the black box". This again could hinder innovation if companies cannot provide their source codes due to contractual obligations or trade secret considerations and would thus rather avoid implementing algorithms which are subject to certification.

---

38 Directive 2014/65/EU of the European Parliament and of the Council of 15 May 2014 on markets in financial instruments and amending Directive 2002/92/EC and Directive 2011/61/EU, O.J. EU L 173, 349 et seq.

39 E.g., the Digital Services Act, see https://www.euractiv.com/wp-content/uploads/sites/2/2020/12/Digital_Services_Act__1__watermark-3.pdf and the Digital Markets Act, see https://ec.europa.eu/commission/presscorner/detail/en/QANDA_20_2349.

40 See, e.g., https://algorithmenethik.de/2017/09/11/was-die-wahlprogramme-ueber-maschinen-sagen-die-menschen-bewerten/ and https://www.spd.de/fileadmin/Dokumente/Regierungsprogramm/SPD_Regierungsprogramm_BTW_2017_A5_RZ_WEB.pdf, 73.

To date, there is no known concept for the implementation of this kind of certification. Instead, the German Federal Government created an AI Observatory which is supposed to analyse potential effects and risks of AI in the context of work and society[41] which leans towards the solution discussed in this paper: Regulating specific situations or application contexts,[42] not specific types of algorithms.[43]

Algorithms of AI (mostly machine learning algorithms) for example, tend to be complex structures and their outcomes can be hard to predict, especially for non-machine-learning-specialists. Moreover, there is not just one kind of AI algorithm. Developers and data scientists frequently are coming up with new approaches and applications for machine learning. Regulating with regard to situations and environments could therefore be especially helpful when dealing with AI, since it does not need the regulator to anticipate future developments, but instead shifts responsibilities to the makers and creators of such algorithms. These are then required to ensure that their systems meet transparency and accountability requirements.

The regulations described above show how this aim can be achieved. It is not advised to impose a general "law on AI", since this would, on the one hand, be confined to technology as-is, and on the other hand, might be circumvented by the use of algorithms which are similarly damaging, but which do not fall under the definition of AI, if there even is one. The European Commission White Paper on Artificial Intelligence suggests creating a regulatory framework which should be applicable to all products and services making use of AI,[44] and then dives into the issue of defining AI. This could be avoided by taking the situation-centered or application-centered approach, therefore taking into account the effect algorithms have, irrespective of their type or implementation. The EC aims at developing a risk-based approach,[45] but restricts this risk-based approach to AI. It is questionable whether this pre-selection of algorithms is necessary.

Nevertheless, situation specific regulation also has its limits in that it seems impossible to address all situations individually (e.g., face recognition can have various applications: supporting immigration agents, identifying fugitives in large crowds, detecting people in traffic situations or

---

41 See https://www.denkfabrik-bmas.de/en/projects/ai-observatory.

42 See also AI Ethics Impact Group (2020) 35.

43 For the suggestion of a situation specific requirements' matrix as a basis for regulation, see Martini (2019) table at 76.

44 European Commission (2020) 16.

45 Ibid. 17.

tagging friends in picture collections, just to name a few). Such regulation therefore needs to carefully consider broader contexts in which such situations potentially arise, such as the GDPR is dealing with all situations where personal data is being automatically processed.

IV. Improving the Image of Algorithms Outside of Legal Regulation

Laws are not the only means of guiding the development and use of algorithms. The image – as in the public perception – of an algorithm might already be improved by voluntarily providing information on the use and functionality of algorithms. This section will present two suggestions of such rather self-regulative measures.

1. Algo.Rules

The first of these non-regulatory schemes is "Algo.Rules"[46] by the German group algorithmenethik.de in cooperation with irights.lab. These rules were created in a joint conversation that involved almost 500 participants from the areas of science and research, industries and organisations, civilians, NGOs, politics and administration. "Algo.Rules" provide guidelines on how to incorporate these rules into algorithmic projects, including detailed questionnaires.

To just point out of some of them: The very first rule would be to strengthen competency, addressing the issue that decision makers and developers alike need to understand both the functioning of the algorithm as well as the effects it could have when put into practice. In addition, safeguarding manageability addresses the issue of the algorithm staying in control of a human, something which we already saw in the HLEGs requirements of trustworthy AI. Moreover, ensuring intelligibility – like the requirement of explicability – tries to manoeuvre the algorithm away from being regarded as a black box into the direction of understandable and explainable decisions.

With regard to the above suggested situation-specific regulation, these rules are a tool to guide developers in creating algorithms which comply with said regulation. The rules heavily focus on anticipating effects, en-

46 All of those rules are described in-depth and accompanied by practical recommendations online at https://algorules.org.

suring transparency and maintaining accountability and therefore complement situation-specific regulation.

2. Google model cards

The second suggestion is a visualising approach, i.e., using images to improve the image of their algorithms. This is similar to food labels informing consumers about the contents and nutrition facts. In a similar way, algorithms could be labelled to give users a quick overview of how the algorithm functions, what its limitations are, and perhaps even provide the means to easily test it on their own data. Of course, simply stating that whatever system has "AI inside" or even naming the machine learning algorithm used, is not guaranteed to provide transparency to users, since they might not be aware of the features of specific algorithms, or the effect of automatic processing in general.

Google suggested these so-called "model cards"[47] for systems using machine learning models.[48] Two model cards are currently available, one for a model on Face Detection and one for Object Detection, both of which target machine learning algorithms detecting face and objects in images The model cards describe what kind of input a model requires, the expected outcome (e.g., whether the model will highlight the area of the input image which lead the model to detect a face), and its limitations. It is more a proof of concept now than an established mechanism, but it is a concise suggestion which could be integrated into a software development process if it reaches a status of "best practice".[49]

---

47 See https://modelcards.withgoogle.com/about.

48 In the context of machine learning, models are the trained or trainable structures used for making predictions or generating creative output. These models are used in the context of the executing computer program and roughly represent the underlying statistical algorithm.

49 A similar approach was suggested by GI (2020), https://gi-radar.de/276-beipackzettel-fuer-ki/; also demanding an obligatory AI label https://www.n-tv.de/panorama/Maschinen-ueberwinden-Schreibblockade-article22201094.html?utm_source=pocket-newtab-global-de-DE.

V. What Comes Next?

So, what comes next? Do we need a centralized "code for code",[50] unifying all of those far-spread different sprinkles of regulations of algorithms? For example, the Data Ethics commission suggested a "horizontal basic rule by means of an EU directive for algorithmic systems" on the European level to be accompanied by sector specific national legislation.[51] According to the German AI Enquete Commission, sector specific legislation might then be extended by AI specific provisions.[52] This seems like a reasonable approach: Identifying relevant sectors, situations or applications of algorithms, and then – if necessary – enriching regulation by provisions taking into account potential specific issues of AI. In this way, practitioners especially in the software development business could focus on legislation pertaining to their domain of application, without the need to assemble fragments of regulations according to their use of algorithms.

It should also be discussed whether industry guidelines, putting money into certifications (who do we trust to issue such certifications?), or laws are the preferred means of regulation. How much control is wanted and needed? How much responsibility is desired and required – and who should be responsible at all? How can one steer clear of over-regulation, taking into consideration constitutional rights such as freedom of opinion?

In conclusion, the image of algorithms might be improved by strict regulation, insofar as subjects to algorithms increasingly trust the legislators in protecting them from potential harm. However, while this supposed trust might seem to be comforting, it does not change the image of algorithms per se, since demonstrating a strict regulative approach might even emphasize the dangers and threats associated with the use of algorithms.

One should be aware of the potential manipulative and sometimes unconscious effects algorithms might have both on an individual's life and on democracy. But computer literacy might also go a long way, enabling users to better understand what potential threats they might be faced with, thus raising awareness and addressing the issue bottom-up in addition to the top-down approach of regulation.

---

50 Discussing a "Lex Algorithmica" in France, see GI (2018) 113.

51 Data Ethics Commission (2019) 180

52 See the summary of the German AI Enquete Commission report at https://dserver.bundestag.de/btd/19/237/1923700.pdf.

References

AI Ethics Impact Group (2020): 'From Principles to Practice – An interdisciplinary framework to operationalise AI ethics' (2020; https://www.ai-ethics-impact.org/resource/blob/1961130/c6db9894ee73aefa489d6249f5ee2b9f/aieig---report---download-hb-data.pdf)

BEUC (2020): 'The Use of Big Data and Artificial Intelligence in Insurance' (2020; https://www.beuc.eu/publications/beuc-x-2020-039_beuc_position_paper_big_data_and_ai_in_insurances.pdf)

Brennan, Tim/Dieterich, William/Ehret, Beate (2009): 'Evaluating the predictive validity of the COMPAS risk and needs assessment system', 36 Criminal Justice and Behavior, No. 1 (January 2009) 21–40

Brosnan, Mark J. (2002): *Technophobia – The Psychological Impact of Information Technology* (London: Routledge 2002)

Data Ethics Commission of the Federal Government of Germany (2019): 'Opinion of the Data Ethics Commission' (2019; https://www.bmjv.de/SharedDocs/Downloads/DE/Themen/Fokusthemen/Gutachten_DEK_EN.pdf?__blob=publicationFile&v=1)

De Streel, Alexandre/Bibal, Adrien/Frenay, Benoit/Lognoul, Michael (2020): 'Explaining the Black Box: When Law Controls AI' (2020; https://cerre.eu/wp-content/uploads/2020/03/issue_paper_explaining_the_black_box_when_law_controls_ai.pdf)

European Commission (2018): High Level Expert Group on Artificial Intelligence: *Ethics Guidelines For Trustworthy AI* (2018, https://ec.europa.eu/newsroom/dae/document.cfm?doc_id=60419)

European Commission (2020): 'Whitepaper on Artificial Intelligence – A European approach to excellence and trust' (2020; https://ec.europa.eu/info/sites/info/files/commission-white-paper-artificial-intelligence-feb2020_en.pdf)

Federal Government of Germany (2018): 'Artificial Intelligence Strategy' (2018; https://www.ki-strategie-deutschland.de/home.html?file=files/downloads/Nationale_KI-Strategie_engl.pdf), cited as: German AI Strategy

Gesellschaft für Informatik (2018): 'Technische und rechtliche Betrachtungen algorithmischer Entscheidungsverfahren – Studien und Gutachten im Auftrag des Sachverständigenrats für Verbraucherfragen' (2018; https://www.svr-verbraucherfragen.de/wp-content/uploads/GI_Studie_Algorithmenregulierung.pdf)

Hajian, Sara/Bonchi, Francesco/Castillo, Carlosn(2016): 'Algorithmic Bias – From Discrimination Discovery to Fairness-Aware Data Mining', KDD '16 – Proceedings of the 22nd ACM SIGKDD International Conference on Knowledge Discovery and Data Mining, 2125–2126 (2016; https://dl.acm.org/doi/pdf/10.1145/2939672.2945386)

Heron, Simon (2009): 'Advanced Encryption Standard (AES)', Network Security (2009) 8–12

Kolany-Raiser, Barbara/Heil, Reinhard/Orwat, Carsten/Hoeren, Thomas (2019): *Big Data* (München: C.H. Beck 2019)

Künstner, Kim Manuel (2019): 'Preissetzung durch Algorithmen als Herausforderung des Kartellrechts', Gewerblicher Rechtsschutz und Urheberrecht (2019) 36–42

Luthe, Ernst-Wilhelm (2017): 'Der vollständig automatisierte Erlass eines Verwaltungsaktes nach § 31a SGB X', Die Sozialgerichtsbarkeit (2017) 250–258

Malgieri, Gianclaudio (2019): 'Automated Decision-Making in the EU Member States – The right to explanation and other "suitable safeguards" in the national legislations', 35 Computer Law & Security Review (2019) 2–26 (https://reader.elsevier.com/reader/sd/pii/S0267364918303753?token=5D8EBF5DD9AFA9741959E608A623E0693A93E5DDFF29D24384EFB9A93DB4670DF78A331FEF74DCE05DEB4EBE8503613)

Martini, Mario (2019): 'Fundamentals of a Regulatory System for Algorithm-based Processes' (2019; https://www.vzbv.de/sites/default/files/downloads/2019/07/19/martini_regulatory_system_algorithm_based_processes.pdf)

Paal, Boris (2019): 'Missbrauchstatbestand und Algorithmic Pricing', Gewerblicher Rechtsschutz und Urheberrecht (2019) 43–53

Pasquale, Frank (2015): *The Black Box Society. The Secret Algorithms that Control Money and Information* (Cambridge, Mass.: Harvard University Press 2015)

Schätzing, Frank (2018): *Die Tyrannei des Schmetterlings* (Cologne: Kiepenheuer & Witsch 2018)

Simon, Herrmann/Butscher, Stephan A. (2001): 'Individualised Pricing: Boosting Profitability with the Higher Art of Power Pricing', 19 European Management Journal, Issue 2 (2001) 109–114

Smid, M.E./Branstad, D.K. (1988): 'Data Encryption Standard – Past and Future', 76 Proceedings of the IEEE, Issue 5 (1988) 550–559

Stone, Harold S. (1971): *Introduction to Computer Organization and Data Structures* (New York et al.: McGraw-Hill 1971)

Thomas, R. Guy (2012): 'Non-Risk Price Discrimination in Insurance – Market Outcomes and Public Policy', 37 The Geneva Papers on Risk and Insurance – Issues and Practice (2012) 27–46

Part 6
Ethics and Fundamental Rights

Chapter 20
The Constitutional Protection of Images

Johannes Eichenhofer

I. Preliminaries

1. What "images" are we talking about?

Talking on an abstract level about the constitutional protection of images is not an easy task. To be honest, constitutional law scholarship has not come very far in this regard. Although (constitutional) law and images are interrelated in many ways[1], images have hardly been made an explicit subject of (constitutional) jurisprudence or (constitutional) law scholarship so far.[2] In particular, constitutional law does – unlike (cultural) philosophy[3], psychology[4], media- and image studies[5] – not (yet) know a theory of images. This finding is not directly surprising for a text-oriented discipline like jurisprudence. But it is in some ways remarkable *how* little attention jurisprudence, and especially constitutional jurisprudence, has actually paid to images so far compared to other "media of law."[6]

Certainly, copyright law, trademark law or, in part, data protection law deal with non-textual visual objects (such as photos, logos, etc.) on an ongoing basis. Here, however, the legal sciences' access usually appears to be *object*-related rather than *media*-related. Hereby I mean that an image becomes a copyright, trademark, or data protection issue not because it belongs to the media type "image", but because of the *object* it depicts

1 To give just one example: on the one hand, law can be the object of images (e.g. images of Justitia), on the other hand, images can be media of law (e.g. traffic signs).

2 See, however, for the first attempts in German-speaking countries Vismann (2007); Boehme-Neßler (2010); Dreier (2019); On the specific aspect of the "staging" of law, see Münkler/Stenzel (2019).

3 See, e.g., the contributions by Boehm, Pichler and Weising in: Seitz/Graneß/Stenger (2018) 21 et seq., 39 et seq. and 55 et seq.

4 See, e.g., Beach (1993).

5 See, e.g., Mitchell (1994); Belting (2001); Bredekamp (2010).

6 See Vesting (2011–2015).

(e.g., a copyrighted photograph, a trademark-protected logo, or an image of a person that meets the requirement of a personal data).[7] Apparently, images are so commonplace to us due to their ubiquity that we always (subconsciously) "think" about them but have hardly ever made them the subject of a media-specific jurisprudential consideration.[8]

The present text cannot possibly tackle the Herculean task to develop a constitutional theory of images on its own, but it aims to make at least a modest contribution. The starting point is a conceptual sharpening. So, what are we talking about when we speak of "images"? Only when these conceptual foundations are clarified, it is promising to abstractly consider its constitutional status or how constitutional law affords them protection. In the following, I would like to propose a terminological and phenomenological distinction between "inner" and "outer" images on the one hand, and "self" and "foreign" images on the other (I.3.). Starting from this distinction, we will then examine how constitutional law deals with these types of images. The article then aims to show (II.), in a rather associative way, where "inner" and "outer", as well as "self images" and "foreign images", are dealt with in Italian and German constitutional law (with respect to our Italo-German cooperation). Following on from this, the article devotes itself to dealing with these types of images by means of a comparative case study (III.). With regard to our Italian-German cooperation, I have chosen one Italian and one German case, whereby the latter has even involved the European Court of Human Rights (ECtHR). Both cases concern media reports about celebrities, namely Princess *Soraya of Persia* (Italian case) and Princess *Caroline of Hanover* (formerly *Monaco*) (German case). Since both cases date back some time, the question of whether and, if so, what effects digitalization will have on this case law, will have to be examined under a specific section (IV.). The article will then conclude with some remarks on the constitutional requirements for dealing with digital images (V.).

7 In copyright law, however, not only the object but also the image itself can constitute a protected work.

8 See, however, Dreier (2019), 13 et seq., who refers to the discipline of "law and images" practiced in the UK and in the USA.

2. *Depictions, illustrations, data, information, metaphors, imaginations: the multiformity of the concept of image*

The concept of the image must be distinguished from both the depiction and the object depicted. While the depicted object represents a person or an item that was either found in the real world (as in the case of photography and paintings of real life objects) or originated in the imagination of the creator (as in the case of paintings of objects which merely existed in the phantasy of the painter), the depiction is the result of the process of image creation (e.g., the photograph or portrait). Images, on the other hand, represent an intermediate stage between the object and its image, so to say the idea of the picture, which arises in the viewer through the contemplation of the image.[9]

In the sense of illustrations, images (or pictures[10]) are furthermore used to illustrate a certain fact. In the visual arts, images occur as paintings, drawings or graphics. In photography, an image usually refers to the optical reproduction of an object. And in film, an image is a single component, the juxtaposition of which creates the (moving) film (a movie). In this respect, it seems as if images were always the result of artistic creation, which would assign them to the freedom of art[11] from the perspective of constitutional law. However, images extend far beyond the artistic context. One might think of images that are shown in the press, on broadcasting media or in advertising – or how they are posted billions of times on social networks, at the latest since the invention of the smartphone. In this respect, too, a common denominator seems to be identifiable from a constitutional point of view: images always appear to be subject to the freedoms of communication.[12]

---

9 See on this Dreier (2019), 30 ed. seq., 191.

10 Following, I understand both terms as synonyms.

11 This freedom is, for instance, guaranteed by Article 13 of the Charter of Fundamental Rights in the European Union (CFR): "The arts and scientific freedom shall be free of constraint (…)".

12 One can think, for example, of Article 10 of the European Convention on Human Rights (ECHR) on the "Freedom of Expression". For the protection of images under the ECHR see Neukamm (2007).

Against this background, it would seem logical to adopt a purely technical viewpoint and treat images as special forms of data[13] or information[14], which, as such, can form the basis of communication[15]. Constitutional law is familiar with dealing both with information and communication. For example, German constitutional law recognizes a right to informational self-determination, while European constitutional law recognizes a fundamental right to data protection (Art. 8 CFR). Beyond that, however, information is omnipresent in constitutional law (as well as in law in general): it could even be said that law is all about information processing. Then, however, it is hardly possible to make general statements about the relationship between data, information and (constitutional) law. If, then, the same does not apply to the relationship between (constitutional) law and images as to the relationship between (constitutional) law and data or information, we must now look for the properties that distinguish images from other information.

Such a differentiation from other information could start on a semantic[16], a semiotic and a syntactic level.[17] The most obvious difference might be the syntactic one: pictures do not transport information by means of text, but by means of other data (e.g., color spots, etc.), i.e., pictorially. Probably even more significant – and this is what makes them so interesting for (constitutional) law – is their semantic richness. Pictures are often used as legal rules to clearly indicate a certain rule as, which, for example, even small children or illiterate people can understand (e.g., standing traffic light = stop, walking traffic light = walk). However, the semantic content of images is likely to be even higher than that of texts, since images are linked to an even greater extent to cognitive dispositions, prior knowledge,

13 For the term "data" see, e.g., the definition to be found at https://www.encyclopedia.com/science-and-technology/computers-and-electrical-engineering/computers-and-computing/data. Images can also constitute personal data if they can be used to identify a person (such as in the case of passport photographs); see the legal definition of personal data in Article 4 No. 1 of the General Data Protection Regulation (GDPR). For the classification of portraits as either images or personal as personal data, or both, see Müller-Tamm (2022).

14 On the difference between data and information, see for example https://www.encyclopedia.com/social-sciences-and-law/law/law/information.

15 On the concept of communication, see for example https://www.encyclopedia.com/religion/encyclopedias-almanacs-transcripts-and-maps/communication-philosophy.

16 See for example Boehm (2015).

17 See Zech (2012); for a summary see Raue (2022).

prior understanding, and prior cultural imprints.[18] Therefore, images can, on the one hand, condense information, but on the other hand, distribute it like a fan and set communication processes in motion that a text can never achieve due to its relative "unambiguousness".

At this point, another meaning of images must be mentioned. Images cannot be reduced to this feature as ambiguous carriers of information embodied in an object. Rather, in linguistics, images are synonymous with metaphors[19], i.e., expressions that bring a word into a different context of meaning. This also includes the so-called "guiding images" (in German: "Leitbilder"), which will be discussed in a moment (II.1.b)). Finally, psychology teaches us that there are also images in the inner world of humans. This also distinguishes them from other information carriers in the outer world. They are also called conceptions (imagination). Apart from the fact that thinking in general is, to a large extent, pictorial[20], human consciousness also functions in such a way that it collects images from the outside world and processes them into its own images. In this way, "self-images", i.e., ideas of one's own self (personal identity), are created. This is essentially based on self-perception, as well as the feedback of external perception. By measuring an actual condition against a target condition (the ideal image), it greatly controls how a person thinks, feels, and behaves.

3. *Wording in the following: "inner" and "outer" images, "self-images" and "foreign images"*

Despite these diverse meanings – which are expressed especially in the German language[21] – some general characteristics of images can be sum-

---

18 See for example Seitz/Graneß/Stenger (2018), who emphasize that images are "never purely epistemic or aesthetic objects, but always carry ethical as well as political implications and may even exercise agency." (Translation by the author; in the original: "Bilder können niemals rein epistemische oder ästhetische Gegenstände darstellen, sondern immer auch ethische sowie politische Implikationen mit sich führen und womöglich gar Handlungsmacht ausüben..."). The autonomy of the image is also the guiding thesis of Bredekamp (2010).

19 On this, see Münkler (2016).

20 For the "image of thinking" see Deleuze (1968/1972).

21 Here the word "image" is a component of numerous nouns, such as "Selbstbild" ("self-image"), "Weltbild" ("worldview"), "Leitbild" ("mission statement"/"guiding principles/images"), "Vorbild" ("role model"), "Bildung" ("education"), "Abbildung" ("illustration"), "Ausbildung" ("education"), "Einbildung" ("imagina-

marized: an image is a semiotically,[22] often artfully composed source of information of great semantic value. In this context, it is always to be regarded as something "holistic", as a unity, which cannot be broken down into individual parts, without a loss of information. However, this does not contradict the fact that images can be sub-divided into meaningful individual parts or even bits of information.[23] A further result of the previous considerations is apparent in the fact that images can be understood both as objectified data and information carriers of the physical or "outside world" (in the following: "outer" images) and as conceptions in the "internal world" of a human being (in the following: "inner" images). Furthermore, a distinction can be made between images of oneself and images of others or of objects ("foreign" images).[24] Accordingly, one can identify four different variations of images (Table 1):

	Self-image	**Foreign image**
Inner image	Imagination of oneself or a community one belongs to	Imagination of others or of objects
Outer image	Depiction of oneself (e.g., self-portrait, selfie) or a community one belongs to	Depiction of others or of objects

Table 1: Four variations of images

When "outer" images, which means images located in the "outside world", speak to us and thereby evoke "inner" images, such as ideas, one could speak of the "internalization of the outside". Conversely, when "inner" images leave the inner world and enter the outer world, as is the case, for example, with self-portraits or "selfies", an "externalization of the inner" is achieved. These crudely formed categories are undoubtedly no more than

tion") and verbs, such as, "bilden" ("(to) build, form") in the sense of building/producing an object, but also an intellectual achievement, such as an opinion, a judgment, etc. Perhaps this is the reason why, in particular, Germans are interested in the general relationship between image and law.

22 For a socioethics of image fakes built upon semiotics see Leone (2022).

23 For the example of information contained in the parts of a map stored in the form of a database see CJEU, case C- 490/14 of 29 October 2015, ECLI:EU:C:2015:735- *Verlag Esterbauer*.

24 See Dreier (2019) 71.

heuristics of a (constitutional) jurist, that do not even come close to achieving the complexity of contemporary image theory. Image theorists may forgive it. For the further course of the article, however, the author hopes that some interesting insights can be generated based on these distinctions.

II. Points of Reference

Constitutional law encompasses several norms and figures to which the typology of images just proposed can be linked. For a better overview, a distinction will be made here between state organization law (1.), i.e., those constitutional norms, which regulate the actions of state organs (e.g. the Parliament, the Government, or the Constitutional Court), and fundamental rights (2.).[25]

1. State organization law

a) State symbols

The law of state organization, also regarded as an ensemble of norms for the self-regulation of a state community, is familiar with both "inner" and "outer" images, "self-images" and "foreign images". Relevant "inner" images in this context are individual people's ideas about one's own role in the community or the community as a whole. They can be "self-images" (e.g., images of a "good citizen") or "foreign images", i.e., external attributions of the community as a whole or of its individual organs (in themselves already an image in the sense of a metaphor), procedures or sections of community life. If these "inner" images have been "externalized" and thus have become "outer" images, they can in turn influence the individual viewer – and, for example, trigger a feeling of belonging to a collective identity of such a community. Examples of these kinds of externalized "inner images" are national symbols, such as national emblems or flags,

25 This distinction is quite common in German constitutional law, whereas the Author is aware that other Countries follow a different pattern to differentiate constitutional law.

which are the subject of separate constitutional articles in, for example, the Italian[26] or the German[27] constitution.

b) *"Guiding images" of the state or individual state organs*

While the legal content of such state symbols as externalized collective self-attributions is rather limited[28], there are other forms of externalized inner images, which can have considerable normative effects. We are talking about the so-called "guiding principles" or "images" (in German: "Leitbilder"). These are not usually externalized through images, but through language. But even through their linguistic externalization, guiding images appear as objects of the external world. They are perceptible to the senses and can contribute to generating internal ideas. As objects of the "outside world" they can in turn – by way of constitutional interpretation – generate quite considerable normative effects.[29] For example, the guiding image of a "lean state" articulates the normative demand for de-regulation, i.e., the reduction of public duties with a simultaneous reduction in taxes. Similarly, the guiding image of the "night watchman state" (in German: "Nachtwächterstaat") expressed the idea that the state must limit its intervention in the societal self-determination to a minimum. Often, these kinds of "guiding images" are also formulated for specific state organs[30] or their members, which can then establish further normative specifications beyond the competences and duties written into the constitution. An example from German Constitutional law is the guiding image for every Member of Parliament.[31]

---

26 Article 12 of the Italian Constitution of December 27, 1947 states: "La bandiera della Repubblica è il tricolore italiano: verde, bianco e rosso, a tre bande verticali di eguali dimensioni." ("The flag of the Republic is the Italian tricolor: green, white and red, with three vertical bands of equal size.").

27 Article 22 (2) of the German Constitution ("Basic Law") of May 23, 1949 states: "Die Bundesflagge ist schwarz-rot-gold." ("The federal flag is black-red-gold.").

28 For the federal flag see, e.g., Classen (2018) notes 23 et seq. Here, the first issue is the competence to design the federal flag, as well as the flag management. The second issue is the protection of the federal flag.

29 See Volkmann (2009). On guiding principles in administrative law, see, e.g., Baer (2004).

30 On the origin and meaning of this metaphor see Münkler (2016).

31 BVerfG ruling 2 BvE 1–4/06 of 11 October 2006 = BVerfGE 118 277, paras 214 et seq.; for additional examples, see Volkmann (2009) 159 et seq.

"Guiding images" are insofar problematic as they evoke (pre-legal) ideas of justice and order of society that have not been "juridified". As such, although they are not the subject of constitutional law, they can influence constitutional law and – by way of interpretation by the constitutional courts – become applicable constitutional law.[32] On the other hand, precisely because they appeal to supra-legal notions of justice, they can also provide beneficial orientation in the often difficult interpretation of abstract constitutional norms.

c) *Dealing with "outer" images beyond states symbols and guiding principles ("image regimes")*

A question to be distinguished from constitutional symbols (1.a) and "guiding images" (1.b) is that of the visibility and invisibility of images in law[33] or of "image regimes"[34]. Here, the question is to which extent a state is entitled to express its own collectively formed values through outer (self-) images – and to which extent individuals are entitled to defend themselves against these images. This rather abstract question has become very concrete in a German law case of the permissibility on the hanging of crosses (crucifixes) in schools or other public buildings. Although the German Constitutional Court ("Bundesverfassungsgericht", in the following: BVerfG) held[35] that such an exposure of religious symbols is prohibited because it violates the pupils' and teachers' religious freedom, in 2018, the Bavarian state government required crosses to be displayed in official buildings.[36] The Bavarian Constitutional Court rejected the decision's appeal due to a lack of legal standing.[37] Particularly in the judiciary, this kind of externalized "self-images" of a state (in the sense of the crucifix: as a Christian state) can have the effect of a "performative practice".[38] The resulting regulatory effect is difficult to determine under constitutional law. Although the overall disappearance of images and symbols as an element

32 For German law, see § 31 (1) of the Law on the Federal Constitutional Court (Bundesverfassungsgerichtsgesetz).
33 See Damler (2019) 97.
34 See Vismann (2007).
35 BVerfG ruling 1 BvR 1087/91 of 16 May 1995 = BVerfGE 93, 1.
36 General Rules of Procedure of the authorities of the Free State of Bavaria para. 28.
37 See BayVerfGH, Vf. 8-VII-18 of 3 April 2020.
38 See Müller-Mall (2012) 173 et seq.

of the state's self-representation is clear[39], the question of its admissibility is still of high constitutional relevance. It expresses a fundamental conflict between the democratic self-determination of the majority and the rights of a (cultural) minority. However, the resolution of this conflict is not a question of state organization law, but of fundamental rights.[40]

2. *Fundamental rights*

Images are the subject of fundamental rights provisions in many respects. "Outer" images such as portraits, photographs or other sorts of pictures, or more precise, their usage, can be protected by freedom of opinion, freedom of the press or freedom of broadcasting. This includes circumstances where they are used to express an opinion or are printed in a press product of broadcast on the radio, TV or the web. If they are the result of an artistic-creative process, both the process and the presentation / dissemination of the images are protected by artistic freedom.[41] The economic value of a work of art is protected by the fundamental right to property. While for collectors and dealers a picture is treated like any other asset according to constitutional standards, there is a special legal regime of intellectual property for authors in the form of copyright law.[42]

However, not only "outer", but also "inner" images are subject to fundamental rights. It must be assumed that the entire inner life, i.e., the formation of thoughts and feelingsis not accessible to the law.[43] The production of "inner" (be they "foreign" or "self-") images typically becomes legally relevant and in need of regulation only when an action derives from them. For example, when the thought of killing someone else is actually put into action. Then this action (the act of killing) must be regulated (forbidden or

---

39 See for the example of the courts: Behrmann (2019) 87: "Die moderne Justiz versteht sich als bilderloser Ort der Neutralität und Unabhängigkeit." ("The modern judiciary sees itself as an imageless place of neutrality and independence").

40 In BverfG 1 BvR 1087/91 of 16 May 1995, the negative freedom of religion of the pupils guaranteed by Article 4 (1) GG was opposed to the freedom of the school guaranteed by Article 7 GG in connection with the positive freedom of religion.

41 The first dimension is referred to in German law as the "work area" ("Werkbereich"), the second as the "effective area" ("Wirkbereich"); see, e.g., BVerfG ruling 1 BvR 435/68 of 24 February 1971 = BVerfGE 30, 173 (189); BVerfG ruling 1 BvR 712/68 of 5 March 1974 = BVerfGE 36, 321 (331); BVerfG ruling 1 BvR 816/82 = BverfGE 67, 213 (224).

42 Instructive about this Goldhammer (2012).

43 See Gusy (2003) 104.

prevented in the case of killing). Furthermore, many constitutions of European states and on the intra-European level recognize a fundamental right to self-presentation[44]. This grants everyone the right to defend themselves against the dissemination of images of others if they contradict their own self-image.

3. *Prospect on the further argumentation*

In the following section, this article will focus precisely on this right to self-presentation. A constitutional law scholar has far more to say about its development, its scope, and its balancing with competing fundamental rights (such as freedom of expression, freedom of the press, and freedom of broadcasting) than, for example, about the intricacies of copyright law. This is because the latter is largely left to the parliamentary legislature, so that copyright law is determined by constitutional law only through a relatively little extent.[45] Instead, the most important statements are found in statutory law[46] (and increasingly in European secondary law). Furthermore, focusing on the right to self-presentation and the conflicting fundamental rights allows to illustrate a conflict between inner self-images and outer foreign images. In other words, except for "outer self-images" (e.g., selfies), all forms of images are included.

This article seeks to illustrate this conflict between the right of self-representation and the freedoms of communication, between "self" and "foreign" images, based on two famous court cases, one Italian and one German. The aim is to show how the Italian and German courts resolved this conflict and what can be learned from it regarding the relationship between "self" and "foreign" images. Both cases are likely to be well-known beyond their respective national borders. The plaintiffs, Princess *Soraya Esfandiary* of Persia, and Princess *Caroline* of Monaco (and Hanover, respectively), are not only particularly famous but also persistent ones. Both plaintiffs repeatedly commenced legal action against the media coverage

---

44 For an in-depth analysis of German Constitutional law, see Britz (2008).

45 See, however, Geiger (2022); Depenheuer/Froese (2018) notes 148 et seq. For the importance of the Charter of Fundamental Rights of the EU see the recent decisions by the CJEU of 29 July 2019, cases C-476/17, ECLI:EU:C:2019:624 – *Pelham et al.*; C-469/17, ECLI:EU:C:2019:623 – *Funke Medien NRW* and C-516/17, ECLI:EU:C:2019:625 – *Spiegel Online*. On U.S. Constitutional Law, see Goldhammer (2012).

46 Comprehensive on German copyright law, e.g., Dreier/Schulze (2022).

of their private lives. *Soraya* eventually appealed at the Italian Supreme Court (Corte di Cassazione[47]), and *Caroline*, even twice to the European Court of Human Rights (ECHR). The decisions issued in this regard are undoubtedly among the "classics" of privacy protection in general. After all, they have set a new fundamental course.

Thus, in the *Soraya* ruling, the Italian Constitutional Court recognized for the first time a fundamental right to privacy ("*diritto alla riservatezza*") that clearly went beyond the right to one's own image ("*diritto all'immagine*") already codified by law (see III.1. below). While the first *Caroline* case still concerned rather detailed aspects of the right to a counterstatement[48], the second Caroline ruling[49] of the German Constitutional Court (Bundesverfassungsgericht, BVerfG) is well known to many German jurists because it is one of the very few cases in which a complainant was filed against a decision of the BVerfG before the European Court of Human Rights (ECtHR). In its first decision of 2004, the BVerfG adjusted the relationship between freedom of the press and private life significantly more in favor of the plaintiff, so that the first BVerfG decision was declared contrary to the Convention in this respect.[50] In a second proceeding[51], however, the ECtHR upheld the decision of the BVerfG and thus dismissed Caroline of Monaco's complaint (III.2.).

III. Case Study: Soraya vs. Caroline – A Legal Comparison Between Italy, Germany and Europe

1. Soraya before the Italian courts

Before the *Soraya* decision is discussed, a few remarks on Italian law should be noted. Since 1941, Italian legislation on the protection of copyright and related rights, provides for special portrait rights ("diritti relativi al ritratto") which include the right to one's own image.[52] According to

---

47 Cass., 27.5.1975, n. 2129, *Giust. Civ.* 1975, I, 1686, 1696.

48 BVerfG ruling 1 BvR 1861/93, 1864/96, 2073/97 of 14 January 1998 = BVerfGE 97, 125 – *Caroline von Monaco I.*

49 BVerfG ruling 1 BvR 653/96 of 15 December 1999 = BVerfGE 101, 361 – *Caroline von Monaco II.*

50 ECtHR, 24.6.2004, No. 59320/00 – *Caroline von Hannover I.*

51 ECtHR (Grand Chamber), 7.2.2012, No. 40660/08 – *Caroline von Hannover II.*

52 See the law of April 22, 1941, No. 633 on the protection of copyright and related rights, Part II.

Art. 96, the likeness of a person may not be exhibited, reproduced or placed on the market without that person's consent. Exceptions are regulated by Art. 97, p. 1 which states that consent is not required if the reproduction of the image is justified. This can encompass the fame of the person depicted or from the exercise of a public office. Further, Art. 21 of the Italian Constitution postulates a fundamental right to freedom of expression and freedom of the press[53], while also failing to include neither a written fundamental right to privacy ("riservatezza") nor a general right of personality. Following the U.S. role model[54], various methodological approaches to standardizing such a (fundamental) right have been discussed in Italian legal literature since the 1950s. There was agreement that the simple "diritto all'immagine" left various gaps in protection that needed to be closed with the right to privacy. As will be shown in a moment, such a gap existed in the case Princess *Soraya Esfandiary-Bakhtiary* of Persia (1932–2001).

The princess, born in Berlin to a Persian father and a German mother, became the Queen of Persia after marrying the Persian Shah *Mohammed Reza Pahlavi* in 1951. The couple divorced in 1958 most likely because *Soraya* was infertile. But even after the divorce, *Soraya* remained a favorite subject of the tabloids as she continued to lead an eventful life. Against this background, the case was ideally suited for the recognition of a general fundamental right to privacy. In contrast to the Court of Appeal in Rome[55], the *Corte di Cassazione*[56] had expressly refrained from taking this step in an earlier decision concerning the broadcast of a feature film about the now deceased opera singer *Enrico Caruso* (1873–1921). In the meantime, however, after the majority of doctrine[57] and the courts[58] favored

53 This provision states: "Tutti hanno diritto di manifestare liberamente il proprio pensiero con la parola, lo scritto e ogni altro mezzo di diffusione. La stampa non può essere soggetta ad autorizzazioni o censure." (Translation by the author: "Everyone has the right to express his or her thoughts freely by word, writing and any other means of communication. The press cannot be subject to authorization or censorship.").

54 In particular, the decisions of the U.S. Supreme Court in the proceedings *Olmstead v. United States* 1928, 277 US 438, 473 et seq. and *Katz v United States* 1967, 389 U.S. 347, 361, were fundamental in this regard.

55 App. Roma, 17.5.1955, Foro it. 1956, I, 793, 797 et seq.

56 Cass., 22.12.1956, n. 4487, *Giust. Civ.* 1957, I, 5 et seq.; 7.12.29160, n. 3199, *Foro it.* 1961, I, 43, 44 et seq.; skeptical on the other hand already Pugliese (1954).

57 See for example Franceschelli (1960) 2.

58 App. Napoli, 20.8.1958, *Giust. Civ.* 1959, I, 1811, 181 et seq.; App. Milano, 5.1.21958, *Giust. Civ.* 1959, I, 1811, 1812 et seq.; 26.8.1960, *Foro it.* 1961, I, 43,

recognizing a right to privacy (*riservatezza*), the *Corte di Cassazione* now expressly concurred for the first time in its *Soraya* decision of 1975.[59]

The facts of this decision can be told comparatively quickly. Repeatedly, Princess *Soraya* was subjected to tabloid media coverage that was devoted in detail to her private life and sometimes concerned the most intimate issues, such as the princess's ability to give birth. The *Corte di cassazione* then recognized a comprehensive right to privacy that not only encompassed the domestic sphere (*intimità domestica*), corresponding to the *right to be let alone*,[60] but also protected acts occurring outside this domestic sphere if they had a clearly private or personal character.[61] The fact that persons in whom there is a public interest could also invoke this right was not seriously doubted by the case law. At most, something else should apply when matters have ceased to be "private" and the work falls within the scope of protection of the right to historical reconstruction (*diritto alla ricostruzione storica*).[62] The right to confidentiality could thus protect broad parts of the personality. It is intended to protect its holders from such interference as is not by lawful means, is not for exclusively speculative purposes, is not contrary to honor, reputation or decency, and is not justified by overriding public interests. Nevertheless, the right to privacy was not conceptualized as a comprehensive right of control, as previously proposed in the literature.[63] This is because the right to privacy only guaranteed an injunction claim, but not a comprehensive entitlement to control one's "own" data.[64]

---

47 f.; Pret. Forlì, 23.10.1970, *Giur. It.* 1971, I, 2, 113; Pret. Roma, 20.2.1971, *Dir. Aut.* 1971, 330.

59 Cass., 27.5.1975, n. 2129, *Giust. Civ.* 1975, I, 1686, 1696.

60 Vicari (2007) 61; Ubertazzi (2004) 57.

61 Corte cass. 27.5.1975, n. 2129, *Giust. Civ.* 1975, I, 1686: "… il diritto alla riservatezza consiste nella tutela di quelle situazioni e vicende strettamente personali e familiari le quali, anche se verificatesi fuori dal domicilio domestico, non hanno per i terzi un interesse socialmente apprezzabile." ("… the right to privacy consists in the protection of those situations and events that are strictly personal and familiar and which, even if occurring outside the home, have no socially appreciable interest for third parties.").

62 Vicari (2007) 86.

63 Ubertazzi (2004) 62.

64 Ibid.

2. *Caroline before the German courts*

As in Italy, Germany also provides a simple legal regulation for the use of images that is much older than the German Constitution (the so-called Basic Law = Grundgesetz, in the following: GG). According to Section 22 of the Art Copyright Act of 1907 ("Kunsturhebergesetz") images may – as in Italian law – only be disseminated or publicly displayed with the consent of the person depicted. However, Section 23 (1) provides for exceptions to this principle. This includes when the person depicted is a person of "contemporary history". Since both Princess *Caroline*, born in 1957 as the eldest child of Prince Rainier III of Monaco and the famous US-American actress Grace Kelly, who spent almost her entire life under the observation of the mass media[65], was classified as such a person by the Federal Court of Justice[66], images of her may be taken and disseminated even without her consent. However, Section 23(2) allows an exception if the dissemination or display of the image violates a legitimate interest of the person depicted. This conception, repeatedly confirmed as constitutional by the BVerfG[67], is intended to take account of the fundamental rights of communication guaranteed in Article 5 (1) GG – i.e., freedom of expression, information, the press and broadcasting – on the one hand, and the "general right of personality" guaranteed by Article 2 (1) in conjunction with Article 1 (1) GG on the other.

This fundamental right, developed by the BVerfG[68], guarantees, in the terminology of *Thorsten Kingreen* and *Ralf Poscher*[69], a right to self-*determination*, to self-*preservation* and to self-*presentation*. While the first dimension involves the freedom to determine one's own identity (for example, to choose a name[70] or to live according to one's sexual orientation[71]), the second dimension contains the freedom to withdraw from the public sphere. To specify this legal position, the BVerfG has developed a three-level protection concept that distinguishes between an inviolable intimate sphere, a

---

65 Her father had already sold the rights to broadcast his wedding with actress Grace Kelly to the production company MGM and arranged for a picture of his just-born first daughter to appear on the cover of "Life" magazine.

66 BGH, 19.12.1995, VI ZR 15/95.

67 BVerfGE 35, 202 (224 f.) – *Lebach*; BVerfG ruling 1 BvR 653/96 of 15 December 1999 = BVerfGE 101, 361 – *Caroline von Monaco II* (para. 90).

68 BVerfGE 7, 198 – *Lüth*; E 54, 148 (153) – *Eppler*.

69 See Kingreen/Poscher (2020), notes 391 et seq.

70 BVerfGE 78, 38 (49) – *Gemeinsamer Familienname*; 109, 256 (266 et seq.) – *Vor(Ehename)*.

71 BVerfGE 47, 46 (73) – *Sexualkundeunterricht*; 121, 175 (190) – *Transsexuelle V*.

private sphere that can only be restricted under strict requirements, and a social sphere that is only weakly protected.[72] Finally, the third dimension, the right to self-*presentation*, includes the protection of personal honour[73], the right to one's own name[74], one's own word[75] and one's own image.[76] Others[77] view the right to one's own image as a subcategory of the right to informational self-*determination*, since it determines what informational value others can derive from an information carrier.[78] A distinction must be made between these legal positions and the constitutional protection against *statements* that are likely to detrimentally effect the individual's public image.[79] Additionally, in these cases the beneficiary requests that the creation of certain (inner) images be prevented. However, these "inner" images, which emerge in the statement recipient's mind, are not created by using "outer images" (e.g., photos) as information carriers, but by written or oral utterances, which give rise to the mental images in our imagination.

The numerous court cases that Princess Caroline of *Monaco*[80] conducted before the German courts, however, concerned not only the written statements about her, i.e., the textual reporting, but also the images that were published to illustrate these texts, in the Boulevard press. The first court case that *Caroline* commenced at the ECtHR concerned the publication of pictures in German tabloids showing the princess with her children and/or a male acquaintance in recognizably private situations in public (such as sporting activities, a visit to a restaurant or a market). While the lower courts approved the publication of the pictures, remarking that Caroline was a person of "contemporary history", the German Federal Court of Justice[81] ("Bundesgerichtshof", BGH) prohibited the publication of a picture showing the princess together with her male acquaintance exchanging inti-

72 BVerfGE 6, 32 – *Elfes*; 32, 373 (379) – *Ärztliche Schweigepflicht*; see, Gusy (2003) 104.
73 BVerfGE 54, 208 (217) – *Böll*.
74 BVerfGE 104, 373 (387) – *Ausschluss von Doppelnamen*.
75 BVerfGE 54, 148 (155) – *Böll*.
76 BVerfGE 35, 202 (220) – *Lebach*.
77 See, e.g., Britz (2008) 71.
78 This is a recognizable continuation of the view mentioned above (I.2.), according to which (external) images are to be treated like other data or information.
79 BVerfGE 99, 185 (193) – *Scientology*; 114, 339 (346) – *Mehrdeutige Meinungsäußerungen*.
80 Who since her (third) marriage with Prince Ernst August of Hanover in 1999 is known as Caroline of *Hanover*.
81 BGH, 19.12.1995 = BGHZ 131, 332.

macies on the terrace of a garden restaurant. Although the terrace was public, the princess had recognizably withdrawn to the "local seclusion" and thus expressed her desire for privacy and her trust that this expectation of being left alone would be respected by third parties. The remaining images, however, could be published. The constitutional complaint filed against this judgment was only successful insofar as the BVerfG[82] upheld the decision of the BGH and additionally prohibited the publication of images showing the children of the princess. In addition to the general right of personality, the right to family (Art. 6 (1) GG) was affected.[83] The publication of the other images, on the other hand, was – according to the BVerfG – covered by freedom of the press.

3. *Caroline before the European Court of Human Rights (ECtHR)*

Caroline then filed an individual appeal against this decision with the ECtHR, arguing that it violated her right to respect for private life under Art. 8 of the ECHR. For the ECtHR, such a case was uncharted territory as there was only one previous case on video recordings of unknown persons in public spaces.[84] With *Caroline* of Hanover, however, the ECtHR were dealing, for the first time, with a prominent complainant who simultaneously held no public office. This is significant because in previous decisions, the Court was inclined to recognize a legitimate interest in reporting on such public officials, such as members of government,[85] because the transparency of their actions is an important element of democracy. In contrast, reporting on a private person – albeit a famous one – who does not exercise sovereignty could only be recognized under very strict conditions.[86] In doing so, the ECtHR clarified that the social status of a person, except for sovereign activity, had no effect on whether the scope of Art. 8 ECHR is affected.[87] However, a person's celebrity may be a consideration

---

82 BVerfG ruling 1 BvR 653/96 of 15 December 1999 = BVerfGE 101, 361 – *Caroline von Monaco II*.

83 Ibid. 385 et seq.

84 See for instance ECtHR, 17.07.2003, No. 63737/00 para. 37 – *Perry*; ECtHR, 4 May 2000, No. 28341/95 para. 43 et seq. – *Rotaru*; ECtHR, 28 January 2003, No. 44647/98 para. 53. – *Peck*.

85 See for instance ECtHR, 23 April1992, No. 11798/85 para. 46 – Castells; ECtHR, 25 June 2002, No. 51279/99 para. 56 – *Colombani (King of Morocco)*; Neukamm (2007) 228 et seq.

86 ECtHR, 24 June 2004, No. 59320/00 para. 72. – *Caroline von Hannover I*.

87 Ibid. paras. 50–53; EGMR, 21 February 2002, Nr. 42409/98 – *Schüssel*.

in weighing the freedom of the press.[88] Furthermore, the ECtHR made it unmistakably clear that the right to privacy protects not only conduct within a spatially secluded private sphere, but also activities in public[89], if a person may reasonably trust that this will be respected, which was the case here.[90]

Regarding the balance between *Caroline's* private life and the freedom of expression and freedom of the press (Art. 10 ECHR), the ECtHR held that since Caroline did not exercise sovereign powers, she was not a public figure and therefore enjoyed the same protection of privacy as all other private persons.[91] There was hence no general public interest in the private life of such a private person. This merely served one single purpose, namely "... to satisfy the curiosity of a particular readership regarding the details of the applicant's private life"[92]. Consequently, both the text and the photo coverage of *Caroline's* private life had to be prohibited.

The case clarified that it must be taken into account to what extent the person concerned actively shields himself or herself from photojournalism or, on the contrary, may have "attracted" the photojournalism in the first place through correspondingly permissive behavior.[93] In general, the circumstances under which the pictures are taken must also be considered. The more it becomes apparent that the taking of the photographs was perceived as a nuisance for those depicted, the more priority is to be given to the protection of privacy.[94] Furthermore, the intention with which the images are used is also important. If the pictures only serve to satisfy the curiosity of uninvolved third parties[95] (e.g., the readers of a newspaper) and thus to achieve an economic profit[96], priority is to be given to private

88 ECtHR, 24 June 2004, No. 59320/00 paras. 54 et seq. and 61 et seq. – *Caroline von Hannover I.*

89 Ibid. para. 69.

90 Ibid. paras. 51, 53, 69.

91 ECtHR, 24 June 2004, No. 59320/00 para. 62 – *Caroline von Hannover I.*

92 Ibid. para. 65. – Contrary to the German BVerfG, the EctHR thus limited the legitimacy of reporting on individuals' private lives to the private life of politicians, ibid., para. 63 (only in the case of politicians "the press exercises its vital role of 'watchdog' in a democracy by contributing to 'impart[ing] information and ideas on matters of public interest'").

93 According to BVerfG ruling 1 BvR 653/96 of 15 December 1999 = BVerfGE 101, 361 (385) – *Caroline von Monaco II* the person who actively seeks the public has lost his protection of privacy.

94 ECtHR, 24.06.2004, No. 59320/00 paras. 59, 68 – *Caroline von Hannover I.*

95 Ibid. paras. 65, 68.

96 Ibid. para. 77.

life. And finally, it also depends on the range of effects of the dissemination. The wider this range is, the more privacy is to be protected.

4. *Comparison between the three decisions*

All these decisions have granted the famous complainants protection of privacy outside their own four walls and thus a right to "privacy in public". Here the ECtHR went significantly further than the BVerfG which merely required an active effort to ensure privacy. Simultaneously, the ECtHR set higher standards for photojournalism than, for example, the BVerfG, by stating that a legitimate interest in persons who are not politically active "cannot in principle be denied".[97] The importance of the information should only be taken into account in the process of balancing the right to privacy with other rights such as the freedom of the press or other legitimate interests under Art. 8 (2) ECHR.[98] Under Italian law, the legitimate interest must in turn be checked to ensure that it does not harm the reputation, honor or standing of the person depicted. The decisions of the three courts are therefore quite close in terms of their analysis.

However, the legal construction of the acknowledged right to "privacy in public" is different. The Italian *Corte di Cassazione* was comparatively brief in its general comments, as the right to privacy ("*riservatezza*") primarily serves as a barrier to the conflicting fundamental rights of communication. This construction makes the protection of the privacy of the person depicted more of a concern to be weighed up than an independent fundamental right. This legal construction of a "right to privacy" as a barrier of other rights has prevailed until today.[99] The ECtHR likewise tends to respect the specific needs for privacy protection by balancing the right to a private life (Art. 8 ECHR) with and other human rights. However, the ECtHR also provides a more detailed instruction on how to execute the balancing. For example, one can consider the negative effects of (adverse) image reporting on the private life of the person depicted, which can result both from making (keyword: harassment) and publishing the images. German constitutional law however has more extensive requirements on the use of images. The general right of personality protects, in the form of the

97 BVerfG ruling 1 BvR 653/96 of 15 December 1999 = BVerfGE 101, 361, para. 101 – *Caroline von Monaco II*.

98 Ibid.; BVerfGE 34, 269 (283) – *Soraya*.

99 Ubertazzi (2004) 72–79.

right to self-*determination* and self-*presentation*, not only the right to create one's own "self-image", but also to communicate and maintain this image to the outside world. The result can be a right to suppress "outer" images that deviate from the "self-image" and are embodied in photographs, to suppress the emergence of certain foreign images that contradict the self-image.

It is recognized, however, that there is not and cannot be a general claim to suppress "foreign images", may they be "outer" (e.g., photos) or "inner" (e.g., imaginations) images[100], since "foreign images" are not only an important prerequisite of all communication; they are ultimately unavoidable, true to Paul Watzlawick's saying, "You cannot not communicate."[101] A legal system can therefore only be concerned with suppressing *certain* images of others. For example, because they were obtained under circumstances that violate the private (as in the case of *Caroline*), the intimate sphere of the person depicted, or because they are linked to characteristics that should not be linked based on the prohibition of discrimination so that racist or misogynistic images of others are not created.[102] It is therefore not a question of guaranteeing the *identity* of the "self-image" and the "foreign images". This would indeed be incompatible with the communication freedoms of third parties. Rather, the aim is to suppress such images of others that are based on the unlawful acquisition or transmission of information. As a result, constitutional law, and statutory law, which together decide the illegality of the acquisition and transmission of information, become the decisive medium for conveying the claims to "self-images" and "foreign images".

IV. Soraya and Caroline 2.0: The Impact of Digitalization

It is no coincidence that the two princesses, *Soraya* and *Caroline*, sued major tabloid newspapers with their lawsuits. After all, these tabloids were particularly capable of distorting the plaintiffs' "self-image". This is probably due not only to the high circulation of tabloid newspapers, but because they make extensive use of "outer images" (in this case: photos) to support their reports. And these *outer* images are particularly suitable for creating or changing "inner" images (imaginations) in the recipient

---

100 Britz (2008) 62.

101 http://www.ciando.com/img/books/extract/3456956002_lp.pdf.

102 See on this Britz (2008) 62 et seq.

about the person depicted, hence they modify their "foreign images" in the public. Here, it is exposed to a principally unlimited communication, during which it can take on constant new meanings. The release of this communicative force in turn may explain why a "turn to the image" has been noticeable in mass and individual communication for several decades. This is essentially due to two developments: first, to an increased use of "outer" images in communication (photos, movies, but also new forms like emojis), and second, to an increasing penetration of more and more areas of social life by images. Against this background – especially in philosophy and cultural studies – the desideratum of an "image science" has been formulated. This desire is expressed in the (more or less, strongly) programmatically intended buzzwords "imagic turn" (*Ferdinand Fellmann*[103]), "pictorial turn" (*W.J.T. Mitchell*[104]), "iconic turn" (*Gottfried Boehm*[105]) or "visualistic turn" (*Klaus Sachs-Hombach*[106]). In the following, it will be shown to what extent digitalization additionally promotes and accelerates these developments. In doing so, the paper intends to focus on the effects of digitalization on "outer" (1.), "inner" (2.) and the relationship between outer and inner images (3.).

1. *Impact on "outer" images*

Digitalization and especially Internet-based information and communication technology (ICT) creates entirely new possibilities for creating and disseminating "outer" images. Nowadays, practically everyone carries a smartphone and thus a photo camera around with them to use it at any time. The "outer" images obtained in the process are made accessible to certain third parties or a basically unlimited public via the numerous channels provided by the Internet. This has resulted in a veritable "flood of

---

103 Fellmann (1991), who sees images no longer merely as systems of symbols, but as relational structures that can provide an adequate foundation for a theory of mind.

104 Mitchell (1994) 11 et seq., and (1997). Mitchell is concerned with an analysis of the use of images in everyday culture and in the sciences with the aim of rehabilitating thinking in images.

105 Boehm (1994) who is more concerned with immunizing the "aura" (Walter Benjamin) of artworks against the inflationary use of images.

106 Sachs-Hombach (2009) who is skeptical about the term "turn", at least if it is supposed to refer to a similar upheaval as the "linguistic turn" initiated by Wittgenstein and others, which at least resulted in a turn of philosophy away from the philosophy of consciousness towards linguistics.

images"[107], the evaluation of which probably depends on the perspective. For professional photographers and other creators, the insight that digital photography makes it possible for every user to become a photo artist without further ado[108] could be described on the one hand as the "democratization" of art, but on the other hand also as its "banalization". For recipients, the increasing visualization of communication – for example, through photos, videos, emojis or memes – can be perceived as either a gain in information, or a sensory overload. And finally, the evaluation of the increasing communication of *outer* images (e.g., photos of individuals published online) from the perspective of those portrayed probably depends decisively on the extent to which the communicated image of others is compatible with self-images.

Analysing this phenomenon a little further, let us first turn to the effects of digitalization on outer *foreign* images. Much of what has been said could also apply to outer *self-images* which have gained astonishing popularity in the age of digitalization in the form of the "selfie"[109]. Regardless of whether they are foreign or self-images, digital images are always "outer" images in the sense of digitally encoded data or information. As such, they are accessible via the World Wide Web within a very short time to an audience of hitherto unknown dimensions all over the world – and at any time. What represents a phenomenal progress from the point of view of communication freedoms is an enormous problem from the perspective of protecting personality and privacy (see IV.2 below).

In relation to the individual ("outer") image, the conclusion seems obvious that it is in danger of being lost in the flood of images. This is likely to lead to an even greater loss of the "aura" of the image than *Walter Benjamin* stated at the beginning of the age of photography.[110] Indeed, as a data and information carrier, each digital image is a set of data without an embodied potentially accessible by any computer connected to the Internet. At the same time, the modern technology of digital image processing offers numerous possibilities for image manipulation[111] which may once again contribute to discrediting the aura of images even more. Finally, images – especially because of their emotional resonance – can be commer-

107 Dreier (2019) 36 and 313 ("Bilderflut"); see also Ullrich (2022).

108 Ohashi (2018) 241 et seq.

109 This is emphasized, e.g., by Wulf (2018), 196 et seq; see also Ullrich (2019).

110 Benjamin (1935/1996) 11 et seq.

111 See the contribution by Hägle (2022), as well as the various contributions in: Dreier/Jehle (2020); Baudrillard (1991), 112 points out the danger of a "hyperreality" in this context.

cialized[112] through various online channels to an even greater extent than previously. On the other hand, precisely because of their ubiquity, digital images are also able to achieve effects that "analogue" images can only achieve with difficulty. Because they can be transmitted and retrieved globally, they easily cross not only national borders, but also cultural contexts. Also, it is typically no longer individual people who "steer" the "fate" of an image, but at best emergent collectives of people.[113] However, one could also formulate the assumption that images are increasingly taking on a life of their own in the age of digitalization.[114]

2. *Impact on "inner" images*

The ubiquity of ("outer") images described above is likely to have an impact in many respects on the emergence of "inner" (foreign and self-) images. What exactly these effects are is a question that should be answered by (media) psychologists or cultural scientists. A (constitutional) analysis of these effects must limit itself to some tentative assumptions[115]: first, it is conceivable that the ubiquity of "outer" images leads to a loss of "inner" images, for example in the form of a lack of imagination. Incidentally, something similar could be said for the reduction of other mental performances, such as those of memory: if the Internet, due to the circumstances just outlined (Section 4.1), really does not forget[116], it functions as an externalized collective memory whose reservoir of outer images can then be accessed on an occasion-related basis.

The information value of images, as already stated above[117], is to be judged as ambivalent. On the one hand, images seem to be suitable to simplify complex issues and to communicate information independently of the medium language. This is likely to be an invaluable advantage, especially in a globally networked world. However, this could also entail the danger of reducing the ambiguity inherent in the language of the text and thus contributing to a "unification of the world"[118]. On the other hand,

---

112 Dreier (2019) 185.
113 See, e.g., Münker (2009).
114 To that effect already Bredekamp (2010).
115 For a summary of the argument developed in this article from a constitutional see Chapter V.
116 Dreier (2019), 44.
117 See I.2.
118 See Bauer (2018).

there are many indications that images can convey far more information than text, so that a global discourse on images could perhaps even enable entirely new sensory horizons and forms of communication.[119]

3. *Impact on the relationship between the "inner" and "outer image"*

While one may only speculate about the effects of digitalization on the emergence of "inner" images from the perspective of (constitutional) jurisprudence, it is at least possible to make somewhat more substantial statements about the effects of digitalization on the relationship between "inner" and "outer" images. First, the Internet, with its unimaginably large quantity of (outer) images, leads to their increasing internalization, i.e., their reception by a previously unknown quantity of people. At the same time, inner images can also be digitally externalized (e.g., selfie) making them accessible again for internalization in this form. Digitalization thus offers the fundamental rights of communication – both those of the "sender" and those of the "recipient" – previously unimagined potential for development. The use of digital image technology poses a threat above all to the fundamental rights of those who are depicted in foreign (third-party) or self-images or whose (intellectual) property owns the outer images, namely if third parties use these images against the consent of the holders of the fundamental rights. Clear and effective rules for dealing with digital images are needed to protect the fundamental rights to privacy, general personal rights and property that are affected in this respect, and these rules must be outlined in the following concluding section.

V. *In the End: Constitutional Requirements for the Dissemination of Digital Images*

Constitutional law protects both the use of "outer" and "inner" images. "Outer" images can be an important medium of fundamental communication rights (e.g., freedom of expression, freedom of the press or freedom of art), while the formation of "inner" images falls under the constitutional protection of privacy. This fundamental right, which – with varying scope

119 See in this respect, e.g., the attempts of an intercultural theory of images by Seitz/Graneß/Stenger, Bildtheorie und Interkulturalität (2018) 1 et seq.

and based on different legal constructions – is recognized in German, Italian and European law, also protects the freedom to form an (inner) "self-image". At the same time, this freedom does not extend so far as to interfere with the freedom of others to form a foreign image of others. There is therefore no constitutional claim to the identity of self-image and image of the other. However, the right to privacy does offer protection, as the *Caroline* case in particular demonstrates, against extremely distorting images of others. For example, against extreme deviations from self-image and image of others, whereby the conflicting fundamental rights of communication must also be observed in this respect. Thus, it is not the case that the European and the Member States' (fundamental) legal systems do not yet have rules for resolving these conflicts of fundamental rights. On the contrary, the comparative case study (IV.) has just shown that the Italian, the German, and the European constitutional law have found dogmatic ways to resolve the conflict between private life and the protection of personality with fundamental rights of communication. Despite all the disruptions, it has caused, digitalization does not directly give cause to reject the aforementioned models of balancing the affected interests. The need to use "outer" images as a means of communication has remained just as relevant in the digital age as the need to create "inner" ("self" and "foreign") images. At most, it would be worth considering making certain adjustments where digitization has shifted the "balance of power" between privacy or protection of personality and communication freedoms.

One such attempt is the "right to be forgotten" developed in the literature[120], adopted by the CJEU[121] and now codified in Article 17 of the General Data Protection Regulation (GDPR). This right responds to the fact that information (may they be text or images) circulating on the Internet is typically stored not only on one web server, but several servers or end devices. This information can also be shared again from these sources at any time. This is to be expressed with the sentence that the Internet "does not forget". In this respect, the right to be forgotten is not just a conventional right to delete a digital image (or other sorts of information) on a website from the respective content provider. Rather, the right to be forgotten also obliges service providers such as search engines to delete the corresponding links, thus making it more difficult to access these images. Thus, to find a corresponding digital image, one must firstly know of its existence and secondly, the website on which it was published.

120 Mayer-Schönberger (2011).

121 ECJ, Case C-131/12 of 13.5.2014 – *Google Spain*.

The extent to which further requirements for dealing with digital images arise from European or member state constitutional law on the protection of private life or personality protection depends on the respective constitutional legal system. The higher the requirements are, the greater the need for action. If – as in Italian law, for example – only the dissemination of degrading or defamatory images is to be prohibited, such a rule is easier to achieve than the high standard of "image sovereignty"[122] that underlies the German right to informational self-determination. As far as can be seen, German, Italian and – except for the "right to be forgotten" – European constitutional law has so far relied on the balancing models developed for the "analogue world" and lack standards that would respond specifically to the changing digital "reality of images" (IV.). If further standards were applied by the courts, it would make sense, in the opinion of the author, to closely review the intention for which the image was published or disseminated. If, for example, an image is only used to harm others, as it happens often in the context of "hate speech", this should weigh in favour of the privacy of the person depicted. This applies above all – evidently – to manipulated images. In contrast, the dynamic and rapid dissemination of images on the Internet means that it is probably only possible to determine the target group of an image ex post, i.e., at a point in time when it is already too late. Finally, the standards of (image) ethics could provide orientation. Here, the authenticity / genuineness of the image would come to mind, which would be expressed in the current consideration model at best under the aspect of intention. Thus, if an image is recognizably manipulated, for example to use it for "hate speech" or "fake news" purposes, then this intention must be utilized in favour of privacy when weighing it against freedom of expression. For other aspects, the (legally non-binding) press code for print journalists (NPPA Code of Ethics) could serve as a model. Ultimately, however, it is solely up to the constitutional courts, the ECtHR and the CJEU to establish these rules.

---

122 Critical on this Belting (2001) 50: "... der Mensch" sei "nicht als Herr seiner Bilder" anzusehen, "sondern als Ort der Bilder, die seinen Körper besitzen." (quoted from Dreier (2019) 32). ("… man (is not to be regarded) as the master of his images, but as the locus of the images that possess his body").

References

Baer, Susanne (2004): 'Schlüsselbegriffe, Typen und Leitbilder als Erkenntnismittel und ihr Verhältnis zur Rechtsdogmatik', in: Schmidt-Aßmann, Eberhard/Hoffmann-Riem, Wolfgang: *Methoden der Verwaltungsrechtswissenschaft* (Baden-Baden: Nomos 2004) 223–251

Baudrillard, Jean (1991): *Der symbolische Tausch und der Tod* (München: Mattes & Seitz 1991)

Bauer, Thomas (2018): *Die Vereindeutigung der Welt: Über den Verlust an Mehrdeutigkeit und Vielfalt* (Stuttgart: Reclam 2018)

Beach, Lee Roy (1993): 'Image theory – A normative alternative to decision theory', NA Advances in Consumer Research Vol. 20 (1993) 235–238 (https://www.acrwebsite.org/volumes/7441/volumes/v20/NA-20)

Behrmann, Carolin (2019): 'Gericht aus Glas', in: Münkler, Laura/Stenzel, Julia: *Inszenierung von Recht, Funktionen – Modi – Interaktionen* (Weilerswist: Vellbrück 2019) 74–94

Belting, Hans (2001): *Bild-Anthropologie – Entwürfe für eine Bildwissenschaft* (München: Wilhelm Fink 2001)

Benjamin, Walter (1935/1996): *Das Kunstwerk im Zeitalter seiner technischen Reproduzierbarkeit. Drei Studien zur Kunstsoziologie* (ed. Frankfurt: Suhrkamp 1996, originally published 1935)

Boehm, Gottfried (2015): *Wie Bilder Sinn erzeugen – Die Macht des Zeigens* (Berlin: Berlin University Press 4th edition 2015)

Boehm, Gottfried (1994): *Was ist ein Bild?* (München: Wilhelm Fink 1994)

Böhme-Neßler, Volker (2010): *BilderRecht – Die Macht der Bilder und die Ohnmacht des Rechts – Wie die Dominanz der Bilder im Alltag das Recht verändert* (Berlin/Heidelberg: Springer 2010)

Bredekamp, Horst (2010): *Theorie des Bildakts* (Frankfurt: Suhrkamp 2010)

Britz, Gabriele (2008): *Freie Entfaltung durch Selbstdarstellung – Eine Rekonstruktion des Allgemeinen Persönlichkeitsrechts aus Art. 2 I GG* (Tübingen: Mohr Siebeck 2008)

Classen, Claus Dieter (2018), 'Commentary of Article 22', in: von Mangoldt, Herrmann/Klein, Friedrich/Starck, Christian, edited by Huber, Peter/Voßkuhle, Andreas: *Grundgesetz-Kommentar* (C.H. Beck 7th edition München: 2018)

Damler, Daniel (2019): 'Sichtbarkeit und Unsichtbarkeit im Recht des 20. Jahrhunderts', in: Münkler, Laura/Stenzel, Julia: *Inszenierung von Recht, Funktionen – Modi – Interaktionen* (Weilerswist: Vellbrück 2019) 95–124

Deleuze, Gilles (1968/1992): *Differenz und Wiederholung* (München: Wilhelm Fink 1992, originally published 1968)

Depenheuer, Otto/Froese, Judith (2018): 'Commentary of Article 14', in: von Mangoldt, Herrmann/Klein, Friedrich/Starck, Christian, edited by Huber, Peter/Voßkuhle, Andreas: *Grundgesetz-Kommentar* (München: C.H. Beck 7th edition 2018)

Dreier, Thomas (2019): *Bild und Recht – Versuch einer programmatischen Grundlegung* (Baden-Baden: Nomos 2019)

Dreier, Thomas/Jehle, Oliver (eds) (2020): *Original – Kopie – Fälschung* (Baden-Baden: Nomos 2020)

Dreier, Thomas/Schulze, Gernot (2022): *Urheberrechtsgesetz, Verwertungsgesellschaftengesetz, Kunsturhebergesetz* (München: C.H. Beck 7th edition 2022)

Fellmann, Ferdinand (1991): *Symbolischer Pragmatismus – Hermeneutik nach Dilthey* (Reinbek: Rowohlt 1991)

Franceschelli, Bruno (1960): *Il diritto alla riservatezza* (Napoli: Jovene 1960)

Geiger, Chrisophe (2022): 'Contemporary Art on Trial – The Fundamental Right to Free Artistic Expression and the Regulation of the Use of Images by Copyright Law', in: Dreier, Thomas/Andina, Tiziana: *Digital Ethics – The issue of images* (Baden-Baden: Nomos 2022) 387–415

Goldhammer, Michael (2012): *Geistiges Eigentum und Eigentumstheorie – Rekonstruktion der Begründung von Eigentum an immateriellen Gütern anhand der US-amerikanischen Eigentumstheorie* (Tübingen: Mohr Siebeck 2012)

Gusy, Christoph (2003): 'Grundrechtsschutz des Privatlebens', in: Zehetner, Franz: *Festschrift für Hans-Ernst Folz* (Wien/Graz: Neuer wissenschaftlicher Verlag 2003) 103–118

Hägle, Olivia (2022): 'From Copy & Paste to Deep Fakes – Digital Collaging and Image Manipulation', in: Dreier, Thomas/Andina, Tiziana: *Digital Ethics – The issue of images* (Baden-Baden: Nomos 2022) 207–227

Kingreen, Thorsten/Poscher (2020), Ralf: *Grundrechte – Staatsrecht II* (Heidelberg: C.F. Müller 36th edition 2020)

Leone, Massimo (2022): 'Semioethics of the Visual Fake', in: Dreier, Thomas/Andina, Tiziana: *Digital Ethics – The issue of images* (Baden-Baden: Nomos 2022) 187–205

Mayer-Schönberger, Viktor (2011): *Delete – The Virtue of Forgetting in the Digital Age* (Princeton: Princeton University Press 2011)

Mitchell, W.J.T. (1994): *Picture Theory* (Chicago: University of Chicago Press 1994)

Mitchell, W.J.T. (1997): 'Der Pictorial Turn', in: Kravagna, Christian: *Privileg Blick – Kritik der visuellen Kultur* (Berlin: Ed. ID-Archiv 1997) 15–40

Müller-Mall, Sabine (2012): *Performative Rechtserzeugung – Eine theoretische Annäherung* (Weilerswist: Vellbrück 2012)

Müller-Tamm, Lorenz (2022): 'Portrait or Personal Data – The Rivalry of Image and Data Protection Legislation', in: Dreier, Thomas/Andina, Tiziana: *Digital Ethics – The issue of images* (Baden-Baden: Nomos 2022) 239–252

Münker, Stefan (2009): *Emergenz digitaler Öffentlichkeiten – Die sozialen Medien im Web 2.0.* (Frankfurt: Suhrkamp 2009)

Münkler, Laura (2016): 'Metaphern im Recht – Zur Bedeutung organischer Vorstellungen von Staat und Recht', 55 Der Staat (2016) 181–211

Münkler, Laura/Stenzel, Julia (2019): *Inszenierung von Recht, Funktionen – Modi – Interaktionen* (Weilerswist: Vellbrück 2019)

Neukamm, Kathrin (2007): *Bildnisschutz in Europa – Zugleich ein Beitrag zur Bedeutung der Verfassungsüberlieferungen der EU-Mitgliedstaaten und der EMRK für die Auslegung der Unionsgrundrechte* (Berlin: Duncker & Humblot 2007)

Ohashi, Ryosuke (2018): 'Bildkunst und Kunstbild – Befinden wir uns im Zeitalter des "Weltbildes" oder der "Weltbilder"?', in: Seitz, Sergej/Graneß, Anke/Stenger, Georg: *Facetten gegenwärtiger Bildtheorie – Interkulturelle und interdisziplinäre Perspektiven* (Wiesbaden: Springer VS 2018) 231–242

Pugliese, Giovanni (1954): 'Il preteso diritto alla riservatezza e le indiscrezioni cinematografiche', Foro italiano, 1954, I, 118–120.

Raue, Benjamin: 'The Multi-Layered Information in a Digital Image', in: Dreier, Thomas/Andina, Tiziana: *Digital Ethics – The issue of images* (Baden-Baden: Nomos 2022) 229–237

Sachs-Hombach, Klaus (2009): 'Einleitung', in: Sachs-Hombach, Klaus: *Bildtheorien – Anthropologische und kulturelle Grundlagen des Visualistic Turn*, Frankfurt a.M.: Suhrkamp 2009) 7–16

Seitz, Sergej/Graneß, Anke/Stenger, Georg (2018): 'Bildtheorie und Interkulturalität', in: Seitz, Sergej/Graneß, Anke/Stenger, Georg: *Facetten gegenwärtiger Bildtheorie – Interkulturelle und interdisziplinäre Perspektiven* (Wiesbaden: Springer VS 2018) 1–18

Seitz, Sergej/Graneß, Anke/Stenger, Georg (2018): *Facetten gegenwärtiger Bildtheorie – Interkulturelle und interdisziplinäre Perspektiven*, Wiesbaden: Springer VS 2018)

Ubertazzi, Tommaso Maria (2004): *Il diritto alla privacy, natura e funzione giuridiche* (Pavia: Casa Editrice Dott. Antonio Milani 2004)

Ullrich, Wolfgang (2022): 'From Works to Living Means of Communication – The Digital Image and the "Iconic Turn"', in: Dreier, Thomas/Andina, Tiziana: *Digital Ethics – The issue of images* (Baden-Baden: Nomos 2022) 127–135

Ullrich, Wolfgang (2019): *Selfies – Die Rückkehr des öffentlichen Lebens* (Berlin: Wagenbach 2019)

Vesting, Thomas (2011–2015): *Medien des Rechts – Sprache* (Volume 1), *Schrift* (Volume 2), *Buchdruck* (Volume 3), *Computernetzwerke* (Volume 4) (Weilerswist: Vellbrück 2011–2015)

Vicari, Marcella (2007): *Das Informationsrecht und das Recht auf Privatsphäre in Italien* (Baden-Baden: Nomos 2007)

Vismann, Cornelia (2007): 'Bildregime des Rechts – Rechtsregime des Bildes', in: Joly, Jean-Baptiste/Vismann, Cornelia/Weitin, Thomas: *Bildregime des Rechts* (Stuttgart: Edition Solitude 2007) 15–32

Volkmann, Uwe (2009): 'Leitbildorientierte Verfassungsauslegung', 134 Archiv des öffentlichen Rechts (2009) 157–196

Wulf, Christoph (2018): 'Bilder des Menschen: Die Visualisierung des Unsichtbaren – Materielle, informative und ikonische Perspektiven', in: Seitz, Sergej/Graneß, Anke/Stenger, Georg: *Facetten gegenwärtiger Bildtheorie – Interkulturelle und interdisziplinäre Perspektiven* (Wiesbaden: Springer VS 2018) 193–212

Zech, Herbert (2012): *Information als Schutzgegenstand des Rechts* (Tübingen: Mohr Siebeck 2012)

Chapter 21
Contemporary Art on Trial – The Fundamental Right to Free Artistic Expression and the Regulation of the Use of Images by Copyright Law

Christophe Geiger[*]

I. Copyright, Appropriation Art and Artistic Freedom

1. Appropriation art's discontents with copyright

Undeniably, copyright – or authors' right, as the legal protection of authors is called in countries following a continental European tradition – aims to protect the interests of authors of creative works. In this sense, the interest of *all* authors should be protected, including those that have created and those who will create or are already in the creative process. However, recently, authors of visual arts are increasingly at odds with copyright legislation. The reason is that copyright legislation, based on traditionalist author's rights conceptions, clearly privileges initial creations over any form of copying, partial taking, repetition or creative reuses of protected works. This is highly problematic for many forms of contemporary art expressions which stem from a long-standing artistic tradition: from Marcel Duchamp's famous ready-mades to Andy Warhol's use of famous brands, commercials or photographs of pop culture icons, different forms of appropriation art have become the main characteristic of a whole array of artistic activities in postmodern times.[1] In fact, many artists frequently use such a process, primarily by reworking elements protected by intellectual property rights (copyright, trademark, or designs rights) for the purpose of criticism or homage, their aim being to trigger artistic reflection on society and its current icons. Appropriation therefore plays a central role in the modern and contemporary art movements, original

---

* This contribution draws from and is building upon previous articles by the author on the same subject; see Geiger (2021); Geiger/Izyumenko (2019) and (2020a).

1 On this issue, see already Bauer (2022) and (2020); see also before the turn of the century, e.g., Sandler (1996).

works being sometimes modified, transformed, or even reused without any alterations in a new artistic context.

Fortunately, most creative appropriations are not subject to copyright infringement litigation because, given their frequency, such litigation would likely lead to seizure of the contemporary art collections of many of the world's major museums.[2] Without doubt, these artistic activities tremendously benefit from the ease of copying by way of digital technology; however, as technology became a central component of everyday life, artists also incorporated digital technology and its evolutions – including the opportunities and dangers of it – in their artistic discourse.[3] Appropriation and copying became an essential tool to reflect on the control of images and on the role that copyright itself plays in our information society.[4] "Infringing" copyright is then even sometimes "elevated" to a militant act and is used to expose the negative effect of the copyright system on society.

However, such cases (fortunately) only occasionally end up before the courts, usually when two factors are present, sometimes in combination.[5] The first is extrinsically linked to the success of the derivative work in question. If it is successful, the author of the appropriated work is likely to consider him or herself entitled to a share of the fruits of that success. The second is when the appropriation harms the reputation of, or is contrary to the idea behind, the original work or is simply objected to by the original

---

2 Museums can in addition to the artists also be liable for copyright infringement, to the extent an exhibition can be considered as an act of communication to the public.

3 For an example see the first Strasbourg biennale of Contemporary art on the topic "Touch me – Being a citizen in the Digital age" organized at the end of 2018, "inviting the public to consider our relationship with new technologies and how the internet has profoundly affected our behavior and society" (https://biennale-strasbourg.eu/en/).

4 See for example the fascinating work of artists such as Paolo Cirio, who are putting appropriation at the core of their artistic and politic message (see https://paolocirio.net/). For example, in his 2019 work called "Property", Paolo Cirio "examines images as a form of capital accumulation, bound by intellectual property laws, trade agreements, legal contracts, and litigations" in order to "reflect on the stock photography company Getty's dominance in the market, capitalization, and control of images on the Internet" and in order to do so, the artist "adopts the semantics of appropriation art through transforming images into compositions of colored shapes and texts, which overlay with the prints of the original photos appropriated from Getty's websites". Copying therefore becomes a necessary part of an artistic reflection and a way to expose the negative impact of the abusive use of legal tools such as copyright.

5 For more detail of some of these cases see Geiger (2018b).

author. The latter occurs primarily in cases in which the derivative work contains a criticism of the primary work.

To illustrate the problem appropriation art faces when confronted with copyright law in the courtroom, exemplary reference shall be made to one very prominent case adjudicated by the French courts. The facts of the case are as follows: The painter Peter Klasen, a member of the artistic movement known as Narrative Figuration,[6] incorporated into his paintings three photographs from an Italian fashion journal showing the face of a young model after colouring them blue (Figs. 1 and 2).

Figs. 1 and 2: Left: Alix Malka, photograph for the Fashion magazine "Flair" (2005); Right: Peter Klasen, Painting

Justifying his appropriation of the photographs as symbols of excessive consumption, Peter Klasen stated that the objective of his artistic approach was to use advertising images in his paintings to provoke reflection by the spectator, thereby placing the initial work in a new context and expressing something entirely new and unexpected. Whereas in the first instance

6 On this artistic movement, which often intends to give art a political dimension, see Pradel (2008); Wilson (2010).

the Paris District Court held that the photographs lacked originality,[7] the Paris Court of Appeal overruled that decision, finding that the photographer's choices reflected genuine aesthetic decisions that were an imprint of his personality as an author and, consequently, that the photographs at issue were deserving copyright protection.[8] The application of the parody, quotation, and incidental use exceptions were all rejected. The only remaining defence available to the painter was to claim it was a legitimate use supported his fundamental right to free artistic expression. However, the Court of Appeal dismissed this argument, holding that there was no higher public interest that would justify the rights of a derivative artist prevailing over those of an original work's author. The court held that freedom of expression can be limited to protect other individual rights, and that the reworking of visual material in Klasen's work could not reasonably permit him to ignore the rights of the original photographer. The French Supreme Court however surprisingly reversed the Court of Appeal ruling based on Article 10 of the ECHR.[9] The Supreme Court criticized the appellate judges for not having explained "*in the specific case* the manner in which the search for a fair balance between the fundamental rights at issue required the decision as pronounced" (emphasis added).

2. *The traditional approach: narrow interpretation of exceptions and internal control by fundamental rights*

Before discussing the French Supreme Court's reversal of the Paris Court of Appeal decision in more detail, it should be noted that traditionally fundamental rights played a limited role when deciding copyright cases for mainly two reasons: first, according to the traditional author's right doctrine, exceptions to copyright should be interpreted narrowly which does not leave room for extensive interpretations in the light of, e.g., free-

7 Tribunal de Grande Instance Paris (Paris Court of First Instance), of 31 January 2012, No. 10/02898 (Fr.).

8 Cour d'Appel de Paris (Paris Court of Appeal), Pole 5, 1st Chamber, 18 September 2013, No. 12–02480 (Fr.).

9 Cour de Cassation (French Supreme Court), 1st Civil Chamber, 15 May 2015, Bull. Civ. 1, No. 13/27391. – It seems however worth mentioning that already at the end of the 1990s, in the "Utrillo"-case, the Paris District court had allowed the use of copyright protected work to report on current events based on the fundamental right to information protected by Art. 10 ECHR, Tribunal de Grande Instance of Paris, 3rd chamber, 23 February 1999, No. 98–7053. On this issue see Geiger (2007).

dom of expression.[10] This doctrine was by and large accepted by French courts, but also, initially, the European Court of Justice (CJEU).[11] This is despite significant doubts regarding its legitimacy raised by scholars against this traditional approach.[12] Moreover, it was traditionally assumed that any balancing of fundamental rights which affected the interests of the parties involved had already been undertaken by the legislature, when crafting within copyright legislation the limitations and exceptions, such as those contained in Article 5 of the Information Society Directive.[13] In other words, the control of conflicts which touched upon the protection and balancing of fundamental rights only takes place *internally* within the copyright law itself.[14]

As a result, once a reproduction or communication to the public was found and no limitations or exceptions applied, the facts of the case proved to be immune against any additional *external* fundamental rights control. That is, unless national copyright law provided for some additional limitation to the adaptation right, such as the so-called "free use" according to Section 24 of the German Copyright Act, which permitted partial taking of someone else's copyrighted work, if the taking was made particularly for purposes of freedom of information and freedom of the arts.[15]

10 See on this issue Geiger/Schönherr (2014), Geiger (2010) and (2016), criticising this approach of restrictive interpretation of limitations and exceptions often used by national courts in continental author's right countries or the CJEU, but which is not mandated by the copyright legal and theoretical framework nor the rationale of copyright law. For detailed analysis see also recently Rendas (2021).

11 See only CJEU, C-5/08 of 16 July 2009, ECLI:EU:C:2009:465 – Infopaq.

12 See, e.g., Geiger/Schönherr (2012); Geiger (2010) and (2016b).

13 Directive 2001/29/EC of the European Parliament and of the Council of 22 May 2001 on the harmonisation of certain aspects of copyright and related rights in the information society, O.J. EU L 167 of 22 June 2001, 10 et seq.

14 See for example in this sense the French Supreme Court of 13 November 2003, Bull. Civ. I, No. 01-14385 (Fr.). For comment, see Geiger (2004b); Belgian Supreme Court of 25 September 2003, Auteurs et médias 2004, 29, holding in an abstract manner that "the freedom of expression guaranteed by Article 10 of the European Convention on Human Rights and by Article 19 of the International Treaty concerning Civil and Political Rights does not prevent the protection of a literary or artistic work by copyright".

15 For comment, see, e.g., Loewenheim (2020) notes 1 et seq.; Schulze (2018) notes 1 et seq.

II. External Control in the Light of Freedom of Artistic Expression

However, recently an increasing use of fundamental rights in copyright disputes in many civil law countries can be observed.[16] This development challenges the assumption that copyright interests can only be balanced against fundamental rights internally, not externally. In addition, this development raises the question whether a sort of "fair use" limitation modelled after the US precedent[17] is not already in place through the weighing of interests and use of the proportionality test, which are both required when the judiciary is applying fundamental rights.[18] This change in approach by the courts can be witnessed in many civil law jurisdictions across Europe, and even by the CJEU, thus strengthening the argument for the introduction of an open clause for limitations in EU copyright law.

1. Fundamental Rights and the CJEU

Whereas in the beginning, the CJEU largely left the national Member States to balance conflicting rights,[19] after the adoption of the European Charter of Fundamental Rights in 2012, the CJEU, in its judgements, not only continuously referred to European fundamental rights, but increasingly applied and balanced them in the cases referred to the Court.[20]

As can be seen from the three recent decisions *Funke Medien*, *Pelham*, and *Spiegel Online*,[21] as a matter of principle, the CJEU, in essence, adopts quite a liberal position towards the national courts' interpretation of existing copyright norms in the light of the freedom of expression require-

---

16 More generally on this trend, see Geiger (2006), (2009) and (2012).

17 Title 17 U.S.C. § 107. – For discussion of the U.S. "fair use"-test see below, IV.1.

18 For further discussion of the principle of proportionality, see Christoffersen (2015); Afori (2014); Geiger/Izyumenko (2018) and (2020).

19 See only, regarding the conflict of copyright, i.e., property protection, with the protection of personal data before the adoption of the General Data Protecting regulation (GDPR), CJE, case C-275/06 of 29 January 2008, ECLI:EU:C:2008:54 – Promusicae.

20 See, e.g., CJEU case C-314/12 of 27 March 2014, ECLI:EU:C:2014:192 – UPC Telekabel Wien (also regarding copyright and data protection). Since the cases are too numerous to be cited here, for further references, see only Geiger (2016b); Griffiths (2018); van Deursen/Snijders (2018).

21 CJEU, cases C-469/17 of 29 July 2019, ECLI:EU:C:2019:623 – Funke Medien NRW; C-476/17 of 29 July 2019, ECLI:EU:C:2019:624 – Pelham and others; and C-516/17 of 29 July 2019, ECLI:EU:C:2019:625 – Spiegel online.

ments. The Luxembourg judges fully accept that fundamental rights take part in shaping copyright law in the EU. The CJEU explicitly refers to the need to interpret at least copyright law's *internal* norms in such a manner that freedom of expression, including freedom of the press and freedom of artistic creativity, are sufficiently protected and balanced against each other.[22] The CJEU goes even as far as to term the exceptions listed in Article 5 of the Information Society Directive not as "exceptions" as such, but as self-sufficient "rights" of users of copyright-protected subject matter.[23]

However, as further discussed below,[24] it may not be overlooked that the great emphasis on fundamental rights, did not hinder the CJEU to limit their consideration to the interpretation of copyright's *internal* limitations and exceptions, thus unequivocally rejecting any *external* free-wheeling application of fundamental rights. This position taken by the CJEU openly conflicts with the stance taken by another European Court on the same matter: the European Court of Human Rights (ECtHR).[25]

2. *Fundamental Rights and the ECtHR*

The ECtHR determined in *Ashby Donald*[26] that a prohibition on the communication of works on the Internet, even in breach of copyright, might constitute a violation of freedom of expression. Hence, even where there has been a clear copyright infringement, it is always necessary to evaluate whether the resulting restriction to freedom of expression is "necessary in a democratic society". After pointing out that "freedom of expression constitutes one of the essential bases of a democratic society, one of the basic conditions for its progress and the development of each individual," the ECtHR confirmed that "it involves exceptions that in any event require a narrow interpretation, and the need to restrict it must be established convincingly."[27] The court thus clarified that intellectual property rights must be interpreted as exceptions to freedom of expression and that, given the great importance of that freedom within the framework of a democrat-

22 See Jütte (2020) 481–482.
23 For an extensive comment see Geiger/Izyumenko (20201); Dreier (2020).
24 See below, III.2.
25 For a discussion see Goldhammer (2021).
26 Ashby Donald v. France, App. No. 36769/08, of 10 January 2013; see also the so called "Pirate Bay" decision (Neij & Sunde Kolmisoppi v. Sweden, App. No. 40397/12 of 19 February 2013).
27 Ashby Donald v. France, App. No. 36769/08, para. 38.

ic society, judges need to be very careful in the presence of a restriction, particularly when it comes to political and artistic speech.[28]

3. Other national jurisdictions

Even in France, considered an exemplar of traditional reasoning in copyright matters, a recent and highly commented-upon decision of the French Supreme Court concerning the balancing of freedom of artistic expression with copyright has paved the way for a judicial *in concreto* assessment of copyright limitations. In the *Klasen v. Malka*-case already referred to above,[29] the French Supreme Court reversed the Court of Appeal ruling based on Article 10 of the ECHR. By doing this, the French Supreme Court ended a debate that had been raging for over 15 years on the application of fundamental rights in the intellectual property arena and, more precisely, on the manner in which a fair balance is to be struck between copyright and freedom of expression, even outside existing internal copyright limitations and exceptions.

Courts in other jurisdictions have also gone into the same direction. One should also mention the German Constitutional Court, which stated in two cases that the proper legal understanding of the quotation exception must be expanded and interpreted more extensively to guarantee the protection of artistic freedom. This would reinforce the notion that copyright exceptions must be read in the light of such freedom to strike a balance between various interests.[30] In sum, there is a clear tendency to apply the principle of proportionality in copyright to legitimize the freedom of artistic expression in diverse situations of creative appropriation.

---

28 In this sense, see Geiger (2004a); Porsdam (2007); Geiger/Izyumenko (2014).

29 Cour de Cassation, 1e civ., May 15, 2015, Bull. Civ. 1, No. 13/27391.

30 The first case decided by the German Constitutional Court (Bundesverfassungsgericht, BVerfG), 1 BvR 825/98 of 29 June 2000, Gewerblicher Rechtsschutz und Urheberrecht (GRUR) (2001) 149, concerned an extensive interpretation of the quotation right in a theatrical play (for non-official English translation, see Adeney/Antons (2013)); the second case, 1 BvR 1585/13 of 31 May 2016, Gewerblicher Rechtsschutz (GRUR) (2016) 690 – Metall auf Metall about the sampling of snippets of someone else's phonogram. – For other jurisdictions, see Geiger (2021) 179 et seq.

III. *Resistance to Change and the Internalization of a (Limited) Flexibility by Way of Fundamental Rights*

1. *Resistance to change: the improper use of the proportionality test by the judiciary in copyright cases*

However, despite this tendency to apply the principle of proportionality in copyright to legitimize the freedom of artistic expression in diverse situations of creative appropriation, a number of trial courts have continued to support a more restrictive approach. These include the *Koons v. Bauret* decisions by the Paris District Court[31] later confirmed by the Paris Court of Appeal,[32] the *Koons v. Davidovici* decisions by the Paris District Court[33] also recently confirmed by the Paris Court of Appeal[34], and the remittal decision by the Versailles Court of Appeal in the case *Klasen v. Malka.*[35] However, only a few cases shall be briefly discussed here to serve as examples of the pitfalls when it comes to improperly referring to fundamental rights.[36]

Koons v. Bauret centered on a postcard featuring a black-and-white photograph of two naked children holding hands, taken in 1970 by Jean-François Bauret (Fig. 3), that the American artist Jeff Koons had used as inspiration in 1988 in designing the porcelain sculpture Naked as part of his "Banality" series (Fig. 4).

The Paris District Court welcomed the argument that Article 10 ECHR protects the freedom of artistic creativity, stating that assessing the facts on a case-by-case basis is required to guarantee a fair balance between copyright and freedom of expression. The Paris District Court began the justification of

31 Tribunal de Grande Instance [TGI] de Paris (Paris District court of first instance), 3rd Chamber, *Succession Bauret c. Jeffrey Koons et le Centre national d'art et de culture Georges Pompidou*, 9 March, 2017, No. 15–01086 (Fr.).

32 Cour d'appel de Paris (Paris Court of Appeal), Pole 5, 1st Chamber, 17 December 2019 (No. 152/2019). The Court of Appeal simply confirmed the decision of the Paris District court and the factual assessment by the first instance judges without much argumentation, far from a proper proportionality analysis required by article 10 ECHR. Therefore, the following developments will concentrate on the Paris district court decision, not on the Appeal decision.

33 Tribunal de Grande Instance [TGI] de Paris (Paris District Court of First instance), 3rd Chamber, 8 November 2018, *Koons and Centre Georges Pompidou vs Davidovici* (No. 15/02536).

34 Cour d'appel de Paris (Paris Court of Appeal), Pole 5, 1st Chamber, 23 February 2021 (No. 034/2021); for comment see Sutterer (2022).

35 Cour d'appel (CA) de Versailles (Versailles Court of Appeal), 1st Chamber, 16 March 2018, No. 15/06029, Dalloz IP/IT (2018) 300.

36 For more detailed discussion, see Geiger (2021) 185 et seq.

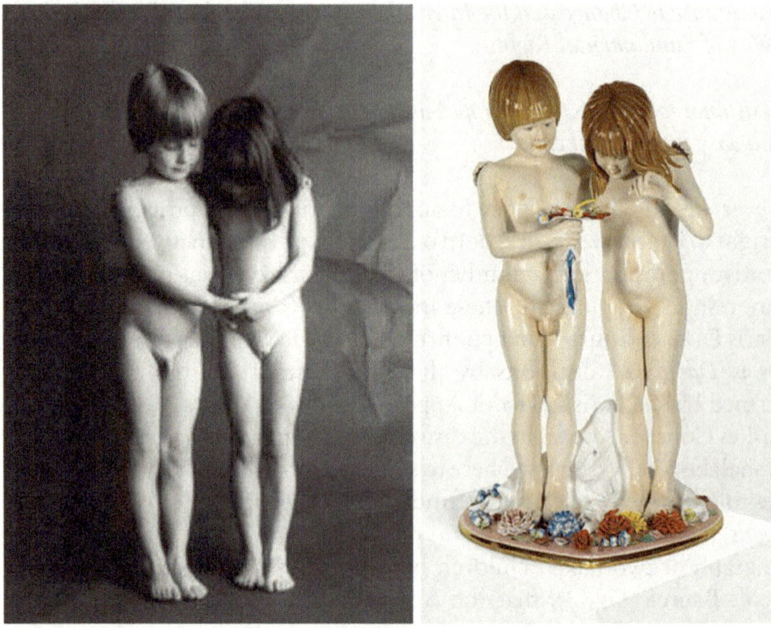

Figs. 3 and 4: Left: Jean-François Bauret (photograph, 1970); right: Jeff Koons, "Naked" (porcelain sculpture, 1988)

its ruling by highlighting that the weight of the right to freedom of expression is intrinsically linked to the type of discourse used in the given circumstance (political speech enjoying greater protection than commercial speech). The judges considered it necessary to ascertain whether the situation concerned the reuse of copyright for commercial intent or for a higher public interest purpose in order to properly measure the impact on that fundamental right. This stance was clearly a consequence of the ECtHR's approach and the aforementioned *Klasen*-decision of the French Cour de cassation. However, in appreciation of the particularities of the case, the court concluded that the creative use in question should not be allowed, as Koons had failed to justify the imperative necessity of using Bauret's photograph without seeking the photographer's prior authorization. It seems worth noting that to arrive at this conclusion, the Paris court surprisingly reversed the burden of proof. Rather than placing the burden on the photographer to demonstrate that the restriction of free speech by invoking his copyright was justified, the Paris Court placed the burden on the creator of the artistic reuse, who was to prove that the restriction was indeed necessary and imperative for the benefit of a democratic society. This is an incorrect understanding of how Article 10 ECHR should be applied in copyright cases, as it implies that the artist must justify his creative choices to the court. Moreover, neither the argument concerning the particularities of the artistic movement of which the work of art was a part of, nor the description of the aim of the individual sculpture or series of sculptures was evaluated with the attention it deserved. Instead, the Paris judges came rather close to judging the artistic merits of the sculpture in question, and even the pertinence and legitimacy of the art movement to which Koons belongs.

Thus, the judges seemed to be assessing his art rather than limiting themselves to matters of law,[37] which entails a strong risk of interfering in the artistic process, potentially leading to a denial of the artist's intellectual and creative freedom. Rather, judges should be extremely prudent in their rulings when asking for artistic justifications, such as in the U.S., where the Court of Appeals for the Second Circuit, overturning a decision of the lower trial court, concluded that the appropriation by the artist Prince in the way of inserting a photograph taken by Patrick Cariou of a Rastafari man (Fig. 5) constituted "fair use" (Fig. 6).[38] As Valérie-Laure Benabou has pointed out, the judges in these two French cases seemed alarmingly interested in assessing the merits of particular works of art, which has traditionally been considered undesirable when it comes to copyright, as judges are not to play the role of art critics.[39]

Moreover, the Paris court held that for an artist's reuse to be justified by Article 10 ECHR, the public must have knowledge of the primary work, as only then can the reuse provoke a reflection. However, on the facts, the primary work was unknown to a broader audience.

It thus seems that the Paris court confused the requirements of the parody exception, for which a reference to the original work is of major importance, with those of artistically creative re-appropriation, which is protected under Article 10 of the ECHR. In this respect, the judges seemed to imply that Koons had run out of inspiration and wanted to save himself the effort of creating something new. However, this way of reasoning not only fails to understand the process behind creative appropriation, but also the notion that the core of a new work is based on an existing work of art. Such reasoning not only deprives French citizens of access to a major piece of art by a

---

37 Sharing this concern, see Treppoz (2017) 440.

38 United States Court of Appeals for the Second Circuit in *Cariou v. Prince* 714 F. 3d 694 (2d Cir. 2013).

39 Benabou (2018).

renowned 20th-century artist, but also prevents the artist from publicly conveying his artistic message.

Figs. 5 and 6: Left: Patrick Cariou, photograph from "Yes, rasta" (2000); Right: Prince, work from "Canal Zone" (2008)

In the *Klasen v. Malka*-case, the Court of Appeals reasoned similarly. First, the court stated that Peter Klasen, who had invoked his freedom of expression in defence, must establish the extent to which a fair balance between the protection of his rights and those of the original work's right-holder should be sought to justify his failure to obtain authorization for use of that work. Second, because of that failure, the court considered that Klasen's unauthorized use of the photographs in question had not been indispensable for the exercise of freedom of expression he was claiming. Although Klasen admitted that the primary work was perfectly capable of being substituted by any other advertising photographs of similar kind for achieving the same means, he nevertheless explained sufficiently well that his rationale for using the photographs was to expose how cultural materials convey a message about consumer society. However, in the eyes of the court, this justification was not sufficient. It held that the painter had failed to explain exactly why he had chosen these particular photographs, even though his explanation made it clear that the appropriated material was part of his creative process, if not the heart of his artistic speech. In addition, quite like the Paris District Court in its *Koons v. Bauret*-decision, the Versailles Court of Appeal based its decision on the additional argument that the photographs appropriated were not known to the public. Using notoriety as a yardstick to measure the level of protection a work of art deserves is rather odd. In reality, it is not the notoriety of a piece of art that might permit its appropriation, but rather the artistic reasoning behind that appropriation.[40] If this stance had been adopted in the two aforementioned cases, the uses would undoubtedly have been deemed permissible.

Figs. 7 and 8: Top: Franck Davidovici, photograph from 1985 used in a commercial of the brand "Naf-Naf" entitled "Naf-Naf. Le grand méchant look"; Bottom: Jeff Koons, "Fait d'hiver", porcelain sculpture, taken from the serie "Banality", 1988

40 Benabou (2018) 301.

These same surprising arguments were re-used by the Paris Court of first instance and of Appeal[41] in the *Koons and Centre Georges Pompidou vs Davidovici* case, where it was alleged that Jeff Koons had infringed the copyright of a photographer when using the image of an advertisement campaign (Fig. 7) as a point of departure for one of his sculptures (Fig. 8).

The Paris court found no violation of Article 10 ECHR and that there was no disproportionate restriction of the artist's freedom of artistic expression, as no artistic dialogue was possible since the original work was unknown. Very surprisingly, the court considered that the artist just wanted to spare a creative effort.

Regarding the freedom of artistic creativity and its protection in the case, the Paris Court of Appeal had another surprising argument. According to the Court, the message by Jeff Koons was an act of artistic creation and not political or related to questions of general interest, and would thus benefit from a weaker protection with regard to Article 10 ECHR.[42] Because Jeff Koons was a top selling artist, the Court held that his artistic project had a commercial nature.[43] Noting that commercial speech is less protected then political speech, the Court thus considered, with regard to the European Convention, that copyright justified a proportionate and necessary restriction of Jeff Koons artistic freedom. Such a position seems to misunderstand completely the case law of the European Court of Human Rights on the issue of freedom of artistic expression.[44] On the contrary, according to the Strasbourg Court, "freedom of artistic expression [...] affords the opportunity to take part in the public exchange of cultural, political and social information and ideas of all kinds [...]. *Those who create, perform, distribute or exhibit works of art contribute to the exchange of ideas and opinions which is essential for a democratic society.* Hence there is an obligation on the State not to encroach unduly on the author's freedom of expression [...]."[45] Works of art benefit on the contrary from a particular

41 See the references supra, notes 33 and 35.

42 Cour d'appel de Paris (Paris Court of Appeal), Pole 5, 1st Chamber, 23 February 2021 (No. 034/2021) 22; see also note 34.

43 The Court of Appeal even cites the price paid for the sale of one of Jeff Koons' works: "En outre, comme le relève à juste raison M. DAVIDOVICI, qui produit un article extrait du site internet du Monde en date du 16 mai 2019 qualifiant l'artiste de '*commercial hors pair*' et faisant état de la vente d'une de ses oeuvres, 'Rabbit', adjugée au prix record de 91,1 million de dollars, la démarche artistique de Jeff KOONS n'est pas dénuée de caractère commercial" (ibid., p. 22).

44 For more detail see Geiger (2018a).

45 ECtHR, *Alınak v. Turkey*, no. 40287/98, 29 March 2005, para. 42 (emphasis added).

strong conventional protection. The fact that the art is sold (and even very well sold!) does not diminish in any way the public interest dimension of the artwork. Nor does the fact that a newspaper is sold diminishes the protection that journalists enjoy by freedom of information.

Typically, commercials or advertising are considered commercial expressions.[46] Categorizing Jeff Koons' artwork as commercial is not only contrary to the artistic understanding of his role (and other artists from the same appropriation-art movement) in contemporary art, but it is moreover dangerous and discriminatory as it implies an artistic judgement of the judges on the merit of his work, denying him a public interest dimension. When copyright is used as a vehicle for taste, we are close to censorship and the darkest hours of our civilization. It is thus very much hoped that Jeff Koons will take the case to the French Supreme court who should, in accordance with its *Klasen* decision, ask for a better motivation from the Appeal judges to restrict freedom of artistic creativity, as there have been manifest errors in the proportionality analysis of the Paris Court.

2. *CJEU: Internalization of a (limited) room to manoeuvre using fundamental rights*

Although the CJEU has recognized that the freedom of expression and its balancing factors play a crucial role in shaping the contours of copyright, and although in applying freedom of expression to EU copyright, the CJEU has largely relied on the case law of the European Court of Human Rights,[47] the Luxembourg Court nevertheless indicates in its recent decisions *Funke Medien*, *Pelham*, and *Spiegel Online*[48] that an externally introduced flexibility (by means of complementing that already existing in the EU list of exceptions) could be harmful to copyright harmonization and legal certainty. Therefore, despite having taken a more favourable position on the possibility of shaping EU copyright by fundamental rights norms, the CJEU does not completely adopt this approach since it considers, in quite categorical terms, that an *external* exception of freedom of expression beyond the exhaustive list of limitations of Article 5 of the Information So-

46 Geiger/Izyumenko (2020b) 580, noting that advertising is one of typical forms of commercial speech protected by the European Convention on Human Rights.

47 See above, II.

48 CJEU, cases C-469/17 of 29 July 2019, ECLI:EU:C:2019:623 – Funke Medien NRW; C-476/17 of 29 July, 2019, ECLI:EU:C:2019:624 – Pelham and others; and C-516/17 of 29 July 2019, ECLI:EU:C:2019:625 – Spiegel online.

ciety Directive is clearly unacceptable. According to the CJEU, copyright's own internal mechanisms present sufficient safety valves for balancing with freedom of expression.

Even if *Funke Medien* and *Spiegel Online* did not involve the artistic use of images, in both cases fundamental rights were at stake, namely freedom of information and of the press.[49] The former related to the publication of internal governmental reports and the latter to the republication of an older book. Similarly, in *Pelham*, the court addressed the conflict between the property right of copyright owners and freedom of the art as a two-second snippet was taken from a phonogram of the German band "Kraftwerk" in the song of another German pop artist and played on loop.[50] However, the rejection of an external application of fundamental rights outside the exceptions listed in Article 5 of the Information Society Directive – and, one might add, the additional exceptions to copyright's exclusive right created by Articles 4–6 of the Digital Single Market Directive[51] – undoubtedly also applies to copyright protected images.

The problem with the CJEU's approach, however, is that the list of copyright exceptions and limitations contained in Article 5 of the Information Society is both limited and exhaustive. According to this approach, unless the existing exceptions for "quotations for purposes such as criticism or review", and for "the purpose of caricature, parody or pastiche"[52]

---

49 Article 11(1) second sentence of the European Charter of Fundamental rights (freedom of information) and Article 11(2) of the Charter (freedom of the press).

50 Article 17(2) of the Charter (protection of intellectual property), and Article 13 of the Charter (Freedom of the arts and sciences).

51 Directive (EU) 2019/790 of the European Parliament and of the Council of 17 April 2019 on copyright and related rights in the Digital Single Market and amending Directives 96/9/EC and 2001/29/EC, O.J. EU L 130 of 17 May 2019, 92 et seq.

52 Article 5 (3) (d) and (k) of the Information Society Directive. See in this sense the interesting recent decision by the First instance Court of Rennes (Tribunal judiciaire de Rennes), 2nd civ. Chamber, 10 May 2021, *Société Moulinsart v. Xavier Marabout*, involving paintings by a French contemporary artist showing Tintin (the famous comic figure created by Hergé) in the environment of the painter Edward Hopper (the 1950s in the US) together with sexy girls. The Court considered that the conditions for parody were fulfilled: immediate identification of the work subject of parody, humor or criticism (here the mixture of the asexual Tintin put in the universe of US 1950s with reference to Hopper), as well as no confusion with the original work. The Court also considered that since parody is justified by freedom of expression, there is a need to assess on a case by case basis if a fair balance has been found between the interest of the artist and those of rightholders. It concluded, quoting almost verbatim a famous decision

can be made operational, artistic uses of someone else's copyrighted material cannot be justified. There is only one other limitation which provides for some sort of flexibility, but apart from only allowing takings of "minor importance", the exception is limited to analogue uses and does not apply to digital uses. Moreover, such exceptions are only permissible if they have been part of national law prior to the adoption of the Information Society Directive in 2001.[53] But not all artistic uses can be described as "quotations for purposes such as criticism or review", or for "the purpose of caricature, parody or pastiche", unless such exceptions are broadly interpreted in the light of fundamental rights.

To provide sufficient flexibility in this respect, the German Copyright Act contains a limitation which allows so-called "free uses" of copyrighted material were permissible if the material taken "faded away" behind the new work.[54] The CJEU, however, declared this national provision to be incompatible with EU law.[55] Rather, in *Pelham*, the CJEU assumed that the freedom of the arts may well limit the scope of the exclusive rights which in this case was the reproduction right of a phonogram of Article 2(c) of the Information Society Directive. However, the court accepted such a limitation of the exclusive right only in cases where the material taken was "unrecognizable" to the consumer.[56] Needless to point out that this is not a true limitation of the exclusive right based on the freedom of artistic creation, since if what has been taken from the existing work is not recognizable in the new work, by definition no copyright infringement exists in the first place.

In sum, regarding artistic works which are not covered by any of the named copyright exceptions and limitations of Article 5 (3) of the Information Society Directive, the CJEU only seems to pay lip service to the

---

of the German Constitutional court on the interface of freedom of the arts and copyright law (see above, note 30): "The potential violation of copyright is of small range and entails only a small if not hypothetical financial loss for the claimants. In this case, the freedom of artistic expression and the artist's interest to use the work freely in the context of an artistic confrontation must prevail over the simple financial concerns of the claimants". The exception for parody is thus read "in the light" of freedom of expression to allow the use in question, showing that extensive interpretation of the existing exceptions can help to justify some contemporary art uses.

53 Article 5 (3) (o) of the Information Society Directive.

54 Sec. 24 of the German Copyright Act. For discussion see Bauer (2022).

55 CJEU, case C-476/17 of 29 July 2019, ECLI:EU:C:2019:624, paras. 56 et seq. – Pelham and others.

56 Ibid. para. 31.

freedom of the arts as enshrined in the European Charter of Fundamental Rights. Although, admittedly, the CJEU is the last arbiter in these questions, it is argued here that the opinion of the CJEU itself which relies on the fact that the legislature has anticipated all the potential conflicts between copyright and higher-ranking norms such as fundamental rights, might be incompatible with the EU legal order. It remains to be seen, how the conflict between the position taken by the CJEU on the one hand, and of the ECtHR on the other hand,[57] will be resolved in light of the future pending accession of the EU to the European Convention on Human Rights.[58] Hence, a different solution is needed, given the protection and importance fundamental rights deserve.

IV. Proposal of a European Style "Fair Use" Grounded in Freedom of Expression

It is apparent that unless one adopts a reading of the CJEU decisions which not only considers fundamental rights when interpreting statutory exceptions to the exclusive rights, but also when determining the scope of the exclusive rights in the first place, the internal control of copyright through fundamental rights remains rather limited. If the fundamental right to free artistic creativity and the use of images by copyright law are to be sufficiently supported, this present contribution advocates that the legislator introduce into the EU copyright framework an open provision based on the freedom of expression balancing-test.[59]

It should be noted, however, that such internalization through the implementation of a new exception for uses made for creative purposes is not a totally new idea. In fact, it was clearly considered to be a potentially viable option by the European Commission[60] a good decade ago, and was also envisaged as a possibility by the European Parliament in a resolution dated July 9, 2015.[61] In the same spirit, a group of European academics

57 See above, II.2.

58 For discussion see Geiger/Izyumenko (2020a) 301 et seq.

59 For a more detailed discussion see Geiger/Izyumenko (2019). – On an economic merit of reflecting on open, "fair use" like clauses, see, among others, Flynn/Palmedo (2017).

60 Commission of the European Communities (2008).

61 European Parliament Resolution (2015) para. 42, in which the European Parliament "notes with interest the development of new forms of use of works on digital networks, in particular transformative uses, and stresses the need to examine solutions reconciling efficient protection that provides for proper remuneration and fair compensation for creators with the public interest for access

working on the European Copyright Code project proposed the adoption of a general clause covering all uses justified by freedom of expression that are not provided for by existing EU legislation.[62] In a similar vein, scholars have proposed to implement a new use privilege for User-Generated Content which, combined with the obligation to pay equitable remuneration, would satisfy all requirements of international copyright law such as the three-step test and create a new revenue streams for creators.[63]

Even if currently an EU "fair use" does not as such (yet) exist, the search for possible theoretical models of its construction might, however, be unnecessary. Surprising as it may seem, in Europe we might already have some sort of "fair use". As highlighted above,[64] in recent years it has been gradually shaped by courts through the application of the right to freedom of expression and information to copyright disputes. The fundamental right to freedom of expression is characterised by a developed list of balancing factors that have been elaborated throughout the years of the human rights jurisprudence in Europe.

V. The U.S. "Fair Use" Exception

Overall, these balancing factors of the courts resemble to the American "fair use" factors. In the EU, these factors include: 1) the character of expression (commercial or not; artistic; etc.); 2) the purpose and nature of expression/ information at stake (political; cultural; entertaining; otherwise in the general interest); 3) the status of a counterbalanced interest and the degree of interference with it; 4) availability of alternative means of accessing the information; 5) the timing/ "oldness" of speech; 6) the status of the speaker/ user (active or "passive"; press; etc.); 7) the form of expression; 8) the medium of expression (notably, the Internet); and 9) the nature and severity of the penalties; etc.[65]

It should be noted that these factors reveal some striking similarities with the fairness factors to be found in the US "fair use doctrine". US "fair use" includes four factors which are non-exhaustive (meaning that new

---

to cultural goods and knowledge". For a comment, see Geiger/Bulayenko/Hassler/Izyumenko/Schönherr/Seuba (2015).

62 Wittem Project (2010); see, in particular Dreier (2013).

63 See only Senftleben (2020); Quintais (2017), in particular chapter 6, 365 et seq.

64 See II.

65 Geiger/Izyumenko (2014).

additional factors can be identified by the courts) and some of which split, in turn, into several important subfactors[66].

Factor 1 is the purpose and character of the use. It encompasses the following subfactors: commerciality of the use; transformativeness; and correspondence of the use to one of the preambular purposes or the purposes analogous to them. Preambular purposes include criticism, comment, news reporting, teaching, scholarship, and research. Educational purpose is further identified in the wording of factor 1 itself. Non-commercial, transformative use for one of the purposes considered to be socially valuable would tilt towards the finding of fair use in American case law.

Factor 2 deals with the nature of the copyrighted work. Here again, two important subfactors stand out: the published or unpublished nature of the work and its fictional or factual character. More protection is usually given to creative/fictional works and to those works that have not yet been published (although some case law to the contrary exists as well).

Factor 3 concerns itself with the amount and substantiality of the copyrighted work that has been used (quantitatively and qualitatively[67]).

Finally, factor 4 looks at the effects of the use on the potential market for or value of the copyrighted work. Alongside transformativeness and commerciality, it is often claimed to be one of the most influential factors.

Some further factors have sometimes been identified in addition to the statutory ones. Those include: how long the copyrighted work has been on the market; the refusal to license; the existence of a market failure; the availability of alternative means (or, almost along the same lines, necessity or availability of a work to a user); custom; failure to utilize the technical protection measures; acknowledgement of source material; good faith or "propriety of the defendant's conduct"; social desirability of the transfer of use to the defendant; and impact of an award of fair use on the incentives to create of the plaintiff copyright owner.

---

66 Several scholars have for example analyzed problems posed by appropriation art in particular in the context of the "fair use" defence of US copyright law, as in the US a certain number of copyright cases dealt with the delicate issue of what can be appropriated or not in the copyright context. See, e.g., Greenberg (1992); Jaszi (2009); Bresler (2003); Landes (2000); Hick (2013); Morley (2015); Adler (2016). For a comparative approach, see Geiger (2018a); Lucas/Ginsburg (2016); Westenberger (2018).

67 Taking even of small parts can be considered excessive if what is taken is the "heart" of the work; see, e.g., *Harper & Row v. Nation Enterprises*, 471 U.S. 539 (1985), at 600.

VI. A proposal for a European "Fair Use" Test

Admittedly, the mere transplant of a U.S.-type fair use provision would not be ideal, as the copyright systems on the two sides of the Atlantic, despite certain convergences,[68] remain different in scope and spirit.[69] Thus, as has been recently proposed, a more promising way forward – and one that is more compatible with the EU legal system – might be to codify the criteria already used by judges when balancing fundamental rights and copyright law and introduce a European fair use provision based on freedom of expression in the EU *acquis* in addition to the existing list of exceptions.[70] Such a European "fair use" grounded on freedom of expression would be not the four-factor test known from the US law but, rather, would subsist in the proportionality test. It can further be combined with an already existing list of limitations as found, currently, in Article 5 of the Information Society Directive. One possible proposal of how such a clause could be worded is presented hereby:

"1. Any other proportional use for the purpose of freedom of expression and information is permitted. In determining whether the use made of a work in any particular case is proportional, the factors to be considered shall include:
   a) the character of the use, including whether such use is commercial or transformative;
   b) the purpose of use (in the common interest or not);
   c) the nature of the information at stake;
   d) the degree of interference with the property of copyright holder, including whether the fair remuneration was paid;
   e) the availability of alternative means of accessing the information; and any other factor that might be relevant for the circumstances of the case.
2. All factors are considered in an overall assessment. In the case of 1.4), the payment of a fair remuneration subsequent to the use can

---

68 See Davies (1995).

69 See in this sense Torremans (2012). – For a detailed comparison of the different factors of the US "faire use" exception and with the factors influencing the balancing with Article 10 ECHR, see Geiger/Izyumenko (2019).

70 For more details on this text proposal see Geiger/Izyumenko (2019) 72; Calling for the introducing of an open-ended limitation in EU copyright law, see also, e.g., Senftleben (2017); Hugenholtz (2017).

re-establish its proportionality when otherwise freedom of expression and information would be unduly restricted."

Implementing an open-ended copyright clause in EU copyright law would not only be possible, but more transparent than the currently functioning external limitations to copyright (including fundamental rights) to which the judges have to recourse in the situation of a lack of appropriate legislative provision. Furthermore, a codification of the criteria of the freedom of expression balancing test would ensure a better predictability and thus an increased legal security with an ensuing harmonising effect. Finally, the "fair use" clause grounded in the European human rights tradition is, by definition, supranational, which is important in view of the EU legislator's intention of harmonisation, or even unification of IP laws, particularly significant of course in the online environment. Such clause can also reconcile, in view of the upcoming European Union's accession to the European Convention on Human Rights,[71] the current European legal framework for intellectual property rights with Europe's human rights law obligations.

VII. Conclusion

Whatever solution is adopted, it would be desirable to increase the flexibility of and the role granted to freedom of artistic expression within copyright law to better adapt legal provisions to the factual circumstances of various art movements. The failure of copyright law to take sufficient account of fundamental values such as freedom of expression ultimately risks the rejection of the entire system by creators and the general public alike if no appropriate solution is implemented.[72] In this context, the argument put forward by the EU Commission and the CJEU that flexible exceptions are not within the continental tradition, and risk increasing legal uncertainty, is not convincing as numerous other open norms can be found in continental legal systems. Moreover, the uncertainty that an open provision can generate should not be overestimated. Even in the United

---

71 See Article 6 (2) TEU as amended by Article 1 (8) of the Treaty of Lisbon, and Article 59(2) ECHR as amended by Article 17 of Protocol No. 14 to the ECHR. Although the CJEU rejected the latest draft agreement of EU accession to the ECHR (Opinion 2/13 of 18 December 2014, EU:C:2014:2454), this only delayed the accession, which remains binding on the EU.

72 See Geiger (2020).

States, whose copyright system is often presented as difficult to predict owing to the fair use clause, empirical studies over the past decade have shown that the solutions adopted by the courts can be forecast in most cases, largely disproving certain preconceived ideas on the matter.[73] The fact that more than 40 countries worldwide have adopted open clauses within the copyright arena,[74] and that many of those countries boast flourishing cultural industries, should serve to mitigate concerns and definitively permit a different view concerning open-ended clauses to limit copyright.

Of course, more fundamentally, it might be necessary to think ahead and carry out a more in-depth review of the mechanism of exclusivity in the context of derivative creations, even if doing so means considering other options for the remuneration of a work's original authors.[75] This fascinating, albeit complex, issue is, however, beyond the scope of this contribution.[76]

Whatever solution is adopted, it must necessarily guarantee that copyright cannot under any circumstances be misused for the purpose of censorship, regardless of whether the expression in question has political, cultural, or artistic intent.[77] All in all, one thing appears quite obvious: it can hardly be considered compatible with free artistic creativity in a democratic society to demand that artists seek authorization before creating a new work, or to ban its work later on from a museum because of copyright claims of contestable legitimacy. Consequently, the dissemination of contemporary art in museums and galleries could be in serious danger, as these institutions will be tempted to refuse showing certain artists in order to avoid copyright claims. At a time when even the core principles of copyright law are subject to artistic reflections and that appropriation is used as a vehicle for an artistic discourse about creativity, it is crucial to

73 Sag (2012); Beebe (2008); Samuelson (2009).

74 For the list of these countries and their legislation, see Band/Gerafi (2015).

75 On this issue see Geiger (2010), (2017) and (2018), advocating a "limitation based"-statutory remuneration system for commercial creative uses, administrated by an independent regulation authority which could solve ex post disputes between original and derivative creators on the price to be paid for the transformative use via mediation, taking into account the existing and expected revenue streams for the derivative work.

76 For a fundamental reflection, see Frosio (2018), examining the long history of creativity in order to demonstrate disparity between cumulative mechanics of creativity and modern copyright policies.

77 On the issue of censorship by way of copyrights exclusive rights, see Ortland (2021); see also Geiger (2016a).

ensure that copyright law continues to serve creators without becoming a tool for cultural censorship.

References

Adeney, Elizabeth/Antons, Christoph (2013): 'The Germania 3 Decision Translated – The Quotation Exception Before the German Constitutional Court', 35 European Intellectual Property Review (2013) 646–657

Adler, Amy (2016): 'Fair Use and the Future of Art', 91 NYU Law Review (2016) 559–626

Afori, Orit Fischman (2014): 'Proportionality – A New Mega Standard in European Copyright Law', 45 International Review of Intellectual Property and Competition Law (2014) 889–914

Band, Jonathan/Gerafi, Jonathan (2015): *The Fair Use/Fair Dealing Handbook* (polix-cybandwidth March 2015), http://infojustice.org/wp-content/uploads/2015/03/fair-use-handbook-march-2015.pdf [https://perma.cc/489F-MYUK]

Bauer, Eva-Maria (2020): *Die Aneignung von Bildern – Eine urheberrechtliche Betrachtung von der Appropriation Art bis hin zu Memes* (Baden-Baden: Nomos 2020)

Bauer, Eva-Maria (2022): 'Fairness Aspects of Techniques of Referencing Cultures', in: Dreier, Thomas/Andina, Tiziana: *Digital Ethics – The issue of images* (Baden-Baden: Nomos 2022) 137–157

Beebe, Barton (2008): 'An Empirical Study of U.S. Copyright Fair Use Opinions, 1978–2005', 156 University of Pennsylvania Law Review (2008) 549–624

Benabou, Valérie-Laure (2018): 'Comment of the decision of the Versailles Court of Appeal, 1st Ch., March 16, 2018', Dalloz IP/IT (2018) 300

Bresler, Judith (2003): 'Begged, Borrowed or Stolen – Whose Art is it Anyway? An Alternative Solution of Fine Art Licensing', 50 Journal of the Copyright Society of the USA (2003) 15–40

Christoffersen, Jonas (2015): 'Human Rights and Balancing: The Principle of Proportionality', in: Geiger, Christophe: *Research Handbook on Human Rights and Intellectual Property* (Cheltenham: Edward Elgar Publishing 2015) 19–38

Commission of the European Communities (2008): 'Green Paper – Copyright in the Knowledge Economy', COM 466 (2008)

Davies, Gillian (1995): 'The Convergence of Copyright and Authors' Rights – Reality or Chimera?', 26 International Review of Intellectual Property and Competition Law (1995) 964–989

Dreier, Thomas (2013): 'The Wittem Project of a European Copyright Code', in: Geiger, Christophe: *Constructing European Intellectual Property – Achievements and New Perspectives* (Cheltenham: Edward Elgar Publishing 2013) 292–313

Dreier, Thomas (2020): 'The CJEU, EU Fundamental Rights and the Limitations of Copyright', 69 Gewerblicher Rechtsschutz und Urheberrecht – Internationaler Teil (2020) 223–224

European Parliament (2015): 'Resolution of 9 July 2015', P8_TA-PROV(2015)0273

Flynn, Sean/Palmedo, Mike (2017): *The User Rights Database – Measuring the Impact of Copyright Balance*, Program on Information Justice and Intellectual Property (PIJIP), American University Washington College of Law (CC-BY), available at: http://infojustice.org/archives/38981 (2017)

Frosio, Giancarlo (2018): *Reconciling Copyright with Cumulative Creativity – The Third Paradigm* (Cheltanham: Edward Elgar 2018)

Geiger, Christophe (2004a): 'Fundamental Rights, a Safeguard for the Coherence of Intellectual Property Law?', 35 International Review of Intellectual Property and Competition Law (2004) 268–280

Geiger, Christophe (2004b): 'France: Intellectual Property Code, Art. L. 122–5–3; European Convention on Human Rights, Art. 10 – "Utrillo"', 35 International Review of Intellectual Property and Competition Law (2004) 717–726

Geiger, Christophe (2006): '"Constitutionalizing" Intellectual Property Law? – The Influence of Fundamental Rights on Intellectual Property in Europe', 37 International Review of Intellectual Property and Competition Law (2006) 371–406

Geiger, Christophe (2007): 'Author's Right, Copyright and the Public's Right to Information – A Complex Relationship', in: Macmillan, Fiona: *New Directions in Copyright Law Vol 5* (Cheltenham: Edward Elgar Publishing 2007) 24–44

Geiger, Christophe (2009): 'Copyright's Fundamental Rights Dimension at EU Level', in: Derclaye, Estelle: *Research Handbook of the Future of EU Copyright* (Alphen aan den Rijn: Kluwer Law International 2009) 27–48

Geiger, Christophe (2010): 'Promoting Creativity through Copyright Limitations – Reflections on the Concept of Exclusivity in Copyright Law', 12 Vanderbilt Journal of Entertainment and Technology Law (2010) 515–548

Geiger, Christophe (2012): 'Fundamental Rights as Common Principles of European (and International) Intellectual Property Law', in: Ohly, Ansgar: *Common Principles of European Intellectual Property Law* (Tübingen: Mohr Siebeck 2012) 223–238

Geiger, Christophe (2016a): 'Copyright as an Access Right, Securing Cultural Participation through the Protection of Creators' Interests', in Giblin, Rebecca/Weatherall, Kimberlee: *What if We Could Reimagine Copyright?* (Canberra: ANU Press 2016) 73–109

Geiger, Christophe (2016b): 'The Role of the Court of Justice of the European Union – Harmonizing, Creating and sometimes Disrupting Copyright Law in the European Union', in: Stamatoudi, Irini: *New Developments in EU and International Copyright Law* (Alphen aan den Rijn: Kluwer Law International 2016) 435–446

Geiger, Christophe (2017): 'Statutory Licenses as Enabler of Creative Uses', in: Liu, Kung-Chung/Hilty, Reto M.: *Remuneration of Copyright Owners – Regulatory Challenges of New Business Models* (Berlin/Heidelberg: Springer 2017) 305–327

Geiger, Christophe (2018a): 'Freedom of Artistic Creativity and Copyright Law – A Compatible Combination?', 8 University of California at Irvine Law Review (2018) 413–458

Geiger, Christophe (2018b): 'Appropriation créative et droit d'auteur – Réflexions sur les évolutions récentes de la jurisprudence française à la lumière du droit de l'Union et du droit comparé', in: *Mélanges en l'honneur du professeur Claude Witz* (Paris: LEXISNEXIS 2018) 325–348

Geiger, Christophe (2020): 'Reconceptualizing the Constitutional Dimension of Intellectual Property – An Update', in: Torremans, Paul: *Intellectual Property Law and Human Rights* (Cheltenham: Edward Elgar Publishing 4th edition 2020) 117–168

Geiger, Christophe (2021): '"Fair Use" Through Fundamental Rights in Europe – When Freedom of Artistic Expression Allows Creative Appropriation and Opens Up Statutory Copyright Limitations', in: S. Balganesh, Shyamkrishna / Ng-Loy, Wee Loon/Sun, Haochen: *The Cambridge Handbook of Copyright Limitations and exceptions* (Cambridge: Cambridge University Press 2021) 174–194

Geiger, Christophe/Bulayenko, Oleksandr/Hassler, Théo/Izyumenko, Elena/Schönherr, Franciska/Seuba, Xavier (2015): 'The Resolution of the European Parliament of 9 July 2015 – Paving the Way (finally) for a Copyright Reform in the European Union?', 37 European Intellectual Property Review (2015) 683–701

Geiger, Christophe/Izyumenko, Elena (2014): 'Copyright on the Human Rights Trial – Redefining the Boundaries of Exclusivity through Freedom of Expression', 45 International Review of Intellectual Property and Competition Law (2014) 316–342

Geiger, Christophe/Izyumenko, Elena (2018): 'Intellectual Property before the European Court of Human Rights', in: Geiger, Christophe/Nard, Craig Allen/Seuba, Xavier: *Intellectual Property and the Judiciary* (Cheltenham: Edward Elgar Publishing 2018) 9–90

Geiger, Christophe/Izyumenko, Elena (2019): 'Towards a European "Fair Use" Grounded in Freedom of Expression', 35 American University International Law Review (2019, available at https://ssrn.com/abstract=3379531) 1–74

Geiger, Christophe/Izyumenko, Elena (2020a): 'The Constitutionalization of Intellectual Property Law in the EU and the Funke Medien, Pelham and Spiegel Online Decisions of the CJEU – Progress but Still Some Way to Go', 51 International Review of Intellectual Property and Competition Law (2020) 282–306

Geiger, Christophe/Izyumenko, Elena (2020b): 'Shaping Intellectual Property Rights through Human Rights Adjudication – The Example of the European Court of Human Rights', 46 Mitchell Hamline Law Review (2020) 527–612

Geiger, Christophe/Schönherr, Franciska (2012): 'Defining the Scope of Protection of Copyright in the EU – The Need to Reconsider the Acquis regarding Limitations and Exceptions', in: Synodinou, Tatiana-Eleni: *Codification of European Copyright Law – Challenges and Perspectives* (Alphen aan den Rijn: Kluwer law Internationel 2012) 133–168

Geiger, Christophe/Schönherr, Franciska (2014): 'Limitations to Copyright in the Digital Age', in: Savin, Andrej/Trzaskowski, Jan: *Research Handbook on EU Internet Law* (Cheltenham: Edward Elgar Publishing 2014) 110–142

Goldhammer, Michael (2021): 'Taking Constitutionalization Seriously – European IP Law, Weak Fundamental Rights and the Network of Courts', 70 Gewerblicher Rechtsschutz und Urheberrecht – Internationaler Teil (2021) 544–553

Greenberg, Lynne A. (1992): 'The Art of Appropriation: Puppies, Piracy and Post-Modernism', 11 Cardozo Arts and Entertainment Law Journal (1992) 23–33

Griffiths, Jonathan (2018): 'Taking Power Tools to the Acquis – The Court of Justice, The Charter of Fundamental Rights and European Union Copyright Law', in: Geiger, Christophe /Nard, Craig Allen/Seuba, Xavier: *Intellectual Property and the Judiciary* (Cheltenham: Edward Elgar Publishing 2018) 144–174

Hick, Darren Hudson (2013): 'Appropriation and Transformation', 23 Fordham Intellectual Property Media and Entertainment Law Journal (2013) 1155–1195

Hugenholtz, P. Bernt (2017): *Flexible Copyright – Can EU Author's Rights Accommodate Fair Use?*, in: Okediji, Ruth: *Copyright Law in an Age of Limitations and Exceptions* (Cambridge: Cambridge University Press 2017) 275–291

Jaszi, Peter (2009): 'Is There Such A Thing As Postmodern Copyright?', 12 Tulane Journal of Technology and Intellectual Property (2009) 105–121

Jütte, Bernd Justin (2020): 'Finding the Balance in Copyright Law – Internal and External Control Through Fundamental Rights', in: Torremans, Paul: *Intellectual Property Law and Human Rights* (4th ed., Alphen aan den Rijn: Kluwer Law International, 2020) 461–483

Landes, William M. (2000): 'Copyright, Borrowed Images, and Appropriation Art – An Economic Approach', 9 George Mason Law Review (2000) 1–24

Loewenheim, Ulrich (2020): 'Commentary on § 24 of the German Copyright Act', in: Schricker, Gerhard/Loewenheim, Ulrich: *Urheberrecht* (München: C.H. Beck 6th edition 2020)

Lucas, André/Ginsburg, Jane (2016): 'Copyright, Freedom of Expression and Free Access to Information', 249 Revue internationale du droit d'auteur (2016) 4–153

Morley, Jacqueline (2015): 'The Unfettered Expansion of Appropriation Art Protection by the Fair Use Doctrine – Searching for Transformativeness in Cariou v. Prince and Beyond', 55 IDEA (2015) 385–416

Ortland, Eberhard (2022): 'Algorithmic Censorship of Online Visual Content – Ethical, Political, and Economic Rationales', in: Dreier, Thomas/Andina, Tiziana: *Digital Ethics – The issue of images* (Baden-Baden: Nomos 2022) 323–334

Porsdam, Helle (2007): 'On European Narratives of Human Rights and Their Possible Implications for Copyright', in: Macmillan, Fiona: *New Directions in Copyright Law Vol. 6* (Cheltenham: Edward Elgar Publishing 2007) 335–358

Pradel, Jean-Louis (2008): *La Figuration Narrative* (Paris: Hazan 2008)

Quintais, João Pedro (2017): *Copyright in the Age of Online Access: Alternative Compensation System in EU Law* (Alphen aan den Rijn: Kluwer law International 2017)

Rendas, Tito (2021): *Exceptions in EU Copyright Law – In Search of a Balance between Flexibility and Legal Certainty* (Alphen aan den Rijn: Kluwer Law International 2021)

Sag, Matthew (2012): 'Predicting Fair Use', 73 Ohio State Law Journal (2012) 47–91

Samuelson, Pamela (2009): 'Unbundling Fair Uses', 77 Fordham Law Review (2009) 2537–2621

Sandler, Irving (1996): *Art of the Postmodern Era – From The Late 1960s To The Early 1990s* (New York: Basic Books 1996)

Schulze, Gernot (2018): 'Comment on § 24 of the German Copyright Act', in: Thomas Dreier/Gernot Schulze: *Urheberrecht* (München: C.H. Beck, 6th edition 2018)

Senftleben, Martin (2017): 'The Perfect Match – Civil Law Judges and Open-Ended Fair Use Provisions', 33 American University International Law Review (2017) 231–286

Senftleben, Martin (2020): 'User-Generated Content – Towards a New Use Privilege in EU Copyright Law', in: Aplin, Tanya: *Research Handbook on Intellectual Property and Digital Technologies* (Cheltenham: Edgar Elger Publishing 2020) 136–162

Sutterer, Moritz (2022): 'Paris Embraces Modern Art – But Not in Court: Opinion on the Cour d'Appel de Paris Decision Jeff Koons v Franck Davidovici', 71 Gewerblicher Rechtsschutz und Urheberrecht International (2022) 131 – 138

Torremans, Paul (2012): 'The Perspective of the Introduction of a European Fair Use Clause', in: Synodinou, Tatiana-Eleni: *Codification of European Copyright Law – Challenges and Perspectives* (Alphen aan den Rijn: Wolters Kluwer 2012) 319–338

Treppoz, Edouard (2017): 'Retour sur la dénaturation contextuelle du Dialogues des Carmélites – Comment on Cass. 1re civ., 22 June 2017 – G. Bernanos et al. c/ D. Techerniakov, Bel Air Media et al.' (Montrouge: Légipresse 2017) 438

van Deursen, Stijn/Snijders, Thom (2018): 'The Court of Justice at the Crossroads – Clarifying the Role for Fundamental Rights in the EU Copyright Framework', 49 International Review of Intellectual Property and Competition Law (2018) 1080–1097

Westenberger, Paula (2018): *Cultural Palimpsests: Artistic Reuses in Brazil in the Context of Copyright and Human Rights* (London, unpublished Ph.D. dissertation: Queen Mary University of London 2018)

Wilson, Sarah (2010): *The Visual World of French Theory – Figurations* (Nw Haven, CT: Yale University Press 2010)

Wittem Project (2010): *European Copyright Code* (http://www.copyrightcode.eu April 2010)

Photo credits

Fig. 1: Alix Malka/Flair; https://ipkitten.blogspot.com/2018/03/french-court-finds-appropriation-of.html

Fig. 2: Peter Klasen; https://ipkitten.blogspot.com/2018/03/french-court-finds-appropriation-of.html

Fig. 3: Jean-François Bauret; https://ipkitten.blogspot.com/2019/12/paris-court-of-appeal-confirms-that.html

Fig. 4: Jeff Koons; https://i.dailymail.co.uk/1s/2019/12/22/02/22545666-7817383-image-a-45_1576980529527.jpg

Fig. 5: Patrick Cariou; http://www.artistrights.info/cariou-v-prince

Fig. 6: Prince; http://www.artistrights.info/cariou-v-prince

Fig. 7: Franck Davidovici; https://ipkitten.blogspot.com/2021/03/jeff-koons-loses-again-in-france-his.html

Fig. 8: Jeff Koons; https://ipkitten.blogspot.com/2021/03/jeff-koons-loses-again-in-france-his.html

About the authors

Gianmaria Ajani is Professor of Comparative Law and Law & Art and past Rector at the University of Turin, Italy. He has published monographs and articles on Law & Arts, Legal Theory, Law and Language as well as Legal Reforms in post-Socialist Countries. He has taught EU Law at UC Berkeley and worked as expert and consultant for various international organisations such as the IMF, the EU Commission, the Council of Europe, the UNDP, the GIZ and the ILO. He served as an expert on legal reforms in PR of China, Russia, Albania, Kosovo and Vietnam. He is author of numerous articles for national and international journals and co-founder and co-editor of the journal "Brill Research Perspectives in Art and Law". Prof. Ajani was awarded an honorary doctorate from the University of Savoie (Chambéry). Moreover, he is Guest Professor at the Univerity of Bergen and Honorary Professor at the Shanghai Normal University and at the Zhonghan University of Economics and Law, Wuhan. Likewise, he was a Fellow at the Käte Hamburger Kolleg "Law as Culture" in Bonn. Major publications comprise: *Contemporary Artificial Art and the Law – Searching for an Author*, Brill Research Papers, Art and Law, 2019; *Russian Liberalism and the Rule of Law – Notes from Underground*, in R.M. Cucciolla (ed), Dimensions and Challenges of Russian Liberalism, Springer, 2019; *Transplants, Legal Borrowings and Reception*, in Encyclopedia of Law and Society (Gen. ed. D. Clark), New York, 2007, vol. 3; *Law and Economic Reform in the Transition from Plan to Market*, Int. Encycl. of Comparative Law, vol. XVI State and Economy, R. Buxbaum, F. Madl (ed), Mohr, Tübingen, 2006; *Das Recht der Länder Osteuropas*, Berliner Wissenschafts Verlag, 2005.

Tiziana Andina is Full Professor of Philosophy at the University of Turin, Italy (https://labont.it/people/tiziana-andina/). She is an expert in metaphysics and ontology with a specialization in social ontology. Since 2016, she has been the director of the research center, LabOnt – The Laboratory of Ontology at the University of Turin (www.labont.it). Her recent publications concern social ontology, transgenerational actions, relationship between generations and problems of social justice, fostering the interdisciplinary research between philosophy, social sciences and law. She is co-editor of the international journal *Brill Research*

Perspectives in Art and Law and since 2020, she is the editor of Rivista di Estetica. As fellow at the Columbia University (2008–2009), Käte Hamburger Kolleg, University of Bonn (2015), ITMO University, Russia (2014) and Saint Petersburg State University (2015 and 2016), University of Nanjing and University of Wuhan (2019), she started several international collaborations with leading institutions in the field of the social ontology, cultural studies, political philosophy and philosophy of law, making LabOnt one of the leading European centre in the field of social ontology. Among the most recent titles are: As editor, *Bridging the Analytical Continental Divide. A Companion to Contemporary Western Philosophy*, Brill 2014; *Post-Truth, Philosophy and Law*, Routledge, 2019; *Institutions in Action: The Nature and the Role of Institutions in the Real World*, Springer 2020; as author, *An Ontology for Social Reality*, Palgrave-Macmillan, 2016, *What is Art? The Question of Definition Reloaded*, Brill, 2017 and *A Philosophy for Future Generations. The Structure and Dynamics of Transgenerationality*, Bloomsbury Academic 2022.

Eva-Maria Bauer is a postdoctoral research assistant at the Center for Applied Legal Studies at the Karlsruhe Institute of Technology (KIT). After her studies in Law and German Language and Literature in Freiburg, Hong Kong and Karlsruhe, she obtained her First Legal State Examination (2016) and her Ph.D. degree (2020) at the University of Freiburg and her Second Legal State Examination (2021) at the Higher Regional Court Karlsruhe. Her main research focus is on copyright and digital communication. Her major publication is *Die Aneignung von Bildern – Eine urheberrechtliche Betrachtung von der Appropriation Art bis hin zu Memes* (*The Appropriation of Images – A Copyright View from Appropriation Art to Memes*, Baden-Baden: Nomos 2020).

Davide Dal Sasso is Postdoctoral Research Fellow in Philosophy at the University of Turin, Italy. He holds two Masters' degrees (Philosophy and Art History) and was awarded his Ph.D. in Philosophy from the University of Turin in 2017. He is a member of Labont – Center for Ontology, and Curator of *Dialoghi di Estetica* (Dialogues of Aesthetics), the philosophy and art section of the magazine *Artribune*. His research focuses on the relationship between philosophy, aesthetics, and contemporary arts, with a particular focus on questions concerning conceptualism, expression and representation, and the role of practices in the arts. He is the editor of the new edition of Ermanno Migliorini, *Conceptual Art* (Mimesis 2014), the author of *Nel segno dell'essenziale L'arte dopo il concettualismo* (Rosenberg & Sellier 2020) and of *The Ground Zero of the Arts: Rules, Processes, Forms* (Brill 2021).

Thomas Dreier is Professor of Civil Law and Questions of the Information Society at the Karlsruhe Institute of Technology (KIT). He is also Honorary Professor at the University of Freiburg, and Senior Fellow of the Käte Hamburger Center for Advanced Studies "Law as Culture" in Bonn, Germany. After his studies in law and art history in Bonn, Geneva and New York, he obtained an LL.M.-degree from New York University School of Law (1983) and his Ph.D. degree (1990) as well as his habilitation (2000) at the University of Munich. Before joining the KIT, he worked as Senior Researcher at the Max Planck Institute for Foreign and International Patent, Copyright and Competition law (now Max Planck Institute for Competition and Innovation) in Munich. His main research focus is on copyright and the regulation of images. He is Co-founder and Co-editor of the online open access *Journal of Intellectual Property, Information Technology and Electronic Commerce Law* (JIPITEC). He also is co-editor of the series of monographs *Bild und Recht – Studien zur Regulierung des Visuellen* (*Image and Law – Studies on the Regulation of Images*). Major publications include commentaries of the German Copyright Act, Dreier/Schulze, *Urheberrecht*, 7th ed., Munich: C.H.Beck 2022, and Dreier/Hugenholtz (eds), *Concise European Copyright*, 2nd edition, Alphen aan den Rijn: Wolters Kluwer 2016); *Bild und Recht*, Baden-Baden: Nomos 2018; *Law and Images*, Brill Research Papers, Art and Law 3.1, Leiden/Boston 2019; Dreier/Jehle (eds), *Original, Kopie, Fälschung*, Baden-Baden: Nomos 2020; *Copyright – Urheberrecht versus Netzkultur*, Berlin: Wagenbach 2022.

Johannes Eichenhofer is a private lecturer ("Privatdozent"), currently representing the Chair for Public Law at the law faculty of the University of Bielefeld, Germany. His research and teaching activities focus mainly on fundamental and human rights, especially in the areas of migration and integration, as well as privacy and data protection. He studied law at the Freie Universität Berlin and the Humboldt Universität zu Berlin, as well as at the Università degli Studi di Siena (Italy). After obtaining his First Legal States Exam from in Berlin (2009), he wrote his dissertation on the *Concept and Conception on Integration in the German Integration Act*, which was published in 2013 by Nomos. In 2013, he also completed his legal Clerkship (2011–2013) at the Higher Regional Court in Berlin. From 2014–2019 he was as a postdoctoral fellow at the University of Bielefeld, where he was mainly involved in an interdisciplinary research project on the "Strukturwandel des Privaten" ("Transformation of Privacy"). In May 2020, he habilitated at the University of Bielefeld with the thesis *E-Privacy – theoretical and doctrinal foundations of a European* *privacy protection*, Tübingen: Mohr Siebeck 2021. In the winter term 2019/20 he represented the Chair of Public Law and Legal Philosophy at the Albert-Ludwigs-University in Freiburg. Following, until the winter term 2020/21 he was affiliated with the Institute of Information and Economic Law at the Karlsruhe Institute of Technology (KIT).

Maurizio Ferraris is Full Professor of Philosophy and he is the President of the LabOnt – Center for Ontology and Deputy Rector for Humanities Research at the University of Turin. He is columnist for "La Repubblica", for "Neue Zürcher Zeitung", and for "Libération". He is also the director of "Scienza Nuova", an institute of advanced studies – dedicated to Umberto Eco and uniting the University and the Polytechnic of Turin – aimed at planning a sustainable future, both from a cultural and from a political point of view. He wrote more than sixty books that have been translated into several languages. The last one is *Documanità. Filosofia del mondo nuovo* (Laterza 2021).

Christophe Geiger is Professor of Law at Luiss Guido Carli University, Rome. Previously, he taught at the Centre for International Intellectual Property Studies (CEIPI) of the University of Strasbourg (France), which he leaded as Director General and Director of the Research Department for 11 years. In addition, he is an affiliated senior researcher at the Max Planck Institute for Innovation and Competition in Munich (Germany), as well as Spangenberg Fellow at the Spangenberg Center for Law, Technology & the Arts, Case Western Reserve University School of Law in Cleveland (US). He specializes in national, European, international and comparative intellectual property (IP) law, acts as external expert for the European Parliament and the European Union Intellectual Property Office (EUIPO), has drafted reports on IP for the European and international institutions and taught as visiting professor in several universities. In 2019, he has been elected President of ATRIP, the International Association for the Advancement of Teaching and Research in Intellectual Property (2022–2024). He has published numerous articles as well as authored and edited many volumes in this field, such as *Criminal Enforcement of Intellectual Property: A Handbook of Contemporary Research* (2012), *Constructing European Intellectual Property: Achievements and New Perspectives* (2013), *Research Handbook on Human Rights and Intellectual Property* (2015), *Intellectual Property and the Judiciary* (with Craig Nard and Xavier Seuba, 2018), *Research Handbook on Intellectual Property and Investment Law* (2020), with Edward Elgar Publishing; *What Patent Law for the European Union?* (2013), *The Contribution of Case Law to the Construction of Intellectual Property in*

Europe (2013, in French); *Intellectual Property Law in a Globalized World* (with Caroline Rodà, 2014), *The Intellectual Property System in a Time of Change: European and International Perspectives* (2016), *Trade-Related International Intellectual Property Law: The TRIPS Agreement, Assessment and Perspectives* (2017, in French), *Computer-Implemented Inventions: Issues, Practices and Perspectives* (with Matthieu Dhenne, 2019, French/English) with LexisNexis; and *Penser le droit de la pensée: Mélanges in honor of Michel Vivant* (with J.-M. Bruguière, 2020), with Dalloz.

Werner Gephart is Senior Professor at the faculty of sociology at the University of Bonn, Germany. Besides being a legal scholar, sociologist he also is an artist. In 2014, alongside with German artist Amselm Kiefer, he was awarded an honorary doctorate in Philosophy by the University of Turin. In 2021–2022 he is Senior Fellow of the the Institut Michel Villey pour la culture du juridique et la philosophie du droit at the University of Paris II (Panthéon-Assas). Prof. Gephart is Founding Director and currently co-directing the Käte Hamburger Center for Advanced Study in the Humanities "Law as Culture", in Bonn. He has held numerous visiting professorships, among others the Fulbright Distinguished Chair for German Studies at Washington University, St. Louis, a visiting professorship at the IDC (Herzlyia, Israel), numerous invitations as professor in Tunis, as well as the Chaire Alfred Grosser at SciencesPo, Paris. In 2019 he was appointed as President of the Jury Senior of the Institut Universitaire de France (IUF). He is the editor of the series "Law as Culture" (25 vol.) and co-editor of the volume "Recht" ("Law"), which is part of the Max Weber Gesamtausgabe (MWG I/22–3). His further publications are centered on the cultural analysis of law (*Recht als Kultur*, Klostermann 2006), the sociology of religion (*Religion und Identität*, 1998), and aesthetics (*Law and the arts* 2016). In addition, he is co-editor of the international journal *Art and Law, Brill Research Perspectives in Art and Law*. – As an artist he has held numerous exhibits in cities including Paris, Düsseldorf, Cologne, Bonn, St. Louis, Houston, Bloomington, Minneapolis, Tunis, New Delhi, and London. From 2016 to 2017, Werner Gephart was honorary artist at the Dickson Poon School of Law during his exhibition *Some Colours of the Law* at King's College in London (Somerset House).

Olivia Hägle is a Ph.D. student at the Albert-Ludwigs University of Freiburg and a research assistant at the Institute of Information and Economic Law of the Karlsruhe Institute of Technology (KIT), Germany. After her High School graduation, she studied law at the University of Freiburg (2014–2019) with a focus on Intellectual Property Law and

Chinese Law. In October 2019 she has joined Professor Dreier at the Karlsruhe Institute of Technology (KIT) and is writing her Ph.D. thesis on Deep Fakes in the context of Information Law. Since 2021 she has been collaborating with researchers of other KIT Institutes in a project on interdisciplinary approaches to deep fakes. Her main research focus is on Information Law, including Copyright Law and personal rights.

Wybo Houkes is Professor of Philosophy of Science and Technology at the Department of Industrial Engineering & Innovation Sciences of the Technical University Eindhoven (TU/e). After studying theoretical physics and philosophy in Amsterdam and Leiden, he defended a Ph.D. thesis on Kantianism in early 20th century philosophy at the University of Leiden (2000). Until 2004, he was a post-doctoral researcher in the program "The Dual Nature of Technical Artefacts" funded by the Netherlands Organization for Scientific Research (NWO). In 2008, he was awarded a Vidi fellowship for a project on evolutionary theories of technology. His research interests include technical artifacts and their functions; cultural-evolutionary models of technology; scientific modelling; and the interrelations between technology, individual users and societal practices. He (co-)authored Houkes/Vermaas, *Technical Functions* (Dordrecht: Springer, 2010), and articles in peer-reviewed journals such as *The British Journal for the Philosophy of Science*, *Design Studies*, *The Monist*, *Philosophy of Science*, *Research Policy*, *Studies in History and Philosophy of Science* and *Synthese*.

Lisa Käde is a postdoctoral research assistant at the Center for Applied Legal Studies at the Karlsruhe Institute of Technology (KIT). She studied law in Freiburg and Ottawa as well as business IT (B.Sc., B.A. (hons.)) at the Baden-Wuerttemberg State University of Co-operative Education (DHBW) Stuttgart. Her Ph.D. thesis *Kreative Maschinen und Urheberrecht – Die Machine Learning-Werkschöpfungskette vom Training über Modellschutz bis zu Computational Creativity*, published in 2021 with Nomos focuses on artificial intelligence and machine learning in the context of computational creativity and copyright. She has been a regular contributor to ifrOSS (Institute for Legal Issues of Free and Open Source Software) since 2012. She has been using her experience as a passionate web developer to join the legal tech community in several hackathons. Recent publications included research on explainable artificial intelligence (Computer und Recht 2020) and machine learning model manipulation (Zeitschrift zum Innovations- und Technikrecht 2020).

Massimo Leone is Full Tenured Professor ("Professore Ordinario") of Philosophy of Communication and Cultural Semiotics at the Department of Philosophy and Educational Sciences, University of Turin, Italy, Permanent Part-Time Visiting Full Professor of Semiotics in the Department of Chinese Language and Literature, University of Shanghai, China, and Associate Member of Cambridge Digital Humanities, University of Cambridge, as well as Director of the Bruno Kessler Foundation, Trento. He is a 2018 ERC Consolidator Grant recipient. He graduated in Communication Studies from the University of Siena and holds a DEA in History and Semiotics of Texts and Documents from Paris VII, an MPhil in Word and Image Studies from Trinity College Dublin, a Ph.D. in Religious Studies from the Sorbonne, and a Ph.D. in Art History from the University of Fribourg (CH). He has been visiting professor in several universities and research centres around the globe. His work focuses on the semiotic study of cultures, with particular emphasis on religion and images; his ERC project bears on the meaning of the face in the digital era. Massimo Leone has single-authored fifteen books, (*Religious Conversion and Identity: The Semiotic Analysis of Texts*, London and New York: Routledge, 2004; *Saints and Signs: A Semiotic Reading of Conversion in Early Modern Catholicism*, Berlin and New York: Walter de Gruyter, 2010; *On Insignificance*, London and New York: Routledge, 2019; etc.), edited forty collective volumes, and published more than five hundred peer-reviewed articles in semiotics, visual studies, and religious studies. He is the chief editor of Semiotica (De Gruyter), the chief semiotics journal in the world, and of the SCOPUS journal *Lexia*, and editor of the book series *I Saggi di Lexia* (Rome: Aracne), Routledge/FACETS Advances in Face Studies and *Semiotics of Religion* (Berlin and Boston: Walter de Gruyter).

Lorenz Müller-Tamm is a Ph.D. candidate in legal studies at the Albrecht-Ludwig University in Freiburg, Germany. The topic of his doctoral thesis is on the legal issues of street photography. After studying law at the Humboldt-University in Berlin and at the Queen Mary University in London, he joined the law firm Noerr as a research assistant in the IP/IT department. His main research areas include the regulation of images, data protection law and copyright law.

Eberhard Ortland is Research Associate in the Collaborative Research Centre 1385 "Law and Literature" at the University of Münster (WWU) and coordinator of the *Encyclopedia of Law and Literature*. He has studied philosophy, art history and German literature in Bochum, Berlin and Kyoto, obtained an M.A. from FU Berlin (1993) and a Dr. phil.

from the University of Potsdam (2002). He taught philosophy at the Universities of Hildesheim, Münster and Magdeburg and worked as scientific coordinator for a research group on the Ethics of Copying at the Institute for Advanced Study, Center for Interdisciplinary Research in Bielefeld. He is the editor of Theodor W. Adorno's Lectures on Aesthetics (2009; English translation 2018; French translation 2021) and the author of numerous articles on aesthetics, ethics, and copyright law; most recently (in English): "A Moral Need for Censorship, Access Restrictions, and Surveillance? The Ethics of Copying and the Freedom of Communication", *Annual Review of Law and Ethics* 26 (2018); "Copies of Famous Pictures in Tadao Andō's 'Garden of Fine Art' in Kyōto", in: C. Forberg/Ph. Stockhammer (eds), *The Transformative Power of the Copy*. Heidelberg 2017; "Blurred Lines: A Case Study on the Ethics and Aesthetics of Copying", in: D. H. Hick/R. Schmücker (eds): *The Aesthetics and Ethics of Copying* (London/New York: Bloomsbury 2016).

Benjamin Raue is Dean of the Law Faculty and Professor of Private Law, Law of the Information Society and Intellectual Property Law at the University of Trier, as well as Director of the Institute for Digital Law Trier (IRDT). After studying law in Hamburg and Bordeaux, he obtained his Ph.D. degree in 2010 (*Nachahmungsfreiheit nach Ablauf des Immaterialgüterrechtsschutzes?*, Göttingen: V&R unipress 2010) and his habilitation in 2015 (*Die dreifache Schadensberechnung*, Baden-Baden: Nomos 2017), both from Christian-Albrechts-University of Kiel. Prof. Dr. Raue has clerked at the Higher Regional Court of Hamburg, the German Federal Ministry of Justice, and law firms specializing in intellectual property (2009–2011). Prof. Dr. Raue practiced law at an intellectual property and media law boutique in Hamburg (2011–2012). After his habilitation and before joining the University of Trier in 2016, he acted as temporary professor at the Chair of Civil Law, Trade, Business & Corporate Law at Karlsruhe Institute of Technology (KIT) from 2015–2016. His main research focus is on the consequences of digitalisation on law, especially on copyright and IT law. He is co-founder and co-editor of the open access journal *Recht und Zugang* (*Law and Access, RuZ*).

Cosetta Saba is professor of *Film Analysis* and *Audiovisual Practices in Media Art* at the University of Udine where she is vice-coordinator of Ph.D. in "Storia dell'Arte, Cinema, Media Audiovisivi e Musica". She is member of the Scientific Committee of International Network for the Conservation of Contemporary Art – INCCA Italy and also of the Italian Group of International Institute for Conservation. Her main research interests focus on the languages of art in all its forms and audiovisual manifestations, and on the archiving and preservation models of videos, films and installations. She has published studies dedicated to the analysis of the relationships between cinema, video and art, including *Unstable Cinema. Film and Contemporary Visual Arts* (2007), *Art in Videotape. Art / tapes / 22, ASAC collection – La Biennale di Venezia* (2007), *MATTHEW BARNEY. Polimorfismo, multimodalità, neobarocco* (with Nicola Dusi, 2012), *Preserving and Exhibiting Media Art: Challenges and Perspectives* (with Julia Noordegraaf, Barbara Le Maître, Vinzenz Hediger, 2013); *Cinéma: immersivité, surface, exposition* (with Francesco Federici, 2013), *Archivio Cinema Arte* (2013), *Carmelo Bene. Cinema, arti visive, happening, teatro* (2019).

Reinold Schmücker is Professor of Philosophy at the University of Münster, working on fundamental problems in aesthetics, ethics, and political philosophy. After his studies in philosophy, German literature, and theology in Tübingen and Hamburg, he obtained his Ph.D. degree (1997) from the University of Hamburg. Before joining the University of Münster (2009), he has been an assistant professor of philosophy at the University of Hamburg (1997–2004) and served as founding executive secretary of the Alfried Krupp Wissenschaftskolleg Greifswald (2004–2009), an institute of advanced study. In 2015–16, he was a principal investigator and convenor of the research group *The Ethics of Copying* at the Center for Interdisciplinary Research (ZiF) in Bielefeld (Germany). In his recent research, he has been particularly interested in the philosophy of artifacts, meta-ethics and applied ethics. As well as numerous articles he has authored *Was ist Kunst? Eine Grundlegung* [What Is Art? A Groundwork] (1998, rev. ed. 2014) and *Gibt es einen gerechten Krieg?* [Is There a Just War?] (2021). His (co-)edited books and special issues include *Kunst und Kunstbegriff* [Art and the Concept of Art] (2002, 4th ed. 2017), *Identität und Existenz. Studien zur Ontologie der Kunst* [Identity and Existence. Studies in the Ontology of Art] (2003, 4th ed. 2014), *Aesthetics and Ethics of Copying* (2016, Paperback ed. 2017), *Law and Ethics of Copying* (2018).

Enrico Terrone is Associate Professor of Aesthetics at Università di Genova. He received a degree in Electronic Engineering from the Politecnico di Torino and then a Ph.D. in Philosophy from the Università di Torino. He was visiting researcher at Institut Jean Nicod in Paris, and Juan de la Cierva Postdoctoral Fellow at LOGOS Research Group, Universitat de Barcelona. He works on philosophical issues concerning fiction and depiction. His primary area of research is philosophy of film. He published papers in international journals such as *The British Journal of Aesthetics*, *The Journal of Aesthetics and Art Criticism*, *Erkenntnis*, *Ergo*, *The Monist, Dialectica*. His last book, co-authored with Luca Bandirali, is *Concept TV – An Aesthetics of Television Series* (2021).

Wolfgang Ullrich is cultural scientist and freelance author in Leipzig. From 1986 he studied philosophy, art history, logic/science theory and German language and literature in Munich. He obtained his Master's degree in 1991 with a thesis on Richard Rorty, and his dissertation in 1994 on the late work of Martin Heidegger. Afterwards, he undertook freelance work as an author, lecturer, and consultant. From 1997 to 2003 he was the assistant professor at the Academy of Fine Arts in Munich, and then held guest professorships at the Hochschule für Bildende Künste in Hamburg and at the University of Arts and Design in Karlsruhe. From 2006 to 2015 he was a professor of art history and media theory at the University of Arts and Design in Karlsruhe. His research areas are the history and critique of the concept of art, the sociology of images, digital imagery, and consumer theory. Major publications of the last years: *Siegerkunst. Neuer Adel, teure Lust*, Berlin: Wagenbach 2016; *Der kreative Mensch. Streit um eine Idee*, Salzburg: Residenz 2016; *Wahre Meisterwerte. Stilkritik einer neuen Bekenntniskultur*, Berlin: Wagenbach 2018; *Selfies. Die Rückkehr des öffentlichen Lebens*, Berlin: Wagenbach 2019; *Feindbild werden. Ein Bericht*, Berlin: Wagenbach 2020; *Die Kunst nach dem Ende ihrer Autonomie*, Berlin: Wagenbach 2022.

Special thanks of both the editors and the authors for copy-editing the contributions to this book go to ***Georgia Jenkins***, Herchel Smith Doctoral Researcher, Research Associate, Queen Mary Intellectual Property Research Institute, Centre for Commercial Law Studies, Queen Mary University of London. The editors and authors are likewise grateful to ***Melissa Ducar***, research assistant at the Institute for Information and Economic Law of the Karlsruhe Institute of Technology (KIT), for reading the proofs. Thanks also go to ***Marco Ganzhorn***, Deputy Head of Legal Publishing at Nomos, for his reliable support of the series of the "Bild und Recht" monographs, as well as to ***Eva Lang*** from the Nomos Production Department.

The links listed in the contributions of this book have last been accessed on 6 April 2022.